AF655890

CHALLENGES IN HIGHER EDUCATION: AN INCLUSIVE PERSPECTIVE

Professor Karamjeet Singh

Dr. Navleen Kaur

GAURAV BOOK CENTRE PVT LTD

DELHI

Publisher
GAURAV BOOK CENTRE PVT LTD
4832/24,Prahlad Lane,S-207 Ansari
Road, Daryaganj, Delhi-110002
Ph.: 43570976, 23278261
Email: gauravbookcentre@gmail.com

Edition: 2015

© Author

ISBN: 978-93-83316-03-8

Laser Typesetting
JEE-VEE Graphics, Delhi

Price: 1495/-

Printed
Vikas Computers, Delhi

FOREWORD

Education is as old as the evolution of the human race. Right from the time of its progression, education began from gaining knowledge and skills related to the fulfillment of basic human needs. These were passed on to the next generations in an informal manner. With the growth of civilization, the need of formal education for the development of the individual as well as the society was realized and gradually education got institutionalized.

Ever since, education has not remained stagnant but it has undergone wider transformation through the course of time. Expansion of education has helped in the intensification in the ability of our educational system. This includes the increasing number of aspirants, expansion of physical facilities for imparting education, and diverse forms and types of education taking place due to rapidly expanding knowledge base, resulting in new specialized areas of knowledge. This growth is in response to the rapidly changing socio-economic changes in the present world.

The higher education has been characterized by: increasing demand in higher education ; emergence of a demand for life-long learning; emergence of open and distance learning system as important provider of education; emphasis on ICT's aided learning; growing emphasis on dual mode education system where-in conventional education system also provide education through distance mode; increasing commercialization of education through ICT's; proliferation of "education for profit" private education providers, especially the technical and professional sectors; proliferation of foreign universities campus; etc.

Expansion in higher education has been unparalleled during the last six decades. The assorted qualitative expansion of higher education facilities has fulfilled many goals and produced human resource required for diverse segments. At the same time it raised many issues, posed a number of challenges and problems and resulted in a crises situation on many aspects. In this backdrop, an attempt has been made to collect views from experts regarding challenges confronting Higher Education.

Editors

Professor Karamjeet Singh

And

Dr. Navleen Kaur

Contents

1

Higher Education in India: A Perspective of Twelfth Five Year Plan

*Professor Karamjeet Singh**

"The illiterate of the 21st century will not be those who cannot read and write, but those who cannot learn, unlearn, and relearn."

—**Alvin Toffler**

Abstract

Higher Education in India faces challenges on several fronts including low and inequitable access to higher education, shortage of faculty, deficient infrastructure and low-quality and inadequate research. Today, a key concern for India is the creation of an employable workforce to harness its demographic dividend to the maximum extent. In this paper, effort is being made to evaluate the strategy of Twelfth Five Year Plan to meet the challenges of excellence, expansion and equity. Further, legislative initiatives aimed at restructuring the higher education system have also been examined.

Introduction

In the beginning of 21st Century, it was suddenly realized that population, which was considered as a major stumbling block in India's growth trajectory, is a blessing and key to future growth. As populations in western countries are ageing, India's huge pool of young people is being considered as its biggest strength. Due to globalization and industrialization, there is a huge demand for young skilled, efficient and effective workers, resulting in a gap between demand and supply. There are lot of jobs available for younger generation at global level and this is a great opportunity for Indian young population. But, what

* Director, Academic Staff College and Professor, University Business School, Panjab University, Chandigarh

type of young people India need at this moment of time? Are we ready to fill the gap?

Unfortunately, India is far from having its act together when it comes to figuring out how to educate these young people. Government data suggests that only one out of every seven children born in India goes to college. What's more, the nation suffers from both a crippling quantity, as well as a quality, challenge when it comes to higher education. Yes, of late, there is a mention of improved ranking of Indian University and Panjab University Chandigarh came into the bracket of 226-250 in recent *'The Times Higher Education World Rankings'*.

Unfortunately, we are not even nearer to World's Top Educational Institutions. For instance, the QS World University Rankings, an annual listing of the world's top universities, had no Indian Universities are in the top 400 of its recently released global list for 2013. Only IITs are amongst 400 listed, which are: IIT Delhi (222), IIT Bombay (233), IIT Kanpur (295), IIT Madras (313), IIT Khargpur (346). University of Delhi came in the bracket of 441-450. Although some experts argue that the standards set up and used by the accrediting agencies are not conducive with Indian education system. But, it is also a time proven fact that Indian Universities concentrate on generating the 'BABUS' and not scientists or good thinkers. With specific reference to the Engineering field, our approach is to churn out the budding engineers from the age old set syllabus & not to permit new entry or approach to the developing field to meet the expectation of industry in applied science or future trend in pure science. On one hand, we don't produce graduates with requisite skills required by the industry; on the other hand, there is a sizable section of population, who drop out after primary or secondary school education and could not get higher education. In fact, India has one of the poorest Gross Enrolment Ratios (GER) for higher education in the world. According to 2010 data, India's GER was a meagre 13.8 percent, compared with the global average of around 26 percent. Australia, Russia and the U.S., to name a few examples, have GERs upwards of 75 percent. Although the Ministry of Human Resources & Development had set a target of a 30 percent GER for India by 2020, that target is unlikely to be met. At the current rate of GER growth, India is looking at a GER of around 19 percent. To find out how India got to this point, and how it can climb out of its educational abyss, *an attempt has been made in this paper to examine the present status of higher education in India, issues and challenges confronting higher education in the present day milieu, the steps taken by the Government of India in the twelfth plan and possible ways to come out of this impasse.*

Present Status of Higher Education in India

India's higher education system is the third largest in the world, next to the United States and China. The main governing body at the tertiary level is the University Grants Commission, which enforces its standards, advises the government, and helps coordinate between the centre and the state. Accreditation for higher learning is overseen by 12 autonomous institutions established by the University Grants Commission. There has been phenomenal growth of higher education in India since independence. There were only 20 Universities and 500 Colleges at the time of independence. These number have increased by 29 times (i.e. 574) in the case of the Universities and 71times (i.e. 35539) in the case of Colleges. Similarly, there has been tremendous growth in the enrolment also. At the beginning of Academic year 2011-12, the total number of students enrolled, in the formal system, in the Universities and Colleges has been reported to be 203.27 lakhs. Similarly, there has also been growth in different programmes in Technical Education as such, during 2011-12 about 13507 Programmes/Institutes are running and for the year 2011- 12, the intake has been 30.14 lakhs. Thus, the above statistical overview of the higher education system clearly shows that there has been phenomenal growth in Institutions (Universities, Colleges, Technical Institutions) as well as in intake, enrolment etc. since independence.

The higher education landscape is changing very rapidly in India. With permission to allow entry of private universities in India, the whole game has been changed and a new dimension has been added. It is better for some and worse for many. Many new institutions of medicine, science, technology and others have been introduced. But the majority of the youth would never get to study in these, shackled as they are by poverty. Only 10 per cent of the relevant age group is enrolled for higher education compared to 40-50 per cent in developed economies. With many state universities in terminal stages, private institutions are mushrooming. This state of disrepair is because of the lack of research facilities, un-enterprising teachers, outdated methods, abysmal infrastructure and unrealistic cut offs. Some of the brilliant child, who scored 75 per cent or more in their 12th exams, couldn't get admission into college of their choice. One year down the line, they start doing odd jobs. Their dreams of becoming an entrepreneur are on the wane. Moreover, India's social pitfalls also affect the higher education sphere. As reported in Indian Express on March 14, 2012, Balmukund Bharti and Anil Meena committed suicide because both belonged to scheduled castes and were unable to face the discrimination prevalent in Indian educational institutions. Balmukund was a Dalit studying to be a doctor, who killed himself at the AIIMS campus in Delhi. Anil Meena, born in a tribal family in Rajasthan, did the same. "We are singled out, both by the faculty and the students. A couple of boys in my class called me 'Kalu' for the entire month I was at AIIMS. I ignored the insults, until they said something derogatory about my parents, which is when I left," said Bala S Sridhar of Chennai.

Poverty is the main killer of dreams of higher education for a large number of aspiring students in India. Much of rural India cannot access reputed institutions in cities as distance becomes an issue. Discrimination on basis of caste and gender are rampant. There are too many students and too few 'good quality' seats in reputed institutions. There is a vicious circle. If you aren't educated, you can never rise out of poverty. To escape poverty, you need education, to which, most people don't have access. Hence your contribution to the country's growth can never be optimum, and hence its overall market value suffers

Challenges of Higher Education

Although the country has the largest higher education system in the world in terms of the number institutions and the second-largest in terms of enrollment, it still faces challenges on several fronts including low and inequitable access to higher education, shortage of faculty, deficient infrastructure and low-quality and inadequate research. Today, a key concern for India is the creation of an employable workforce to harness its demographic dividend to the maximum extent. To achieve this, the country needs an education system that can deliver quality in terms of a skilled and industry-ready workforce, without diluting focus on world-class research and innovation. Prime Minister Manmohan Singh rightly remarked in 2007 that "Our university system is, in many parts, in a state of disrepair...In almost half the districts in the country, higher education enrolments are abysmally low, almost two-third of our universities and 90 per cent of our colleges are rated as below average on quality parameters... I am concerned that in many states university appointments, including that of vice-chancellors, have been politicised and have become subject to caste and communal considerations, there are complaints of favouritism and corruption." Similarly, looking at the facts, Mrs. Pratibha Patil remarked in her inaugural address in a seminar at Mumbai that "it is a worrying sign that even though the 3rd largest number of graduates in the world every year is produced in India, only 15 percent of our boys and girls passing out of college have the skills required to become employable! This brings in concerns that students are getting degrees, but not getting employable hands-on skills". Students are not taught what they need or the contents required in the practical, but are being taught traditional syllabi framed four decades ago. The same concern was raised by Mr. Kishore B, Lead Researcher, Tata Institute of Social Sciences (TISS) that "The faculty at colleges has limited quality industry experience. The best practice may be to get significant bits of training, at least 25%, to be delivered by actual industry experts" Thus, there is a problem not only on contents but on delivery mechanism also.

Keeping into mind all these issues, 12th plan summed up Challenges on three fronts — excellence, expansion and equity. The 12th plan has laid down a blueprint and made a strategy on these three fronts. The strategy as envisaged has been explained in the following paragraphs.

On The Front Of Excellence

A. Infrastructure and technology

1. **Establishing Meta Universities** framework to promote inter-institutional collaboration and designing of innovative interdisciplinary programs. This framework would encourage the use of Massively Open Online Courses (MOOCs) and access to content, teaching and research support for all the members of a network.

2. **Strengthening National Mission on use of ICT.** In the 12th Plan, the proposal is to upgrade broadband connectivity of universities and colleges to 10 GBPS and 1 GBPS, respectively; building computer labs with increased availability of laptops, low-cost access devices for faculty and students and smart classrooms (classrooms with video-conferencing facility linking meta-universities and affiliating universities). Development of virtual labs, establishing a single national-level consortium for propriety content and creating open-access content repositories will be a proiority. Further, efforts will be made to train faculty in creation of instructional design content, implementation of capacity-building measures to adopt technology-mediated pedagogy in classrooms.
3. **Technical Education Quality Improvement Programme (TEQIP):** Phase-3 of TEQIP is to be launched to introduce diversity in curricula and scale sector-wide programs. This phase will focus on the development of an "eco-system" by supporting State Technological Universities, strengthening AICTE and scaling up sector-wide programs.

B. Faculty

1. **Overcoming faculty shortages:** The Government aims to double faculty at HEIs by the end of the Twelfth Plan period from 0.8 million at present to 1.6 million at the end of the Plan. The Government also wants to tap the pool of retired experts, who can function as adjunct faculty and also enroll for doctoral degrees.
2. **Undertaking Faculty Training and Development:** A "National Mission on Teachers and Teaching" would be launched in the 12th Plan to pool all the existing and new initiatives on faculty development under one umbrella. The Government would also launch a program to fund doctoral students and enable them to study at international institutions. The institutional weaknesses of Academic Staff Colleges (ASCs) are slated to be eliminated through qualitative change in the content and methodology of development of faculty. More Faculty Development Programs along with improvements in hiring practices and working conditions are expected to lead to the enhanced performance of

casual and part-time academic employees. In order to provide global exposure to Indian faculty, the Government plans to launch the International Faculty Development Programme, under which: Indian faculty will be sent to the best universities in the world for 3 to 6 months' internship, around 40–50 annual workshops are expected to be conducted by leading international teachers and researchers for selected Indian post-doctoral students and faculty. The Government seeks to establish 50 Teaching and Learning Centres (TLCs) to promote research activity and training of faculty in the country.

C. Infrastructure and Technology

1. **Shifting from annual to semester examination system:** All Indian universities would be encouraged to shift from the current annual examination system to semesters with choice-based credit system (CBCS), comprehensive and continuous evaluation and regular revision of curricula to ensure updated and relevant curricula
2. **Promoting Holistic Undergraduate Programmes:** Four-year undergraduate courses (in place of three-year courses) will be promoted, to provide holistic education and opportunities for intellectual exploration, and will include hands-on research, experiential learning, as well as ethical and leadership education, community service, creative thinking, education on acquiring
3. **Creating active learning environment:** The Government plans to create professional networks of institutions and individuals, similar to the 'Network of Social Work Education' and the mathematics initiative of the University of Delhi. Subject-specific curricula and packaged, re-usable digitized content would made available to students to create a knowledge repository

D. Accreditation:

Setting up of a National Accreditation Regulatory Authority for Higher Educational Institutions is under consideration to strengthen India's accreditation system. The capacities of existing agencies (e.g., NAAC and NBA) would also be enhanced. Indian institutions would be encouraged to obtain accreditation from international accrediting bodies to create competitive pressure on

Indian accrediting bodies. Multiple accreditation bodies would be set up to handle the large volume of applications for accreditation

E. Internationalization:

India would adopt a clearly articulated strategy for internationalization of higher education, which will include faculty and students exchange programs, institutional collaboration for teaching and research, induction of diverse teaching learning models and enhanced use of technology. A globally compatible academic credit system and internationally recognized curricula and processes would be put in place. The India International Education Centre, a professional national agency, would be created to support selected institutions to help them establish dedicated internationalization units.

F. Research and innovation:

The Government plans to invest up to 2% of the country's GDP in research activity during the 12th Plan (from 1% at present). The increased investment would be used to develop institutions and create centers of excellence in research and research training. Research universities that are able to participate in research and teaching in multiple disciplines will be promoted. A legislative framework for setting up "Universities for Research and Innovation" is being considered. The Government intends to have 20 such universities, which are either created or converted, by the end of the Twelfth Plan. The creation of 20 Centers of Excellence (CoEs) as a long-term investment in selected areas of national importance is expected to attract and retain research talent. In addition, 50 centers of training and research will be established in frontier areas of science and technology, social sciences and humanities. Boosting entrepreneurship, enhancing innovation capacity, and encouraging innovation will be the focus.

On The Front Of Expansion

A. **Central institutes to become the epitome of quality:** Government's initiatives will focus on strengthening the infrastructure of Central and state institutions and on establishing research-based institution. The Central Government proposes to establish and support research and innovation based institutes. Some Central institutions would be upgraded during the 12th plan. These include: ISM Dhanbad that is to be upgraded to the level of an IIT, BESU Shibpur that is to be upgraded to an Indian Institute of Engineering, Science and Technology, NIFFT Ranchi that will be a premier institution for forging and foundry technology. The idea is to ensure that Central institutions should become role-models for other institutions in all aspects including governance, faculty, curricula and infrastructure.

B. **State Higher Education Systems to be strengthened:** State higher education systems would be provided more central funding as compared to previous plans. There will be a strategic shift in the manner in which higher education in the States is supported by the Central Government. Under Rashtriya Uchhatar Shiksha Abhiyan (RUSA), Central funding will be linked to the academic, administrative and financial reforms of a state's higher education system. This is essential for modification of Central support and intervention based on the needs of each state. Central funding will be allocated for a state's education system as a whole, flowing through individual institutes via the UGC. The UGC will play a more strategic role in disbursal of Central funds, particularly in funding strategic investment plans proposed by institutions. State system-wide planning is needed for higher education in the country to benefit from synergies between state and central funding.

C. **Private sector investments to be encouraged:** 'Not-for-profit' status in higher education should be re-examined to allow for-profit entities (which are currently not permitted in higher education) in selected areas where there are acute shortages, subject to requisite oversight and accreditation. Innovative ways have to be found to encourage infusion of capital in not-for-profit higher education. Some proposals in this direction include:

   a. Permission for private institutions to raise funds through public offerings of bonds or shares

   b. Allowing all types of institutions to be established as Section 25 companies and permission given to convert existing trusts and societies to Section 25 companies

c. Designating higher education as "infrastructure" to allow similar legal and tax treatment as other infrastructure projects

Government could support non-profit private institutions by extending student financial aid to accredited private institutions, providing access to research funding on equal footing with public institutions. New models of PPP will be encouraged especially for the establishment of research and innovation institutes. Innovative PPP models could be used to transform public institutions that are failing to meet set standards.

D. **Skill-based and distance learning:** Added emphasis will be laid on increasing skill-based programmes. The framework of community colleges (based on the model established in North America) is being developed. These colleges will provide flexibility of entry and exit to students, linkages with higher education and curricula based on national occupation standards. Technical support would be given by philanthropic foundations and the Indian Centre for Research and Development of Community Education (with 230 community colleges under it) to create a framework for skill-based education. Enhanced provision of open and distance learning will be made to widen access in a flexible and cost-effective way. Government support to IGNOU, state open universities, and other institutions of distance education will be increased to expand their access traditional institutions will be encouraged to promote blended learning by offering part of their curriculum online.

On The Front Of Equity

A. **Increased funding support:** The Government would increase public spending on students' financial aid funding to increase scholarship amounts. All students' financial aid schemes under the MHRD would be consolidated under Student Financial Aid Programme (SFAP). Scholarships and student loans with government guarantees would be universalized. A student loan guarantee corpus under the Credit Guarantee Trust would be created by the Government to meet the increased demand for student loans. This should reduce defaults for lending institutions and decrease the rate of interest for students.

B. **Differential response to address dimensions of inequalities:** Schemes for establishing model colleges, community colleges and polytechnics in low GER districts may be modified to include minority-concentrated districts and Fifth Scheduled Districts. Special schemes will be devised to draw students from the Muslim community .These schemes will have to provide special incentives to potential students from these communities and pro-actively identify the potential beneficiaries with the help of non-governmental organizations. Setting-up of additional women's colleges in small towns as well as giving high priority to women hostels.

C **Consolidation of several schemes and initiatives:** All equity-related schemes in higher education across the different ministries under the Central Government would be brought under one umbrella, Equal Opportunity for Higher Education Initiatives. All existing and several new initiatives for inclusion of persons with disabilities will be brought under an umbrella, National Initiative on Inclusion of Persons with disabilities.

D. **Other Initiatives:** Individual-oriented schemes will be linked to a multi-dimensional "Index of Disadvantage," which gives due weight to caste, community, gender, poverty and rural background, to address the intersectional dimensions of inequality. A mechanism, called the "Diversity Index" could be used to measure the performance of institutions in increasing the participation of disadvantaged groups and link this to budgetary incentives. A mechanism, called the "Diversity Index" could be used to measure the performance of institutions in increasing the participation of disadvantaged groups and link this to budgetary incentives.

Major Legislative Initiatives In Higher Education

Several legislative initiatives aimed at restructuring the higher education system (general/technical) have been taken during the last three years which are at various stages of finalization/consideration as given below:—

Title of Legislative Proposal(s)	Objectives
Higher Education and Research Bill 2011	The proposed Bill will cover all areas/ disciplines of learning and disciplines including general, technical and professional education. Only agricultural education is excluded from its purview since agriculture falls within the State List in 7th Schedule of the Constitution.
The Educational Tribunals Bill, 2010	The Bill aims to provide a mechanism for adjudication of disputes involving stake-holders in the higher education sector including students, teachers, employees of higher educational institutions universities and institutions and statutory regulatory authorities, so as to reduce litigation in courts involving universities and higher education institutions.
The Prohibition of Unfair Practices in Technical Education Institutions, Medical Educational Institutions, and Universities Bill, 2010	This Bill provides for prohibition of certain unfair practices in respect of medical and professional educational institutions and universities, in order to protect the interests of students and applicants seeking admission to such institutions and for allied matters
The National Accreditation Regulatory Authority for Higher Educational Institutions Bill, 2010	The Bill is for mandatory accreditation of all higher educational institutions through accreditation agencies registered by a regulatory authority created for the purpose at the national level.

The National Academic Depository Bill, 2011	The Bill provides for creation of a National Electronic Database of academic awards and its maintenance by anauthorized depository.
The Universities for Research and Innovation Bill, 2011	The Bill provides a framework for the establishment of Universities for Research and Innovation, which will be set up in the public mode, purely privately funded, as well as Universities in the PPP mode.
The Foreign Educational Institutions (Regulation of Entry and Operations) Bill, 2010.	This Bill is in the public interest which aims to maintain the standards of higher education within the country as well as to protect the interest of the student's community.
Amendment of Indian Institutes of Technology Act, 1961	This Bill envisages (a) inclusion of eight new IITs within the purview of the Institutes of Technology Act, 1961 and (b) conversion of the Institute of Technology, Banaras Hindu University (a constituent unit of the Banaras Hindu University, a Central University), into Indian Institute of Technology (Banaras Hindu University), Varanasi and integrating it with the IIT system in the country. Institute of Technology Act, 1961 has been amended to bring the eight new Indian Institute of Technology (IITs) at Bhubaneshwar, Gandhinagar, Hyderabad, Indore, Jodhpur, Mandi, Patna and Ropar within the ambit of the Act and convert the Institute of Technology – Banaras Hindu University(IT - BHU) to Indian Institute of Technology – Banaras Hindu University (IIT–BHU), Varanasi. The amended Act, has been into force with effect from 29th June, 2012.

Amendment to the Architects Act, 1972	The Architects (Amendment) Bill, 2010 was introduced in the Rajya Sabha on 31st August, 2010 to provide for- (a) Amendment of section 6, so as to amend sub-section (1) with a view to omit certain words therefrom and insert a new sub-section (6) with a view to provide for the notification of the names and addresses of the Members of the Council in the Official Gazette; and (b) Insertion of new sections 10A and 10B with a view to make provision for issuance of directions by the Central Government and to provide for supersession of Council on certain grounds and for a total period not exceeding two years.
National Institute of Technology (Amendment) Bill, 2010	To make National Institute of Technology Act, 2007 more comprehensive and effective, necessary amendments were moved on the following accounts:- (i) To incorporate 10 new NITs located in the States of Sikkim, Arunachal Pradesh, Manipur, Nagaland, Meghalaya, Mizoram, Uttarakhand, Delhi, Goa and Pondicherry as Institutions of National Importance. (ii) To strengthen exısting transitional provisions of the NIT Act, 2007. (iii) To give representation to nearby premier Central Institution in the Board of Governors of NITs. (iv) To amend the procedure for appointment of Deputy Director in NITs; and (v) To incorporate Indian Institutes of Science Education and Research(IISERs) in the NIT Act by making suitable provision in the NIT Act, 2007.

	The NIT (Amendment) Act, 2012 received assent of the President of India on the 7th June, 2012 and since then the 10 new NITs and five IISERs are functioning under the ambit of the NIT Act, 2007.
Indian Institute of Information Technology Bill, 2012.	To ensure uniformity and autonomy in governance in respect of all the IIITs, as also to declare them as institutions of national importance a Bill, namely, Indian Institutes of Information Technology Bill, 2012 has been formulated. The Bill will be a novel experiment as both the Central Government institutions and the institutions set up in partnership with the State Government and industry are sought to be covered under a single legislation. It recognises the need to develop new knowledge in information technology and to provide manpower of global standards for the information technology industry which would in turn contribute to the development of industries.

After analyzing various steps taken by the Government, it could be summed up that there are basically three big challenges in Higher Education in the present day scenario, i.e. ensuring sustainable higher education systems at the time when public funding is decreasing and competitiveness is increasing, improving the quality of the total student experience even as the demand for participation is growing and strengthening knowledge and innovation as drivers of growth while ensuring that multi- and cross-disciplinary critical inquiry is maintained. This is a herculean task. We need funds and for a long time we were happy with the public, government-owned system. Unfortunately, in higher education, we were too focussed on the few good institutions we have, such as the IITs (Indian Institutes of Technology) and the IIMs (Indian Institutes of Management) (none of which are in the QS Top 200, though). It's a step forward that at least now we recognise the scale of the challenge. But, there is no way such magnitude of scale can be achieved by the government. It will need the private sector's active participation. Right now, the private sector accounts for 59 percent of enrolment in higher education. And there are some worthy examples of quality – institutes such as BITS (Birla Institute of Technology and Science), Manipal University and FLAME (Foundation for Liberal and Management Education). Over the past decade, to cater to the huge supply-demand gap, people who didn't know enough about education, and had no aspirations to be in education – mostly business people from industries such as real estate who knew how to get large pieces of land allotted or had surplus cash – started to create private colleges and universities. Given that they were not academically oriented people, or who didn't understand education, even if they were well-intentioned they didn't know how to create an environment for education. They saw themselves as providing a service, and the service was providing somebody a degree that could not get them a job. Thanks to the demand fuelled by the rise of IT, BPOs (business process outsourcing firms) and our services industry, this "service model" of education worked well enough to attract large numbers of students. This led to a mushrooming of many mediocre private universities that definitely provided many students an option, but there was little incentive for these universities to improve. That will have to change. India needs to make sure that only those private universities are to be encouraged, who have academic bent of mind. The Government of India should discourage low quality foreign institutions, but make efforts to encourage the world's Top 400 universities to set up campuses in India. This will not only provide opportunities to Indian scholars, but also give competitive environment to the existing institutions. India's higher education system can be expected to be better aligned to industry and global practices, and be more transparent and inclusive by the end of Twelfth Plan period, provided the Government is able to create an enabling regulatory environment and put in place robust implementation, monitoring and quality assurance mechanisms.

Conclusions

It has been rightly pointed out in the Annual Report of UGC 2012-13 that within the context of globalization and developments in technology, higher education is undergoing unprecedented changes. In addition to questions of access and equity, institutions of higher education are called upon to cut costs, improve quality and compete in an environment of cross-border educational provision. Employability is the key to any reform. Making education-industry relevant and practical would be the right way to ensure a highly employable talent pool. Financial support to needy and meritorious student is required as we have to ensure inclusive growth. Thus, we must have merit-based student financing. This should ensure admissions to meritorious students independent of financial background. Teaching standards should be of international level. As in future, we will not be producing graduates for traditional government organizations, but for the global organizations. Whole world is a global village and young Indians should keep an eye on all organizations across the world. As in times to come, it will not be nationality, but competence level as deciding factor to get a job. So there is a need for internationalization of education. This would entail aligning different aspects of education (curriculum, faculty, etc) to international standards and enabling research environment. This would involve creating adequate means of research funding and practical application of research. Improved technology is required for delivery of education. Leveraging technology for enhancing the teaching-learning experience will ensure better outcomes. All this is possible if we can ensure high quality faculty in higher education. The need of the hour is to create a conducive environment and provide incentives to attract and retain high quality faculty. Academic administrators have to respond to these challenges and steer the course of their institutions to provide world class education and training to their students. The UGC proposes to address this issue by creation of a structured system to impart training and development opportunities to the staff, administrators and senior functionaries in the various universities and colleges with the broad goal of attaining excellence in academic governance. For this, there is scope for Academic Staff College to impart training to faculty for achieving excellence.

Bibliography

1. "India Country Summary of Higher Education". World Bank.
2. "Higher Education", National Informatics Centre, Government of India". www. education.nic.in.

3. http://www.ey.com/Publication/vwLUAssets/Higher_Education_in_India/$File/EY-FICC_Higher_Education_Report_Nov12.pdf
4. "Latest Statistics on Indian Higher Education". DrEducation.com.
5. http://www.ugc.ac.in/ugcpdf/740315_12FYP.pdf
6. http://planningcommission.nic.in/plans/planrel/12appdrft/appraoch_12plan.pdf

2

Exclusive Aspects In Inclusive Society: From Theory To Practice In Higher Education

Dr. Navleen Kaur*

Abstract:

Indian education system has come a long way from the days of the Gurukuls where the students had to stay with the Gurus in their ashrams, till they were educated and mastered certain amount of skills and knowledge. The post independence era has seen expansion of education at all levels, be it primary, secondary and higher education. The manifold qualitative expansion of higher education facilities has fulfilled many goals and produced manpower required for various sectors. At the same time it has raised many issues, posed a number of challenges and problems and resulted in a crises situation on many aspects. The marginalized groups remained exploited, degraded and deprived of access to the existing socio-economic resources. The educational deprivation of the marginalized and their inclusion in mainstream education and their empowerment has raised a lot of interest among the thinkers and the policy makers to relook at the education system in the country.

Key Words: *Indian Education System; Expansion: Marginalized; Inclusion*

Introduction

According to Mohandas K. Gandhi, "In human society, all violence can be traced back to these seven recurrent blunders: wealth without work, pleasure without conscience, knowledge without character, commerce without morality, science without-humanity, worship without sacrifice, and politics without principles". Indian education

* Chairperson and Associate Professor, Department of Community Education and Disability Studies, Panjab University, Chandigarh.

system has been, by its very nature, elitist and exclusionary from the ancient times. In the vedic period, education was linked exclusively to caste and gender. The Brahmins, reckoned to be the 'ritually pure agents', were the custodians of the religious texts. The lower castes, in no case could seek education, being 'non-sacred'. Hindu women were denied access to formal education. The situation of the Muslim women was a shade better. They went to religious schools but were not granted entry to formal secular schools. With the coming of the British in India, the non-discriminatory educational institutions were started. This broke the monopoly of education held by the elite and the upper castes. The formulators of the Constitutiion Sustem;on odian Educatf free and independent India understood the significance of education in terms of enhancing equality and social mobility. Thus, several constitutional provisions to enable free and fair access to the formal education to all groups came into force. But still the problems and challenges are quite evident when children belonging to the marginalized groups have not gained social acceptance, equal respect and treatment in the school by teachers, administrators and students. To improve access and enrolment, measures need to be taken to retain them for long to complete the full cycle of education. The excluded sections have shown trends of poor performance as compared to the advantaged groups, an issue to be pondered over by making reforms in the education system. The present paper intends to:

- explore the reasons for exclusion of the disadvantaged groups from the mainstream education;
- suggest measures for inclusion of all marginalized groups in mainstream education.
- examine the role of higher education in promoting inclusive education.

Towards Inclusive Society:

Every society has its own obligation for the social development of their diverse segment of the population through diverse means. These obligations are to be met through various institutionalized resources. Education is one of the vital means for the upliftment of the community, its well- being and effectual instrument for social development. In the World Development Summit of 1995, all heads of the states of the

United Nations Organization (UNO), committed themselves to make education a tool for empowerment of the marginalized. They have also committed themselves for 'Education For All'.

According to the World Declaration on Education for All, "Every person—child, youth and adult—shall be able to benefit from educational opportunities designed to meet their basic learning needs. These needs comprise both learning tools (such as literacy, oral expression, numeracy, and problem solving) and basic learning content (such as knowledge, skills, values and attitudes) required by human beings to be able to survive, to develop their full capacities, to live and to continue learning. Moreover, whether or not expanded educational opportunities will translate into meaningful development-for an individual or for society -depends ultimately on whether people actually learn as a result of these opportunities, i.e. whether they incorporate useful knowledge, reasoning ability, skills and values. The focus of basic education must, therefore, be on actual learning acquisition and outcome, rather than exclusively upon enrolment and completion of certification requirements. Active and participatory approaches are particularly valuable in allowing learners to reach their fullest potential."

Subscribing to this notion, the Human Development Report of India(2001) recognizes that education 'is only a means to enhance human capital and productivity but also a critical invasive instrument for bringing about social, economic and and political inclusion and a durable integration of people, particularly those excluded from the main stream of society' . The Human Development Report 2005 clearly states that human development is about freedom and about building capabilities which encompasses the range of things that people can do and what they can be. This range becomes narrowed when conditions of poverty, illness, illiteracy, social and economic discrimination, and unrest prevail. The basic aptitudes for human development are, leading a long and healthy life, being educated, having adequate resources for a decent standard of living, and social and political participation in society.

Nevertheless due to several social, economic and historical reasons all segments of the population have not acquired equal access to education. Even among the literate or educated sections only a few have got access to higher, professional and technical avenues of knowledge. As a result these vast sections of the population have remained deprived of the avenues and processes of human development and capacity building for upward social mobility. The state and the society have also remained deprived of the human potentials of these sections of society. Inequality in access to education has been historically rooted and socio-culturally circumscribed. In India, e.g. traditionally only the upper castes have had access to education at all levels. Such situations are available in many other parts of the world as well e.g. in North America also the blacks and the indigenous people have delayed educational achievements.

Higher education is a process of imparting knowledge and skills to individuals and empowers them to; participate in development, decision making and democratic process. Effective education takes place when students are able to participate fully and benefit from that education. Higher education has been perceived as a privilege of the few intellectuals or the rich and therefore those with disabilities are denied accessibility. Persons with disabilities are unable to access higher education due to barriers outside the institutions and those within. Such barriers include narrowly-defined set of legibility criteria, negative attitude, and inaccessible environments. Inclusive education approach is instrumental in addressing these barriers in order to open higher education for students with disabilities and all those who are currently denied access on racial, ethnic, health, linguistic and cultural grounds.

For long the role of education has been confined to awareness generation and at best opening opportunities for employment and thus providing security of income. This limited scope of education swallows- up the empowerment of the poor and the marginalized. When people become empowered to make choices, take decisions for themselves, and challenge the decisions of the administrators, governance becomes intricate. In fact for this reason the plan documents have expressions like 'capacity building', 'community participation', 'people's movements' which convey a sense of decentralization. These documents are prepared by the bureaucracy who have no understanding of the social reality of those for whom the plans are made. Dreze and Sen (1995) very rightly affirmed that the education system has served to safeguard the interests of the privileged and powerful groups of people leaving behind the socially and economically disadvantaged.

According to Rampal (2000) 'If education is really to be a means of reducing social inequities and redressing the skewed course of development followed in the last few decades, it shall have to relocate the power to critique and change – the power also to decide what shall count as legitimate content for curricula, to choose enabling pedagogies, negotiated when, where and ultimately for what purpose. The educational discourse would need to consciously give voice to the silenced majority and redefine its objectives by valuing their lives on their terms. Strong and visible affirmative action in favour of the disadvantaged and disempowered will have to redefine the educational priorities of the countries in this region."

As Sapon-Shevin (2003) very expressively states, "Inclusion demands that we ask, what kind of a world do we want to create, and how should we educate students for that world?" He propagates the 'Creating of an Inclusive Society'. An inclusive society is a society that over-rides differences of race, gender, class, generation, and geography, and ensures inclusion, equality of opportunity as well as capability of all members of the society to determine an agreed set of social institutions that govern social interaction. (Expert Group Meeting on Promoting Social Integration, Helsinki, July 2008).

The World Summit for Social Development 1995 defines an inclusive society as a "society for all in which every individual, each with rights and responsibilities, has an active role to play. Such an inclusive society must be based on respect for all human rights and fundamental freedoms, cultural and religious diversity, social justice and the special needs of vulnerable and disadvantaged groups, democratic participation and the rule of law". It is promoted by social policies that seek to reduce inequality and create flexible and tolerant societies that embrace all people. This speaks of social integration and social inclusion,and to achieve this the voices of people and their needs and concerns, need to be attended to. Not only some but all members of society with different backgrounds must have a say and a stake in 'their shared society'. This inclusiveness of society creates and maintains stability as well as a readiness to embrace change when necessary. In indispensable terms, the international human rights law requires governments to respect individuals' civil and political rights – such as their rights to free speech, fair trial, and political participation – and to promote their economic, social and cultural rights – such as their rights to health care and education." In an inclusive society, members not only have the right to education or the right to political participation but actually take part in the process, using the right to education and having a vote that actually counts in a political process. What is most significant in creating an inclusive society is the engagement of the individual in the process by which society is managed, ordered and represented.

It has long been realized and recognized that lack of education and unequal access to education has emerged to be a potential cause of socio-economic backwardness, poverty, ill-health and all forms of human deprivation. Since the significance of and disparities in access to education have widely been recognized, there have been several obligations to enhance access to education both by the state, international bodies and the civil society organization. These obligations aim to:

- Recognize education as the foundation of social and human development;
- Enhance access to education to all sections of the populace;
- Endow with special provisions for ethnic, religious and linguistic minorities;
- Provide special attention for children, women and other vulnerable sections of society;
- Provide adequate resources for expansion of education;
- Save education as a tool for national integration;
- Use education as a tool for mainstreaming the marginalized;
- Increase and sustain diversity among students, staff, and faculty based on race, sex, ethnicity, sexual identity, differently abled and international origin
- Increase the number of courses that contain a diversity component in their curriculum and will generate, as economically suitable, proposals for new related programs.
- These courses and programs shall include content and issues related to race, sex, ethnicity, sexual identity, national origin, disability, age, religion, and social class.
- Increase the diversity of students who participate in higher

education by providing both co curricular and curricular curriculum.

- ❖ Create an institutional structure that will sustain the diversity and substantive equality initiatives.
- ❖ Assure substantive equality in a diverse community. This involves achieving impartial outcomes, as well as equal opportunity. It focuses on the acceptance of many identities, desire for inclusive engagement, and assurance that entitlements, opportunities, and access are distributed fairly and justly throughout any educational institution. It builds on cultural pluralism, defined as a condition of community in which numerous distinct ethnic, religious, or cultural groups interact constructively.
- ❖ It views the classroom as an inclusive learning community where pedagogy addresses and involves all learners.

So, poverty and marginalization are major causes of exclusion. Households in rural or remote communities and children in urban slums have less access to education. Disabled children suffer from blatant educational exclusion, those belonging to indigenous groups and linguistic minorities, nomadic children and those affected by HIV/AIDS are among the vulnerable groups.Once identified, strategies can be developed to get them into school and keep them there. The challenge is to implement policies and practices to overcome the sources of exclusion. Efforts to expand enrolment must be accompanied by policies to enhance quality at all levels of education. It is a process that involves addressing and responding to the diverse needs of learners. This has implications for teaching, the curriculum, ways of interacting and relations between the schools and the community. The overall goal is to ensure that school is a place where all children participate and are treated equally. This involves a change in how we think about education. Inclusive education is an approach that looks into how to transform education systems in order to respond to the diversity of learners. It means enhancing the quality of education by improving the effectiveness of teachers, promoting learning-centred methodologies, developing appropriate textbooks and learning materials and ensuring that schools are safe and healthy for all children. Strengthening links with the community is also vital: relationship between teachers, students, parents and society at large are crucial for developing inclusive learning environments.

An inclusive curriculum addresses the child's cognitive, emotional and creative development. It is based on the four pillars of education for the 21st century - learning to know, to do, to be and to live together. This starts in the classroom. The curriculum has an instrumental role to play in fostering tolerance and promoting human rights and is a powerful tool for transcending cultural, religious and other differences. An inclusive curriculum takes gender, cultural identity and language background into consideration. It involves breaking gender stereotypes not only in textbooks but in teachers' attitudes and expectations. Multilingual approaches in education, in which language is recognized as an integral part of a student's cultural identity, can act as a source of inclusion.

The way teachers teach is of critical importance in any reform designed to improve quality. A child-centred curriculum is characterized by a move away from rote learning and towards greater emphasis on hands-on, experience-based, active and cooperative learning. Introducing inclusion as a guiding principle has implications for teachers' practices and attitudes – be it towards girls, slow learners, children with special needs or those from different backgrounds.

Adequate pre-service and in-service teacher training is essential to improve learning. A new curriculum cannot be introduced without familiarizing teachers with its aims and contents. Assessment can help teachers to measure student performance and to diagnose difficulties. But teachers need to understand the value of good assessment practices and learn skills to develop their own tests.

Exclusion starts very early in life. A holistic vision of education and a comprehensive early childhood care and education programmes improve children's well being, prepare them for primary school and give them a better chance of succeeding once they are in school. It is evident that the most disadvantaged and vulnerable children benefit most from such programmes. Linking inclusion to broader development goals will contribute to the reform of education systems, to poverty alleviation and to the achievement of all the Millennium Development Goals. An inclusive system benefits all learners without any discrimination towards any individual or grou on values of democracy, tolerance and respect for difference.

Education plays the central role towards economic development, technological advancement, effective social and political participation of people by paving the way for human resource development, upward social mobility collective conscientisation of society. Education as an enabling mechanism is a result of the processes of empowerment and an important component of power. As a liberated force, it has always been recognized as a means to improve personal and collective endowment and capacity, enhance human capital, and expand the basis of opportunities and choices of individuals and groups.

Social dimension promotes social inclusion, reduces inequalities and raises aspirations and the level of knowledge, skills and competence in society. It also covers social diversity with regard to participation in and completion of higher education at all levels. The reason for it being marked as dimension is, almost all decisions made in higher education have a social impact. It has its own advantage and disadvantage. On the one hand, it provides the opportunity for people to interpret the social dimension according to their own regional needs or circumstances, and on the other hand, it can be a barrier gas the steps involved are unclear. Access to higher education is still a social problem. In countries like the UK, Ireland and the Netherlands it is easy to predict a person's future simply by looking at his or her postal code. It is a clear indicator of existing social segregation.

There is no universal solution to how to improve access to higher education, simply because different under-represented groups need different solutions. But the socio-economic background of people is the biggest factor hindering access to higher education. The solution to that problem is to provide loans to students, while forgetting that students need to pay back their debts. The financing of education is a big part of the Social Dimension. Many students have already dropped out of the education system before they have the chance to enter higher education. Therefore it is important to develop inclusion schemes at the early stages of education. Starting at secondary level may prove to be too late. Social Dimension would not only be a source of equality but also a source of justice.

In the name of offering quality education, universities and other colleges of higher learning end up isolating members of society who are different. Students who are different are seen in a negative context and same as inequality. In this case inequality in higher education is regarded as normal and continues to exist. Exclusion of certain students in higher education is based on the principle of those who are different in terms of disability, ethnic/racial, cultural, linguistic, and rural has no regard for individual differences. Higher education has always been associated with specific outcomes such as good employment opportunities and high income but with the dwindling economy many students finish their university and college education without getting any employment. Universities and colleges are also competing for most bright students and those with resources to fill the limited spaces available in universities and colleges. Institutions for higher education still perceive disability from the basis of medical model rather than social model making it rather difficult for them to understand that the student's learning problem is as a result of interaction between impairment and contextual barriers. The few vulnerable students especially those with disabilities who complete high school are in special education institutions where the quality of education offered is low due to the negative attitude of teachers.

Impediments to Inclusion:

Barriers faced by students before enrolling into higher education include;

- Social exclusion and stigmatisation by the society
- Higher education institutions catering for those with disabilities are not available in every community.
- Environments where higher education institutions are situated are not disability friendly and the facilities within the community that they are expected to use are also inaccessible.
- Admission criteria to higher education institutions are complex, inflexible and stringent for vulnerable students intending to be enrolled.
- Most vulnerable students intending to enroll into higher education are coming from poor economic background.

When students meet all the requirements for admission into higher education they still face certain barriers within higher education institutions. These barriers within the institutions include:

- ❖ Rigid curriculum and examination systems
- ❖ Lack of appropriate teaching methodology
- ❖ Feeling of inadequacy by teachers
- ❖ Content based teaching
- ❖ Rote and memorisation learning
- ❖ Tuition and coaching of students who can afford
- ❖ Exams are one-sided to discriminate students

Barriers to inclusion in higher education include:

- ❖ The implementation of inclusive education in institutions of higher learning has been affected mainly by the negative attitude of teachers and other stakeholders.
- ❖ Inclusion requires flexible teaching-learning and assessment based, flexible and accessible curriculum that is sensitive to individual differences.
- ❖ Socioeconomic aspect is another factor that affects inclusive education in higher education. Education in universities and colleges is not free and the cost is unaffordable for an ordinary citizen.
- ❖ There is lack of policy guideline on admission criteria of vulnerable students into higher learning institutions and the type of learning and financial support given to them when they are enrolled in higher education.
- ❖ The Universities and colleges need to provide; course materials in accessible formats, ensure buildings and materials, are accessible, encourage flexible teaching methods, provide support during exams, and allow additional time to complete courses. Students will also need assistance on a daily basis; interpret words in sign language, take notes for students, helping students to overcome physical, language and cultural barriers.

Conclusions:

Hence, higher education institutions need to become sensitive and responsive to the diverse students conditions. They have a responsibility of promoting lifelong learning that enables an individual to participate in the process of development and decision making, by making education accessible to all through elimination of all forms of barriers from both within higher education institutions and in the society. Higher education must ensure that all courses offered must be aware of the needs of vulnerable members of society. It is its responsibility to restructure its programmes to include the marginalized; providing assistive devices, academic flexibility, supporting aids and services, modification of the classroom environment, sign language interpreters and note takers among others. Formulation of higher education policy should involve people from diverse backgrounds and with disability in planning, implementation and its evaluation. This would lead to the creation of an inclusive society.

Bibliography

1. Ambedkar, B.R. (1972) Emancipation of the Untouchables, Bombay: Thacker and Co.
2. Amnesty International (2001) Racism and the Administration Of Justice, Amnesty International Publication, UK,
3. Amnesty International (2001)Using The International Human Rights System To Combat Racial Discrimination, Amnesty International Publication, UK.
4. Altbach, Philip G. (2006) The Private Higher Education Revolution: An Introduction. University News. January 2-8, 2006. Vol. 44 No.01.
5. Anandakrishnan, M. (2006) Privatization of higher education: Opportunities and anomalies. 'Privatization and commercialization of higher education' organized by NIEPA, May 2, 2006., New Delhi
6. Anittos, M. and McLuskie, L.(2008). On Track Toward Inclusive Education. Central Queensland, Australia Commonwealth Consortium for Education. Opportunities for Partnerships

in Education in the Commonwealth. Paper for the 15th Commonwealth Conference of Education Ministers: Edinburg, 27-30 October 2003

7. Agarwal, Pawan (2006) Higher Education in India: The Need for Change (ICIER Working Paper No. 180). New Delhi: Indian Council for Research on International Economic Relations.
8. Barnes; C. Oliver, M. and Barton, l. 'disability,, the academy and the inclusive society'. In C., Barnes et al., (eds.) Disability Studies Today, pp, 250-260, Cambridge, Polity (2002).
9. Barnes, C., (2007). 'Disability, higher education and the inclusive society', The British Journal Of Sociology Of Education, volume 28, number 1. January, pp.135 – 145
10. Barnes, C. 'Disability Studies: What's the Point? Intersticios: Revista Sociológica de Pensamiento Critico, Volume 1, Number 1.
11. Devy, Ganesh N. public lecture series, Inclusive education A view of higher education in India. national institute of advanced studies Iisc campus, bangalore-560012
12. Govinda, R.(2002) India Education Report, New Delhi: Oxford University Press.
13. Hardman, M. L., Drew, C. J. & Egan. M.W. (2005)Human Exceptionality. Allyn and Baco, Boston
14. Heward, W. L. (2006). Exceptional Child: An introduction to Special Education. Pearson, Merrill Prentice Hall,
15. Human Development Report of India 2001, GOI ,New Delhi
16. Human Development Report of India2005, GOI ,New Delhi
17. Jonsson, T. (2001). Inclusive education: Dream or Necessity? Asia Pacific Disability Rehabilitation Journal Vol. 12 N. 2, (106 – 112)
18. MHRD (2006) Annual Report. Ministry of Human Resource Development, Department of Secondary and Higher education. Government of India. New Delhi.
19. National Knowledge Commission, Report to the Nation 2006. New Delhi: National Knowledge Commission, 2007 (cited as

NKC2007) (http://knowledgecommission.gov.in/report2006/default.asp)

20. Higher Education in India: Issues, Concerns and New Directions http://www.ugc.ac.in/pub/heindia.pdf.
21. Nambissan, Geetha B. 2000, Dealing with deprivation. Seminar September
22. Ncube, J. & Macfadyen, P. (2006). Young Voices on the UN Convention on the Rights of Persons with Disabilities. Leonard Cheshire International, London
23. Planning Commission (1999) Approach paper to the Tenth Five-year Plan (2002- 2007). Planning Commission. New Delhi.
24. Rampal, A. 2000. Education for Human Development in South Asia, Economic and Political Weekly, July 22:2523-2531.
25. Rustemier, S. (2002). Inclusion Information Guide. Writen for Centre for Studies on Inclusive education, CSIE, London.
26. Sen, A. 2000, "Social Exclusion: Concept, Application and Scrutiny". Social Development Papers No.1, Asian Development Bank, June
27. Stephen J. Ball 2004 "Education for sale! The co-modification of everything. King's Annual Education lecture2004, Institute of Education, University of London.
28. Sen, A. and J. Dreze, 2002 India: Development and Participation, New Delhi: Oxford University Press.
29. UN. United Nations declaration and international convention on the elimination of all forms of racial discrimination. United Nations Department of Public Information, USA, 1997.
30. Singha Roy, D.K.2003 Social Development and the Empowerment of the Marginalised: Perspectives and Strategies, Sage Publication: New Delhi
31. UGC (2005) Research Handbook: Towards nurturing research culture in higher education institutions in India. University Grants Commission. New Delhi.
32. UN. (2008). Convention on the Rights of Persons with Disabilities: a call for action on poverty, discrimination and lack

of access. Report of a Joint Conference organised by Leonard Cheshire Disability and United Nations Economic Commission for Africa, Addis Ababa

33. UNESCO. (2005). Guidelines for Inclusion: Ensuring Access to Education for All. Paris.
34. UNICEF, (2009). Learning Guide on the Convention on the Rights of Persons with Disabilities
35. UNESCO (1994). The Salamanca Statement and Framework on Special Needs Education, Paris: UNESCO

3

HIGHER EDUCATION IN INDIA: PROBLEMS AND PROSPECTS

Dr. Ashwani Sharma*

ABSTRACT

Higher Education has assumed so much importance in the post-liberalization reforms in India that it is virtually impossible to think of competing with other developed nations of the world without having well defined agenda under higher education. Unfortunately we have been grappling with the same old age problems under higher education which we had in the pre-independence period where we had higher education for the elite section of the society. No doubt higher education has expanded tremendously since independence and more so after 1991 but despite this we have somewhere compromised with the quality and made it accessible, like earlier, to the rich section of the society which is causing serious concern in academics. In the present paper an attempt has been made to highlight factors which are responsible for poor quality of education under higher education in India resulting in higher unemployment rate causing frustration among the youth which directly or indirectly has its serious repercussions for India and its endeavors for development as we notice that some of those who, even, acquire education from reputed institutions like IITs and IIMs are unable to find job opportunities forcing them to go abroad for either education or employment causing brain drain. This paper highlights the shortcomings in Indian higher education system and in the concluding part make some recommendations its improvement and further investigation.

INTRODUCTION

Higher Education in India has a history of its own when Britishers during their colonial rule in India, for the first time, introduced

* Associate Professor, Department of Community Education & Disability Studies, Panjab University, Chandigarh

higher education in 1857 by establishing three universities at Bombay (Mumbai), Calcutta (Kolkata), and Madras (Chennai). No doubt these Universities were established on the pattern of University of London but the objectives were not to enable Indians to acquire knowledge but to introduce the Indian elite to the European culture and seeking their support and help to spread British culture to every nook and corner of India. It was aimed at producing a class of Indians fully equipped to serve the British administration in India and practice the professions like Laws, medicine and teaching according to British rules and regulations. In these institutions only those disciplines – Laws, Medicine, History, Philosophy and Literature- were introduced which were suitable to the British Government. It is ironical to say that these Universities never, in practice, encouraged a critical enquiry or logical thinking so vital to the advancement of knowledge. They introduced solely the English language as medium of instructions. Not only this, they withdrew support to the indigenous crafts, skills and professional practice where India was highly advanced in areas like textiles, architecture and medicine. Together these policies slowly and gradually created a climate where indigenous knowledge was rejected and links with traditional learning were broken.

This distanced the Indians from their own culture, restricted economic growth and their continued dependence on the British for knowledge

All these developments led to the determination on the part of Indian leadership, even before independence, to free higher education from the colonial dominance when country was very close to independence. Hence, when India got freedom, the leadership decided to take education on priority as principle instrument of India's transformation from a poor, dependant and technologically backward imperial colony into an advanced nation. In this context higher education was mandated with two responsibilities:

Higher education was required to provide manpower for economic growth and for efficient delivery of services such as healthcare, community welfare and communication, and to contribute to the advancement of knowledge in an manner which can place India at par with developed states of the world.

Higher education was to function as an instrument of equality where everyone will have the opportunity to acquire education irrespective of the fact which class, caste, creed they belong to.

It was recognized that these objectives were the opposite of those that universities in British India had served. It was believed that by instituting appropriate policies and facilities it would not be difficult to gear Universities to the new objectives.

It is in the light of this argument that we find the growth of higher education in India in the post-independence period which is considered to be the third largest in terms of students' enrolment after China and America. In India under higher education 11 % of the youth gets education in institutions of higher learning which have shown enormous growth since independence as we find that number of government recognized universities have gone up to 507 which includes 243 state Universities, 53 state private Universities, 43 Central Universities, 130 Deemed Universities, 33 Institutions of national importance under the act of parliament and 5 institutions established under various legislations. In addition to these, there are 25951 colleges including 2565 women colleges. In all these institutions 136.42 lakh students are getting education out of which 16.69 lakh (12.24%) are acquiring education in University departments and 119.73 lakh (87.765) in affiliated colleges. Nearly 5 lakh teachers are teaching in these institutions.

But despite all this unprecedented growth in higher education in India, our higher education system is plagued with serious fundamental problems which makes it unable to match with the global quality standards. Periodic evaluations undertaken by the public and private sector agencies and organizations from time to time which includes eminent academicians have highlighted the grey areas in higher education particularly in increasing unemployment, de-motivating the students and more so of the demoralizing effect of irrelevance and purposelessness of the most of the syllabi's being taught. The current scenario is that the world class institutions in India are in scarcity except the Panjab University Chandigarh which has recently been ranked no. one in BRICS countries by Times Higher Education, London.. This is due to the lack of quality research, under-investment in libraries, information technology and laboratories. This needs to be seriously looked into by the University Grants Commission which is a regulatory body at the apex level. There is a need to ensure that all possible measures are taken by the institutions of higher learning in a highly professional and judicious way. With changing economic equations and world economic order under globalization, there is immense scope to make higher education worthwhile for the younger generation of this country. Other regulatory bodies like AICTE, RCI, MCI, NCTE and NCERT etc. have equal responsibilities to share in maintaining quality standards in higher education. It is time for those who are actually associated with planning, policy making and implementation to revitalize the very thinking on higher education and put it back on the horse.

With a projected growth rate of 6% as announced by the Indian Finance Minister in his budget speech in Parliament on February 16, 2014, India now emerges as fast developing economy at the global level. It is also a producer of high skilled manpower other than doctors, engineers and scientists who are making substantial contribution to the foreign economies by migrating to countries like America, England, Australia, New Zealand and Canada etc., thus causing huge losses to their own native which who invested substantial amount of resources –economic to be more specific—on their education. To large extent institutions of higher learning are to be blamed for this as they have failed to cultivate a sense of commitment among students to serve their own country. At the same time we find rampant poverty, mass scale illiteracy and increasing unemployment which are considered to be serious deterrents to realize the potential for its human resources. Time and again world organizations like the World Bank and UNESCO have observed that education, particularly higher education, leads to more productivity and hence increases people's earnings which have direct impact on nation's social and economic development. In the light of globalization we need to concentrate on three key areas like expansion of qualitative higher education system, inclusive policy and excellence thereby enabling India to compete with the global economies in terms of manpower inputs in production and research & development including other key areas which can march India towards super power status with potential in knowledge economy. No doubt dreams are high but efforts are not very serious as they should be with the result that we are left with no choice but to open the doors to private sector educational institutions in higher education system to cope up with the increasing demand of higher education particularly in professional courses. This has been expanding very fast particularly after the economic reforms initiated after 1991. But at the same time it has started a serious debate in academic circles that to what extent these private institutions in higher education are doing justice to their existence in India so far as quality if higher education is concerned and to what extent they are relevant to the emerging Indian social structure under globalization and modernization.

Least we not forget that this country needs highly skilled manpower in the form of engineers, doctors, technocrats and managers etc. for which high quality higher education is a pre-requisite to meet. Hence we need to equip and upgrade our higher education system with market oriented courses and produce world class skilled manpower. So there is a need to diversify to those disciplines which can generate interest and employment also. No doubt we have the best brains but they need to be used optimally in the professions they qualify for. We need to de-politicize and de-commercialize our education system. Therefore, under higher education qualitative reforms are urgently required to bring back higher education on the track as this will definitely increase qualitative Gross Enrolment Ratio (GER).

We must admit that since last 2-3 decades Indian higher education system is facing major challenges in both quality and quantity as we find its detailed description in a Report to the Nation 2006 of the National Knowledge Commission which concludes that there is 'a quite crisis in higher education in India that runs deep' and that it has to do with both the quantity and quality of higher education. On this Indian Prime Minister Dr. Manmohan Singh also expressed his serious concern particularly on the deteriorating standards in higher education. Reflecting on the NAAC (National Assessment and Accreditation Council) report, he further "expressed his concern about the poor quality of education which is being imparted to the younger generation by highlighting the facts that most of the Indian Universities are academically very poor as they are teaching traditional courses with poor faculty background. Most of the courses being taught have lost their relevance in today's market, particularly courses in social sciences and languages. Qualitative research is what is lacking in both these disciplines. Situation is quite dismal in sciences also where we find, according to Science Report of UNESCO-2010, India's contribution to the world research publications is much lower (3.7%) than countries like China (10.6%) and USA (27.7%) – to name few. However, if Indian students aspire to get absorbed into the research centers on completion of their graduate studies and to add value to research projects, then they must have had enough opportunities to develop required knowledge and skills during their course works at university level. According to UNESCO-2010 report one of the major challenges for India in the coming years will be to improve both quantity and quality of scientist and researchers. Serious concern in this regard has also been shared by Bharat Ratna Prof.CNR Rao during his visit to PGI Chandigarh on March 3, 2014 when he said that research standards in education particularly in Sciences are deteriorating which is quite alarming for a nation like India who aspires to become a competitive developed economy in the coming years. This whole exercise to improve academic standards in higher education needs structural reforms at the University level. Knowledge is the base for overall growth and development of any nation and if we have to be competitive and at par with globalized world then we will have to respond to the global market needs and forces accordingly.

Challenges for the nation to tackle higher education are many as we notice that since 1947 many governments have come and gone, many education commissions-University Education Commission of 1948-49 and Kothari Commission of 1964-66- have been constituted and Education policies- 1968, 1986 and Program of Action-1992- have been in place to bring fundamental qualitative reforms in overall education but still we find that nation is grappling with unimaginable problems in higher education system. India can no longer continue with the age old model of general education as it has been persisting in for the large bulk of the student population. The new emerging economic equations at the regional and global level pose unprecedented challenge to higher education in India. In this context University Grants Commission has stated many a times that "Universities have a very crucial and important role to play in promoting fundamental changes in our curriculum. It must be designed in a way that it leaves impact on society if it is to gain popularity, legitimacy and public support".

Another important challenge to higher education is to improve the deteriorating standards in research. Government funding in research has come to the lowest ebb now. Condition of colleges in the rural areas is more pathetic as there is very poor quality of infrastructure which is responsible for low turnout of students. Government is fully aware of all these shortcomings through inspections and interventions but instead of finding solution to problems it has added more confusion in higher education. We hardly find any well informed reform agenda for remediation in higher education. Continuous curriculum up gradation is the most essential element in the qualitative improvement in higher education in order to keep pace with the rapid growth of science and technology, market driven forces under globalization and more significantly redefining the role of private institutions dealing with higher education to maintain standards and meet the needs of society at large because concentration of student enrolment is more in such institutions. Nevertheless, we still have large population of students who still do not have access to higher education for the reasons well known to us. But we must remind our policy makers and administrators that higher education needs to be viewed as a long term social investment for the promotion of economic growth, cultural development, social cohesion, equity and justice. In order to meet the 12th Plan objective of inclusive growth and to ensure endogenous and sustainable development along with social justice and equity, the higher education has to play a crucial role, especially in generating research based knowledge and develop a critical, educated and skilled manpower as is the need being felt under globalization. In this context the emerging modern Indian society has high hopes and expectations from higher education where quality of higher education needs to be sustained at the desired level.

Time has come when we need to have a highly skilled professional manpower which can take India forward and enable it to compete with the developed world. This would happen only when we create world class infrastructure in higher education along with employment opportunities within the country so that we can retain these people in our own country. Fundamental systemic changes are the need of the hour particularly in the context of partnership between industry and institutions of higher learning so that demand driven courses, as per requirement of the industry, can be introduced with full assurance to the students that their placements are secure once they pass out from such institutes. Mobilization of economic resources is equally important to strengthen the basic infrastructure and ensuring education at subsidized cost to those who cannot afford higher education as statistics shows that majority of the students do not have access to higher education due to its high cost factor. This will help us to attract deserving students. There is a need to have very strong interface between Institutions, Industry and National Laboratories. Government can ensure partnership between three through an appropriate policy. In this context UGC and MHRD need to come together and play a constructive role in developing a meaningful interface.

Bibliography

1. Aggarwal,P : Higher Education In India-the need for a change, Indian Council on International Economic Relations, 2006
2. Bhattacharya,I & Sharma,K :India in th Knowledge Economy-an electronic paradigm, International Journal of Educational Management. vol.21,No.6, 2007, pp543-68
3. 3.Carl, Dahlman & Anuja: India and the Knowledge economy-Leveraging strengths and Opportunities, World Bank Report, 2005.
4. Das,Ajay: Global Educational Reforms (Pearls,New Delhi), 2010
5. Laurence, James C: Educational Problems (Rajat,New Delhi),2010
6. Mishra, H.P.: Higher Education-New Challenges and Emerging Roles, Odisha Review, July 2012.
7. Pandey,V.C.(ed): Education and Globalization (Kalpa,New Delhi),2001
8. Rashtriya Uchchtar Shiksha Abhiyan-National Higher Education Mission-2013.
9. The World University Ranking in Times Higher Education Report-2013-14 (London)
10. UGC Annual Reports (2005-12).
11. National Knowledge Commission, Report to the Nation-2006 in www.knowledgecommission.gov.in/report 2006.
12. www.nature.com/04 November 2008

13. www.wikipedia.org.Higher_Education_in_India
14. www.ugc.ac.in August 2011
15. www.wikipedia.org./wiki/history_of_education_in_the Indian _subcontinent.
16. Ministry of Human Resource Development, India, 2007 in www.education.nic.in
17. Center for Distance Engineering Education Program, India,2007 in www.edeep.iitb.ac.in

4

Assessing Academic Performance Of Teachers In Higher Education: Dealing With Non-Linear Situations

*Dr. Jayanti Dutta**

Abstract

This paper tries to examine the parameters of faculty performance measurements in higher education and focuses on significance of the non-linear nature of teachers' roles, responsibilities, duties, nature and multiplicity of duties, diversity of disciplines, nature of knowledge, creativity and individuality. It argues for a more thoughtful, holistic, diverse and creative assessment index which is indispensible for bringing in the much desired quality in higher education.

Introduction

Parameters of measurement of faculty performance in higher education have been framed and changed from time to time as per the wisdom of the policy makers. The notification of the University Grants Commission (Minimum Qualifications for Appointment of Teachers and other Academic Staff in Universities and Colleges and Measures for the Maintenance of Standards in Higher Education) Regulations (The Gazette of India, 2010) is presently being used for the assessment of academic performance of teachers in colleges and universities in India. This is for the first time that a detailed pre-set Academic Performance Indicator (API) has been put into practice in Indian higher education scenario. This system has generated a lot of discussion in the academic circles and has enforced further amendments.

* Deputy Director, Academic Staff College Panjab University, Chandigarh,

The All India Federation of University and College Teachers' Organisation (AIFUCTO) has pointed out several flaws in the system and had protested nation-wide against the Performance Based Appraisal System (PBAS) based on API. Rumors that this system might also be scrapped and replaced by another new system are rife while the authorities are all out for implantation of the API without further delay. The UGC has amended it twice (The Gazette of India, 2011, 2013). Several universities and state governments have already implemented the API while many other universities are mulling over it. These conflicting reactions are an indicator of the challenges of framing a good measurement of faculty performance system with minimum flaws and maximum effectiveness. Though a flux is expected, the solution to settle down the unrest is to look at the issue at hand deeply and within the context of indigenous situations.

The parameters prescribed to assess teachers are not some ordinary guidelines, detached from the rest of the academics. In fact, these ultimately decide the quality of teaching, research and other academic activities in higher education institutes which has a direct bearing on the quality of students that are produced, which in turn determines the kind of society we will have. Therefore, setting the parameters of teachers' performance is a serious, significant and complicated process which must be given due thought by the policy makers before setting it loose on the academia. It is obvious that several crucial factors have been overlooked the most significant of them is the non-linearity of teachers' roles, responsibilities, duties, nature and multiplicity of duties, diversity of disciplines, nature of knowledge, creativity and individuality and hence the solution to this multi-dimensional and dynamic situation cannot be a linear one.

The need to assess academic performance of teachers in Higher education is a recent phenomenon as compared to the times when teachers were considered equivalent to God and hence beyond reproach, criticism and evaluation. Till recently teachers were needed to show only a few published papers in order to get promoted to the higher grade. Now, however, it has become mandatory for a teacher to go through a tedious routine of evaluation and assessment of preset activities in order to claim their due, increments, promotions, career advancement or just to stay in job. For the authorities a detailed rubric to assess teachers' academic performance is needed to set a certain benchmark or create a hurdle which a faculty has to jump in order to catch the hefty pay packet on the other side. The stake-holders/ society need it to keep an account of contribution of the academics in the welfare of the society. Institutes need to measure the performance of faculty for reasons of administration, recruitment and promotion, personnel decisions and as an essential aspect of the institute's accountability towards the funder, the nation and its citizen. Evaluation of a teachers work can be used by the faculty for improvement of their performance, to bring positive changes in their professional work and to check from time to time the direction their work is proceeding towards, to steer it as per the requirement of discipline, institute and society (Braskamp and Ory, 1994). In these multiple agenda the prime issue of achieving excellence in the teaching learning process becomes a non-issue and the whole purpose is defeated. Since the goals and objectives of assessment of teacher's academic performance are non-linear and not uniform the challenge can be dealt with by finding a common meeting ground where the prime consideration should be quality education. The administrators, policy holders, authorities, stakeholders and faculty have to be clear about the reason to assess academic performance of faculty and linking of this reason to overall development of the student in particular and the institute in general The measurement of faculty performance can be drafted in a way that the institutional and individual uses of assessment do not clash but compliment and support each other and is able to address both individual and institutional missions.

While in other professions performance can be based on quantitative parameters such as number of targets achieved, number of patients/ clients/consumers dealt with, products sold/manufactured, teaching does not offer such easy equations. The duties of a teacher have been defined as teaching, research and extension. These sweeping terms include infinite number of tasks that faculty must perform. Teaching can involve, on the one extreme, giving instructions in the classroom and performing administrative duties, on the other. Research can include doing lab-work on one end of the spectrum to inviting tenders and quotations on the other. Similarly extension can mean writing popular articles and also on-the- field activism. In short, faculty work is extremely complicated and non-linear. Therefore, any academic performance index consisting of a simple rubric to calculate credits for a few pre-defined activities cannot reflect the whole spectrum of actual achievement and hence will remain incomplete and flawed.

Whatever assessment criteria are marked as important for evaluation will be the parameter on which the teacher will be motivated to work on. This is a very natural implication. In case, the index values classroom teaching, the teachers would willy-nilly start emphasising on the pedagogical techniques and improvement in this domain will take place. On the other hand if research parameters are highlighted the faculty would focus on that area. The challenge is to find a fine balance between the assessment of the two equally important areas of teaching and research. However, since research is easier to be measured quantitatively on the basis of number of publications, citations, impact factor, number of authors, sequence of authorship etc. and since we are yet to develop quantitative rubrics for measuring the quality of classroom teaching, the index is lopsided towards research and totally ignores pedagogy. This skew can have detrimental consequences for quality teaching in higher education institutes. Research indicates that across institutional types and different fields of study, faculty who spend the least time on teaching and the most on research receive the highest salaries (Fairweather, 1996). The stakeholders would have to give this aspect a serious thought as to whether the assessment criteria of faculty is in tune with the expectations we have in the area of teaching. Otherwise, since faculty rewards are rarely linked to teaching innovations such as creating student-centered classroom learning environment, focus on active learning, development of pedagogical content knowledge (Lazerson, Wagener and Shumanis, 2000), it is highly likely that faculty stops spending time on such non-productive work of teaching (from the perspective of assessment) which competes with research in allocation of faculty time (Austin, 1996). Discipline-specific rationales for restructuring evaluation and reward teaching in ways compatible to research are available in literature (Diamond and Adam, 2000) and can be further developed as per our indigenous situations.

Even when research is being assessed it is important that we base the evaluation on sound foundation. Publication of research papers/articles in reputed journals has become an important factor in assessment of the academic performance of teachers. One of the measures of reputation and academic standard (rank or importance) of a journal is the so-called 'Impact Factor.' Detailed statistical analysis of journal impact factors across the disciplines finds that if it is used to assess the academic performance of individuals (for the purpose of selection, promotion, etc) without bearing in mind that due to vast differences in the nature of distribution of impact factors across the disciplines they are not justifiably comparable, a below average scholar in the one discipline will rank higher and will be honored (and benefitted) more than another scholar in some other discipline (wherein the journal impact factor is adversely skewed) (Mishra, 2009).

There are specializations with low impact factor journals and others with very high impact factor journals. The teachers/researchers of different specializations in the departments compete with each other for promotion. In this milieu, the researchers with an unfortunate specialization (wherein the journal impact factor is mingy or adversely skewed) would receive injustice is plainly predetermined. Therefore, other measures quantifying the quality as well as productivity of an individual author/scholar would be more appropriate than the journal impact factor.. Nevertheless, even these indexes would not be appropriate to the purpose of interdisciplinary or inter-specialization comparisons. A more informed and balanced judgment of the expert committee for selection, appointment and promotion purposes will continue to be extremely important (Mishra, 2009).

The nature of faculty performance is further diversified depending on the disciplines they are dealing in. Disciplinary differences affect the relative emphases on teaching and research goals of undergraduate education, perspectives on curriculum, and teaching methods and practices and students ratings of teachers (Braxtons and Hargens, 1996; Cashin, 1995; Paulsen and Wells, 1998; Smart, Fieldman and Ethington, 2000). Disciplinary differences also affect the nature and construction of pedagogical content knowledge as well as how it should be evaluated (Hutchings and Shulman, 1999; Shulman, 1993). Since institutional goals are manifested through the departments and each department has situation specific goals (Austin, 1996) hence faculty should be actively involved in articulating and negotiating department specific faculty responsibilities and criteria and methods to evaluate the teacher's role (Arreola, 2000). In fact, each department should be granted the liberty to design specific evaluation criteria instead of thrusting a generic, broad and all encompassing performance index which ignores the non-linearity of each discipline.

A teacher's performance is also impacted by the uniqueness of their own intellect, their temperament, the opportunities/ chances they have got in their career and several factors out of the control of the faculty. The performance index that does not acknowledge, recognize and respect this uniqueness is perilous for our education system. According to Wergin and Swingen (2000) faculty members should be able to focus their efforts on those activities that best match their own interests, skills and experience by negotiating with their colleagues how they can best use their talents to contribute to the collective work of their department. An extremely significant aspect of academic work is colleague-ship or collegiality. Assessment parameters should be such as promotes collegiality, does not damage team work and nourish rivalries. Measurements which discourage collaborations, team work, credit sharing, and cooperation are sure to destroy the academic culture and prove highly acidic to the environment so conducive to the nurturing of teaching and research. Though this seems to be an ideal situation and may pose logistic difficulties in real life yet similar mechanisms need to be experimented with and developed. In fact, there cannot be a single, rigid, fixed and non-flexible dictate to mark the performance of the entire faculty whether they are teaching mathematics or dance, whether they have put in 12 years of service or 24 years, whether they have flair for teaching or for research. One size fits all is not a good assessment index.

Finally, the assessment index should be administered in a totally threat-free, bias-free platform where faculty is not judged but should provide formative inputs. In fact the Latin root of the word 'Assessment' means 'to sit beside'. It is well known that panic stricken individuals perform at a lower level than usual; they become less creative, less innovative, and more rigid. How can such a teacher contribute positively for the academic upliftment of the institute? Therefore, it is in the welfare of everybody- students, institutes, society that the measurement of faculty performance takes cognizance of the subtleties of teaching profession specially its non-linear character and does not devalue it through some hastily drafted, sketchy rules.

There is a huge body of research on performance based assessment system in the countries where it is in vogue for quite some time now. When we are bent upon implement of academic performance index in a vast and diverse country like India where the non-linearity of teaching situations becomes yet more acute, it would be wise to first introduce it on a pilot basis, weed out its flaws after rigorous research, creation of scientific measures for evaluation of teaching and research and only then put it into practice on a pan India basis. Otherwise, the haste in implementing the operation can backfire and result in irreconcilable harm to our education system, students and stakeholders which is not desirable at all.

Bibliography

1. Arreola, R. Developing a Comprehensive Faculty Evaluation System: A Handbook for College Faculty and Administrators on Designing and Operating a Comprehensive Faculty Evaluation System. Bolton, Mass.: Anker, 2000.
2. Austin, A. "Institutional and Departmental Cultures: The Relationship Between Teaching and Research." In J. Braxton (ed.), Faculty Teaching and Research: Is There a Conflict? New Directions for Institutional Research, no. 90. San Francisco: Jossey-Bass, 1996.
3. Braskamp, L.A, and Ory, J.C. Assessing Faculty Work: Enhancing Individual and Institutional Performance, San Francisco: Jossey-Bass, 1994
4. Braxton, J., and Hargens, L. "Variation Among Academic Disciplines: Analytical Frameworks and Research." In J. Smart (ed.), Higher Education: Handbook of Theory and Research. Vol. 11. New York: Agathon Press, 1996.
5. Cashin, W. E. Student Ratings of Teaching: The Research Revisited. Idea Paper, no. 32. Manhattan, Kans.: Center for Faculty Evaluation and Faculty Development, Kansas State University, 1995.
6. Diamond, R. M., and Adam, B. E. (eds.). The Disciplines Speak II: More Statements on Rewarding the Scholarly, Professional,

and Creative Work of Faculty. Washington, D.C.: American Association for Higher Education, 2000.

7. Fairweather, J. S. Faculty Work and Public Trust: Restoring the Value of Teaching and Public Service in American Academic Life. Boston: Allyn & Bacon, 1996.

8. Gazette of India UGC (Minimum Qualifications for Appointment of Teachers and other Academic Staff in Universities and Colleges and Measures for the Maintenance of Standards in Higher Education) Regulations, Part III, Sector-4, F-3-1/2009 (EC/PS) Vol. II September 18, 2010

9. Gazette of India UGC (Minimum Qualifications for Appointment of Teachers and other Academic Staff in Universities and Colleges and Measures for the Maintenance of Standards in Higher Education) Regulations, Part III, Sector-4, MS 1-2/2009 (EC/PS) Vol. II February 11, 2011

10. Gazette of India UGC (Minimum Qualifications for Appointment of Teachers and other Academic Staff in Universities and Colleges and Measures for the Maintenance of Standards in Higher Education) Regulations, Part III, Sector-4, NoF1-2/2009 (EC/PS) V(i) Vol. II, June 13, 2013

11. Hutchings, P., and Shulman, L. "The Scholarship of Teaching: New Elaborations, New Developments." Change, 1999, 31(5), 11–15.

12. Lazerson, M., Wagener, U., and Shumanis, N. "Teaching and Learning in Higher Education, 1980–2000." Change, 2000, 32(3), 13–19.

13. Mishra,SK Does the Journal Impact Factor help make a good indicator of Academic performance?, Munich Personal RePEc Archive, deposited October 7, 2009.

14. Paulsen, M. B., and Wells, C. "Domain Differences in the Epistemological Beliefs of College Students." Research in Higher Education, 1998, 39(4), 365–384.

15. Shulman, L. S. "Teaching as Community Property: Putting an End to Pedagogical Solitude." Change, 1993, 25(6), 6–7.

16. Smart, J., Feldman, K., and Ethington, C. Academic Disciplines:

Holland's Theory and the Study of College Students and Faculty. Nashville, Tenn.: Vanderbilt University Press, 2000.

17. Wergin, J. F., and Swingen, J. N. Departmental Assessment: How Some Campuses Are Effectively Evaluating the Collective Work of Faculty. Washington, D.C.: American Association for Higher Education, 2000.

5

Alienation and Depression among Students in Higher Education: An overview

Dr Komila Parthi*

Abstract

Attaining higher education is a major challenge among students and a dream to fulfill for the parents. No amount of adversities deters the students or the parents from achieving their goal. However, with the change of environment and lack of social support, students get alienated which in turn increases the likelihood of depression among them.

Objective: *To explore the relationship of alienation and depression among students in higher education.*

Conclusions and implications: *It is vital for college/university campus to be equipped with well functioning counseling cells. It is imperative to closely observe and conduct surveys within the campus to identify high risk students. Peer counselors should be identified within each class to be able to identify and rectify behavior problems within peers.*

Introduction

Attaining higher education is a major challenge in the life of a student and a dream to be fulfilled for the parents. To achieve this goal, adversities do not deter the student or the parents, considering the potential benefits it brings with it. It may also include movement from a rural hamlet to a city which brings with it a change in the environment and social support (Bugra & Ayonrinde, 2004). Students face challenges such as living independently for the first time, making new friends, and

* Assistant Professor, DAV College Sector 10, Chandigarh

deciding on an academic major (Towbes & Cohen, 1996). They often suffer from a 'relational deficit' (Sawir et al., 2007), issues of personal autonomy (Baker & Siryk, 1986) and the recreation of identity in the new setting. Often, the physical and cultural environment is very different, with new social customs and norms. (Church,1982). The student starts to get a feeling of being different from the rest thereby getting alienated. In this the individual experiences low self-esteem and aspires to become another person, which can lead to psychological problems (Kalekin-Fishman, 2006). These problems may begin with stressors of everyday life such as transportation, financial burdens, and interpersonal conflicts (Staats, Cosmar & Kaffenberger, 2007). It is reported that the millennial generation (also referred to as the Y generation—is defined as those born between 1982 and 2003. This generation was proceeded by Generation X (defined as those born between 1961 and 1981) are experiencing higher college related stress as compared to the previous generation (Howe & Strauss, 2007). Stressful life events can also increase the likelihood of occurrence of depressive symptoms among students (Kadison & DiGeronimo, 2004; Sokratous, Merkouris, Middleton & Karanikola, 2013).

Thereby, a need was felt to understand the causes of alienation and depression among the students in higher education, particularly those living away from home. Thus the objective of the present study was to explore the relationship of alienation and depression among the students in higher education.

Alienation

Alienation plays a vital role in the adjustment of students in college (Pound, 1987). Victims of social alienation were less effective socially, had fewer friends, felt lonelier, and participated less in extra-curricular activities. They were also less likely to have personal contacts with others on campus or to become integrated into the social systems within the institution (Pound, 1987). Mann (2001) also described it as the state or experience of being isolated from a group or an activity to which one should belong or in which one should be involved. According to Fullilove (1996) an individual requires a "good enough" environment in which to live. They are linked to that environment through three key psychological processes: attachment, familiarity, and identity. Each of these psychological processes-attachment, familiarity, and place identity-is threatened by displacement, and the problems of nostalgia, disorientation and alienation may ensue. Alienation has been defined as "a separation or distance among two or more entities and involves a sense of anguish or loss, resulting in a student viewing life and school as fragmentary and incomplete" (Brown et al. (2003, p.4). Four fundamental aspects of student alienation have been defined as: (Newman, 1981) powerlessness, normlessness, meaninglessness, and social isolation.

Powerlessness refers to student perception of absence of personal control in learning.

Normlessness reflects lack of appropriate rule-governed behavior (e.g., academic dishonesty).

Meaninglessness describes alienated students' interpretation of curriculum as irrelevant to their current and future needs.

Social Isolation defines a feeling of being alone.

In the recent past alienation has also been described as student's estrangement in the learning process (Brown, Higgins, & Paulsen, 2003). Thereby recognizing the five meanings of alienation put forth by Seeman (1959). Thus, it is an umbrella concept that is sometimes used interchangeably with other terms such as isolation or anomie (Seeman, 1991). Research literature also supports that alienation is linked to "gang activity, violence, vandalism, absenteeism, truancy, and other forms of deviant behavior" (Brown et al., 2003, p.4) which may lead to school dropouts and students can suffer from social alienation even as adults. Alienation has also been correlated with anxiety, deviant behavior, substance abuse, low participation in school activities poor social skills, low academic motivation, low self-esteem, psychological distress, and depression (Newman & Newman, 2001; Claes, 2003; Rose-Sepowitz & Thyer, 2004; O'donnell, Schwab-Stone, & Ruchkin, 2006).

Depression

Depression is emerging in epidemic proportions in modern society (Seligman, 1991) and according to World Health Organization by 2020 it will be the second most common prevalent condition worldwide.

Research conducted on students in higher education reinforce that depression is a mental health problem that frequently occurs (Adams, Wharton, Quilter, & Hirsch, 2008; S. J. Cho et al., 2002; E. H. Lee, 2004; Roh et al., 2006). The prevalence of depression through different studies conducted in Korea reveal that depression varied between 14.3 percent to 26.8 percent among college students (S.J. Choi, 2003; Kim, 2004 ; E.H. Lee, 2004). In Iran, in a study conducted among high school and Pre-University students results reported that 34 percent of them were depressed according to cut-off score of BDI 16 (Modabber-Nia et al., 2007). While in a study in India the prevalence among college going girls was reported to be 29 percent (Nair et al., 2004).

Literature on depression also reveals that females report more depressive disorders as compared to the males (American Psychiatric Association, 1994; Nolen-Hoeksema, 2001; Kessler et al., 2003; H. Y. Kim, 2004; E. H. Lee, 2004; Roh et al., 2006; Lin et al., 2008; Nolen-Hoeksema & Hilt, 2009; Ryba & Hopko, 2012). A number of factors account for this difference such as biological influences, psychosocial variables such as more frequent victimization and trauma in childhood, gender role factors (e.g., competing social roles, role restrictions), interpersonal orientation such as increased vulnerability to the emotional pain of others, being more prone to rumination, differential attributional styles, and greater reactivity to stress in terms of biological responses, self-concept, and coping styles (Bierut et al., 1999; Steiner et al., 2003;Nolen-Hoeksema & Hilt, 2009). Females are also vulnerable to stress related to establishment of identity, formation of close relationships, getting a job, marriage, pregnancy, and delivery (Jung, 2009; Park, 2003). In a study conducted on 2163 college students from the University of Puerto Rico, Reyes-Rodríguez et al., (2013) concluded that the model that best explained the variance of Beck Depression Inventory scores among females was the presence of suicide risk, relationship break-up, illness, and relocation for college, whereas for males a similar model without the relationship break-up variable resulted in a better fit.

Sokratous et al., (2013) attempted to link the depressive symptoms among Cypriot university students and concluded that a high number of stressful life events were more likely to manifest clinical depressive symptoms. An increase in depressive symptoms such as hopelessness, anxiety and poor quality of life may also report suicide ideation among students (Farabaugh, 2012; Nyer et al., 2013).

Alienation and Depression: Interlinked

Research reveals that alienation emerged as an important mediating variable, having a significant effect on depression and suicidal thoughts. It was also reported that depression was indirectly affected through alienation by school attachment, peer relationships, and academic performance. Suicidal thoughts were also greatly affected by depression, and were directly and indirectly influenced by alienation (Lee, 2007). Safipour (2011) also reported a strong association between the feeling of alienation and having more self reported mental health problems; this suggests the mediating role of the feeling of alienation between mental health and physical health of students.

In a study conducted by the author comparing the students from North India and North East India on depression and alienation, the results revealed an overall high score on alienation for all four groups, which indicate a syndrome, rampant over the campuses. However, a deeper insight into the results reveal that female students from North India were relatively less alienated as compared to their male counterparts and even the North East females (t=2.604**). A number of reasons could be attributed to the significant differences emerging between the two groups. Some of the reasons can be viz., having distinct physical features, language, religion and cultural variations in terms of festivals and rituals performed which could be alienating the female students from North East. While the girls from North Indian regions perhaps have no such problems marring their absorption in the local social milieu.

The results also reveal higher scores on depression among males as compared to the females. This may be due to the fact that males experience a higher turbulence as compared to the females as there are pressures of unrealistic demands to achieve success from themselves and from others in the family. Females as such are known to have better communication skills, interpersonal dealings and social values (Aufora et al., 1994). They also most likely are more steadfast, socially wise, more stable and mature as compared to their young male counterparts. This might indicate better social adjustments and adaptability of these girls in a land away from home. More so, all these factors might facilitate better adjustment and more effective stress coping social strategies for girls especially in the Indian culture, where in spite of all westernization, still girls enjoy a more protective and generous attitude of the society. While in the West, owing to their stress on 'independence', it is apparently the same kind of social status that persists for both the genders, in a way explaining the opposite results in non-Indian samples, where girls exhibit more depression.

Conclusions

Research literature supports the view that alienation may reinforce deviant behaviors. It also plays a mediating role in developing depressive disorders among students in higher education. To meet these emerging needs among students in higher education it is imperative to undertake immediate measures. The stigma attached to seeking psychological help needs to be worked upon by authorities by providing counseling cells on the campus. Empowering vulnerable students psychologically and building their confidence will prepare them to face the challenges offered on the campus. Peer counselors should be selected within each class to be able to identify and rectify behavior problems within peers. It is essential to closely observe and conduct surveys within the campus to spot high risk students. For students to excel in academics, a feeling of acceptance by teachers and peers for students away from home is necessary. To inculcate this feeling, a close knit environment with sensitivity, support and an empathetic shoulder need to be developed. Interventions in terms of therapy, individual and family counseling sessions and referrals in case of serious disorders can be arranged to reduce depressive disorders among students.

Bibliography

1. Adams, T. B., Wharton, C. M., Quilter, L., & Hirsch, T. (2008). The association between mental health and acute infectious illness among a national sample of 18- to 24-year-old college students. Journal of American College Health, 56, 657-663.
2. American Psychiatric Association, Diagnostic and Statistical Manual of Mental Disorders, Author, Washington, DC, USA,4th edition, 1994.

3. Aufora, A. et al., (1994). Personal vs.social values in Romanian students. Revue Roumaini de Psychlogie, Jan.-Jun., Vol.38 (1), 25-32.
4. Baker, R. W., & Siryk, B. (1986). Exploratory intervention with scale measuring adjusting to college. Journal of Counseling Psychology, 33, 31-38.
5. Bierut, L.J., Heath, A.C., Phil, D., et al., (1999). "Major depressive disorder in a community based twin sample. Arch Gen Psychiatry, 56; 557-563.
6. Brown, M. R., Higgins, K., & Paulsen, K. (2003). Adolescent alienation: What is it and what can educators do about it? Intervention in School & Clinic, 39(1), 3-7.
7. Cho, S. J., Jeon, H. J., Kim, J. K., Suh, T. W., Kim, S. U., Hahm, B. J., Cho, M. J.(2002). Prevalence factors of suicide attempts in junior and high school adolescents. Korean Journal of Neuropsychiatric Association, 41, 1142-1155.
8. Choi, M. K. (2003). Symptoms, depression, and coping behaviors of university students. Journal of Korean Academy of Public Health Nursing, 33, 433-439.
9. Church, A. T. (1982). Sojourner adjustment. Psychological Bulletin, 91, 540-572.
10. Claes, M. (2003). Theoretical structure of adolescent alienation: A multi-group
11. confirmatory factor analysis. Adolescence, 10. Retrieved from www.highbeam.com/library/docfreeprint.asp?docid DOI: 10.1177/1028315307299699
12. Farabaugh A, Bitran S, Nyer M, Holt DJ, Pedrelli P, Shyu I, Hollon SD, Zisook S, Baer L, Busse W, Petersen TJ, Pender M, Tucker DD,Fava M. (2012). Depression and suicidal ideation in college students. Psychopathology, 45(4):228-34. doi: 10.1159/000331598. Epub 2012 May 22.
13. Fullilove, M.T. (1996). Psychiatric implications of displacement: contributions from the psychology of place. Am J Psychiatry, 153 (12):1516-23 8942445 (P,S,G,E,B) Cited:3

14. Howe, N. & Strauss, W. (2007). Millennials go to college. Life Course Associates, United States.

15. in a community-based twin sample: are there different genetic and environmental contributions for men and women?" Archives of General Psychiatry, vol. 56, no. 6, pp. 557–563.

16. Israel, J. (1971). Alienation; from Marx to modern sociology; a macrosociological analysis. Boston: Allyn and Bacon.

17. Jung, D. H. (2009). The effects of stress coping on life stress and it's related anxiety and depression in university students. Journal of Research in Education, 33, 221-244.

18. Kadison, R. & DiGeronimo, T. F. (2004). College of the overwhelmed. San Francisco: Jossey-Bass.

19. Kalekin-Fishman, D. (2006). Studying alienation: Toward a better society? Kybernetes, 35(3/4), 522_530.

20. Kessler, R.C., Berglund, P., Demler, o., et al., (2003). "The epidemiology of major depressive disorder: results from the National Comorbidity Survey Replication (NCS-R)," Journal of the American Medical Association, vol. 289, no. 23, pp. 3095–3105.

21. Lee, E. (2007) Construction of a structural model about male and female adolescents' alienation, depression, and suicidal thoughts. Taehan Kanho Hakhoe Chi Jun; 37(4):576-85.

22. Lee, E. H. (2004). Life stress and depressive symptoms among college students: Testing for moderating effects of coping style with structural effects of coping style with structural equations. Korean Journal of Health Psychology, 9, 25-52.

23. Lin, H. C., Tang, T. C., Yen, J. Y., Ko, C. H., Huang, C. F., Liu, S. C., & Yen, C. F. (2008). Depression and its association with self-esteem, family, peer and school factors in a population of 9586 adolescents in southern Taiwan. Psychiatry Clinical Neurosciences, 62, 412-420.

24. Mann, S. J. (2001). Alternative perspective on the student experience: Alienation and engagement. Studies in Higher Education, 26, 7-13.

25. Mau, R. Y. (1992). The validity and devolution of a concept: Student alienation. Adolescence, 27 (107), 731-744

26. Modabber-Nia MJ, Shodjai-Tehrani H, Moosavi SR, Jahanbakhsh-Asli N, Fallahi M. (2007). The prevalence of depression among high school and pre university adolescents: Rasht, Northern Iran. Arch Iran Med. 2007 ; 10:141–6. [PubMed]

27. Nair MK, Paul MK, John R. (2004) Prevalence of depression among adolescents. Indian J Pediatr. 71:523–4. [PubMed]

28. Newman, B.M., & Newman, P.R. (2001). Group identity and alienation: Giving the we its due. Youth and Adolescence, 30(5), 515_538.

29. Newman, F. M. (1981). Reducing student alienation in high schools: Implications of theory. Harvard Educational Review, 5 (4), 546-564.

30. Newmann, F. M. (1981). Reducing student alienation in high school: Implications of theory. Harvard Educational Review, 51, 117-129.

31. Nolen-Hoeksema, S. & Hilt, L.M. (2009). "Gender differences in depression," in Handbook of Depression, I. H. Gotlib and C. L. Hammen, Eds., pp. 386–404, Guilford Press, New York, NY, USA, 2nd edition.

32. Nolen-Hoeksema,, S. (2001). "Gender differences in depression," CurrentDirections in Psychological Science, vol. 10, no. 5, pp. 173–176.

33. Nyer M, Holt DJ, Pedrelli P, Fava M, Ameral V, Cassiello CF, Nock MK, Ross M, Hutchinson D, Farabaugh A.(2013). Factors that distinguish college students with depressive symptoms with and without suicidal thoughts. Ann Clinical Psychiatry, 25 (1):41-9.

34. O'donnell, D.A., Schwab-Stone, M.E., & Ruchkin, V. (2006). The mediating role of alienation in the development of maladjustment in youth exposed to community violence. Development and Psychopathology, 18(1), 215_232.

35. Park, K. (2003). The effect of negative life stress and interpersonal

problem on woman's depression. Korean Journal of Health Psychology, 8, 581-593.

36. Pounds, A.W. (1987). Black students needs on predominantly white campuses. In D. Wright (ed.) Responding to the needs of today's minority students, 29-33. San Francisco: Jossey-Bass.
37. Redden, C.E. (2002). Social alienation of African American students: Implication for social support system. Paper presented at the National Convention of the Association for Counselor Education and Supervision, Park City, UT.
38. Reyes-Rodríguez ML, Rivera-Medina CL, Cámara-Fuentes L, Suárez-Torres A, Bernal G.(2013). Depression symptoms and stressful life events among college students in Puerto Rico. J Affect Disord 2013 Mar 5; 145(3):324-30. doi: 10.1016/j.jad.2012.08.010. Epub 2012 Aug 29.
39. Roh, M. S., Jeon, H. J., Lee, H. W., Lee, H. J., Han, S. K., & Hahm, B. J. (2006). Depressive disorders among the college students: Prevalence, risk factors, suicidal behaviors and dysfunctions. Korean Journal of Neuropsychiatric Association,45, 432-437.
40. Rose-Sepowitz, D.E., & Thyer, B.A. (2004). Adolescent mental health. In L.A. Rapp-Paglicci, C.N. Dulmus, & J.S. Wodarski (Eds.), Prevention interventions for children and adolescents (pp. 67_84). Hoboken, NJ: Wiley.
41. Ryba, M.M. & Hopko, D.R. (2012). Gender Differences in Depression: Assessing Mediational Effects of Overt Behaviors and Environmental Reward through Daily Diary Monitoring. Depression Research and Treatment, Volume 2012, Article ID 865679, 9 pages, doi:10.1155/2012/865679. Hindawi Publishing Corporation
42. Safipour, J. (2011). Self-reported health and social alienation in Swedish adolescents: A cross-sectional study among high-school students in Stockholm. Published by Karolinska Institutet. Printed by [universitet service -AB] © Jalal Safipour, 2011 ISBN 978-91-7457-503-3.
43. Sandhu, D. S. (1995). An examination of the psychological needs of the international students: Implication for counseling

and psychotherapy. International journal for the advancement of counseling, 17, 229-239.

44. Sawir, E., Marginson, S., Deumert, A., Nyland, C & Ramia, G. (2007). Loneliness and International Students:An Australian Study. Journal of Studies in International Education, Vol. XX No. X, Season XXXX xx-xx (2007)

45. Seeman, M. (1975). Alienation studies. Annual Review of Sociology, 1, 91_123.

46. Seeman, M. (1991). Alienation and anomie. In J.P. Robinson, P.R. Saver, & L.S. Wrightsman (Eds.), Measures of personality and social psychological attitudes (Vol. 1, pp. 291_371). San Diego, CA: Academic Press.

47. Seeman,, M. (1959). On the meaning of Alienation .American Sociological Review 24, 783-791.

48. Seligman, M. E. P. (1991). Learned optimism. New York: Knopf.

49. Sokratous S, Merkouris A, Middleton N, Karanikola M. (2013). The association between stressful life events and depressive symptoms among Cypriot university students: a cross-sectional descriptive correlational study. BMC Public Health 2013 Dec 5; 13:1121. doi: 10.1186/1471-2458-13-1121.

50. Staats, S., Cosmar, D., & Kaffenberger, J. (2007). Sources of happiness and stress for college students: A replication and comparison over 20 years. Psychological Reports, 101, 683-696.

51. Steiner, M., Dunn, E., & L. Born,L. (2003). "Hormones and mood: from menarche to menopause and beyond," Journal of Affective Disorders, vol. 74, no. 1, pp. 67–83.

Vredenburg,K., O'Brien,E, and Krames, L. (1988). Depression in college students: personality and experiential factors. Journal of Counseling Psychology, Vol.35.No.4, pp 419-425.

6

Retention of Faculty in Institutions of Higher Education

*Dr. Yajvender Pal Verma**

Abstract:

Faculty and its quality have an enduring impact on the quality of higher education. In India, teachers have been accorded the highest esteem in the society. However, over the past few decades, the academic profession is facing a sever crisis. Attracting and retaining highly qualified human resource is essential for the success and growth of any organization. It is equally important for the academic institute and any corporate sector to leverage and nurture these assets for continuous growth of the organization. The excellence of an educational institute depends on the kind of faculty it can attract and retain because it is the faculties that take any educational institution to the acme of success. The recruitment of faculty has become a major challenge for higher educational institutions, yet a much bigger challenge is to retain faculty, since a number of faculty members switch organizations due to want of good working environment. The sudden loss of intellect faculty impacts negatively on existing academic plans of institute. Therefore, it is very important that educational institutions frame and adopt policies and regulations so as to compete well in education sector to attract and retain for them the best faculty talent.

Keywords-*Retention, Faculty, Higher Education.*

Introduction

Higher education has an important and crucial role in India's ability to succeed in the present global economic system. The number of institutions serving the sector and student enrolments in India

* Assistant Professor, University Institute of Engineering & Technology, Panjab University, Chandigarh.

have expanded very rapidly in recent decades. The excellence of educational institute depends upon many factors. However, there are three important factors which are responsible for the excellence of any educational institution. First is the quality of its faculty members which include their research work, their exposure and their teaching methodologies etc. The second is the infrastructure facilities available in the institute which include research labs, journals, books and funds to carry out the research. The third most important factor is the learning environment which sets the tone for the excellence in education and research. The increase in educational attainments have contributed significantly to the high economic growth rates in the services sector that have increased the economic performance of India in the last decade. Yet higher education institutions and their performance are faced with many problems, and this has been a major factor of policy concern. Most of the higher education institutions in India face serious problems of faculty shortage and in maintaining the quality of education. However, each institute follows different methods or strategies to tackle these problems. The actions of one type of institution can impact the decisions and policies of other institutes significantly. These impacts can be either positive or negative. Hence, in order to develop strategies for addressing the problem of faculty shortage, it is important for the policy makers to take an overall systemic view of how the higher education sector functions, and hence to assess how different components would respond to policy interventions.

Faculty Demand Determinants

In India, after liberalization a rapid increase was observed in the number of higher educational institutions particularly in professional courses. The demand for faculty in these higher educational institutes increased drastically. The extent of faculty shortage in percentage terms is believed to be substantial, varying between 25 to 45 per cent. There are a large number of unfilled vacancies for faculty in both universities and colleges. Typically, faculty shortage is estimated by the number of unfilled positions as a proportion of the sanctioned posts. However, there is very little knowledge even among experts and policy makers on the degree of faculty shortage that prevails in different academic disciplines. The number of sanctioned positions in any higher education institution is administratively determined, and these numbers generally remain fixed for long periods. Thus, the number of sanctioned positions does not necessarily reflect the actual demand for faculty prevailing in the academic market. The market demand for faculty resources is determined by the decisions of higher education institutions in response to the demand for higher education from students as depicted in Figure 1. The latter in turn depends on the underlying demographic trends, and economic determinants such as trends in income and employment aspirations, all of which change over time.

Any educational institute of higher education institution has to find the optimum combination between its net operating income and its reputation. These objectives represent short run and long run dimensions of institutional success. It can also significantly enhance the capacity of the academic institution to earn a higher income. This arises from their improved ability to attract students, charge higher tuition fees, innovate and create new academic programmes and/or courses, to win research projects and to earn consulting incomes. High reputation also makes it easier to attract high quality faculty. The nature and quantity of faculty resources that are demanded by the institutions therefore depends on how they choose to allocate their budgetary resources between net income generating activities and building institutional reputation.

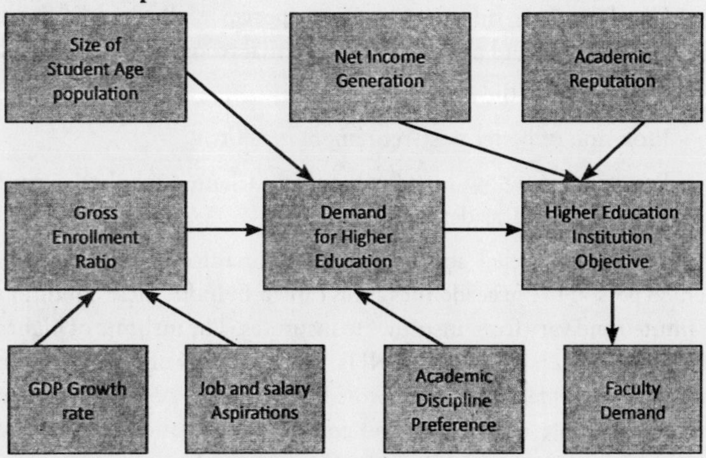

Figure 1 Faculty demand determinants in the education sector

METHODOLOGY TO ATTRACT FACULTY

To evolve a strategy to attract and retain good faculties is not easy. There are many reasons, firstly the academics no more enjoys the reputation and esteem as it was in old time. Besides this, there are better career opportunities than academics for the academically bright students of professional courses. Normally, a person who enters in to academics need to obtain PhD degree which has longer time span as compared to any engineering and other professional degree where one can start earning at very early age. Moreover, there is no efficient and attractive policy for recruitment of the faculty. Huge numbers of faculty members are recruited on contract basis resulting uncertainty in careers. Therefore, very few opt for the teaching as their career. This calls for interventions to improve the standards of post graduate and doctoral education in the country on the one hand and re-look at salary structure and career opportunities of the other. Monetary incentives are not the only, nor perhaps the most significant influence on the decision to take up an academic career. Besides salaries, other important structural determinants of the supply of faculty resources include [6]:

- Better Service conditions such as justified teaching work load, better opportunities for research and administrative facilitation.
- Attractive salaries structure comparable to other professions and employment.
- Good career advancement prospects, skill up gradation programmes and possibilities of external recognition of research.
- Reputation of the institution.
- Provision of better post-retirement benefits.
- Provision of fellowships for inducting talented scholars towards PhD work and academic careers

The factors mentioned above play an important role in attracting a talented person to opt academics as his career. In India, these conditions are limited and vary from institutes to institutes. The institute of highest reputation like IITs, IIMs, IIITs, NITs, IISc and many other universities are able to attract faculty as they provide a good career option for them. However, in state universities and colleges the situation is not good. The condition of private colleges and universities barring a few is very bad. In these institutions, the faculty members are not paid adequately, they have limited resources and facilities for career growth and most of the time their career of job is on the mercy of their management. The talented faculty will feel suffocated this environment and prefers to shift frequently as and when he or she gets and opportunities. In addition to these, in most of the institutions both government and private, the faculty members are hired on contract basis. Thus, there is always an uncertainty in their career and a faculty member join under compulsions and always looks for opportunities elsewhere where one can get stable job.

Methodology for Retaining Faculty

With the growing demand of faculty and attractive pay packages being offered by many private universities, the retention of faculty members have been a challenging task for many institutes. As frequent switching is resulting not only a monetary huge loss but they also suffer academically. There are few practices which an educational institute can adopt to retain its valuable human resource on which institute has already made a significant investment. A number of solutions have been proposed by various authors to retain the faculty [7]. The various steps for retaining the good faculty members are as follows.

- A standard recruitment and selection process should be followed and recruitment be made throughout the year.
- There must be equity in compensation depending upon experience and quality of work. An attractive compensation package must be offered to good faculty.
- Better physical infrastructure (such as residential facilities, ground, gymnasium and others) must be created.
- A formal orientation program must be conducted for fresh recruits where they should be made well aware with the policies & procedures of their institution.
- Conduct Faculty Development Programs for their employees in order to improve their personality & to shape their career.
- Recognize outstanding performances through salary and other forms of compensation, and also, as appropriate, through

opportunities for leadership or for initiatives of special interest to the faculty member and the institution.

- Efforts to provide faculty with the flexibility to accommodate and balance the needs of family and work contribute to their productivity, satisfaction and retention.
- Recognizing the necessity for faculty members to acquire new experiences to enrich their teaching and also to provide time for research projects and writing, sabbatical leaves should be granted for: One semester at full salary; or one academic year at one half of full salary.
- Good reputation attracts better ranked students and good quality of students ensures the quality the research and teaching efforts of the institute's faculty.
- The academic load of faculty members should be communicated well in advance to allow them to prepare well for their classes. Haphazard, planning distracts many faculty members and their research output gets affected.
- Faculty must get reasonable teaching load, should have the availability of latest research literature, Lab facilities and funds to carry out research.
- A transparent performance appraisal of faculty must be adopted and faculty must have the choice to choose the parameters on which his or her performance has to be judged.
- Faculty members must be involved in academic decision making so that they do not feel isolation and neglected.
- Faculty must have the freedom to float a new course in the area of his expertise.
- Management must be proactive to provide world-class experience to its faculty.
- Where ever possible opportunities for spousal employment must be created depending upon their expertise and talent.
- Pro-active retention endeavors must be done to retain any talented faculty leaving the institute due to some non good reasons.
- Exit interview must be conducted as it enables an institute to understand the outgoing faculty's views about the environment,

culture, processes and systems, leadership and managing styles, clarity of roles, commitments or attitudes of associates within the organization.

Conclusions

Talented human resource is very important for the growth of any organization. It equally applies to the institutions of higher education where the excellence of the institute depends upon the quality of its faculty. Thus, it is necessary for policy makers and regulators to keep in view the close connection of faculty shortage with other problems and features of higher education. Without their honest compliance, the effectiveness of policy and regulatory actions would be limited. Administrations in higher education can work on talent management which has been practiced by organizations within other industries and organizations. The institutions can benefit a lot by nurturing the talent within the institute in the current competitive environment for human capital, and the ongoing need of being accountable to its constituent. So, the faculty must be valued and every resignation saved is every Rupee earned. It is the ability and quality of faculty who inculcates the values and nurtures the future of the nation by developing talents of the students as the facilitator and mentor for their self growth as well as for the growth of the nation's economy.

Bibliography

1. Pawan Agarwal, "Indian Higher Education—Envisioning the Future," Sage Publications, 2009.
2. Chiranjib Sen, "A Framework for Analyzing Demand and Supply of Faculty and the Quality of Higher Education" Working Paper No: 350
3. Task Force Report, Chapter III for an assessment of faculty shortage based on the available data.
4. Lavania Dolly, Himanshu Sharma and Nidhi Gupta, "Faculty Recruitment and Retention: A Key for Managing Talent in Higher Education," International Journal of Enterprise Computing and Business Systems. Vol. 1, Issue 2, July 2011.

5. Michael B. Allen. (2005) Eight Questions on Teacher Recruitment and Retention: What does the research say?

6. Task Force Report, "Faculty Recruitment and Retention", May 31, 2001.

7. Manoj Kumar, "Attracting and Retaining Faculty in Technical Educational Institutions," Fourth AIMS International Conference on Management December 28-31, 2006. Paper Id. A528.

7

Challenges of Indian Legal Education in the Era of Globalization: A Critique

*Dr. Anil Kumar Thakur**

Abstract

In the history of humankind, a civilized society without law and a legal system is almost unimaginable. Rather a society can claim to be civilized only when it has established some kind of mechanism for regulating the behavior of the members in the society. In many sense a legal system is a reflection or manifestation of various civilizational aspirations and being civil. Therefore the legal education occupies a significant place in any society which is the fountain of law and legal system in any country. If it is true that the law plays a crucial role in shaping future of the country then it is equally true that legal education do shape the law and future of the country to the same extent. Traditionally there have been some challenges of the legal education in India, but recently Globalization has added new dimensions to the challenges of legal education in India, however it is also asserted that it has offered a chance to confront the status quo, which is necessary requirement for bringing any transformation. At the same time it is alleged that lately the forces of globalizations have succeeded in twisting the direction and the destination of legal education as per their interest which is a deviation from one of the traditional goal of legal system and education, which used to be aiming at establishing a society based on justice. It is in this context this paper examines some of challenges of legal education in India, which the forces of globalization have posed to it.

Key words: *Law, Education, Globalization*

* Assistant Professor, Department of Laws, Panjab University Chandigarh

Setting the agenda of legal education: Sate vs. Agents of globalization

(Who is setting the agenda of legal education?)

In every country, the legal profession as well as legal education is influenced and determined by a set of social norms and cultural ideology. The society decides that how students are going to be conferred with legal knowledge and what would be the parameter with which the standards of legal profession will be judged. This very idea also indicates towards a lager but specific issues related to the direction and content of legal education. It also brings the issue of selection of legal education providers among public, private, domestic and foreign players.

Like any other modern welfare states, in India also the governments are generally engaged in passing laws, making various kind of appointment which includes judges and civil servants, setting up courts, keeping an eye on administration. They also manage citizen's interface with machinery of the state including the legal system. States also sway the market for legal services by regulating the legal professions monopoly. Moreover, in India it is constitutional duty of state to provide free legal aid to the needy. In fact state is one of the biggest legal service providers in India and there has been a tradition of hiring the lawyers for public purposes. In the given setup and present scenario the influence of state/ governments on law and legal education, is very much apparent and persistent. Governments influence legal education by setting higher education policies, establish the structure of legal education, license educational providers ,provide fund for law faculties, imposes fee on the law students, require legal academics to meet quality standards in their teaching and research and measure the success of law schools in recruiting top students and improving the job prospects of their graduates. Nevertheless, it would be a mistake to take the above mentioned observation for granted and to think that it is only the agency of the state which is setting the destination and direction of the legal education in India. Rather it is very much influenced by the agents of globalization and these forces does much to determine the ends and means of legal education and research.

Globalization is by now shaping the scenario of legal education and profession in developing countries and blurring the boundaries between global and local. Somewhat, India is a suitable place to examine the effects of globalization on legal education as well as legal profession. There is a common perception among the economists that there is a spectacular rise of Indian economy among the nation after the liberalization. The government has been playing a vital role for rolling the red carpet for the phenomenon known as 'LPG'. This is very much reflected in polices of the Indian government adopted since 1991.

Since the 1990s The face of Indian legal profession has gradually started changing which was till then mostly served their client in courts and other judicial bodies by and large represented by individual family lawyer. Now new generations of lawyers have started making their presence felt in Indian legal scenario. However, these corporate lawyers are still confined to metropolitan cities of the country.

In this era of liberalization It is interesting to see that how some of the development is globalizing the knowledge and simultaneously there is globalization of governance. These two developments are going to be very decisive for legal education and legal profession in India or any other country. Here by globalization of knowledge one can simply understand global interchange and transformation of knowledge traditions. In this process globalization of knowledge, there is inclination towards the global rather than local and finally the merger of local identity in to the global. At the same time the globalization of governance indicates towards bigger role of non state in the policy framing.

In India legal education is being conferred basically by the Universities and private college which are affiliated with one or other university. The standard of legal education in India is primarily regulated by the Bar Council of India apart from the rules of regulatory authorities like University Grant Commission and the rules of concerned university. At the same time institution like judiciary is another important stake holder in the legal education.

Till seventies the legal education in India was being conferred under the traditional university system, but somehow standard of legal education was not considered to be up to mark in those days. So many steps were taken to improve and restructure the legal education by the Bar Councils of India at various point of time but those efforts were not very successful. Finally the Bar Council of India took a very decisive and historical step to establish a model law school in the private sector or joint sector to revamp the legal education. That is how the National Law School of India University was established in Bangalore in 1986 and gradually so many others national law schools have come up. Now these new creeds of National Law Schools have also emerged at the national scene. Although these National Law Schools have been established by the State but they are having more autonomy in comparison to traditional universities. Perhaps, that is why they have marked their presence very rapidly at the national scenario. Now more and more private universities are entering into the legal education. Again in 2005 The National Knowledge Commission (NKC) was set up to make India knowledge based economy and society. The National Knowledge Commission also explored the field of legal education as an important constituent of professional education. The working Group on legal education pondered over the issues and made various suggestions regarding legal education ranging from the curriculum development to challenges faced by globalization. It was also realized that with arrival of globalization, it has become more and more significant to incorporate international and comparative law perspectives in to legal curriculum. One of the noted legal scholar professor C. Rajkumar, insist that we cannot ignore four important factors to improve the standard of legal education. "These are: Global curriculum, Global faculty, Global degrees and Global interactions." However there is always a fear of losing the sight of local in the quest for global. So we have to be very cautious while racing for this 'global" thing and all the necessary home work has to be properly done before quenching the thirst of global and globalization.

The new quest of Indian legal fraternity for being global is very much manifested in the newly created National Law Universities (NLUs) through which government wanted to replicate the IIT (Indian Institute of Technology) experiment with legal education. These NLUs were specifically intended to be centers of excellence that would give proficient lawyer who are also socially conscious toward the goal of law as a tool of social change. There is no doubt that the NLUs have produced technically very proficient lawyers but they have perhaps failed to produce socially conscious lawyer who are committed to traditional goals of legal education. Some of the studies conducted on the graduates of these NLU indicate that most of the passes out from these NLU are swayed by the lucrative corporate house career option.

In recent times agents of globalization have not only restructured the economies but it also lead to redesigning of market for legal services. States and its people are equally affected by this phenomenon called globalization. The decline of industrial economies and the rise in one based on information technology and financial services has lead to the growth of large, city firms which serves a global cliental. With this development international and domestic law firms find themselves in competition with other legal service Providers

All of these global players has changed the rules of games by influencing the legal scenario in India where lawyers can potentially play a key role in the preserving the constitutional aim, aspirations and values like sovereignty, Socialism, democracy and providing justice to all. Foreign law firms began showing interest in expanding to India in the early 1990s shortly after liberalization. A direct consequence of this reflects in the form of specific changes in legislation, policy and programmes of states. Legal profession and academia also could not resist the temptation to be the part of this neo liberal restructured design. Very soon flag bearers of legal academia and profession found and coined vocabulary and phrases like, "relevant knowledge" and "practical knowledge" etc. Suddenly some subject became more relevant than others. For instance law colleges and faculty nowadays promote some of the subjects like intellectual property rights, international arbitration etc which are considered to be more sellable in the market. A survey and deep analysis the websites of the law schools in India will probably establish this fact that how some of the leading law colleges are promoting this new found 'relevant knowledge'. The idea of the above observation is not that these so called 'relevant knowledge' should not be taught but it is simply to raise a question that whether such promotion is a part of conscious choice. At the same time it is has been observed that the legal academia and fraternity is so obsessed with this 'relevant knowledge' that some time there is no takers for some of the traditional subjects which are very foundation for any legal education. For instance these days subjects like jurisprudence hardly get any priority among the legal fraternity. Some time it is just a decorative piece in the curricula. It is in this context it is asserted that forces of neo –liberal economy quietly but eventually decides the content of law schools program and syllabi. It is these forces which are filtering the judgments and books which reach to the book shelves of law school and setting the tone and tenor of the research agenda of legal academia.

Now days the word global is selling like a hot cake among the law school all over the world. If one surveys the websites of law schools one would find that most of the so called modern law schools are obsessed with the idea of globalization. Lately even in India some of the law colleges have declared themselves as global law colleges. Where, they hire the international faculties or those who have at least some international degrees or exposure. This obsession reflects in their nomenclatures and other activities like conferences, partnerships, mooting competitions etc. The important question to be examined here is that whether this paradigm shifts in legal pedagogies in the law schools are the result of sustained deliberate discussions to embrace globalization? Or law schools have indeed been forced to bend to invisible hands of market?

Emergence of New Social Ideology and its Ramification on Legal Education

Next immediate question which has to be examined is that whether the promoter and regulators of legal education are playing under the invisible hands by a conscious choice or otherwise? The phenomenon of globalization has not only changed the world around us merely by adopting and adapting tools like public policies, legal practice and legal education to new patterns of market ridden economy but it has actually changed the world view of the societies. This changed world view has laid to the emergence of a new set of social values and ideology. This trend has posed serious questions to legal fraternity about what role laws does play in the society and what is the real objective of law and legal systems and to add legal education? This raises a very fundamental jurisprudential question regarding the whole gamut of legal education.

This ideology believes that governments put hindrances in growth and development of economy by hampering the free flow of goods services and information. In present scenario very few governments dares to challenge this new found ideology. Rather the term "market friendly" has acquired the status of the first principle of governance among majority of the governments in recent years. This attitude reflects in rolling the red carpets for the corporate houses, opening up certain traditional sector for private, disinvestments, deregulating the market etc. in fact, in recent years there have been a trend on the parts of some of the government to support those who are urging for liberalization in this area. Some of them even procured services of foreign lawyers. For example, 'the Karnataka state government engaged the UK firm CMS Cameron McKenna to advise it on privatizing the state-owned electricity distribution system in 2007.' Some developments suggest that direction of legal market and legal education. For instance Indian Parliament passed the Limited Liability Partnership Act 2008. This Act allows foreign law firms to register, establish a place of business in India, and offer consultation services. It does not, however, allow foreign law firms to practice law. These developments will make a far reaching impact on the Indian scene.

Instead most focus on creating a business friendly environment by deregulating markets, decreasing corporate taxes and privatizing certain public services. This changed world view reflects one very noteworthy reversal of role of welfare inclinations of state that represent the public policy in neo liberal economy is that governments in pre cold war era was suppose to get involved in order to make thing better but in post war era state now is suppose to step aside for making things worse. The above line of argument is not an exercise to prove globalization as a villain or evil and social democracy is panacea for all the problems of human Civilization. But it is somewhat an effort to bring the point to home is that how this changed world view which has come as a consequence of globalization has brought a paradigm shift in legal education. This paradigm shift in legal education has reset and reprioritized the goals and objectives of law and legal education. India, like all emerging economies, has an important stake in how globalization will be criticized for increasing corporate political power and working against socio-economic and environmental rights, especially against the interests of impoverished members of society. As advocates for both the instruments of globalization and for those who are affected by its processes, lawyers inevitably play an important role in addressing the adverse consequences or accentuate them will depend upon how both the state and the bar view their respective roles, and upon their ability to mobilize in pursuit of social causes at different levels of governance. The globalization and its impact on the Indian legal education and finally on the profession cannot be said to be a spontaneous development. Rather, some study reflects that it is a conscious choice of those who are at the helms affairs. Most importantly its combination of three dimensional impact of globalization i.e. economic globalization, globalization of knowledge and globalization of governance which are entangled with each other are affecting Indian legal education and as well as profession as never before .

The patterns and design of this paradigm shift can be understood as follows:

- ❖ The trance national will prevail over the national;
- ❖ Market will prevail over the politics;
- ❖ Ultimate goal of law making is to make the world market friendly;
- ❖ Best law- which ultimately dilute the sovereignty of a country with respect to market.(apparently through constitution)

With this new ideology the idea that the law is a valuable tool to achieve social justice has taken a back seat. In fact the promises of globalization have also fascinated the legal fraternity (especially the legal scholars) with its mirage. This fascination is very much reflected with the horizons of their teachings, discussions, research and imagination inside or outside the classrooms of law school. Under these circumstances the protagonists of the Keynesian welfare state have been pushed to the corner and there is growing apprehension, those promoters and regulators of law and legal education like legislators, academician, judges etc are over swayed by forces of globalization which has entered in the constitution of many countries through back door.

This new phenomenon has lead to following developments which are as follows:

- ❖ There is systematic erosion of states/constitutional guarantee regarding citizen's civil and political rights against any kind of abuses by a non state actor or even by state itself. The new ideology focuses more on the protection of economic interests against encroachments by the state. This being done sometime by amending the constitution or law directly or some time silently changing the practice of law while the letter of law remains the same. For instance the preamble of India still vouch for the socialism as one of its important virtue but the policies adopted by concurrent governments after the economic liberalization don't match with the constitutional promises.

- This phenomenon is bound to bring the remarkable change in the legal scholarship and education on so many accounts. There will be a fascination among the legal scholars to rely /depend much more on global legal institutions, and legal scholars will seek legitimacy on the basis of global doctrines and processes in comparison domestic legislation and judicial pronouncement. Perhaps, they will demand changes in their domestic laws and doctrines on the ground that it should be in rhythm with global laws which are suitable to market. Maybe, for future generations of legal scholars the domestic are likely to be a kind of inferior source.
- Generally it is thought that legislature of a country is sovereign in matters of law making but the forces of the market have make dent into this utmost power of the legislatures. Many times the legislature of a country cannot make law which curtails the conditions suitable to the market forces in any sense. Rather there are lobbies inside and outside the legislature to make sure that their interests are intact. It is here that the coming generations from these so called global and modern law schools which will provide the intellectual nutrition for the forces of legal globalization.
- This dilution of the power of legislature in many senses has triggered a constitutional disharmony between the various organs of the state and now the executives have been exercising some power which had been traditionally used to be the domain of the legislatures. In fact legislatures themselves have been authoring the executives to take some serious policy decisions which may be crucial for the economic health of the country.
- Above mentioned constitutional disharmony has widened the role of the judiciary as an independent arbitrator between these two branches of state. However some time is also alleged that the even the judiciary is now not untouched by the phenomenon of globalizations and it is perceived that the tentacles of market has also grappled it into its clutches.

- Since Globalization has a strong tendency toward centralization and therefore it has also brought a disharmony in the federal relationship.
- This disharmony is not limited to the institutions of governance but it has also raised the serious question of cultural identities. The whole gamut of social, economic and cultural fabric of society is being threatened by the uncontrolled and unguided global cultural attack.
- The dilution of the national sovereignty has been to such an extent that actions of the national governments are overshadowed or dominated by some of the global institution. Subjecting to entirely new constitutional constraints. Following examples can help us to understand this global attack on the national sovereignty.
  - Member States of European Union cede part of their sovereignty under the Treaty on the Functioning of the European Union (TFEU) which empowers the EU institutions to adopt laws. These laws (regulations, directives and decisions) take precedence over national law and are binding on national authorities.
  - Many international trade related organizations like WTO etc by entering into treaties with various counties have acquired some specific powers which are considered as curtailment of power of national government on their own resources. Rather they are working as super non-governmental tribunals which can counterbalance laws of national governments which are party of treaties.
- In this whole process the gravest thing which has happened is that the forces of market have succeeded in establishing the fact that the idea of law can be separated from the state. Somehow these perceptions are being given that the law cannot just originate from the state or make a law state is not required at all. The effort has been to undermine the idea inseparability of law and state.
- A survey of trance national corporations sees and their activity can prove it beyond doubt that law without state prevails.

Conclusions

Now, the important question is what is going to be the future of legal education in the light of the above mentioned developments. A quick navigation of law journals and law school syllabi will unfold that market has redefined the very concept of law itself, it has penetrated very decisively in law making as well as legal scholarship and pedagogy. Once this fact is accepted as a norm that non-state actors have if not dominant but is there to play an important role in the key areas of the policies, we will have to be ready to agree to its consequence in other aspects as well. This fact is one of the biggest challenges to legal education in the era of globalization which is going to bring far reaching consequences for the society in general and legal education in particular. In other words this development is going to destroy the hegemony of state in law making and development discussed in the paper are an indicator that how one of the very essence of the state sovereignty is definitely sliding towards the forces of globalization. This development is going to create a new platform as well as a vacuum in legal intellectual ecology for law fraternity. And it here there will struggle between the forces of social solidarity (state) and the forces of globalization to capture this space. In this changing environment each stake holder of legal education including law teachers and law students will have to face the challenges which have been posed by the phenomenon of globalization where by the some of the states are appearing as minnows in front of gigantic transnational corporations.

Bibliography

1. Motivation to write this article has mainly emerged from the article written by Harry W. Arthurs Law and Learning in an Era of Globalization German L aw Journal, Vol. 10, No. 07, 2009 http://www.germanlawjournal.com/pdfs/Vol10No07/PDF_Vol_10_No_07_SI_629-640_Arthurs.pdf.as accessed on 1.12.2013
2. C. Raj Kumar Global legal education in India: opportunity and challengesApril 2009 n 13 http://www.jgu.edu.in/sites /default / files/GlobalLegal30April2009.pdf
3. Chandra KrishnamurthyLegal Education and Legal Profession in IndiaInternational Journal of Legal Information the Official

Journal of the International Association of Law Libraries, Volume 36 Issue 2 Summer 2008 - Global Challenges & theIndian Legal Systemhttp://scholarship.law.cornell.edu/cgi/viewcontent.cgi?article=1136&context=ijli

4. Community.martindale.com/.../Curriculum-of-Legal-Education-to-Meet-.Curriculum of Legal Education to Meet Challenges of Globalization

5. Deepa Badrinarayana, India's State of Legal Education: The Road from NLSIU to Jindal www.swlaw.edu/pdfs /jle/jle633badrinarayana.pdf

6. Globalisation And Legal Education In India Ashwani Tanwar International Referred Research Journal, February, 2012. ISSN- 0974-2832, RNI-RAJBIL 2009/29954;VoL. III *ISSUE-37 http://www.ssmrae.com/admin/images/fb0e8e410a0fbea5889e9e406c63a3cc.pdf

7. John Flood DRAFT Report for the Legal Services Board Legal Education in the Global Context Challenges from Globalization, Technology and Changes in Government Regulation www.johnflood.com/summerschool/Flood_Legal%20Education1.docx

8. K.G. Balakrishnan 'Justice in the 21st century: The challenge of globalization' Introductory note for the plenary session at the Qatar Law Forum http://supremecourtofindia.nic.in/speeches/speeches_2009/challenges_of_globalisation_for_justice_-_qatar_law_forum_may_2009.pdf

9. Law commission report Law Commission of India 184th Report onThe Legal Education & Professional Training and Proposals for Amendments to the Advocates Act,1961 and the University Grants Commission Act, 1956 http://lawcommissionofindia.nic.in/reports/184threport-PartI.pdf

10. Marc Galanteand Nick Robinsonr India's Grand Advocates: A Legal Elite Flourishing in the Era of Globalization http://www.law.harvard.edu/programs/plp/ Hls program on the legal profession Research paper series Number 2013-5 ,November 2013

11. Mary C. DalyThe Ethical Implications of the Globalization of the Legal Profession: A Challenge to theTeaching of Professional Responsibility in theTwenty-First CenturyFordham International Law JournalVolume 21, Issue 4 1997 Article 4http://ir.lawnet.fordham.edu/cgi/viewcontent.cgi?article=1568&context=ilj
12. Mihaela Papa and David B. Wilkins Globalization, Lawyers, and India:Toward a Theoretical Synthesis of Globalization Studies and the Sociology of the Legal Profession http://www.law.harvard.edu/programs/plp/pdf/Globalization_Lawyers_and_India.pdf
13. N.R. Madhava MenonThe Transformationof Indian Legal EducationN.R. Madhava Menon A Blue Paper www.law.harvard.edu/programs/plp/pdf/Menon_Blue_Paper.pdf
14. Pillard, Biondi, Igra, Rittich, Sornarajah, Werro, Why legal education? Center for Transnational Legal Studies37-39 High Holborn, 3rd floor receptionLondon WC1V 6AA, United Kingdom http://ctls.georgetown.edu/documents/CTLS_Why_Transnational_Education.pdf
15. Report of The Working Group on Legal Education National Knowledge Commission
16. www.nludelhi.ac.in, https://www.nls.ac.in, www.nalsar.ac.in, www.gnlu.ac.in

8

Sexual Harassment among Girls in India within the framework of Higher Educational Institutions

Dr Anupam Bahri*

Abstract

Sexual harassment has come to be widely condemned as a form of human rights violation, and as an infringement on life and liberty as defined by the Constitution of India. Such behaviour is seen to transgress common dignity, gender equality, and fundamental rights. Sexual harassment is contrary to anti-discrimination laws [Article 15: "Prohibition of discrimination on grounds of religion, race, caste, sex or place of birth" and Article 19(1)(g): Right to Freedom which upholds a woman's right "to practice any profession, or to carry on any occupation, trade or business"].

Keywords: *Sexual harassment; Human Rights Violation.*

Introduction

Sexual harassment is intimidation, bullying or coercion of a sexual nature, or the unwelcome or inappropriate promise of rewards in exchange for sexual favours. Sexual harassment could take place anywhere, at any time, by anyone and in any form. It could happen at public places, school, educational institutes, workplace, even at home. Sexual harassment can be verbal (comments about your body, spreading sexual remorse, sexual remarks or accusations, dirty jokes or stories), physical (grabbing, rubbing, flashing or mooning, touching, pinching in a sexual way, sexual assault) or visual (display of naked pictures or sex-related objects, obscene gestures). Sexual harassment

* Assistant Professor, University Institute of Legal Studies, Panjab University, Chandigarh

can happen to girls and boys. Sexual harassers can be fellow students, teachers, principals, janitors, coaches, and other school officials.

The victims of sexual harassment are mostly girls/women. It indicates that it is not safe for girls to move out of their houses. They are harassed everywhere might be it an educational institute or workplace. Even age is not a concern. Either a little school going girl or a middle aged lady all are same in the eyes of harassers. Harassers are just like hungry beasts who just want a prey to satisfy their hunger.

Forms of sexual harassment that pertain to a campus environment include; demands for sexual favours accompanied by veiled or open promises of preferential treatment or threats concerning an individual's employment or student status, physical and verbal aggression arising from the above, communicating or displaying obscene letters, posters, cartoons, or photographs, disparaging remarks and gestures made with prejudicial intent in the work or study places, which specifically relate to the issue of gender, harassment through unwelcome telephone calls or E-mail, uninvited chasing or following/blackmailing in or outside the campus.

The majority of women stated that sexual harassment leads to a loss of self-confidence as well as a fear of reoccurrence. Some stated that it even resulted in absenteeism from college. These are severe repercussions of sexual harassment on college campuses and it soon became obvious that preventive measures must be taken. Damage to student's levels of confidence, inculcating fear of repeated harassment and consequent absenteeism from college, are only a few of the effects of sexual harassment on college campuses. Most men students reported that women become angry and self-conscious. They also felt that there is an emotional effect, constant suspicion and absenteeism from college. A few also felt that it lowered grades.

The Objectives of the study are :

1. To assess the level of awareness regarding sexual harassment act.
2. To assess the Perpetrators of sexual harassment
3. To evaluate the measures for preventions of sexual harassment.

Sexual harassment is illegal. If a girl is being harassed then she need not to be afraid but try to fight against it and get the harasser punished.

The Sexual Harassment of Women at Workplace (Prevention, Prohibition and Redressal) Act, 2013

- The Act will ensure that women are protected against sexual harassment at all the work places, be it in public or private. This will contribute to realisation of their right to gender equality, life and liberty and equality in working conditions everywhere. The sense of security at the workplace will improve women's participation in work, resulting in their economic empowerment and inclusive growth.
- The Act uses a definition of sexual harassment which was laid down by the Supreme Court of India in Vishaka v. State of Rajasthan (1997). Article 19 (1) g of the Indian Constitution affirms the right of all citizens to be employed in any profession of their choosing or to practice their own trade or business. Vishaka v. State of Rajasthan established that actions resulting in a violation of one's rights to 'Gender Equality' and 'Life and Liberty' are in fact a violation of the victim's fundamental right under Article 19 (1) g. The case ruling establishes that sexual harassment violates a woman's rights in the workplace and is thus not just a matter of personal injury.
- Under the Act, which also covers students in schools and colleges as well as patients in hospitals, employers and local authorities will have to set up grievance committees to investigate all complaints. Employers who fail to comply will be punished with a fine of up to 50,000 rupees.

Sexual Harassment in Higher Education:

Sexual harassment and violence in educational institutions is an abuse of power by teachers and lecturers and corrupts the education system. It has other severe consequences such as leading to girls and women dropping out.

According to **Fiona Leach**, emeritus professor of education at the University of Sussex, "the authoritarian, hierarchical and gendered culture of most educational institutions facilitates opportunities for the abuse of power and trust".

Police statistics on rape and sexual assault, and media coverage of individual cases; show that in educational settings girls and young women can experience sexual violence, sometimes perpetrated by staff members.

She further added that "Corruption as abuse of power, sexual violence in educational institutions", Leach said while the majority of teachers are dismayed that a small proportion of their colleagues may be guilty of sexual misconduct, it is evident that "every case undermines the integrity of the [education] system".

"Students, especially girls, may be deterred from participating actively in class and seeking academic excellence for fear of attracting unwanted attention from teachers. This creates a stressful and intimidating learning environment, lowers concentration and motivation and contributes to poor performance. And it can create "uncertainty among parents as to the benefits of educating their children, in particular girls", especially in the Middle East and South Asia where such fears may lead parents to terminate their daughters' education at an early age, with implications for future careers and improved socio-economic status.

Perpetrators

Sexual violence in education ranges from low-level gratuitous actions to convey messages of power – such as inappropriate sexualised comments or gestures, or unwanted physical contact such as touching, pinching or groping – through to threats of exam failure, punishment or public ridicule, and sexual assault and rape.

In higher education, it often involves sex in exchange for good grades or leaked exam questions, and sometimes also admission to an institution or to a high-status course. "The price of resistance is likely to be failure or exclusion," said Leach.

Perpetrators can be lecturers or administrative staff. In higher education, female staff are also known to be targeted by predatory male staff and sometimes by male students, Leach said.

Although the report does not cover sexual violence by students, which outnumbers violence perpetrated by staff, Leach noted that "a corrupt system is likely to tolerate high levels of student-on-student violence as well as abuses of power by staff".

Sexual violence in education has been largely ignored by policy-makers, education leaders and law enforcement agencies around the world, according to Leach. "Where it has been addressed, it has targeted peer-on-peer violence without recognizing staff complicity."

It is likely to be greatest in countries with poorly resourced education systems, low levels of accountability and high levels of poverty and gender inequality.

There is also considerable under-reporting by students who fear victimisation, including being failed in tests and exams, stigmatisation or ridicule; or because they believe that no action will be taken against the perpetrator if they report incidents. Women are scared to come forward to make complaints regarding sexual harassment, college managements are often unsupportive and regionalism on campuses is creating rifts between students.

Prevention of Sexual Harassment

How widespread is the phenomena of sexual harassment? A majority of faculty members felt that sexual harassment occurs on a daily basis. The majority of women students reported that they had experienced some form of sexual harassment in or coming to college or university levels.

Following steps for Prevention of sexual harassment of female students, teaching and non-teaching women staff of the University and affiliated colleges/institutes.

- Creation of social awareness about the problems of women and in particular regarding gender discrimination.
- Establishment of committees at the collegiate level and seeking the participation of both male and female students from NCC, NSS and other activities for the prevention of sexual harassment of women.
- Provision of assistance to the College level Women's Development Cell for taking preventive steps in the matter of gender discrimination and sexual harassment.
- Encouragement of the participation of NGOs working in the area of women's development in the activities of the Cell.

- Organization of seminars and workshops at different centres in the University for the creation of general awareness and for the orientation of both male and female teachers for their participation in the activities of the cell.
- Organization of various types of training programs and self-employment schemes for the encouragement of self-reliance among women.
- Prevention of sexual harassment and the promotion of the general well- being of female students, teaching and non-teaching women staff of the University and affiliated colleges/institutes.
- Provision of guidelines for the redressal of grievances of female students, teaching and non-teaching women staff of the University and affiliated colleges/institutes.
- Need for awareness generating programs for faculty and students in colleges with respect to the history behind sexual harassment laws, the University policy and definition of sexual harassment.
- Since seniors were identified as being the main perpetrators of sexual harassment, efforts need to be made to challenge the power associated with seniority on campuses.
- College canteens and maidans need to be patrolled by student groups and guards and made safe for women students.

Grievance Cells

- There is a need for effective advertising of the Women's Development Cells by college authorities
- University authorities in charge of the WDC should hold orientation programs and training workshops on the procedures of setting up and running grievance cells
- University authorities in charge of the WDC should help colleges to set up their Cells by clearly articulating its Policy. It could also periodically enquiry about the Cell and trouble shoot problems.
- Principals of colleges need to appoint interested lecturers and students on a rotation basis to the Cell. The quality and number of events taken up by the Cell depends largely on the interest of the members.

- WDCs need to work towards building credibility with students and making themselves more approachable. This will enable them to dissolve a strongly held belief among students that registering cases will not make a difference.

Conclusions

Even after so many efforts of the Government of India the cases for sexual harassment have seen no decline. The people who are assigned for our help, that is the cops and Government employees, are now they are seen as harassers in many cases. The provisions contain several loopholes which can be exploited easily by the harasser in his favour. Clearly the provisions and laws need to be more comprehensive to provide a means of justice to those who have been victims and a means of protection for those who could be potential victims.

Bibliography

Barak-Erez.D (2012) Feminist Constitutionalism: Global Perspectives.cambridge University Press, USA.

Bare Act: The Sexual Harassment of Women at Workplace (Prevention, Prohibition and Redressal) Act, 2013

Ferguson. S.J (2013) Race, Gender, Sexuality, and social Class: Dimensions of Inequality. Sage Publishing House, London.

Fiona Leach(2014) Harassment, sexual abuse corrupts education worldwide. University world new,Global window on higher education, New York.

Gurusamy. S (2010) Human Rights and Gender Justice. A.P.H. Publoshing Corporation, New Delhi.

Kant, A (2008) Women and the Law. A.P.H. Publishing Corporation, New Delhi.

Sarkar. S and Srivastava. M (2011) Globalization and Gender. Rawant Publications, New Delhi.

Rao. M (2012) Law Relating to Women and Children. Eastern Book Company, Lucknow.

9

Role of Parental Influence on the Values of Females in Higher Education: An Overview

Dr. Rohini Thapar*

Abstract:

The paper aimed to examine the value profiles of the urban Indian upper-middle class female students in higher education; and also the subsequent parental influence on their values. In view of the diverse empirical evidence and studies conducted, it was concluded that Indian parents still have a strong hold on the values of their daughters. The young females exhibited values very similar to value profiles of their parents. Also, a trend for androgynous values was seen both amongst females and males, suggesting an amalgamation rather than a replacement of values between the two genders.

Key Words: *Values, Parenting, Intergenerational communica-tion.*

Introduction:

Values are an enduring set of beliefs concerning preferable modes of conduct or states of existence along a continuum of relative importance (Rokeach,1973).The acquisition of these values and morals begins in childhood, but because of the limited intellectual growth of the child, this process is slow. It is only during adolescence that the individual starts acquiring the array of these values and starts applying them by late adolescence. The values assimilated in childhood influence an individual's opinions, beliefs, attitudes and behavior. In this process of value assimilation the parental role is considered of utmost importance. The child takes all the parental "do's" and "don'ts" in fairly unmodified

* Assistant Professor, D.A.V. College, Sector 10, Chandigarh

form through a process of 'internalization' (Freud,1933), and later these internalized rules guide as parents formerly did.

Research investigating the relationship between children and parental values substantially proves the existence of two contrasting hypotheses. The one, called the "socialization hypothesis", assumed an essential similarity between parents and college going children in attitudes and values, with students reflecting the influence of parents.(Rosen,1964; Tolar, 1969; Weiner,1971; Feather, 1975; Sampson,1977;Barclay etal.,1982; Singh etal.,1984; Georgas,1991; Speicher,1994; Vasudeva and Thapar,2001 etc.). The other, called the "generational conflict" hypothesis, assumed that rebellion by the young against the parental standards was a major cause for dissent and the generation gap. This generational cleavage could be attributed to the rapid socio - political changes and the increasing impact of external social forces and secondary institutions - other than the primary institutions like family. (Ginandes,1969; Wright,1972; Acock et al.,1984, etc.).

Traditionally, substantial research evidence indicated that mothers played a paramount role in value inculcation of the offspring (Bowlby,1969;Phares,1992; Stern,1995; Hojat,1999), and fathers were thought to be peripheral in the job of parenting (Kagan,1978; Fagot,1995; Harris et al.,1998). Research also evinced that fathers' involvement in parenting is a function of mothers' values and beliefs (Simons et al., 1990). In fact, with the shift in gender ideologies, especially in the West, impetus is being laid more on joint "parental role", rather than on individual impact of either mother or father (Veneziano, 2013).

Another most noticeable impact of the rapid social change and modernity has been on the values of women. These shifts in gender roles are evident both in the West (Fiorentine,1988; Freiz,et al., 2006) and in India (Kumari, 1981; Singh et al.,1983; Seth and Vohra, 1994).In the last two decades the Indian society has witnessed subtle replacement of the traditional values by modern ones. Women have acquired value systems akin to men, suggesting an amalgamation rather than the masculinization of feminine value constellations, and narrowing of the differences in values of the sexes. But interestingly, still, one also comes across contradictory evidence endorsing the differences in value structures of males and females and strongly the typical male or female stereotypes (Chakraborti & Kundu, 1981; Segal,1992; Speicher,1992; Rao etal., 1994; Aurora,1994; Thapar, 2002).

In view of such contradictory findings both in case of parental influence on children's values and the changing gender roles, further investigation was deemed pertinent. Thereby, an endeavor was made to assess the value profiles of urban upper middle class females engaged in higher education and of their parents, both fathers and mothers. An attempt was also made to examine the degree of congruence between the values of these family triads, depicting any changing trends in the Indian context, if any (Vasudeva & Thapar, 2000a).

The basis of the study was Value Survey (Rokeach,1973), central to which is the assumption that values can be divided into two meaningful categories i.e. terminal (goals) and instrumental(means) values. 100 female under-graduate students, studying in various colleges of Chandigarh, in age range of 18-21 years, belonging to two parent intact families, were randomly selected and administered an adapted version of S.E.S. Scale (Singh,1974). Out of these, 50 students belonging to upper- middle class, volunteering for the study, along with their 100 parents, both father and mother (age range 40-55years), were administered the Value Survey (Rokeach,1973).

The Objectives of the study:

1. To examine and understand the values of urban women engaged in higher education.
2. To assess the role of their parents in their value inculcation.

For this purpose value profiles of daughters, along with their parents are presented and discussed below. Each profile was based on medians calculated for each value, followed by composite rank orders, thereby giving a set of most, moderately, and least important values. Then, differences amongst the three profiles (based on Median test) were considered to assess the parental influence.

Value Profiles of Daughters:

The female students valued their self respect and freedom the most, followed by family security, happiness, contentedness and true friendships in form of close companionships. Unlike other students

(Thapar, 2001), these young women valued a prosperous life full of all comforts, more than the inner harmony valued by the former. These girls embracing their typical feminine traits liked being polite and helpful the most. But, alongside, they also valued masculine characteristics of ambition, honesty, self- control and responsibility.

On the other hand broader values like a world of beauty, national security, salvation were least valued. They also did not long for making lasting contributions, mature love and an exciting life. These students neither wanted to be imaginative, daring, capable and logical, nor did they embrace socially preferred values of being cheerful, forgiving and clean.

Value Profiles of Mothers:

The mothers held utmost importance for their family security and self- respect like their daughters. Akin to the younger generation, these women also valued comforts of life, along with happiness. But, keeping in line with their age, these elderly females showed a higher preference for wisdom and equality. In case of instrumental values, mothers preferred being honest, responsible, self- controlled and ambitious, which otherwise are considered as male values (Rokeach,1973). Alongside, they also clung to their feminine values of being clean and helpful.

The mothers, similar to their daughters, had given values of a world of beauty, salvation, a sense of accomplishment and mature love a back seat. Their lack of interest in seeking true friendships and pleasure set them apart from the younger generation. Values of being daring, logical, courageous, intellectual, independent and loving were also found lacking in their profile.

Value Profiles of Fathers:

Akin to the females (daughters and mothers), fathers also showed maximum preference for their family security, self - respect and a comfortable life. They shared their wives' mature regard for wisdom and equality but yearned to be free like their daughters. Their disregard for a world of beauty, salvation, mature love matched the female members of the family. Also was seen a lack of interest in seeking excitement and pleasure in their lives.

In regard to the instrumental values, these males valued forgiveness and obedience the most (Chad, 2012), quite unlike the women in their families. Keeping in line with their male traits, they were self-controlled and ambitious. Fathers preferred being courageous and stood up for their beliefs, setting them apart from their spouses and daughters. On the other hand, their lack of concern for typical male values of being responsible, logical, independent and broad minded was intriguing; although lesser importance for being loving and clean was quite expected of these males.

Parental Influence: A Comparative Assessment of Value Profiles:

Median test was calculated to find out significant differences existing between value profile of daughters with that of mothers and also with fathers, respectively. A similar comparison was also drawn between the values of the parents,, i.e. fathers and mothers. Results evinced high degree of congruence between the three profiles. Out of thirty six values, very few significant differences emerged between the three profiles.

When daughters were compared with their mothers, only three significant differences were obtained. Daughters emphasized true friendships (terminal values) and imaginativeness (instrumental values) more than the mothers, who instead laid comparatively more preference on capability.

Significant differences were found on six values, between daughters and fathers. Fathers were higher on the values of a sense of accomplishment, wisdom (terminal values), and capability (instrumental values), while daughters stressed more on true friendship and being loving and polite.

No significant differences emerged between the parents in terms of terminal values. This indicates that perhaps the couples (mothers and fathers) held almost similar goals of life. Subtle differences did arise in terms of instrumental values i.e. the means they adopted to reach these goals. Fathers valued imaginativeness while mothers preferred love and politeness.

Conclusions

To sum up, from an overview of these value profiles and the existence of very few significant differences between them, it can be inferred that values of daughters matched with those of their parents This indicates that role of both the parents is important in moral development of the child (Baptiste,2005). Moreover, it also clarifies that in India, parents still enjoy a strong impact on value inculcation of their offspring, thereby, corroborating the 'socialization hypothesis' (Barclay,et al., 1982; Singh,et al., 1984; Speicher,1994; Vasudeva & Thapar, (2000b); Bahadur et al., 2008; Veneziano, 2013, etc.). The findings might stand against the general observations and enumerable empirical evidences proposing a loosening of parental hold or generation gap. But, from the above account it can be safely implied that in India the institution of family and its influence on children is very deep rooted (Bahadur, et al., 2008). Parents and family traditions still formulate the foundations of lives of the youth.

Though, Indian families are known around the world to be patriarchal, with well defined gender roles (Ahmed et al., 2000; Bhattacharya et al., 20004). Also, here parent child relationships are considered formal and vertical, where communication of authority flow is generally downwards, consistent with hierarchical order of position and status (Baptiste, 2005). But, the above discussed studies (Vasudeva & Thapar, 2000a and Thapar, 2002) challenge these findings done on immigrant Indians living in foreign lands. In India, according to this study, some transitions are happening, at least in the urban upper middle class families. There is evident a positive shift in values of both the males and females. Noteworthy is that this is not a mere replacement of typical gender stereotypes, but more of a convergence of values happening. Today's women (daughters and mothers) place greater value on status-attained goals (independence, ambition, responsibility and discipline) without neglecting their nurturing and other-oriented values (politeness, cleanliness and love). Men are also not hesitant in possessing a milder and feminine value constellation preferring forgiveness, obedience and helpfulness. Therefore, the results confirmed the earlier findings (Singh et al., 1983; Fiorentine, 1988; Seth et al., 1994 and Struch et al, 2002) suggesting an emerging trend of amalgamation rather than replacement of values; where the rigid boundaries of gender stereotypes become more fluid and flexible.

This amalgamation can hew new paths for better adjustments not only within families, but also at work place and in society at large. With more and more women joining the work force and trend for nuclear families with shrunken size, it is the need of the hour to opt for a more inclusive society, where gender stereotypes melt. But, very important is to translate these deep seated changes in values into our attitudes, opinions, beliefs, feelings and behavior.

Bibliography

1. Acock, A.C. and Fuller, T.(1984). The attitude – behavior relationship and parental influence circular mobility in Thailand. Social Forces, June, Vol. 62(4). 973-994.
2. Ahmed, S.M. & Lemkau, J.P.(2000). Cultural issues in the primary care of South Asians. Journal of Immigrant Health,2,89-96.
3. Aurora, A et al., (19940. Personal vs. social values in Romanian students. Revue Roumaini de Psychologie, Jan.- June, Vol. 38(1), 25-32.
4. Bahadur, A. & Dhawan, N. (2008). Social values of parents and children in joint and nuclear families. Jr. of the Indian Academy of Applied Psychology, April, 2008, Vol.34, Sp issue, 74-80.
5. Baptiste, D.A. (2005).Family therapy with East Indian immigrant parents rearing children in the United States: Parental concerns, therapeutic issues and recommendations. Contemporary Family Therapy, 27(3), Sept., 229-251.
6. Barclay, L.K. & Sharp, A.W. (1982). Is there really a generation gap? Value similarities and differences between a group of junior high girls and their mothers. Jr. of Early Adolescence, (sum.), Vol.2(2), 163-171.
7. Bhattacharya, G. & Schoppelrey, S.L. (2004). Pre-immigration beliefs of life success, post immigration experiences and acculturative stress: South Asian immigrants in the U.S. Journal of Immigrant Health, 6, 83-92.
8. Bowlby,J.(1969). Attachment and loss. New York: Hogarth Press.
9. Chad, S. (2012). Chinese vs. Indian Parents: How do they differ? Opinion – Vancouver Staff Blogs, The Vancouver Sun, July 5, Section- Curious Dad.

10. Chakroborti, P.K. & Kundu, R. (1981). Age, sex and type of education as the concomitants of value pattern. Journal of Psychological Researches, May,Vol.25(2),100-104.

11. Fagot, B. (1995). Parenting boys and girls. In M.Bornstein (Ed.), Handbook of Parenting (Vol.1,pp. 163-183).

12. Feather, N.T. & Cross, D.G.(1975). Value systems and delinquency: Parental and generational discrepancies in value systems for delinquent and non- delinquent boys. British Journal of Social and Clinical Psychology, Jan., Vol.14(2),117-129.

13. Fiorentine, R. (1988). Increasing similarities in the values and life plans of male and female college students? Evidence and implications. Sex Roles, Feb. Vol. 18(3-4),143-158.

14. Freiz, I.H., Olson, J.E., Murrell, A.J. & Selvan, M.S.(2006). Work values and their effect on work behavior and work outcomes in female and male managers. Sex Roles, 54(1/2),89-93.

15. Freud, S.(1933). New introductory lectures on psychoanalysis. (trans. W.J. Sprott). New York: W.W. Norton. Georgas, J.(1991). Intra family acculturation of values in Greece. Journal of Cross-Cultural Psychology, Dec., Vol. 22(4), 445-457

16. Ginandes, S. (1969). The generation gap widens in America. International Journal of Offender Therapy, Vol. 13(1), 18-20.

17. Harris ,K. etal., (1998). Paternal involvement with adolescents in intact families: the influence of fathers in the life course. Demography, 31,201-216.

18. Hojat,M. (1999). Theoretical perspectives and empirical findings on the role of the biological mother in human survival and development. Paper presented at the World Congress of Families II Conference, Geneva.

19. http:/www.worldcongress.org/gen99_hojat.htm

20. Kagan,J. (1978).The parental love trap. Psychology Today, August, pp.54-91.

21. Kumari, K. (1981). A study of the effect of personality on value pattern. Indian Psychological Review, Jan., Vol. 20(1), 13-17.

22. Mussen, P.H. (1969). Early sex role development. In A.A. Goslin (Ed.), Handbook of socialization theory and research. Chicago: Rand McNally.

23. Phares,V. (1992). Where's poppa/ The relative lack of attention to the role of fathers in child and adolescent psychopathology. American Psychologist,47, 656-664.

24. Rao, S.N. & Paramesh, S. (1994). Value orientation among Indian college students. Journal of Psychological Researches, Vol. 38(3), 42-51.

25. Rokeach, M. (1973). The nature of human values. New York. The Free Press.

26. Rosen, B.C. (1964). Family structure and value transmission. Merrill-Palmer Quarterly, Vol.10(1),59-76.

27. Rosenkrantz, P., Vogel, S., Bee, H., Boverman, I., & Boverman, D.M. (1968). Sex role stereotypes and self concepts in college students. Journal of Consulting and Clinical Psychology, 32, 287-295.

28. Sampson, R. (1977). Transmission of values within traditional family structure. Family Therapy, Vol. 4(2), 163-170.

29. Segal,U.A. (1992). Values, personality and career choice. Journal of Applied Social Sciences, (Spr.- Sum.), Vol 16(2), 143-159.

30. Seth, G., et al.,(1994). Marriage and family ethics in traditional society: A psychological exploration. Journal of Indian Academy of Applied Psychology, Jul., Vol. 20(2),163-169.

31. Singh, G.J. (1974). Socio-Economic Status Scale: A study of college environment and students personality in medical education. Ph.D.Thesis. University of Delhi.

32. Singh, J.G. & Thapar, G. (1984). Impact of parental values on children. Indian Journal of Clinical Psychology, Mar., Vol.11(0),105-109.

33. Singh,L. & Singh, L. (1983). A study of sex differences in value orientation among postgraduate students. Indian Psychological Review, Vol. 24(2), 7-9.

34. Speicher, B.(1992). Adolescent moral judgment and perceptions of family interaction. Journal of Family Psychology, Dec., Vol. 6(2), 128-138.

35. Speicher, B.(1994). Family patterns of moral judgement during adolescence and early childhood. Developmental Psychology, Sep., Vol. 30(5),624-632.

36. Stern,D. (1995). The motherhood constellation. New York: Basic Books.

37. Struch, N.,et al.,(2002). Meaning of basic values for men and women: A cross-cultural Analysis. Personality and Social Psychology Bulletin, 28(1),16-28.

38. Thapar, R. (2001). A study of values in relation to Machiavellianism, alienation, altruism, family typology and influence of reference groups. Unpublished Doctoral Thesis, Panjab University, Chandigarh.

39. Thapar,R.(2002). A study of gender differences in values. Presented at 27th Annual Conference of Indian Psychiatric Society – North Zone, held at Chandigarh, 19-20th Oct.

40. Tollar, C.J. (1968). An investigation of parent-off spring relationship. Dissertation Abstract International, 28(8-B)3463.

41. Troll,L.E., Neugarten,B.L. & Kraines, R.J. (1969). Similarities in values and other personality characteristics in college students and their parents. Merrill- Palmer Quaterly, Oct., Vol. 15(4), 323-336.

42. Vasudeva ,P. & Thapar, R. (2000a). A study of values: Parental influence on the values of urban middle class female youth. Journal of Behavioral Sciences, Vol. 11, No. 1-2, 5-18.

43. Vasudeva ,P. & Thapar, R. (2000b). A study of value profiles of parents and offspring, and generation gap.

44. Personality Study and Group Behavior, vol. 21,15-29.

45. Veneziano, R.A.(2013). Parental roles encyclopedia of sex and gender: Men and women in the world cultures. Spring Reference, Springer, New Haven, U.S.A.

46. Weiner,I.B.(1971). The generation Gap: Fact and fancy. Adolescence.(Sum.), Vol.6(2),156-166

47. Wright, B. (1973). The generation gap: An intergenerational comparison of values. Dissertation Abstract International, Vol. 33(8). 4552-A.

48. Wylie,R.C.(1968). The present status of self theory. In E.F. Borgotta & W.W. Lambert (Ed.), Handbook of Personality theory and Research. Chicago: Rand McNally.

10

TEACHER EDUCATION AT CROSSROADS IN PUNJAB

Dr. Kanwalpreet Kaur* & Dr. Jatinder Grover**

ABSTRACT

The excellence of education depends on the superiority of the teachers. Recognizing the importance of teachers, the Kothari Education Commission (1964-66) has rightly remarked that 'no education system can rise above the level of its teachers'. So the role of teachers is very important in building the nation. Teacher education is not to teach the teacher how to teach; but it is that knowledge, skill and ability which is relevant to the life of 'teachers' as teacher'. It reshapes the attitudes, remoulds the habits and reconstitutes the personality of a teacher. Today's teacher education is facing various types of challenges worldwide and the India is neither exception of it nor the state of Punjab. The theoretical courses are stereotyped, content are even vague and unrelated to actual conditions, outdated teaching techniques, poor and non-academic environmental conditions, faulty recruitment of teachers for teacher- training institutes, inadequate in-service education facilities and defective methods of admissions etc. are major problems and challenges before teacher education.

INTRODUCTION:

After independence strenuous efforts have been seriously and continuously made for expansion and qualitative improvement of teacher education, because of the fact that quality of school education depends upon to a great extent on quality of teacher education

* Assistant Professor, Institute of Educational Technology and Vocational Education, Panjab University, Chandigarh

** Reader, Dept. of Education, USOL, Panjab University, Chandigarh

programme. There have been several attempts to improve the quality of teacher education. Major concerns of teacher education have been discussed by various commissions and committees like :

- Education and National Development : Report of the Education Commission (1964-66)
- Teacher Education Curriculum Frame work of NCTE (1978).
- UGC panel on Teacher Education – it has been set up to advise on matters related to standards of teaching and research in Education.
- Working group on Teacher Education in the light of the need for value orientation to Education.
- National Commission on Teachers.
- Establishment of Statutory NCTE with effect from 17th August, 1995.
- NCTE Curriculum Frame Work for Quality Teacher Education (2000)
- Some specific issues and concerns of Teacher Education : NCTE (2004)
- National Curriculum Framework on Teacher Education (2009)

These reports have given directions for the intended overhaul of teacher education. The task of bringing qualitative change in institutional efficacy of the teacher education system is large and challenging one. The last five decades have witnessed several attempts to change, modify and indigenize the inherited system of education. But for one reason or the other, the desired outcomes have not been attained or could not be attained (Singh, 2004).

In spite of all the innovations and suggestions made by so many committees and commissions from time to time teacher education as a whole has not risen to a minimum expectation, and as a result of which quality of education from primary level to the university level have been gradually falling. It can be observed from the high rate of drop out, and mass failure in all examination in every year.

Quality of Teacher Education:

The global campaign to universalize the basic education and improve its quality is now very much on the world agenda especially in the developing countries like India. Globally, there is overwhelming concern regarding the quality and relevance of education. Undoubtedly, the quality of school education is the direct consequence and outcome of the quality of teachers and teacher education system. Therefore, quality improvement of our teacher education programme is one of the indispensable needs.

The quality of teachers that determines the overall effectiveness of a system of education depends upon their own education that is popularly known as teacher education. In reality the teacher education is the very sine-quo-non of all educational development. Teacher education means professional preparation of teachers. It is not merely training of teachers. Teacher education is something deeper than mere teacher training. It means the acquisition of that type of knowledge, skills and ability which helps a teacher to discharge his professional duties and responsibilities effectively and efficiently. It means reshaping the attitudes, habits and personality of a teacher. The NCTE Act of 1993 states, "Teacher education means programmes of education, research or training of persons for equipping them to teach at pre-primary, primary, secondary and senior secondary stages in schools and includes non-formal education, part-time education, adult education and correspondence education" (Maheshwari, 2008).

Undoubtedly, the present day teacher training system is the weakest link that refuses to change or even modify in spite of criticism being showered and regulations being tightened from various sources. The worst affected is the secondary teacher training programme popularly known as B.Ed, programme which at best provides, within the limited period of few months, some awareness about teaching as a technique in a routine manner with very little practical or professional content. With the mushroom proliferation of B.Ed. Colleges at every nook and corner without proper and adequate human, material or managerial resources, any worthwhile transformation within the present set up is beyond imagination. Although, as a point of fact each B.Ed. College is affiliated to one or the other university but the present sorry state of teacher education probably underlines the fact that the concerned universities are giving least importance to teacher education in terms of professional preparation of teacher. It is being treated as the hen that lays golden eggs but is destined to die a pre mature death (Chakrabarti, 2005).

To put curbs on commercialization and ensuring quality teacher education NCTE was set up by an Act of Parliament in 1993 which became operational w.e.f. 17th August, 1995. But sorry to say NCTE could not do much beyond granting recognition to new institutions and regulate the already existing institutions. The NCTE thus far, due to large number of applications for opening new colleges is limited to accomplishing regulatory functions and that too, not very satisfactorily. The academic functions, therefore, could not be looked after. Inadequate staffing at NCTE Headquarters and Regional offices is yet another inhibiting factor for NCTE not to perform its functions in totality satisfactorily. NCTE put certain restrictions as to enrolments to the B.Ed but there could be no mechanisms evolved for checking the issuance of 'No Objection Certificate' with the result that there has been mushrooming of colleges of Education disregarding the man-power needs, if we just look into the number of B.Ed colleges in this region alone we will fail to justify the reasons why so many colleges have come up.

Things have changed drastically during the last decade. Could one have even imagined some three years ago recognized teacher preparation institutions giving degrees without any faculty, equipment, laboratory or actual training? It is happening now and everyone knows about it, except those who are responsible to 'regulate' the system (Rajput, 2010).

Further, the new curriculum frame work for school education envisages broad fields for curricular changes like in social science, science and technology etc. which would require integrating various subject areas like History, Geography, Economics, Chemistry, Physics, Botany, Zoology, and technology. This is not just being done anywhere. Graduates in these streams are unlikely to do justice with integrating the knowledge of other subjects with their own field and that too, during one year B.Ed. degree programme. At the undergraduate level the courses that are offered in different combinations do not ensure totality of background knowledge essential for integration. There are yet many more training components which are not mechanically touched upon during the one year training programme leading to B.Ed.

Up-dating the teacher curriculum is a must to face fruitfully the challenge of globalisation. Good teacher education curriculum aims at the development of balanced personalities who are culturally refined, emotionally stable, ethically sound, intellectually alert, socially efficient, spiritually upright and physically strong. It can thus be concluded that "man may be made better not only as a consequence of education, but during the process of education." As information technology has caused many changes in communication network system, the teaching at all levels must be modern, innovative and concurrent with the latest developments so as to face the emerging challenges. The present situation is that there is a hue and cry from the educational planners that existing curriculum in teacher education is outdated, unwieldy, inflexible and does not meet the demands of the contemporary society. The syllabi place maximum premium in bookish knowledge rather than helping to develop different practical skills in teaching (Bajaj, 2008).

At present, practice-teaching is probably the weakest component in the entire teacher-education programme, it needs thorough modernization to enhance skills and competencies of the would be teachers, if the teaching practice as a component of teacher preparation is suitably organised in a more effective way only then the pupil-teacher can acquire composite professional competence. This composite competence will develop in him reflection, creativity and appropriate use of skills and insights, decision-making etc. A very well organised teaching-practice on ultra modern lines would ensure to produce efficient teachers who would be able to compete with the teachers of other countries under the impact of globalization.

Teacher Education in Punjab

In Punjab, teacher education at secondary level is the responsibility of Colleges of Education which are mainly affiliated to three universities i.e. Panjab University Chandigarh; Punjabi University Patiala; and G.N.D.U. Amritsar. Till year 2001, Punjab had only 23 B.Ed. colleges which are either Government or Government- aided. But now till December 2013, there are 231 colleges of Education in Punjab region alone; out of which 208 are self financed colleges. With the wide network of colleges scattered all over state there has been phenomenal growth in the number of students into these institutions and system of teacher education has become a 'mass movement' in Punjab. It is true that some colleges have produced teachers, scholars and educationists of a quality comparable with very best product of universities. However, majority of these institutions have little capacity for original thinking and lack social and national responsibility.

Due to low capital and operation cost; huge profit and funding through management quotas many business houses have entered in teacher education (business) for assured and good returns. They consider education as commodity, students as consumers and educators/ teachers as service providers; hence the focus is on the quantity rather than the quality. Two months into session, in 2007, a number of new B.Ed. colleges were granted approvals raising their numerical strength to 231 with total intake of 25125; 5000 more than that of the previous year. . The present situation of teacher education in Punjab is so alarming that supply exceeds demand and number of seats in colleges of education exceeds number of aspirants who seek to have admission in B.Ed. course.

In the academic session 2008-09, seats remained vacant in almost all colleges of education in Punjab and later on in December, 2008 Government had to permit direct admission to colleges of education thus defeating the very purpose of qualifying test. The role of the universities is also nothing laudable under the prevailing political dispensation where the normal counselling was over on 7th November, in 2009. Again in the session 2009-10, same story has been rewritten as the Punjab and Haryana High Court permitted to hold counselling for filling up nearly 6800 vacant seats from 18-23 December, 2009. But the worst is after year 2010 the entrance test is discontinued in the state and admission is directly on the basis of graduation marks. Although there is some uniformity in terms of students enrolled in colleges, yet wide difference are noticed in the quality of students turned out.

Private college managements are exploiting the students by charging hefty amounts as the degrees would now be provided in five-six months. Students have started making a beeline for these colleges to get admission to B.Ed courses. The counselling was not being done by any centralized agency. Students were being given admission without preparing any merit list. Seats are being "sold" by private managements to the students in the absence of any check by the authorities concerned. The managements, principals and teachers do the bargaining regarding facilities provided on the payment of extra fees i.e. liberty to attend the college and surety of maximum internal assessment (Bhakoo, 2008).

Government nominees are going for inspections only for eye-wash. University is doing its duty but the private managements are hiring the eligible teachers and principals only for the inspection and principals in some colleges are coming only once a month to take their salary. Principals are generally hired from other states who do not know Punjabi & English; because majority of the colleges are run by the management people and principals are only rubber stamps. In education colleges, for a unit of 100 students there are 6 NET qualified or Ph.D. teachers are required, but eligible teachers are only on rolls and ineligible teachers are working and if eligible teachers are there, they have not been paid well.

The managements and principals argued that eligible teachers are not available and the available eligible teachers are not ready to stay in the college for full time. The teachers reported that they are not given the facilities of salary, leave and professional growth as per norms and they have been exploited by the managements. Moreover, the original certificates of the appointed teachers are in the custody of management and teachers have to make hard to get their certificates, if they want to shift.

The education colleges have good infrastructure as the college buildings are well constructed. The classrooms are well built, spacious and in good condition in all the colleges the material is purchased or borrowed for inspection only. Science laboratory, the Language Laboratory and Computer Laboratory are rarely used by the teachers and students. The Internet Facility is only in papers and students are not trained to use the computer and technology equipments in instructions. Libraries in the colleges are not well arranged, books are of substandard, seating capacity not sufficient; and dearth of quality books. However as per NCTE norms the books and titles are there in all the colleges only to complete the number of books and titles. The most important aspect of teacher training is teaching practice. In most of the colleges, teaching practice is organized so haphazardly that its actual purpose got forfeited. This has been causing great concerns to policy makers as well as administrative and it is the need of the hour for qualitative improvement in teacher education (Grover, 2008).

In the 12th FYP, the Government has given emphasis on 3E's (Expansion, Equity and Excellence) but so sorry to say that the most important issue which could have been included as 4th E (Employability) has been left out in the plan.

INSIGHTS TO IMPROVE QUALITY

The quality of education in schools is essentially dependent on the quality of the teaching workforce, because teachers are the most important group contributing to educational outcomes. Only the teachers with high quality can contribute much for moulding the future scientists and researchers. But for that, it's the responsibility of the present day policy planners and thinkers of teacher education to frame a strategy firstly to select the motivated learners to join the teaching profession who must not have only good academic scores but also good interpersonal and communication skills with a deep rooted commitment to teach and work in schools to develop them into effective teachers. The foremost need is to change the selection criteria in the training colleges as in India due to privatization, so many aspirants for teacher training are being selected who have least interest in the teaching profession. There should be some valid selection procedure in pre- service training institutes through a test on subject mastery, pedagogy by means of demonstration of social interaction and communication skills.

Secondly the mode of training need to be changed from one year training to two year training as in one year the knowledge base relating to pedagogy cannot be developed fully and there should be an emphasis on mastery of mainstream subject as well as in didactics. Or the new model of teacher education need to be implemented in true sense in Indian universities as followed in many European countries is a shift towards integrated programmes in teacher education which must include mastery on one or two academic subjects and subject focused pedagogy and research in the selected subject pedagogy. In Indian teacher training programme the major miss is practical training in schools; here the European universities model can be replicated which comprises a rigorous basic teaching practice; then an advanced teaching practice followed by a final teaching practice in different type of schools with a field research having practical solutions to student/ school/ curriculum problems. To achieve the goal of developing effective teachers; teacher training curriculum should be based on a combination of studying of educational theory, content, subject specific pedagogy; and training of teaching skills, research, use of ICT and the most required is practice in real environment in varied type of schools with mastery in one or two of the selected academic subjects. The present paper is an attempt to highlight the procedures and solutions adopted in other universities at international level to select the effective aspirants for teaching and effective didactics with research based practice procedures adopted for the teacher training. (http://www.aft.org/pdfs/americaneducator/summer2011/Sahlberg.pdf)

At the same time, teacher education is now at the critical juncture of eliminating excessive dependence on memory banks and crude craziness with computer fall-outs. Let passivity in learning be eliminated and substantially replaced by fine tunings in teacher education that cares for sense and sensibilities, aesthetics and in depth queries.

Overhauled teacher education programme must also place thrust on active involvement of learners in the process of knowledge construction and teacher as a source of knowledge generation. The concepts of group learning, multi-disciplinary nature of knowledge of teacher education, integration of theory and practice dimensions have to be given due consideration, so that the integral model of teacher education strengthens professionalization of teachers and lead to inculcate the skills of global competence in Indian teachers.

Conclusions

In view of the criticalness of the problem and also because of the fact that over the years in spite of concern being expressed the situation has hardly improved; it is time that a fresh thinking has to be generated and the problems are revisited without any preconceived notions along following lines:

- Develop, guide and also offer integrated teacher education courses at all levels from early childhood to higher education;

- Design multiple models of in-service and pre-service teacher education as per needs and requirements of the field.
- Allow specialization in various types of pedagogies and subject-matter content for those interested in teaching profession.
- Develop short-term, long term specialized as well as integrated courses to suit the emerging needs especially in science, social science and information technology.
- Provide opportunities for high level research in various aspects of education and teacher education.
- Admission to teacher education courses should be highly selective so that only those students who have real aptitude for learning and teaching may enter the institute of teacher education. The Finland Model should be implemented.
- Admission should be strictly made on the basis of the qualifying test and for management quota seats; the centralized admission procedure at university level has to be adopted.
- Mushroom growth of institutes of teacher education without proper infrastructural facilities is one of the principle reasons for decline in excellence of academic standards, so the establishment of such ill planned and ill equipped educational institutions should be effectively checked.
- There is an urgent need to re-examine and consolidate the present ill conceived, ill planned and haphazardly executed, formal teacher education system because the foundations of the present system are not capable to bear the load of upcoming generations.
- In addition to providing quality education focus must be given on other areas like; 4 'C' (Critical thinking, Communication, Collaboration and Creativity) so that this holistic approach will definitely help in increasing the employability among the students.
- Teacher education in India needs to be more skill oriented - both in terms of life skills as well as livelihood skills.
- The Punjab Government, Universities and NCTE have to support each other and have to initiate a process of disciplined rethinking to remove the lacunae of the present system.

- Periodic and surprise monitoring and evaluation by competent and experienced persons can be a good step to improve the quality and to check the impersonation of the principals and teachers.
- Special orientation and refresher courses has to be organized for the teachers and principals of the self financed colleges and it has to be mandatory for the teachers to attend these courses.
- A national curriculum for B. Ed has to be framed and implemented in all universities; and innovations like use of information and communication technology in teaching and learning; imperatives of distance and open learning, online teaching and learning strategies has to be integrated in the curriculum.

The Government, Universities and NCTE has not to compromise with quality due to the political and economic pressures of the business houses otherwise the upcoming generations cannot be guided by the skilled and disciplined teachers. For establishing and sustaining excellence in any system, the representation of all stakeholders toward excellence must be involved and only then our promises for excellent teacher education can be kept without any compromise.

Bibliography

1. Bajaj, K. K. (2008). Challenges in teacher education: Issue of professional development. University News, 46, 15, 14-20, April; 1-5.
2. Bhakoo, S. (2008, December 1). B.Ed. Colleges give merit a pass. The Tribune News Service, Chandigarh; 8.
3. Chakrabarti, M. (2005). Resurging a new era in teacher education. The Employment News, New Delhi, 23-10-2005.
4. Inclusive and Qualitative Expansion of Higher Education: 12th Five Year Plan (2012-17) http://www.ugc.ac.in/ugcpdf/740315_12FYP.pdf
5. Grover, J. (2008). Quality of Teacher Education in Punjab. Research Journal Social Sciences, 16 (2&3), Panjab University, Chandigarh; 37-49.
6. Maheshwari, A. (2008). Crucial issues and emerging concerns in teacher education. University News, 46, 12, 24-30, March; 20-23.

7. Rajput, J.S. (2010, January 31). Elementary Education: Neglect & Deficiencies. The Hindu, New Delhi; 12-18.

8. Singh, M.S. (2004). Quality Impact in Teacher Education. Adhyayan Publishers and Distributors, New Delhi; 66-74.

9. Singh, R. P. (2007). Teacher education today: in search of an identity. University News, 45, 36, 24-30, September; 20-24.

10. The Professional Educator: Lessons from Finland http://www.aft.org/pdfs/americaneducator/summer2011/Sahlberg.pdf

11

THE ROLE OF MISSIONARIES IN HIGHER EDUCATION IN SHILLONG : CAN THE 'LOCAL' COMPETE WITH THE 'FOREIGN'?

Dr Harpreet Kaur Vohra★

ABSTRACT

The relationship that Shillong shares with the Christian Missionaries is an old one, beginning with the first conversion to Christianity that took place in the year 1814. This conversion took place when Krishan Pal from Serampore Mission in Calcutta began his work in this picturesque town. Thereafter, the role that the Missionaries have played in this city altered the religion, outlook, culture and education of this place. The Christian missionaries set up several schools and colleges of repute which made Shillong the hub of education in the region. These institutions have over the years developed a reputation that few have been able to match up with. However, over the years, several colleges have been set up by the government to cater to the growing needs of higher education in the city. Several of these institutes of higher education have been offering newer options to the people in the city and have been adequately arming themselves with the right infrastructure and faculty to compete with the so called foreign institutes. The paper that I am writing seeks to ask the question that can the so called 'local' really compete with the so called 'foreign'. Over the years these centres of learning have been making inroads into the education of the city. Have the newer and the lesser preferred institutes been really able to keep up with the towering stalwarts or is the grand reputation that these institutes

Key Words: *Missionaries, Khasi, Higher Education, Colonial*

★ Assistant Professor, Panjab University Regional Centre, Ludhiana

INTRODUCTION

The relationship that Shillong shares with Missionaries is an old one, beginning from the time various missionaries came to this little city. The immense changes that have taken place over decades have influenced religion, culture, education and even the architecture of this city. Higher Education too has been enormously influenced by the Missionaries with numerous colleges that were set up by them all over Shillong. However, the years have also seen a mushrooming of colleges that have been set up by the Government of the state to cater to the needs and aspirations of the growing population. The proposition that I seek to make through the paper is whether these institutes of Higher Education can compete with those that were set up by the Missionaries decades ago, or have the divisions between the two become blurred because of the long presence of local existence. Is it a case of just the age old reputation or is there really something markedly different in both kinds of institutions?

In their paper Looking for God in the University: Examining Trends in Christian Higher Education the writers have studied Christian Education on the basis of analytical work by Robert Berne to examine the number and nature of colleges and universities that retain and nurture a distinct Christian identity. The results that they have come up with indicate that Christian Higher Education continues to expand throughout the world, challenging the assumed linear trend toward secularization (Glanzer, Carpenter and Lantinga, Abstract). Even though the study was carried out on institutions in Canada and The United States of America, the North-East India also presents such a picture where Christian Education is an integral part of Higher Education especially in Shillong.

An important indicator of progress of a state is the level of Higher Education provided to the population. The quality of Higher Education becomes an important index of predicting levels of employability and job success after employment. Education which is the principle component of human capital contributes to economic development through population control, life expectancy, infant mortality, nutritional status and strengthening of civil institution (Ed Biloris Lyndem and Utpal Kumar De 22). Economics who generally don't agree with each other at least agree on the point that 'social rates of return on investment in all levels of education exceed the long-term opportunity cost of capital (Ibid 22). Thus it becomes imperative for the state to provide these opportunities in plenty so as to secure the future of its citizens. These citizens would use their expertise through their degrees in the job market and would hence be able to secure themselves for the future. Shillong is one such destination in which several opportunities present themselves in the field of Higher Education.

The history of formal education in Meghalaya has been a recent one commencing with the formulation of a Khasi alphabet in 1842 by Rev Thomas Jones, a Welsh Missionary. Thus the Christian Missionaries were the first to start modern education in Meghalaya. The first college though was established in Shillong only in 1924 by the Christian Brothers of Ireland. Being a hill station blessed with bracing weather and having a strong colonial influence, several quality colleges and public schools were established over the years. The geography of the state along with its distinctly different people made it an attractive destination for the Missionaries.

The history of the Missionaries in India naturally begins with the advent of the British. William Carey, who was the founder of the Baptist Missionary Society who reached Kolkata in 1793 and worked in Serampore from 1799 to get the Bible translated into as many local languages as possible was one of the earliest missionaries. (Ed Tanka Subba, Intro xvi). The British annexed Khasi Hills in 1835. The Christian Missionaries arrived in 1841. These events opened up the region to the outside world and along with this there came about several changes. (Pariyaram M Chacko, 1). The Christian Missionaries introduced the Roman script and transformed the Khasi and Garo dialects into written languages. The missionary effort popularized education. Shillong, the state capital is known throughout the North-Eastern region of India as a centre of education. (Ibid,2). The earliest Khasi converts were introduced to Christianity by Krishan Pal of the Serampore Mission. They were from the foothills of Khasi-land and were baptised in 1813. The growth of Christianity was slow in the early years and opposition was often violent (Pichau 155). However, Shillong has slowly evolved as the centre of Christianity with around 70.5% (mapsofindia.com) of its population professing the religion according to the 2011 census. The Missionaries set up several institutions of Higher Learning in the state which continue to attract students. Gradually, several other institutions which were set up by the Government to cater to the growing needs of the larger population also became numerous. They catered to the needs of the larger populace and were slowly trying to keep up with the already long established institutions of Higher Learning.

There has always been a great desire and a subsequent rush to get into the institutions run by the missionaries. The grandeur and the charm that they exude in a heavily colonial looking city has always made them attractive centres of learning. The aura and environs of say a Saint Edmund's College or a Saint Mary's would inspire a heady mix of both intellect and style. Even schools like Loreto Convent and Saint Anthony's in the city have a charm that is unmatched in both their standards of education and the etiquette that they impart to their students. Hence both school and college educations in the city have enjoyed a very enviable position for decades and decades. Victor Bannerjee, the actor, JM Lyngdoh, former Chief Election Commissioner, Amita Malik, late film critic are some of the people who had their education in this picturesque city. Mahatma Gandhi, Rabindranath Tagore and Swami Vivekanand visited Shillong on several occasions, too, adding to its value.

The objectives of the paper are:

1. To briefly look into the history of the Missionaries and their contribution to Higher Education in the capital state
2. To briefly outline the history of Government Institutions and their contribution to Higher Education.
3. To evaluate if the Government Institutions can compete adequately with the older and better funded missionary ones.

Methodology

The following methodology has been used in the paper:

1. Use of secondary data from articles and books in order to understand the contribution of various institutions to Higher Education in the Capital city.
2. Comparative studies of Missionary and Non-missionary Institutes using the following parameters:

i. Year of establishment.

ii. NAAC accreditation.

iii. Colleges of Excellence.

There are several such institutions of Higher Learning in Shillong. It will be interesting to note that the Missionary run colleges have been categorized into Colleges of Excellence. The two colleges that have not been set up by the Missionaries and fall under this category are Lady Keane College and Shillong College. However, it is interesting to note that Lady Keane College is a Government College which was set up by the then Governor of Assam Michael Keane in 1936. It was the first Women's college to have been set up in the entire North-Eastern region. Shillong College is a Government which has also been able to make it to the elite league. The following colleges fall under the category of Colleges of Excellence:

i. St. Edmund's College.

ii. St. Anthony's College.

iii. St. Mary's College.

iv. Lady Keane College.

v. Shillong College.

St. Edmund's College was set up in the year 1924 by the Christian Brothers and was the first college to be set up in the state of Meghalaya. St. Anthony's College was set up in the year 1934 by the Salesians of Don Bosco, Italy and has the distinction of being the first institution of Higher Education by the Salesians worldwide. St. Mary's College was set up in the year 1937 by RNDM missionary sisters.

For my study, I have taken up four other colleges which are:

i. Sankardev College.

ii. Women's college.

iii. Synod College.

iv. Shillong Commerce College.

Keeping in mind the growing demand for Higher Education, new colleges were set up gradually. Sankardev College was set up in the year 1962; Synod College was set up in the year 1965; Women's College was set up in the year 1984 and Shillong Commerce College was set up in the year 1987.

The following table makes a comparison of the selected colleges in the city based on the parameters that I have chosen:

Sr No	Name of College	Year of establish-ment	Missionary/Govern-ment	NAAC Rating
1	Saint Edmund's College	1924	Christian Brothers	A
2	Saint Anthony's College	1934	Salesians, Don Bosco	A
3	Saint Mary's College	1937	RNDM Sisters	A
4	Lady Keane College	1936	Government	B
5	Shillong College	1956	Government	B
6	Sankardev College	1962	Government	B
7	Women's College	1984	Government	B+
8	Synod College	1965	Synod Khasi Jaintia Presbyterian Sepngi	A
9	Shillong Commerce College	1987	Government	B

Note: The data of the colleges in bold in the above table stand for those that have been declared as Colleges of Excellence. The data has been collected from the official websites of the respective colleges.

Findings

From the three parameters that were selected, the following conclusions have been drawn:

1. All the three institutes of Higher Education established by the missionaries have the status of Colleges of Excellence.
2. All three of them have been ranked A by NAAC.
3. All three of them have been running the longest as compared to the other colleges.
4. The other two colleges which are Colleges of Excellence have been ranked B by NAAC.

5. Both the colleges have also been running early as compared to the ones that are not Colleges of Excellence.
6. Synod College stands out as an exception as it has been ranked A even though it is not a College of Excellence. Another interesting point to note is that this college too is run by Presbyterian Missionary.
7. All the other colleges have been graded B by NAAC.

Conclusions

The following may be concluded from the above findings:

1. It is not just the institutes run by the missionaries that have been declared as Colleges of Excellence. Two others, i.e. Lady Keane and Shillong College have also bagged the distinction.
2. Year of establishment seems to be an important factor; so we could probably expect the other colleges to surge ahead with the passage of time.
3. The margin of difference in NAAC grading is not so great. So a B+ could probably overtake an A in some time.
4. The non-missionary run colleges are giving competition to the missionary run colleges.
5. Perhaps the missionary run institutes continue to be popular because of their old reputation.
6. Thus the so called 'local' can compete with the so called 'foreign' as the lines between them are slowly blurring and the divide is becoming less and less discernible.

Bibliography

1. Christianity and Change in North-East India. Ed Tanka Bahadur Subba, Joseph Uthenpurakal
2. and Shaji Joseph Puykunnel. New Delhi: Concept Publishing, 2009.
3. Department of Education, Government of Meghalaya. Megeducation.govt.in/Shillong.html.

4. Accessed on 15.12.13.
5. Education in North-East India. Ed Biloris Lyndem and Utpal Kumar De. New Delhi: Concept
6. Publishing Company, 2004.
7. Glanzer, Perry L, Joel A Carpenter and Nick Laltinga. Looking for God in the University:
8. Examining Trends in Christian Higher Education. Abstract. Published online on 20
9. August, 2010. Springer Science + Business Media BV. 2010. Accessed on 31.12.13.
10. Matriliny in Meghalaya: Tradition and Change. Ed Pariyaram M Chacko. New Delhi:
11. Regency Publications, 1998.
12. Pichuau, Lalsangkina. Church Mission Dynamics in North-east India. International Bulletin of Missionary Research, Vol 27, No 4.
13. http://www.shillongcollege.ac.in/ Accessed on 14.12.13.
14. http://www.smcs.ac.in Accessed on 15.12.13.
15. http://www.sec.edu.in/ Accessed on 15.12.13
16. http://www.anthonys.ac.in/ Accessed on 13.12.13
17. http://www.synod-college.com/ Accessed on 12.12.13
18. http:www.sankardevcollege.com/ Accessed on 15.12.13
19. http:www.ladykeanecollege.edu.in/news.html. Accessed on 14.12.13
20. http://www.mapsofindia.com/meghalaya/. Accessed on 31.12.13.

12

Foreign Languages in Professional Courses with Special Reference to French

Dr. Ramnik Aurora*

Abstract

The importance of foreign languages in the present scenario cannot be ignored. In higher education, on the one hand we are moving towards more specialized courses and on the other, only specialization is not sufficient as there are other skills required for a student to get a good job. Globalization has opened up the horizon with a multitude of opportunities for students no longer confined to a limited job environment. Along with the main subjects, foreign languages are also being taught in various courses in universities and other institutions. This paper aims to focus on the teaching of French in India.

Key words: *Higher education, foreign languages, French, professional courses, syllabus*

What is a foreign language?

The simple dictionary meaning of foreign (adjective) is: relating to a country or language other than your own. (DK Illustrated Oxford Dictionary). Or, Of, or pertaining to, or derived from another country or nation; not native ... (Dictionary.com) So, it is a language which is neither the mother tongue of a person nor a language spoken by the natives of a country to which he or she belongs. In India, where many languages are spoken in the various regions, any language other than the mother tongue, which is spoken by the people of other regions, is sometimes so different and incomprehensible to speakers

* Assistant Professor, Department of French & Francophone Studies, Panjab University, Chandigarh

of a particular mother tongue, that it could just as well be a foreign language for them. Due to the colonial background of our education system, English acquired the status of a second language and even the first language in more and more schools all over the country, and largely the medium of instruction in higher education. Even though English is a foreign language, other languages such as Chinese, Japanese, Spanish, German, French, etc. are taken in this context.

Objectives

A. Why are foreign languages taught?

B. Where are they taught?

C. What is being taught?

D. Is this teaching serving the purpose or purposes?

This paper will be focused on the teaching of French along with other subjects in various professional courses in different disciplines taught at the college and university level.

A. Why

Foreign languages are being taught in many colleges and universities since the last several decades. However, it is mainly in the last two decades of the twentieth century that the study of a foreign language as an optional or compulsory subject was introduced. Even when India was under British rule, French was taught in some colleges in the early 20th. century as in Pune (1932. The two World Wars created the need for teaching foreign languages. India being a colony and Great Britain being one of the European countries involved in war, the army comprising of native Indians fighting in Europe would be faced with the difficulty of new languages. As a matter of fact, Indian soldiers fought for the country in France. Incidentally, it was at the time of the second World War that a method of teaching foreign languages called 'Méthode de l'armée' (The Army Method) was created in the U.S.A., by which the soldiers could learn a foreign language very quickly. Therefore, we see the beginning of need-based teaching of a language.

After the emergence of the United States from World War II as the major world economic leader, the creation and implementation of language curricula in the United States for specific purposes in the international business world assumed increased importance. (T. Bruce Fryer)

To quote D.S. Doyle,

Curricular vision and implementation must always keep a finger on the pulse of the times in order to best prepare students for the world they will encounter upon graduation and in order for academic programs to retain and strengthen their relevance and centrality. (Doyle, 2010)

It is a fairly recent development in higher education in India with more and more professional courses including a foreign language as a compulsory, minor or additional subject. As such, specialization in a certain discipline does not necessarily mean that the student having a degree has the requisite skills for a particular job. Being able to communicate in a foreign language is an added skill.

In this era of globalization, when endless opportunities of jobs are offered in other countries and when several multinational companies are setting up their business in India, the scope of foreign languages becomes wider. The prospect of jobs and business through the internet attracts thousands of educated youth. The emergence of call centres has created openings for those who know a foreign language. In some disciplines, a part of the course pertains to different countries, as in the case of History, Political Science, Economics, Public Administration, Law, International Law, Catering, Tourism, etc. The courses of the subjects mentioned above may include the history of Europe or France; the constitution of different countries such as France; administration in France, etc. In Hotel Management, French in particular has importance as many French terms are used in cookery, catering and service in restaurants and hotels and the students must be familiar with them. Tourism is a domain which has vast scope for growth and capable of creating employment, more so as French is used as an official, first or second language in many countries.

B. Where

Most of the universities of our country offer foreign languages at the graduate or post graduate level. Private universities and institutes have not been taken into account even as they form a large segment of higher education today.

In diverse fields such as Business Management, Hotel Management and Tourism, Public Administration and Law, foreign languages have been introduced in the syllabi. Within the framework of this paper, it would be a mammoth task to undertake a survey of all such institutions of higher learning. Therefore, only a few universities or institutes from various parts of the country have been taken to highlight the importance of French:

- B. A. Marathwada University, Aurangabad
- Himachal Pradesh University, Shimla
- IIT Delhi
- IIT Bombay
- IIT Madras
- Indira Gandhi National Open University
- Kurukshetra University, Kurukshetra
- Panjab University, Chandigarh
- Pondicherry University, Puducherry
- University of Rajasthan, Jaipur

C. What

The contents of the various professional courses show that the maximum number with a foreign language component is that of Hotel Management and Tourism.

In the Five Year Integrated programme of Tourism Management of HPU Shimla, French is taught as the Foreign Language, as is the case with the Bachelor of Hotel Management course in MDU Rohtak. The National Council for Hotel Management and Catering Technology (NCHM, Noida) and IGNOU, have included Restaurant French. In Periyar University B.Sc. Hotel Management, Hotel French is an elective subject with the course divided into units including conversation related to the restaurant and preparing a French menu. BAU, Aurangabad has defined the main objective of the course as communication including French terms used in the hotel industry besides written comprehension, translation and written expression.

French of an elementary level in the 2nd. semester and of the intermediate level in the 3rd. semester is part of the Kurukshetra

University Master of Hotel Management and Tourism course. The MDU syllabus of written French is divided into 4 units, teaching simple communication, whereas the oral part includes role playing, comprehension and conversation.

The French Communication Course in the IIT Bombay consists of two modules with no books prescribed. In Panjab University, French is being taught in several courses: in the Five Year Integrated Course in Laws, from the 4th. semester to the 7th., the written paper being divided into units and a viva voce also included. The book prescribed does not have elements of language for specific purposes. For the M.B.A. (IB) course, the same book used for 3rd. and 4th semesters but the pattern of the question paper is different with no oral examination. French is also being taught in the Tourism and Hotel Management course, with the same book prescribed.

French is included in the BBA (IB) programme of the University of Pune as an optional subject in the third year. Commercial French based on real life situations is taught. Though the book is accompanied by a CD, there is only a written test. This university is also offering Foreign Language as a Generic Elective with 2 credits at the MBA level. Japanese, German, Spanish and Chinese are also taught. The skills of listening comprehension, speaking, reading and writing are aimed at. No specific books are prescribed for French.

Foreign Language is one of the subjects in the Pondicherry University MBA Tourism 1st. semester with 3 credits out of a total of 26 for the course; French is one of the options along with Japanese, German, Spanish and Chinese, as in the case of the University of Pune. Communication is emphasized, with a book accompanied by a CD.

D. Are These Courses Serving The Purpose?

In itself, inclusion of foreign languages is a step towards making students better equipped to face the challenges of a work environment which is ever expanding. The future employee, executive or entrepreneur can use a foreign language to understand some simple sentences or be able to read some instructions or details related to his or her profession. At the same time, this language enables him or her to communicate better with clients who speak that language without having to depend on a translator or interpreter.

Most of the syllabi examined are designed to develop the communication skills of the student in French. Even though many universities do not include the oral test, the objective is generally the same. It is true that emphasis on spoken French must be laid, especially in the case of professions where the future professional will be in an environment where he or she would have to deal with clients or associates speaking that language. Hotel Management, Tourism and Catering are professions where a working knowledge of French is certainly a big asset. In other courses, such as Engineering, the additional knowledge of French enables students not only to have access to French journals and universities in France or other French-speaking countries, but also get job opportunities abroad or in companies established in India. It was found that French or any other foreign language is not being taught along with Engineering or Technology courses, with the exception of IIT's. Since only a limited sample of universities was taken, there are several more which are not included. It must be added that in many universities, French and other foreign languages are being taught separately and a large number of students from professional courses learn them.

Largely, the French language courses analyzed cater to the needs of the students, and lead to better employment opportunities, though in some cases, they are too general in nature.

Conclusion

The teaching of foreign languages in professional courses seems to be an increasing trend in our country. It empowers the students to deal with a much wider work environment or 'market', assuring more employability to the students. Mostly French and German are being taught, with Russian, Japanese, Chinese and Spanish in some institutions. The reason for the inclusion of Japanese and Chinese may be seen as the importance of Japan and China in terms of business. In some cases, the French courses need to focus on a particular profession.

Bibliography

1. Banaras Hindu University, Varanasi www.bhu.ac.in
2. DK Illustrated Oxford Dictionary, Dorling Kindersley; Oxford University Press, Oxford, New York, 2011.

3. Doyle, M.S. (2010) Responsive, integrative Spanish curriculum at UNC Charlotte,Hispania,93,80-84 http://onlinelibrary.wiley.com/doi/10.1111/modl.2012.96.issue-s1/issuetoc
4. Dr. Babasaheb Ambedkar Marathwada University, Aurangabad http://www.bamu.ac.in
5. www.crisolenguas.uprrp.edu
6. www.Dictionary.com
7. Fryer, T. Bruce, Languages for specific Purposes Business Curriculum and Implementation in the United States, The Modern Language Journal 96, Focus issue 2012 http://onlinelibrary.wiley.com/doi/10.1111/modl.2012.96.issue-s1/issuetoc accessed on 11.12.2013
8. Himachal Pradesh University, Shimla www.hpu.acin
9. Indian Institute of Technology Bombay, Mumbai www.iitb.ac.in
10. Indian Institute of Technology Madras, Chennai www.iitm.ac.in
11. www.kuk.ac.in
12. Maharishi Dayanand University, Rohtak www.mdurohtak.ac.in
13. Panjab University. Chandigarh www.puchd.ac.in
14. Periyar University, Tamil Nadu www.periyaruniversity.ac.in
15. Pondicherry University, Puducherry. www.pondiuni.edu.in
16. University of Pune www.unipune.ac.in
17. University of Rajasthan, Jaipur www.uniraj.ac.in

13

Relevance of Soft Skills in Higher Education

Dr. Arunachal Khosla*

Abstract:

The paper aims to discuss the concept of soft skills and identifying the skills covered under the umbrella of soft skills. It explores what is the relevance and need of soft skills among students of higher education. The paper also discusses measures that can be taken by teachers, supervisors and trainers at institutions of higher education to develop the much needed soft skills among students to bridge the gap between the skills that the industry wants and the skills that students possess.

***Key Words:** Soft skills; Measures.*

Introduction

There has been phenomenal growth in the higher education system of India ever since independence. India has created one of the largest systems of higher education in the world. India currently has 43 Central universities, 289 State universities, 94 state private universities, 130 deemed to be universities, 50 institutes of national importance, 611 institutes established under State Legislature Acts and 31,324 colleges. There is a huge need for us to grow our institutions in higher education, both in scope and structure to live up to the projected growth of higher education institutions. They are expected to grow manifold in the coming years. The 11th and 12th Five Year Plans have given immense importance to higher education trying to steer the sector in order to match the requirements of the people and the needs of the growing economy.

* Assistant Professor,University Institute of Applied Management Studies, Panjab University, Chandigarh

However with the system of higher education as large as ours, there are major areas of concern which call for immediate action such as infrastructure, financing, increasing the access to higher education, inclusiveness and relevance of education to the current requirements of the changing socio-economic scenario. All these issues are important for the balanced growth and development of our country as the current and coming times are times of knowledge based societies.

In light of the above concerns, the institutions of higher education have to perform multiple roles such as knowledge creation, developing new skills including hard technical skills and soft people skills. Out of the various concerns of higher education system, the current study focuses on the need and importance of developing soft skills among students of higher education.

The major objectives of the present study are:

1. Describing the concept of soft skills
2. Identifying the different types of soft skills
3. Studying the role and relevance of soft skills
4. Identifying initiatives that can be taken to develop soft skills among students of higher education

Currently there are plenty of job openings in various industries in India namely, IT, ITES, healthcare, pharmaceutical, banking, insurance, etc and are likely to grow manifold in the next 5 years. But there exists a wide gap in the skill set required by the industry and this gap will further widen alarmingly if timely intervention is not made in the current ways of our academic delivery. Time and again various surveys have indicated that lack of these employability skills amongst students of higher education is causing acute shortage of manpower for various industries. Technical education and certification needs to be complemented with the soft skills needed by graduates beyond their academic skills. These skills are generic in nature and exist across the various domains of learning, leading to increase employability and also help successfully compete in the dynamic environment.

Defining Soft Skills

There are two kinds of skills that are required by employees at entry level positions namely technical skills and soft skills. Soft Skills are very important skills for enhancing the employability of the students and also help them to perform their jobs even more effectively. Soft skills refer to all aspects of generic skills that include the cognitive elements associated with non academic skills. They are considered the most critical skills in the current global job market. The term soft skills is used to describe skills that managers and leaders use that are subjective in nature, such as creativity, interpersonal skills, time management, problem solving, team work, etc. They are also alternatively called life skills, people skills or employability skills.

The soft skills have been considered to contribute immensely to the emotional intelligence of an individual. This means that soft skills contribute to a person's ability to manage oneself and relate to other people in a better way. These skills are much more important for job success than technical skills. Research has proved that professional and personal success of a person is largely dependent on his emotional intelligence and not just on cognitive intelligence as was earlier thought and measured by IQ or intelligence quotient.

The following skills are commonly included in the category of soft skills

Communication: It is the process of transfer of message from the sender to the receiver. It involves conveying the content and essence of the message to the receiver in the same way as intended to.

Problem solving skills: It is the ability to identify and anticipate problems and the ability to logically handle problems. It also encompasses the ablility to identify causes for problems.

Team skills: It is the ability to work amicably with a group of people from diverse backgrounds towards a common set of goals. It also includes the ability to handle conflicts, self control, trust and respect for others.

Creativity: It is the process of thinking out of the box and looking at regular things through different perspectives. It is the ability to develop innovative insights and outcomes through imagination.

Leadership skills: It is the ability to influence the subordinates and peers in the process of goal achievement which includes being disciplined one self, being organized and having the ability to motivate others and oneself.

Time management: It is the skill to handle multiple tasks which includes work prioritization, work scheduling, and being able to differentiate between important, urgent, and unimportant tasks. It is the ability to meet deadlines without overstretching and overstressing one self

Presentation Skills: It is the ability to speak before the audience in a well organized and planned way with focus on non verbal behaviour cues such as appearance, body language, tone, etc.

Interpersonal skills: It is the capability to interact and socialize with other people who come from different regions, religions, educational backgrounds, etc

Intrapersonal Skills: These are values and traits that are deeply held within a person such as self concept, self efficacy, self esteem, assertion, and self control which a strong sense of personal well being.

Empathy: it is the ability to understand a situation from the other person's point of view. It is the feeling that you understand another person's experiences and condition

Relevance of Soft Skills

There is a huge skill deficit among students of higher education in India as reported time to time by various surveys conducted. They have been deemed unfit in communication skills, confidence, presentation, problem solving capabilities and generic abilities. Thus development of their soft skills can immensely contribute to expanding their employment opportunities at the macro level which can address dual issues of lack of availability of competent work force and unemployability of qualified graduates.

After having elaborated on the different types of soft skills, it needs to be discussed why they are being considered so important. There are several reasons for this. Technical skills carry little significance in the absence of soft skills. The growth and development in professional life cannot be achieved just through the hard technical skills. These skills are important but an individual is incomplete without the right mix of soft skills and hard skills

During job interviews, good communication skills give a major advantage to the candidates. Good communication skills sometimes may even be able to cover up for some weaknesses in the technical skills. To succeed in a job, candidates definitely need hard skills in the respective fields but soft skills are needed to create further opportunities for oneself.

Soft skills helps in the career advancement since at work the employees are expected to participate in many non technical activities to perform their basic roles and responsibilities. The employees need to interact with people from various departments for compliance and passing instructions. For this one must possess good team skills to be able to work with other colleagues in your work team for efficient and timely completion of assigned goals. The employees interpersonal and leadership skills are put to use during such occasions.

Soft skills, other than just providing better opportunities for work performance and advancement in career, also help in the holistic growth and development of the employees as a person. These are skills that are required by a person for all aspects of our life

The technical skills that a person acquires are no guarantee for a life time. As time and technology changes, the hard skills acquired by a person may start to fail him, but the soft skills stay and support a person much longer. More than just the technical skills, it is the set of soft skills such as problem solving, interpersonal skills, leadership etc. that empower a person and make him more competitive.

Employers prefer those candidates who will be very productive right from the very beginning, having strong communication skills and also having the ability to make good presentation, ability to discuss and talk amicably with customers and colleagues.

To grow as a professional is not the only aspect of an employee, one also needs to grow as a person. One needs to be self motivated and should also be able to motivate others and work along with them productively, shedding negative conduct and becoming more sensitive, peaceful

Developing Soft Skills

The institutions of higher education need to play a major role in imparting soft skills among students. Various other inputs can be given to students at the institutions along with technical education which can result in developing soft skills among them. The assignment of work through group tasks can help the students get an insight into group dynamics, helping them develop their skills of team work and other interpersonal skills such as conflict handling, self control, and respect for others. Participant centric learning processes can be used to foster innovative thinking, creativity and self confidence among the students. Rather than limiting education only to the particular areas of specialization, interdisciplinary and multi disciplinary approach to teaching and learning can be provided to students leading to widening of their horizons and giving them the capability to handle problems in a more holistic way. Developing systems thinking is another way for soft skills development amongst students as it gives them the ability to think critically and to view things from different perspectives. It helps them view a problem and the situation with its interconnectedness rather than in isolation. More involvement of students in the process of classroom management can help students become more responsible and self aware. Also along with imparting theoretical and conceptual training, focus on idea generation and solution orientation needs to be given. The students need to be trained into the practices of change management processes leading to development of leadership and team management. This would lead to substantial build up of communication skills and other soft skills. And finally the teachers need to understand their responsibility as role models. These skills, that the students are being trained for, need to be visible and practiced by their own mentors and teachers at their own institutions, for students to observe and later on practice at their own workplace.

Conclusions

Soft skills are not given their due importance in the present curricula in most institutions of higher education. Thus there is a need to look again at the present curricula, and focus on reorientation of these programmes to enable graduates to perform effectively at their jobs and at the same time have more holistic outlook. This is the need of the hour as it will bridge the gap between the skills possessed and those that the employers expect from students.

BIBLIOGRAPHY

1. Bridgstock, R. (2009). The graduate attributes we have overlooked: enhancing graduate employability through career management skills. Higher Education Research & Development, 28(1), 31-44.
2. Dacre Pool, L & Sewell, P.(2007). The Key to Employability. Developing a practical model of graduate employability. Education and Training 49 (4): 277-289
3. Fugate, M., Kinicki, A. J., & Ashforth, B. E. (2004). Employability: A psycho-social construct, its dimensions, and applications. Journal of Vocational Behavior, 65, 14–38.
4. Harvey, L. (2003). Transitions from Higher Education to Work. A briefing paper prepared by Lee Harvey (Centre for Research and Evaluation,Sheffield Hallam University), with advice from ESECT and LTSN Generic Centre colleagues. Available at http://www.palatine.ac.uk/files/emp/1235.pdf (Accessed 12 May 2013)
5. Ju, S., Zhang, D., & Pacha, J. (2012). Employability skills valued by employers as important for entry-level employees with and without disabilities. Career Development for Exceptional Individuals, 35, 29-38
6. Harvey, L. (2001). Defining and measuring employability. Quality in Higher Education, 7, 97–109
7. Jürgen Hagmann, Connie Almekinders (2003) "Developing 'soft skills' in higher education", in pla notes (eds.), Learning and teaching participation, iied
8. Hillage, J., Pollard, E. 1998. Employability. Developing a framework for policy analysis. DFEE Research Briefing No. 85. Sussex, Institute for Employment Studies.
9. Ogbeide, godwin-charles.(2006). Employability skills and students' self-perceived Competence for careers in the hospitality industry.University of missouri-columbia, Columbia missouri unpublished phd thesis.
10. Rothwell, A., & Arnold, J. (2007). Self-perceived employability: Development and validation of a scale.

14

Vocationally Viable English in Higher Education

Dr. Cute Kharbanda★

Abstract

This paper deals with the necessity of having a professionally fulfilling English language course at undergraduate level in colleges. The course should deal with mostly the linguistic aspects of English language and at the same time, not limit itself to mere theoretical bounds, but also teach the students at a practical level, by the means of language laboratories and role playing in oral classrooms. Such a course would be fruitful in providing real-time knowledge of workplace English requirement, as well as be a career builder as far as job opportunities go. Various career choices are enlisted for the students to take up and indeed they are relatively more in number and scope as compared to learners of English in general compulsory classrooms. The gist of this paper lies in stating the need for making Spoken English Language a career- building skill for students.

Keywords: *Communication, Functional English, Social/Professional Language, Phonetics, Phonology, Language Variation, Psycholinguistics, Non-Verbal communication, Language Laboratories, Role play, Jockeying, Business Process Outsourcing.*

Introduction

Educational institutions nowadays lay stress on the students to develop good Spoken English skills. The effort begins at the school level itself, and is made in the direction of developing interpersonal speaking skills of English so that they are set in line with the trends that are in rage, i.e. good English Language Communication. It is noticeable that the effort

★ Assistant Professor, P.G. Dept. of English, D.A.V. College (Lahore), Ambala City

continues at the college level also but what is stressed upon mainly is the reading and writing part of the language and its grammar. It is undoubtedly true that honing the grammar and a thorough practice of its rules through exercises is a must for a student, in order to have a hold over the errorless production of a language; but what is true at the same time is that competence in a language consists not only the written part, but also the spoken part.

The Objective of this paper is to insist on the fact that certain vocational aspects are imperative in the teaching of English as a compulsory subject at the college level. The point to consider is that the verbal articulation of English is something that has not been given its due in the construction of the syllabi of undergraduate classes. According to Sir Francis Bacon, the chief purpose of education is to make man less animalistic and more humanistic. This metamorphosis is contained in the core of every good English class, and employers too expect nothing less (Rowell 241-242).

It is an unfortunate, yet a ground reality that in colleges where English is taught as a compulsory subject, the curriculum of English and the method and orientation of teaching it is observed to be defective. It is also true that the steady deterioration in the language curriculum is found to be ubiquitous in all regional languages. The defects and deficiencies of language instruction are fraught with grave consequences for higher education. A major problem confronting higher education is the inability of the students to use languages effectively as a means of communication. This explains their absolute dependence on notes and guides, and the degeneration of the lecture system into an exercise in clarifying the notes. There is, therefore, an urgent need to reform language curriculum by giving it a functional orientation, and to train teachers to teach the redesigned curriculum (Jayaram 93-114).

What the teaching community has to understand and focus on, is the fact that the ultimate aim of any kind of learning in today's world of immense competition, is acquisition of a career or growth in ones choice of career. We have been stressing on improving our English speaking skills all the time, but then a practical question arises - what is the big need of the same? Our students might be made to excel in a language of their birth – a vernacular language skill could be considered equally important. But to this, the instant reply would be that English is the need of today. In clichéd terms, it is the global language. As compressed as the world has become, so has grown the need for the young people to master themselves in the language of the world in order to keep pace with the growth rate.

Hence, all arguments and discussions center on the necessity of building conversational English skills among students. Stressing that, let us return to the fact that had been stated earlier. If we acquire a skill, the ultimate purpose of it is acquiring a job or excelling in one's job. The fact applies equally well to the acquisition of English speaking skills. And eventually the question hangs on to the bitter truth that we all must admit that our college education - which is a lead up to a young person's career - does not provide enough opportunity or enough attraction towards developing this basic skill.

The concept of Functional English

Now that the question has been asked, and a problem centered on, the discussion rests on the remedy. And the remedy rests on the concept of Functional English, a course designed to make English into a vocationally viable instruction. The content of such a course should follow a sequence:

1. Know Yourself. Students learn about themselves by completing personality and social inventories, and they co-relate their interests and capabilities to a career. The students also demonstrate an understanding of the English language and its value in the job market.

2. Expressing Yourself. Students learn to communicate successfully by using the correct form in business letters, by conversing politely and confidently with people both face-to-face and on the telephone.

3. Public Media. Students become able to recognize and understand the purposes, uses, and divisions of newspapers and magazines in their daily lives. They recognize general and technical magazines as a source of information both socially and occupationally and use news- papers as a source of information and entertainment.

4. Obtaining a Job. Students identify potential occupations and consider which areas will best suit their interests and skills. They

> become aware of the various methods available to them in locating and securing a particular position, and they also participate in mock interviews with student-designed interview questions. They channel their abilities and interests toward a career area, not necessarily one occupation (Turner 86-87).

Overall the design of the course should be such as to fulfill its real aim of making English language, in both its spoken and written form, practicable in use, to hone the caliber of students in English and, hence its division should be into functional speech and functional writing.

Functional Speech: The idea of developing students in functional speech is to make them understand the nuances of communicative English, and developing competence in the same.

Phonetics and phonemic transcription: We take it for granted that we can write a language with discrete symbols (eg. an alphabet), even though speech is for the most part continuous.(Spratt) Neither the acoustic signal (the sound wave) nor the movements of the speech articulators can be broken down into the kind of discrete limits that alphabetic or other written symbols represent. Hence is necessary the study of phonetics- simply described as the study of articulation, transmission and reception of speech sounds. It is concerned with how speech sounds are produced in the vocal tract (a field of study known as Articulatory Phonetics), as well as with the physical properties of the speech sound waves generated by the vocal tract (a field known as Acoustic Phonetics) (Akmajian, Demers, Farmer, and Harnish).

Then there is the representation of speech sounds-the concept of phonemic transcription. Since English orthography is inadequate as a representation of the current speech sound of English, the transcription system helps write down the sounds produced in speech so that correct pronunciation as well as, remedial learning can be done (Sethi, Dhamija). Word stress, accent, rhythm and intonation in connected speech is an important part of phonetics. Phonology, Syntactic analysis, Language variation, Psychology of language, Speech production, Speech comprehension, Non-verbal communication too are an important part of such a course.

Technical English has several distinguishing features at every level of the linguistic structure. It is a formal variety of language used for specific expressions and not for meeting situations in everyday life. It is a form of language used for transmission, in a systemized manner of particular branch of specialized knowledge pertaining to nature and conditions of life. (Comfort, J., Rogerson, P., Scott, T. and Utley)

Functional Writing

As a holistic approach towards employability skills, the need to include various writing skills as well in such a course. Skills that would help a student complete personal, banking, insurance, contractual, and application forms with accuracy, showing them the importance of prethinking, so that they fully understand all of the steps involved in a task before they can write it down, and also need to be able to review and edit those steps in order to make sure that the directions they have written are complete.

Concept of the Oral-Aural Classroom

The necessity of supplementing the knowledge provided at theoretical level with a practical environment is a must. An oral-aural classroom (and additional visual factor may be included) provides the infrastructure for speech stimulation: microphones. speakers, headphones etc. Also sound proof cubicles for the students to give them the opportunity to practice their speech clarity and ability- and get a feedback in the form of recordings, so that they may make correctional amendments as well.

Role Playing

The activity of role playing can be introduced into the course curriculum for giving the feel of real-time work environment and conversational situations to the students. This makes their learning fun filled and interactive and more at the level of practicing whatever they have learnt in their theory lectures in class.

Aims of the course

It is vital to discuss what we aim to achieve with such a course. As we desire it to be an aid to a potential career opportunity, we must be able to make our student relatively good in the skills of speaking business/outdoor English. It is the type of English that a student has to use in the formal world, outside the confines of his home and the territory of his friends and relations. While developing this on- the- job kind of English, a few skills like- Presentation skills, Skills as a social/ professional language (greetings and introductions, Phoning, Dealing with visitors, Meetings), need to be developed.

Dealing with these aspects of a formal and business settings gives us an idea that English is a form of social language or social communicative form, which can act as a two edged weapon in the hand of the speaker- and the can use it to make or break his career opportunity. Social situations in business are very important in building up confidence between individuals and groups. The role play activities that were a part of the course content section of this paper, are undoubtedly helpful in the above mentioned environment, and could be developed individually with different situations of formality in mind, for the practice of prospective career builders.

Professional Opportunities

When the student is able to communicate fluently and correctly in English by the medium of the functional English course, and his skills successfully tested in the work and formal atmosphere we must seek which sectors open themselves for the English speakers to use their skills for profit.

BPO: In 2008 the ITES- BPO segment employed over 1.1 million Indians (NASSCOM and McKinsey Co), and the number are growing. As the trend is set, the companies which are largely multinational in nature have become aware of where to find their workforce. They are heading straight to the young and learned crowd at colleges- in the from of college placements.

Journalism: The skill of writing and organizing good articles, that is a part of the course content, as suggested above in this paper, helps students to foray into the enterprising field of journalism which could be both news paper and television form of it.

News Anchoring: It requires special language skills and styling of the tongue in a special way to become successful news anchors. The section of the course that deals with pitch, voice modulation, intonation and speech pattern, helps the students gain requisite skills for news reading in front of camera.

Radio Jockeying and Video Jockeying: Though jockeying is also possible in the vernacular, but the demand for English speaking creative young people is high in this field too. Functional English courses offer great help by teaching the students audition analysis, voice modulation, interviewing skills etc.

Editing and Copy Writing: Another career choice for the creative young English learners could be editing for the print as well as screen media. A related employment for the student of functional English would be as a copy writer. Their job involves the use of carefully corrected English, with strong grammar and clarity of useful information (Kaushik)

Conclusions

In the end we come back to the ground reality of the colleges around us, as had been stated in the introduction to this paper, that there is a dire need for he fraternity of English to get together and bring functional English to the fore front of college education. . Research has proved that the most successful undergraduate English learning programs appear to be those which encourage the student to communicate in English. This may be accomplished by providing a setting where the student has a need to use English and is given the motivation to do so (Krashen), which comes from a future job opportunity. Such a program has to be marketed among students, recognized by the course makers, hence a good bet as a part of one's under graduate degree.

Bibliography

1. Turner, Elizabeth A. Vocational English. The English Journal, Vol. 64, No. 1, Resources for the Teaching of English: 1975 (Jan., 1975)
2. Krashen, S. The critical period for language acquisition and its possible bases. Annals of the New York Academy of Science, 1975.
3. Rowell, Bobby G. Vocational English. The Clearing House, Vol. 50, No. 6 (Feb., 1977)

4. Jayaram, N. The Language Question in Higher Education: Trends and Issues. Higher Education, Vol. 26, No. 1, Perspectives on Higher Education in India (Jul.,1993)

5. Comfort, J., Rogerson, P., Scott, T. and Utley, D. Speaking Effectively: Developing speaking skills for Business English. Cambridge University Press, 1994.

6. Spratt, M. English for the Teacher: A Language Development Course. Cambridge University Press, 1994.

7. Akmajian, A., Demers, R.A., Farmer, A. K. and Harnish, R. M. Linguistics: An Introduction to Language and Communication. Prentice Hall of India Pvt. Ltd, 2001.

8. Sethi, J. and Dhamija, P.V. A course in Phonetics and Spoken English. Prentice Hall of India Pvt. Ltd, 2001.

9. Kaushik, S. Script to Screen. Macmillan, 2002.

15

INCREASING COST OF HIGHER EDUCATION IN INDIA: SOME REFLECTIONS ON PROBLEMS AND PROSPECTS

Dr. Dipankar Baidya*

ABSTRACT

The paper has sought to highlight a set of challenges regarding the purpose and outcomes of higher education, each of which is affected by the intertwined pressures of market and government. It focuses on the impact of major external influences on Indian higher education, particularly government and market pressures, and in turn, the impact of resulting institutional decisions in matters such as program choices, tuition charges, and the conduct of research on outcomes of higher education for society at large. Parents in India have been pushed to the corner; they know and appreciate the importance of a college education but affordability hinders most of them from meeting their children's needs. Higher Education's responsibilities for achieving broader societal goals, government's responsibility to provide institutions and individuals the resources, autonomy and flexibility necessary to realize these goals. The demand for college or university education is constantly on the increasing, which implies that prospects of private & foreign participation of universities and colleges are increasing; people desperately need college education. It determines the increasing cost of higher education and its prospects of inclusiveness.

Keywords: *Higher Education, Faculty, Outsource, University, Government*

INTRODUCTION

Until a few centuries ago, education delivered by organized instruction could reach only small selected groups, certain elitesin the society. It is

* Assistant Professor, Department of Commerce, Nowgong College, Nagaon. (Assam)

only in the age of independent political India that education began to spread to wider and wider sections of the society. In a modern society, the educational system tries to embrace as much learner as possible.

The twenty-first century has brought with it profound challenges to the nature, values, and control of higher education in India. Social expectations and public resources for higher education are undergoing fundamental shifts. Changes both within and outside the academy are altering its character – its students, faculty, governance, curriculum, functions, and very place in society. It focuses on the impact of major external influences on Indian higher education, particularly government and market pressures, and in turn, the impact of resulting institutional decisions in matters such as program choices, tuition charges, and the conduct of research on outcomes of higher education for society at large. Parents in India have been pushed to the corner; they know and appreciate the importance of a college education but affordability hinders most of them from meeting their children's needs. In today's competitive world, even simple jobs require bachelor's/ Master/Professional degrees. Consequently, students end up attending colleges far from their hometowns, apply for scholarships or drop out altogether. Despite numerous scholarship offers, some students still miss quality education because they may not qualify for college education. Additionally, those students who attend colleges end up struggling to meet their daily expenses since their parents spend a substantial portion for their incomes on tuition alone.

The five issues discuss here changing answers by the public, policy makers and higher education institutions to central questions about the value, role and control of higher education: Who pays for higher education? Who benefits? Who decides who should benefit, what should be offered, and what the outcomes should be? While each of the five issues raises all three questions, for this discussion they are organized as follows:

Issues examined

Who Pays? — Growing privatization of public colleges and universities — A more commercialized and politicized research system?

Who Benefits? — Who will attend college? Challenges to access — The changing and uncertain job market for Post Graduates

Who Decides? — Accountability, governance, and coordination

The objectives of the study are as below:

1. To identify the problem related to increasing cost of higher education in India.
2. To examine the impact due to increasing the cost of higher education leading to the exclusion of certain lower income groups of people.
3. To examine the increasing cost of higher education and its prospects of inclusiveness.
4. To determine the possible solutions for facing the challenges in higher education.

On the Social perspective of Higher Education in India over 30 years ago, the Education Commission on Higher Education asserted that "benefits from higher education flow to all, or nearly all, persons in the country directly or indirectly, and the costs of higher education are assessed against all, or nearly all, adults directly or indirectly," although benefits and costs are assigned in "quite unequal amounts." Today higher education continues to confer both public and private benefits. Higher education provides high economic returns to individuals, and it develops a skilled workforce and an educated citizen, among other public benefits.

The study aims at looking at the problems and prospects of rising higher education costs. Additionally, it seeks to offer a solution to this reeling problem.

The Problems

Many politicians, Higher Education Departments and College administrators agree on the fact that declining Government support is the main reason behind plunging college costs. The Government is responsible for covering tuition costs. However, tuition costs only take up 33 percent of total educational costs in the aided institutions, Colleges and universities have to take care of these anomalies on their own. Most of them end up increasing tuition costs or reducing the number of programs on offer. This is eventually translated to the students who have to attend college regardless of their financial positions. The situation is further forced by competition among different sectors of the economy.

Rising cost is increasing competition among universities and colleges. Reports such as 'US News and World Report' usually rank Universities and Colleges in terms of the nature and availability of resources. Consequently, many institutions want to show that they are a force-to-reckon-with. Most of them employ very expensive and famous professors, build state of the art dormitories, buildings and expand their sporting facilities. Eventually, the student body has to meet these expenditures. It should be noted that an arms race among deemed universities is also a common.

Rising costs occur because universities and colleges feel that they have the mandate to do so. The demand for college or university education is constantly on the increasing, estimates having shown that the graduating class is increasing day by day. However, seating space and classrooms have remained as they were. This implies that universities and colleges are in charge; they know that people desperately need college education. One of the reasons for this high demand is that income gaps between degree and diploma holders keeps rinsing. Employers have reinforced this perception since they give priority to university-educated individuals. Universities keep increasing their prices because they are aware that this will not reduce their intake levels at all.

Between the years 2002 and 2009, higher education costs have increased by a massive 30 percent, this was a report made by the UGC. Statistics further indicate that tuition costs have risen faster than health insurance, consumer prices and even personal income. Between the years 2006 and 2009 public universities charge a 12, 796 dollars for tuition and boarding fees. Private universities are even more dishonorable; they charge a massive 30, 367 dollars for the same.

As if rising tuition costs are not problematic enough, even government aid has reduced over the past five years. Consequently, there are increasing numbers of college students who have to live on student's loans. This means that they leave college with huge debts. Actually, reports indicate that student's debts have doubled over the past decade. In the year 1999, students with debts had to repay only $9,250 yet debts stand at $19,200 dollars in the year 2010. These numbers have changed by 58 percent after including an adjustment for inflation over these years. Some stakeholders assert that increasing the amount of government aid will only inflate tuition prices further because colleges will always count on government backup.

Scholarships offered to most students only manage to cover about 20 percent of educational expenses. This means that students themselves have to cover the rest. Parents have been forced to use up their emergency savings accounts. Those who happen to have college savings funds are compelled to use up all of it. Despite collecting funds from all sources, students will still graduate from college with debts to the tune of twenty five thousand dollars or more. The rising costs make it very difficult for parents to plan well for their children's education. Repeatedly, parents assert that they have had to add about thousand dollars more each year their children attend college. This makes it very difficult to budget as one cannot anticipate what their child's college will demand from them in the next year.

The mounting cost of education in recent years has eaten into a major part of the household budget. An ASSOCHAM survey showed that 65% of parents spend more than half their take-home pay on their children's education, extra co-curricular activities placing significant burden on their family budget.

According to the survey, parents spending on a single child's education has gone up from Rs 35,000 in 2005 to over Rs 94,000 in 2011 on such items and activities as integral to the school curriculum like fees, transport books, uniform, stationery, building fund, educational trips, extra tuitions and extra-curricular activities. The survey highlights that the rising cost of education, has become a major cause of worry for parents. Majority of parents spend on average more than Rs 18 lakh-20 lakh in raising a child by the time their teen graduates from high school.

The government funding system was set up in order to accommodate and fund students from poor backgrounds. However, this has not been achieved effectively because the students who end up getting government funds are those ones who understand the application process and not the ones who need it the most. It is very difficult for parents to secure scholarship for their students given the fact that most acceptance lists come out in student's final high school years.

Consequently, those who decide on the colleges they would like to attend have to do so hurriedly. Most of them end up choosing the wrong institution or missing out on a scholarship altogether. It should be noted that most of the students who qualify for scholarships are those ones who come from relatively stable backgrounds. In order to be well informed, their parents have to be at a good financial position. Parents hailing from humble backgrounds may not know about the intricacies of application. These same poor families have to deal with the rising education costs. Consequently, such groups have to squeeze their budgets even more.

Prospects For Higher Education

a) Opportunities for Private Participation

The government of India has consistently emphasized the development of science education in the country. There has been increasing budgetary allocation over the various plan periods for higher and technical education. Between the 1st and the 6th Five Year Plans, there was a 20-fold increase in allocation (from Rs. 38 crore to Rs.764 crore) for higher and technical education. Similarly, there was a 12-fold increase between the 6th and 10th Plans (Rs. 8,877 crore) and a 9-fold increase between the 10th and 11th Plans (Rs. 84,943 crore). The 12th Five Year Plan has proposed an outlay of Rs. 184,740 crore. The share of higher education in the total budgetary allocation for education is 11.89%, while the share of technical education is 4.78%. The 12th Plan approach paper has set a target of spending 25% of the total budget on higher and technical education. Similarly, the approach paper also mentions a target of spending 1.0% of GDP on higher education and 0.5% of GDP on technical education. Yet these allocations will not be sufficient to expand access to quality higher education across the country. India needs over 150 billion USD worth of investments in the higher and technical education, over the next decade. The government of India (as well as many states) has recognized the need and importance of private-sector participation to meet the overall demands in the higher and technical education sector. In the past few years, the government is also facilitating the adoption of various public-private partnership models. In a report titled 'Emerging opportunities for private and foreign participation in higher education' in July 2010, it was anticipated that the private sector could, and would, participate in the delivery of higher education.

b) Directly running universities on a not-for-profit basis

This is the route through which the private sector has traditionally participated in the higher education sector. Both small and large industrial houses, as well as their promoters acting in their individual capacities, have established trusts and other non-profit bodies to build and run universities and institutes in accordance with the current regulations governing the higher education sector. However, the reliance on philanthropy as opposed to true investment has restricted this form of capacity addition. Delivering educational services on a for profit basis to students Responding to the opportunities for providing a variety of services both as separate enterprises as well as to formal educational institutions, a large number of entrepreneurs have entered this sector focusing on training, skill development, and employability enhancement – areas that are outside the ambit of regulations governing education. This paper will focuses on the various sub-sectors within the education industry that have witnessed private investments/deal activity.

c) The PPP (Private Public Partnership) model in education

The K.B. Pawar Committee constituted by the University Grants Commission (UGC) has recommended the following four models of PPP in higher education:

Model I – Basic infrastructure model. The private sector invests in infrastructure while the government retains the responsibility for operations and management of the institutions and makes annualised payments to the private investors.

Model II – Outsourcing model. The private sector invests in the infrastructure and also has the responsibility of operations and management of the institutions, while the government pays the private investors for the specified services.

Model III – Equity or hybrid model Investments in infrastructure are shared between the government and the private sector, while operations and management are with the private sector.

Model IV – Reserve outsourcing model Government invests in infrastructure and the private sector takes the responsibility of operations and management.

While there has been considerable amount of experimentation with some success stories in school education and in the vocational-education and skill-development sectors, very few PPP models have been tried out in the field of higher education. In this sector, government-aided institutes are one of the conventional forms of PPP. However, their impact has been felt primarily in addressing issues of access and expansion, with limited or no impact on quality.

The government of Assam has recently attempted a lease-based approach for establishing an engineering institute, and the government of Kerala is in the process of establishing a professional institution under the PPP model. At present, the higher education department has initiated a new PPP scheme for setting up 20 IIITs. MHRD has already announced establishing 14 Innovation Universities, mainly through the PPP model.

d) Opportunities for Foreign Universities in India

While 100% FDI in companies engaged in higher education is allowed under the automatic route, regulatory issues have constrained the actual flow of FDI. The 'not-for-profit' principle and lack of clarity on existing regulations are the major bottlenecks. The foreign educational institutions (Regulation of Entry and Operations) Bill, 2010 which was introduced with a view to regulate the entry and operation of foreign educational institutions seeking to impart higher education, is still pending before the Indian Parliament for the past two years. Accordingly, as an alternate route, the UGC recently gave an in principle approval to regulations on twinning arrangements as discussed in the earlier part of the report. The AICTE has also prescribed regulations for foreign universities undertaking-twinning programs.

The aforesaid regulatory environment has encouraged foreign universities to look for twinning arrangements with Indian educational institutions. This may be the reason for the exponential growth in the number of twinning arrangements forged between Indian institutions and foreign universities in recent times in India, as also the huge interest being shown in this area. Keeping in consideration the parameters of the extant regulatory regime, there are a variety of opportunities for foreign universities in India. The following list, though not exhaustive, illustrates the different models that exist.

- Tie-ups with Indian educational institutions for twinning programs- There could be several variations of twinning programs. Generally, a twinning arrangement operates with a student undertaking a study course at an institution in India for a prescribed period and then subsequently spending equivalent time in the overseas institute.
- Tie-ups with Indian educational institutions for providing services- Foreign universities can enter into tie-ups with Indian educational institutions for providing expertise and services like faculty for teaching, curriculum, affiliations, etc.
- Tie-ups with Indian educational institutions for distance education programs- Another common mode of operation is the e learning or the distant education programme offered by many foreign universities to Indian students. Here, foreign universities deliver their teaching, often on an individual basis, to students who are not physically present in a traditional educational setting such as a classroom, using technologies like the Internet. Distance education in India is regulated by the Distance Education Council, which was established under the Indira Gandhi National Open University Act, 1985. Setting up entity in India or entering into arrangements with Indian parties for assistance with student recruitment activities – where the objective is to attract students from India and encourage them to enroll with the overseas universities
- Tie-ups with Indian educational institutions for student exchange programs- With an intention to enhance cross-cultural exposure and to provide a global perspective to students, these programs encourage Indian students to spend short time periods generally ranging from two weeks to a term or semester at the campus of a foreign university.
- Tie-ups with Indian educational institutions for faculty exchange programs- These programs devised with the intent of enabling the teaching staff to teach or conduct research for short periods at the campus of the Counterpart University or institute. This is often a win-win situation for both the institutions as the teaching staff can benefit tremendously from exposure to a culturally varied and diverse faculty make-up, with an opportunity to exchange ideas and observe a variety of styles.

- Tie-ups with Indian educational institutions for joint research programs- The purpose of these programs is to advance collaborative research between excellent researchers in foreign universities and Indian institutes, while providing opportunities for young researchers to hone their skills. These programs are carrying out in cooperation with overseas science-promotion organizations to respond to the global development of scientific research activities.

e) University/Industry Collaboration:

Between 1995 and 2010, industry funding for university research and development (R&D) in science and engineering grew much more rapidly than any other funding source, nearly doubling as a percentage of total university research, from 4 to almost 8 percent. Although this is a small percentage, industry support plays a much larger role in certain fields, such as chemistry, biotechnology, civil engineering, etc.

Conclusions

These challenges raise questions about the implied social contract between the public, elected officials, and institutions of higher education. Some critics suggest that public officials who are not providing fund sufficient to ensure access, for example, Institutions that have retreated from academic values and from the public realm.

However, this paper has discussed, there has been a marked transfer of higher education's costs from public sources to individual students and parents, as well as increased payments from commercial sources. These changes reflect the growing perception by policy makers and the public that higher education is largely a private benefit, rather than a public good. In turn, this perception risks creating the reality of a private-oriented, market-driven system "detached from the public interest." Policy makers who focus on higher education's benefits to individual "consumers" and "clients" have been more willing to reduce general government support for higher education or make it contingent on loans and specific outcomes.

Rising higher education costs squeeze family budgets and may hinder promising students from joining the good colleges or universities. The government can do a lot to curb this problem; they could introduce price caps for private and public institutions in order to minimize these fluctuations. Additionally, they could introduce direct sponsorship program for needy yet promising students. The government should avoid legislations that reduce state funding. Universities can also do their part by reducing contributions made by low-income parents and by increasing full time grants. Following are the possible solutions for the study:

For instance, increase in cost of higher education in 2009; they made a proposal to reduce interest rates on student loans. However, such an approach may not necessarily be the way forward. Reducing interest rates cannot ensure controlled college costs. Legislations must take the problem head on; Policies need to curb the inflated prices and not just interests on student loans.

The government could increase the amounts they offer in grant systems. This means that there will be more funds available for students both in Government College and private college. Additionally, the Banks could improve their loan repayment options. The field of education is crucial to the Indian economy and should be given some special privileges over and above what other sectors receive. Besides these, the government could assess the system they use for selecting students who qualify for sponsorship. The government should aim at regulating fees from private College to Government College. In this case, Government College refers to those universities with high numbers of low income students. The government should avoid making legislations that increase the burden of payment on parents. Such legislations include scraping student loan consolidation.

The UGC needs to step up their actions against universities or colleges that take advantage of their students. For instance, the government could set a price cap for increasing tuition fees for public universities and private institutions too. They could pass a law that penalizes universities that exceed this amount. The most appropriate penalty in this case is eliminating government funds for such universities or colleges. These price caps could be revised annually to make them in tune with economic conditions.

The private participation in infrastructure development and government retains the responsibility for operations and management of the institutions and makes annualized payment. Also outsourcing model for operations and management of the institutions and other services, while the government pays the investors for the specified services may reduce the cost.

University/Industry Collaboration, industry funding for university research and development (R&D) in science and engineering can provide additional sources of support. Industry support plays a much larger role in certain fields, such as chemistry, biotechnology; civil engineering, and more rapid development and transfer of useful products like vaccines, etc. It becomes a supportive funding for student also. Another common mode of operation is the e learning or the distant education programme offered by many universities to students, MOOC (Massively Open Online Courses). Here, universities deliver their teaching, often on an individual basis, to students who are not physically present in a traditional educational setting such as a classroom, using technologies like the Internet.

Additionally, the government could offer some special financial packages for students who perform well in college & universities. The packages could be made automatic and could be tailored to needy students. Governments are already doing this in certain states and more states can adopt these measures too. Already such types of programs are prepared e.g. RUSA that operates on such a principle.

The government need not be the only party that can cause changes in the higher education sector. Universities and colleges themselves can do the same. They can make individual arrangements to reduce these rising costs.

Bibliography

1. www.ugc.ac.in
2. Lang, S. (2006): How competition for the best students, faculties and facilities sends tuition soaring retrieved from http://www.news.cornell.edu
3. Benassi, F. (2005): Growing over Rising Cost of Higher Education, retrieved from www.standardandpoors.com /ringsdirec
4. Valerie Strauss and John Wagner (2008): Md. Keeps a Lid on Tuition, retrieved from http://www.washigntonpots.com
5. Lederman, D. (2008): A College-Friendly Take on Rising Prices, retrieved from http://www.insidehighered.com

16

E-LEARNING: ROLE IN HIGHER EDUCATION

*Dr. Gagandeep Kaur**

ABSTRACT

In this century, Information Age is changing into the Knowledge Age. Knowledge management in higher education institutions identifies number of existing facilities, systems or projects which contribute to knowledge management in higher education such as libraries, and electronic collections of learning materials, networks for e-mail communication, and management information systems which provide data on the student profile. So e learning helps to obtain, acquire and apply the right knowledge effectively.

Keywords: *Education, Learning, Knowledge, Teaching.*

INTRODUCTION

E-learning means electronically supported learning and teaching. The information and communication systems, whether networked learning or not, serve as specific media to implement the learning process. It includes educational experiences both out-of-classroom and in-classroom by using technology. E-learning is achieved by computer and network-enabled transfer of skills and knowledge. This new technology can change the future of education. It includes all medias in any form of text, image, animation, video, audio etc. E learning can be used as a medium to achieve a particular goal. Knowledge and its efficient management constitute the key to success and survival for organizations in the highly dynamic and competitive world of today.

WHAT IS E-LEARNING?

E-learning is learning via electronic media such as internet. E-learning is a new education concept by using the Internet

---

* Assistant Professor, GGDSD College, Sector 32, Chandigarh

technology. It delivers the digital content, provides a learner-orient environment for the teachers and students. The e-learning promotes the construction of life-long learning opinions and learning society. E-learning is a new educational concept; it may different from the old educational concept. We should provide a new explanation to this new concept. Delivery of the digital content is the main characteristic of e-learning. Internet provides a learning environment for the students and teachers. This environment is learner-oriented, so we can throw out the thoughts of traditionally teacher-center's instruction in classroom. As a new concept of education, e-learning gives a condition for us to realize the life-long learning principle and help us to build a more real learning society. The e-learning plays an important role in high education for the reason of fast need of high education.

E-Learning Goals and Objectives

E Learning presents an innovative shift in the field of learning, providing rapid access to specific knowledge and information. A successful e learning strategy requires analysis, design, development and implementation of teaching-learning strategies and content with context to support a wide range of business and educational goals and objectives. Teaching-learning formats including classroom and web-based professional development with an emphasis on distributed learning environments. It also provides distance learning solutions to help an institution become a strategic e learning organization. It also connects people to people and people to knowledge through the sensible use of technology. Therefore, e learning can be considered from two perspectives: Technology and Pedagogy.

Technology: E Learning is the teaching-training-learning process that involves Authoring, Delivery, Assessment and Management (ADAM) of content via video, audio, CD-ROM/DVD, WWW, Learning (Content) Management System (LMS/LCMS), virtual classroom (Web conference) and/or web 2.0 technologies.

Pedagogy: E learning is another means to literacy using computer networks and multimedia to speed the flow of information, knowledge and understanding from creator to learner anytime anyplace (ATP) in a highly personalized, on-demand fashion in order to speed up an outcome performance in the teaching/training-learning environment and enable the learner to become a creator.

Consequently, instructors, trainers, learners, etc. use a Learning (Content) Management System (LMS/LCMS), Web Conference and/or Web 2.0 technologies to enhance and extend their teaching-learning 24*7 environment through a distributed environment. This indeed is LEARNER CENTRIC. Definition of the goals of an E-Learning solution is driven by the following factors:

Identify task: Determine the tasks to be taught, identify subtasks and other elements involved, and identify the knowledge, skills, and attitudes required to complete the tasks efficiently and effectively.

Identify training needs: Identify the target audience for the training. Identify the shortfall in knowledge, skills, and attitudes of this audience and determine what the target learners need to know.

Evaluate accessible capabilities: Review existing methods and infrastructure for providing training or meeting learning needs.

Establish prospect: Identify concrete expectations and requirements from the desired E-Learning solution. The development of an E-Learning strategy begins by setting goals.

Reduce learning costs: E-Learning requires no papers, no delays, and no travel expenses. To reduce the time required for effective learning Electronic learning is sometimes called "just-in-time" learning. Such learning enables learners to take what they have just learned from their computer screens and apply it to the tasks at hand.

To motivate students: E-Learning is considered an effective way to keep up with new technology, to generate new ideas.

Features of E-Learning

In view of the special needs, abilities and backgrounds of learners, e- learning is becoming more and more popular. Some of the main features of e-learning are outlined below:

Connectivity or Networking

The students are spread over large distances and not confined to a classroom with a teacher teaching them as earlier. This technology (computers and broadband internet) allows people spread over large distances to be connected and networked and will have access to both text and visuals materials. Animation is also entering the educational scene apart from its Omnipresence in the advertisement world. Moreover, in some situations there are a very large number of students – sometimes of the order of 1,000, as happens in open schooling or distance education programmes and this large number would not fit into a classroom in any case. This technology allows all these students to have access to the material available.

Flexibility

Again, because of jobs which students maybe engaged in, students have varied hours of learning – late evenings or early mornings. E-learning can accommodate the needs of such students. Similarly handicapped or ill students who find it difficult to attend regular classes would also be able to benefit.

Inter-Activity and collaboration

Not only is their connectivity between the teacher and the learners, the latter can also be interconnected to themselves for sharing information or for posting comments, etc. There can also be collaboration between different scholars or between teachers and students spread over large distances.

Virtual Learning Environment (VLE)

In view of the special needs of learners and the scope this technology offers institutions and scholars, a virtual learning environment (VLE) or virtual learning portal (VLP) is often created to enable interested persons or learners to have access to educational material like texts, visuals, quizzes, etc available on it. The VLEs created would of course differ from subject to subject

M learning

Mobile learning is learning through mobile computational devices. M- Learning is not just electronic, it's mobile learning. It should be restricted to learning on devices which a lady can carry in her handbag or a gentleman can carry in his pocket. I, therefore, define mobile learning as "the provision of education and training on PDA's/ palmtops/smart phone and mobile phone.

Categories of E-Learning

These are considered as follows:-

Courses: Most discussion of e-learning focuses on educational courses. Educational course materials or courseware are usually modified and added with various different media and are uploaded to a networked environment for online accessing. Today, there are several popular learning management systems (LMS) such as WebCT and Blackboard which are commonly used by educational institutions. E-learning has distinct similarities with classroom environment whereby both of the learners and the instructors are together related to the common course arrangement and flow.

Informal Learning systems: Informal learning occurs in a variety of places, such as at home, work, and through daily interactions and shared relationships among members of society. Informal learning environments are sometimes better than structured ones because what is learned through informal situations are easily absorbed by learners.

Blended Learning: Integrated learning provides a good transition from classroom learning to e-learning. Integrated learning which is also referred to as blended learning is a combination of a face to face and online learning. The productiveness of this method cannot be over emphasized. It encourages educational and information review beyond the classroom settings. Blended learning combines several different delivery methods, such as collaboration software, web-base courses and computer communication practices with face to face instruction. Integrated learning utilizes the best of classrooms with the best of online learning.

Communities: Learning is social. The frequent challenges we battled with in our business milieu are sophisticated and unstable. Because we are in the global era, our methods of problem solving are changing daily. Therefore people dialogue with other members of the same organization or network globally to other organization. Communities strongly contribute to the flow of tacit knowledge.

Knowledge Management: KM efforts leveraged semantic technologies for search and retrieval and the development of e-learning tools for communities of practice. Knowledge management is an essential process which is concern with how to create atmosphere for people to share knowledge on distribution, adoption and information exchange activities in an organization.

Learning Networks: Learning network is a procedure of developing and preserving relationship with people and information and communicating to support each other's learning. Therefore (LN) is enhancing and it offers chances to its members to engage online with each other, sharing knowledge and expertise. States that, the use of pen and paper in our educational system today is producing inadequacy and challenges in the global era that we are in today where subject matter is changing speedily "E-learning provides a new set of tools that can add value to all the traditional learning modes - classroom experiences, textbook study, CD-ROM, and traditional computer-based training." Old-world learning models do not scale to meet the new world learning challenges. E-learning can provide the tools to meet that challenge.

E-Learning Tools

Mainly there are three types of e-learning tools:

Course Tools: These tools are used in schools and colleges to give education. Materials are selected and organized to facilitate class activities. Additional tools, such as discussion forums and online quizzes, are integrated to support collaboration and evaluation.

Digital library Tool: Digital library features usually include search, browsing, and discovering special collections. Search and browsing are used to locate resources and explore related topics. Special collections contain organized materials representing a unique treasure for interested users.

Knowledge Representation Tool: It helps learners to visually review, capture, or develop knowledge. Curriculum tools rely primarily on a text-based, syllabus approach to describing course content. A visualization tool can engage both learners and instructors in an active learning process.

Conclusions

E-learning is among the most important transformation by the internet. To face the challenges of new century,e learning helps the users to gather knowledge and education within productive environments. E learning delivers content through electronic information and communications technologies (ICTs). According to, the use of these facilities, involves various methods which includes systematized feedback system, computer-based operation network, video conferencing and audio conferencing, internet worldwide websites and computer assisted instruction. This delivery method increases the possibilities for how, where and when employees can engage in lifelong learning. This environment takes place with background discussion, assignments and assessment.

Bibliography

1. Tavangarian D., Leypold M., Nölting K., Röser M.,(2004). Is e-learning the Solution for Individual Learning? Journal of e-learning, 2004.
2. Ajayi, I.A. (2008). Towards effective use of information and communication technology for teaching in Nigerian colleges of education. Asian J. Inf. Technol. 7(5): 210 - 214.
3. http://www.resourcebridge.net/Articles/e Learn_Objectives .html
4. Quinn,C. (2000) mLearning: Mobile, Wireless and In-Your-Pocket Learning. Line Zine
5. Hiltz, S.R. and Turoff, M. (2002): " What makes learning networks effective?", Communications of the ACM(45:5) 2002, pp56-59

17

WIDENING THE GATES OF THE INSTITUTIONS OF HIGHER LEARNING UNIVERSITY INSTITUTE OF FASHION TECHNOLOGY

Dr. Rita Kant*

ABSTRACT

Our university system today is in a state of despair. Enrolments are low, quality of education is poor, faculty appointments are politicized, and employability of graduates is abysmal. Our seemingly good but adhoc education policies continue to exclude numbers on the basis of caste, community, gender, economic status and the rural: urban divide. Poor career choices, lack of career guidance passion for professional degrees, absence of entrepreneurial skills, poor governance and management, missing out- of classroom exposure and several more such reasons narrow down the vision of our Higher Education System. However, amidst this gloomy picture there is a ray of light. Our Country is set to reap the dividend of a young working age population; the average age in India by 2020 will be 29 years. We need to widen the gateways of our Higher Education Institutions, making a paradigm shift from the stiffness of classroom instruction to creating adaptive and optimized learning environments, flipping the classroom, providing graduate advisers and teaching assistants and tracking a child's progress across classrooms to evaluate their learning levels and employability. It is these and such Innovative Trends that shall throw the doors of our higher education system open to many more takers, making it more inclusive and worthwhile. Education is an ornament in prosperity and a refuge in adversity..... Aristotle

Keywords: *Entrepreneurial skills; Classroom exposure; Employability.*

* Assistant Professor, University Institute of Fashion Technology, Panjab University. Chandigarh

The objectives of the study are to:

- ❖ Overview the quality of Higher Education System in India.
- ❖ Understand the **inequity and disparity** in our Higher Education System
- ❖ Propose Innovative Education Trends and throw its doors open to all.

Quality of Higher Education System in India: An Overview.

Our Nation is in times when it needs to harness its human resource and mould it into intuitive, analytical individuals with problem solving skills. This objective can be derived through the gateways of higher learning, both universities and colleges.

Our university system today is in a state of despair. In almost half the districts in the country, higher education enrollments are abysmally low; almost two-third of our universities and 90 per cent of our colleges are rated as below average on quality parameters. In many states university appointments, including those of vice-chancellors, have been politicized and have become subject to caste and communal favouritism and corruption.

Recent higher education surveys have documented:

- ❖ Our quantitative expansion has not led to quality enhancement.
- ❖ Employability of our engineering graduates ranges between 20% to 40% and that of Arts and Science graduates are only around 10%.
- ❖ There has been value degradation and decline in gratitude towards our teachers by 61%.
- ❖ 94% of our students go to 33,023 colleges affiliated to 316 universities. The system is, thus, stifling quality enhancement of state universities.

Yet amidst all these gloomy statistics are rays of light. Our Country is set to reap the benefits of demographic dividend with its huge working age population. International Labour Organization has predicted that by 2020 India will have 116 million workers in the age group of 20 to 24 years. The average age in India by 2020 will be 29 years as against 40 years of USA, 46 of Japan and 47 of Europe. It will be a lost opportunity if this dividend is not converted to our advantage. Here lies the significance of widening the gates of Higher Education in India in order to produce an educated empowered productive workforce.

Inequity and Disparity in Our Higher Education System.

What are we aiming at when we aspire to educate our students of higher learning? Are we effectively transforming and elevating them to a level where they can comprehend and critically assimilate whatever they have gathered? Is the learning process for them a nightmare? The answer is No! And Yes!

We believe that education is a great leveler in a society. Thereby we must know that if we do not fix education, we cannot fix inequality and mismatch. As per reliable data, India achieved a Gross Enrolment Ratio of 18.8% in higher education in 2012 through expansion schemes under the XIth Five Year Plan (FYP). However, our education policies seem to be narrower than what they seem to be. This is perhaps the reason why we exclude numbers on the basis of caste, community, gender, economic status and the rural: urban divide.

Our citizens are not being prepared to compete in today's global, hyper-connected economy, and, for lesser privileged class the outlook is especially grim. A recent McKinsey report states that a majority of young Indians are unfit for employment. It also mentions that India will see a deficit of 40 million high skilled and 13 million mid-skilled workers by 2030.Of the 90 million low skilled laborers' that will be available in the country in the next two decades, 27 million will find it difficult to get jobs. As per the experience of Infosys less than 2 per cent applicants they get are employable. Findings of FICCI and World Bank report that two-thirds of our graduates are not employable.

1. **Poor Career Choices:** It is a fact that out of the millions of youngsters who graduate out of institutions every year, only 20 per cent are able to find employment at the end of their course. But

what's startling is that even among those who find employment only 50 per cent are really getting jobs that are relevant to their interest and education. We as parents and teachers fail to provide proper and timely guidance, as per the aptitude of our children, resulting in wrong career choices. This is also how we land up in the grounds of these Institutions of higher learning, as dispassionate and disgruntled teachers.... and this becomes the major reason of the failure of our system The answer lies in one being able to opt out at any juncture and take remedial academic choice.

2. **Professional Education** may be as valuable to education as dessert is to a healthy diet. However, our nation also needs plain stuff: mathematicians, physicists, historians, litterateurs' musicians, geographists, psychologists, economists and political scientist. Higher education of our society, a country of size 1.2 billion cannot consist of management, engineering schools only. In the US there are people doing Bachelor's at Yale in Art History and being hired by Goldman Sachs at 300,000 dollars. And here we continue to produce **supposedly exclusive Engineers and MBA'S**

3. **Governance and Management** of our universities needs to be improved. We must bring transparency in our money matters; where the money comes from and how it is spent. No "profit making" educational institution can deliver quality education. Also, student financing alone cannot sustain the budget of an institution; significant subsidies, whether it comes from government or charity are needed. The public expenditure on higher education in India is very low at 0.6% of the GDP, compared to 2.7% in the USA. We need to step up our expenditure on research to pursue large-scale innovation. Our private sector, which contributes to one-fourth of our country's expenditure on research and development, should increase its share of spending to levels prevalent in nations such as Japan, US and South Korea.

4. **Sense of responsibility among students, faculty and alumni is the need of the hour.** We think that the Vice Chancellor alone who drives a university. Are not the faculty and students the true drivers? We must rethink and see what needs to be corrected to

improve our gurukuls. It will help improve the chances of our youth being hired. It is not likely to happen immediately but sooner than later it will.

5. **Lack of passion among young graduates to learn.** Madhok feels "there is a fundamental problem confronting today's youngsters. They do not realize that learning is a lifelong process and does not end after they graduate or earn a degree. They must realize that skill development is a continuous and sustainable process. One has to constantly and consistently upgrade and update oneself to meet the demands of the profession one is in… he points out..". But who is going to make them realize that? Are we answerable?

6. **Missing real-life learning and industrial training.** For most aspiring professionals, learning and training happens outside the classroom. However we fail to encourage our students to learn outside classrooms from real life experiences. Vice chancellor, University of Cardiff, Prof Colin Riordan has pointed out that students can gain from industrial placements and projects while studying. We must make our students realize the importance of having professional experience combined with classroom experience and aptitude to develop skills that are relevant to their careers.

7. **Absence of Entrepreneurial skills.** India has produced over 500 first generation entrepreneurs, which in the opinion of GD Yadav, Vice Chancellor, Institute of Chemical Technology, is one of the greatest assets and example of what we are capable of. Asha Khemka, chairperson of the Association of Colleges in India, advises students to take part in activities that directly or indirectly promote entrepreneurship. Sharing the success story of IIM-Ahmedabad, Prof Rakesh Basant says that his students were given scores based on their performance in handling responsibilities with start-ups."Start-ups are great places to learn, join one," he urged."You face challenges on a day-to-day basis in startups and this is what develops many skills that make you job-ready," We need to show our students how to generate employment if they cannot find one.

Innovative Trends to Throw Doors Open

Sam Pitroda, Chairperson National Knowledge Commission said, 'there is today a need for transition to a course credit system which provides learners with choices; where degrees are granted on the basis of completing a requisite number of credits from different courses." UGC also recommends curricular flexibility through **Credit Based Courses and Credit accumulation** in its Action Plan for Academic and Administrative Reforms. Aided by modern communication and information technology CBCS has a high probability to be made operational efficiently and effectively.

Efforts are being made to address the mismatch between expansions vis-a-vis quality of employable, value-inculcated graduates via a reforms package evolved by UGC in its XIIth FYP document The Government has come up with Rashtriya Uchchatar Shiksha Abhiyan (RUSA), a centrally sponsored scheme for higher education. It will give an excellent opportunity to the state universities to upgrade educational and research ambience, infrastructure, knowledge resources and skill development expertise to produce international quality manpower. It shall provide strategic funding to State higher and technical institutions to address issues of expansion, equity and excellence. RUSA proposes to allow a maximum of 100 colleges to be affiliated to any university. A total of 316 state public universities and 13,024 colleges will be covered under it.

However, all said and done, the process we adopt to make our students learn is of paramount importance. As progressive educational activist Alfie Kohn notes, great teaching isn't just about content but motivation and empowerment. New trends in education technology are breaking old educational habits and making way for a system that will better prepare our young people for the future while leveling the socioeconomic playing field.

We need to sensitize ourselves and begin to appreciate these new trends in learning process.

1. **Cafeteria Approach:** This can include Seminar instruction vs. classroom with small 8-12 students meeting **at a round table or lounge setting** as opposed to classroom to facilitate the collaboration of ideas and free thinking vs. the stiffness created

in a classroom environment. It can also include Field work/Field trips for the purposes of encouraging, motivating and challenging students to overcome obstacles no matter what they are faced with. For example: Doing a field trip to the Taj Mahal focusing less on the architectural genius of the project and more on the social ramifications of what it meant for India at the time. What are we doing to preserve our history and the future of our society in the face of current socio economic and political obstacles?

2. **Grad Advisors:** Every student should have a grade advisor to guide him her through his career path showing him/her the vertical and horizontal choices that are available to him to exercise.

3. **Teaching Assistants:** Students should be offered paid Teaching Assistantship where they can take up certain designated teaching and non teaching work assignment from a specific subject teacher. This practice can go a long way in developing a holistic personality while helping in assimilation of knowledge learnt.

4. **Flipping the Classroom:** In a traditional classroom we find rows of students staring glassy-eyed at the professor who drones on, paying more attention to the equations he's writing on the board rather than the students he's supposed to be teaching. Digital technology helps to "flip" the classroom. In flipping, students do the homework before class, typically reading course materials or watching videos of lectures online. Class time is spent on individual or small group tutoring, with the lesson plan set by the student; concentrating on areas he has not understood. Research shows that such custom made tutoring is more effective for understanding, mastery, and retention than boring lectures

5. **Creating Adaptive and Optimized Learning Environments:** If Google search results can learn our patterns and preferences, why not education software? This question led the founders of Knewton to develop adaptive learning software to provide personalized content for each student that shifts according to his or her personal strengths and weaknesses. "Optimized learning" adapts not only the content, but also the format, according to a student's learning style. With adaptive learning, each student receives a tailored lesson. By using education optimization,

students can benefit from a "blended classroom" experience that allows them to alternate between adaptive software and small-group learning.

6. **Massive Open Online Courses:** MOOCS is bringing education everywhere through distance learning and massive open online courses. It delivers free, non-credit on line classes. Students can pay a tuition fee and take full credit online classes with a discussion forum where they meet their classmates in a virtual environment to exchange ideas, assignments and critique of each other's ideas and the course work as a whole.

7. **Accountability:** Measuring learning outcomes is important. Institutions used to be gatekeepers of knowledge, and memorization was the key to success. We as teachers measure our students' abilities to regurgitate facts and formulas. We need not do that anymore. We now have digital tools to track several dimensions of student progress. Technology can create a wealth of data for us about each student so that we can easily track a child's progress across classrooms. This gives us time to focus our energy on fostering critical thinking skills and providing extra help to struggling students. Our fraternity must become disciplined and analytical about identifying students' strengths and skill gaps, continuously turning classroom data into a plan of action.

8. **Classroom relationship management:** CRM helps capture anecdotal notes and evidence of student growth. We need to balance between the art and science within teaching. The art is in the relationships we build with our students and the science is purposeful assessment that generates real evidence of their growth.

Conclusions

The concern is whether we want higher education manpower to acquire international-level expertise with high employability or dwindle in mediocrity? And whether we have **wherewithal to be world class?**

We teachers are the backbone of educational reforms. We should pragmatically approach problems and provide collective wisdom for further quality refinement. We need to move towards micro learning moments which foreshadow a much larger transformation; socialstructed learning. But before that we need to inculcate

However the danger of encouraging free thinking is that people will speak and act freely and the question we must ask ourselves is: Are we ready for that?

BIBLIOGRAPHY

1. http://m.fastcoexist.com/1681576/5-disruptive-education-trends-that-address-american-inequality
2. http://m.rediff.com/getahead/slide-show/slide-show-1-career-interview-with-prof-shyam-sundar- yale-zzuniversity/201 3040 9.htm
3. http://www.slideshare.net/tijithomas37/choice-based-credit-semester-system-cbcss-18036976
4. UDC letters January 2008; March 2009

18

Relevance of Moral Education in Higher Education

Dr. Amandeep Kaur Sandhu*

Abstract

Everyone recognizes the need for educating youngsters about the importance of moral values in today's complex world. Teaching moral values to youngsters is easy. Concerted review of literature has revealed that Moral education is becoming an increasingly popular topic in the fields of psychology and education. Media reports of increased violent juvenile crime, teen pregnancy, embezzlements, human rights violation, numerous abuses and suicides have caused many people both within and outside the country. Though not all of these social concerns are moral in nature, and most have complex origins, there is a growing trend towards linking the solutions to these and related social problems to the teaching of moral and social values in both public and private schools and universities. However, considerations of the role universities can and should play in the moral development of youths are themselves the subject of controversy. The task of higher education is made more challenging with its needs to impart and retain traditional values, while at the same time moving towards a knowledge-based society. As the youngsters are to be the future leaders of the country, it is vital to prepare them with the necessary social skills and moral strengths that can help guide their decision-making behaviours. This paper is an attempt to deal with the issues of this major problem and suggesting some remedial measures to inculcate the humane aspect among our youth.

Keywords: *Moral education, Core values, Pro- social approach, Moral compass and Humane element in education*

* Assistant Professor, MTSM College for Women, Ludhiana

Relevance of Moral Education in Higher Education Introduction

The economic development and progress of any nation depends upon its higher education system. India's higher education system is the world's largest next to China and United States. Our contribution to internationalization of higher education is noteworthy. But there is other side of the coin too. Our country is engrossed in high tech culture at the cost of humane and civilized behavior .The economics of education has become more important than morals of education. India has a very rich heritage of moral and cultural values, But the increasing incidents of violence, crimes, gender insensitivity, embezzlements among youth gives a very poor reflection of our moral education system. The system produces followers instead of leaders. No doubt the present educational system is producing doctors, engineers, advocates etc. but fails to produce a good character civilized human being.

The objective of this paper is to highlight the following issues :

- To what extent moral education is required in higher education.
- To know the causes of downfall of moral standards in our youth.
- To highlight the role of educational institutions, teachers, parents and society in inculcating the moral values in the young generations.
- Emphasizing the importance of morality in producing civic human being.

What is Moral Education?

Moral education is the guidance and teaching of good behavior & values. It deals with the development of a person in relation to self awareness, relations with others and the realism of belief.

Reasons for Downfall of Moral Standards in Youth.

- **Lack of accountability and social responsibility**

Our present education is not playing suitable role to sharp future of our youth. It makes students corrupt and teaches them indulgent and self-centered attitude.

Administration and even government is not accountable to youth for their discontentment and stressful life. The meritorious are given importance ignoring the moral development of student. Corporate would not assess the candidate in terms of morality but would grade them on basis of scores achieved by them.

❖ **Materialistic attitude and self-decision making**

It is not surprising that the youth have discarded a few other principles in exchange for material welfare or due to changing cultural environment. We see a nation of self centered ideology where the upcoming generations desire all what their parents have but without the hard work. Because they know when the parents are gone they will inherit what they now have. So why become educated? why work? But actually the aftermath is that parents have to pay heavy for decisions taken by their children.

❖ **Defeating the aim of education**

The main aim of education is to provide moral, ethical, social, intellectual values to students and grooming the child from all vital aspects. John Dewey believed that institutes should impart education while ignoring the spectrum of human differences and continuing the noble profession irrespective of race, class, ethnicity, gender, social conflict and inequality on both teachers and students. Even today a physically disabled child is facing too many problems in normal teaching-learning environment but he/she is still not disable friendly..

❖ **Ineffective evaluation system**

No doubt that the present education system is producing doctors, engineers, advocates but there is lack of moral values. The present system test only what student has crammed or is able to copy. It does not test what the student has learned and what ideas they have for life and work.

❖ **Moral standard under attack**

Mainly in the changing scenario the morals are shaken due to dynamism in society. It does not emphasize on patriotism. and humanity. Youth have very little or no value of our heritage and culture. It only prepares students as job-seekers or job-managers with low value system. People now do not respect humanity. Honesty is now laughed at by people.

Sincerity and hard work are considered as foolish. There is no sense of duty and sacrifice in most of the country's youth.

- **The 'REALITY' of modern times**

We have gone down below the level of beasts. The recruitment and selection authorities are blamed for faulty and biased performances. So, here comes the sentiment of

1. Disbelief
2. Shame
3. Anger
4. Hurt

The final conclusion is, this is not localized. It has become the common man practice all over the world. Surprisingly, this is an epidemic behavior in India also. Can this fetch emotional and moral integration, on the part of educational institutions? This is the fundamental question, which cries for an answer.

- **Lack of total personality development**

The system churns out indifferently trained, poorly motivated students, who have few job prospects. For these students success is having money by whatever means. The education is not able to develop leadership qualities among students.

- **Less emphasis on innovation and research**

There is little scope for research activities and knowledge orientation. The system doesn't inspire students to go beyond what is set to be the limit. Students are not encouraged to take subjects of their interest so they have to crack the nut and moral values are ignored.

- **Defective learning patterns**

There is too much stress on getting marks and this encourage children to mug up and pass exams rather than learning concepts. Institutions are giving more stress on completing syllabus and help the students to pass exams instead of building their character and enhancing their personalities. This education system is detached from the real world. It doesn't prepare the person to face the challenges of life. On account of it students face the work stress while performing jobs.

Essence of Moral Education in Higher Education

Moral education is the brake which is very much needed to control the youth or it serve as a steering wheel which will steer our youth towards a fruitful and meaningful end. The various problems in India like corruption, poverty, superstitions etc, are inter-linked. Moral education helps in solving these problems at the root where they originate. All problems can be solved very easily if the citizens have mastered their mind and are pure, harmonious and sincere. It will help the youth to listen to their inner voice-the conscience. **They will hesitate and have second thoughts before committing a wrong deed say stealing, lying, cheating etc. It will also imbibe in them values like honesty, modesty, sincerity, proper manners and also how to control their urges desires and whims.**

Educational Institutions – DUTY BOUND TO IMPART MORAL EDUCATION

At this point it is time to deliberate on the possible ways and means to stop, avert further deterioration and set thing right. It is obvious that schools and colleges are the organizations that are well equipped to take up this uphill task efficiently. The modern schools and colleges are gradually moving away from this task —marks scored by the students are probably one of the indicators of the true knowledge gained in a school or college.

There is a need to identify the causes of moral decline in our society and our universities and academic institutions must take the lead to meet the moral challenges. Some initiatives to be taken are:

- A way to art of living
- Promote transparency in educational system
- Tackling disputes in education sector
- Removing the chronic corruption
- Ensure a comfort zone to youth
- Avoiding unrest among students

❖ Develop pro-social approach among students.

CME Core Values R³ICH

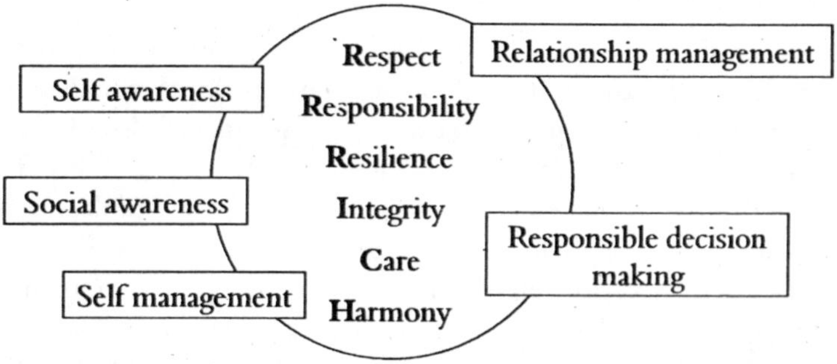

This approach says that if we inculcate the above core values in our youth they will become more self aware, socially aware, self managed, good relationship manager and responsible decision makers.

The Association for Supervision and Curriculum Development, a national organization concerned with curriculum development and the improvement of teaching procedures compiled a report outlining ways to help better the current situation. Additionally, they advocated the incorporation of critical thinking and decision making skills in morality education, and the use of regular assessments of the moral ambiance of schools and colleges.

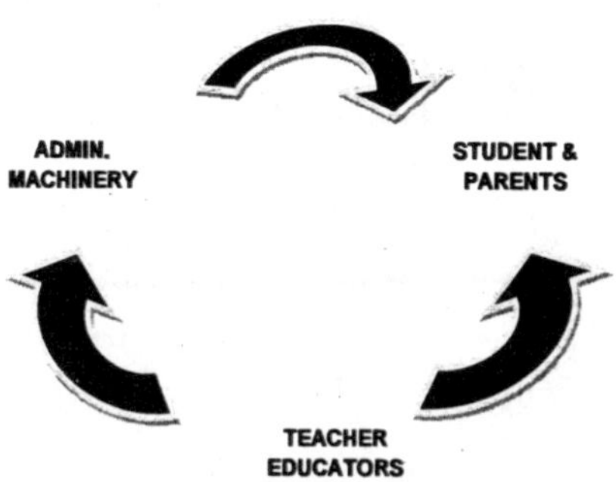

Vital Role on the Part of

❖ **Teachers**

Teachers are always influencing moral attitudes and capacities of their students.

It is we who make the society. If we improve ourselves, we can improve our society. No one is a born criminal or a spoilt person. It's the environment that is deviating the child away from taking the right path. Good teachers can bring the change with good Education imparted to the students.

❖ Education System

There is need for re-structuring of the education system, so as to minimize competition and rivalry and thereby reduce feelings of marginalization and exclusion among low achievers. Also, there is need for reform of the curriculum so as to include universally desirable values that are necessary for producing well rounded, balanced and useful citizens.

Moral education should set to be compulsory in colleges. It can be emphasized through youth festivals as the topics of the fest concerning the social causes such as save earth, save girl child, child labour, gender inequality, corruption etc. This would be a great move on part of colleges as an indirect effort towards moral education. The institutes need to invite some resource persons and professors to teach moral education.

❖ Parents

The parents, consequently, have to assume an active role in the moral development of their children. They need to become fully involved at every stage in the child's mental growth until he/she attains maturity. This involvement includes learning to communicate with the younger generation through their books and reading material. . This is very critical and almost inevitable since there is enormous pressure of studies and competitive scenario.

❖ Administrative Machinery-Use of Power and Not Abuse of Power

Administrative machinery is supposed to be servants of the people. But they take no time in turning into masters over them. Dirty politics enslave humanity and destroy freedom and defeat the very purpose of education system. Thus, it concludes to say; "The only way to bring about a change in the polity is to bring about a change in morality"

❖ Legitimate Role-Government

Government should support the higher education system and frame policies and rules favoring colleges and universities. Govt. should boost the education-system and should design student-centric regulations, adequate funding in education sector.

❖ **Awakening Inner Wisdom**

Within each of us is a centre of wisdom far deeper and greater than we are aware of. When we are willing to open our consciousness to new ideas and new ways of thinking about issues then our lives change for the better. It is a glaring fact that **IF WE ARE NOT PART OF THE SOLUTION, THEN WE ARE THE PROBLEM**.

The concept of morality is very well introduced in schools at elementary, primary and secondary levels. Thus this calls for forwarding the moral education system to Indian higher education system.

Conclusions

"Our Youth Need Roots to Grow and Wings to Fly"

Values are our roots, Success our wings and youth is the **POWER OF NATION**. The combination of these factors means achieving value-based success in life. We can't say that personality of a youth or individual is complete, just because he/she is educated until and unless the knowledge of moral values is there in his/her education. There is still more work to be done in the articulation of moral principles and development of methods to assess their place in higher education system. It is for our universities and other institutes of higher learning to initiate a movement to meet the moral challenges and ensure that our civilization values are once again reiterated. Both parents and teachers can accept the responsibility of inculcating molar values. Only one force of moral harmonization can take us to the sky heights. "If I am not for myself, then who is? And if I am only for myself, then what I am?" The message is clear. If as a citizen, I am not concerned and willing to stand up for my country, then who will? Each one of us, by virtual of being born in this country has to take an unwritten oath to build and uphold the integrity of the Nation and ensure that our civilization values are fully entrenched in our minds.

Bibliography

1. Alwi Hj Azlin, (2006), Changing Student Valuing Of Higher Education, Edith Cowan University, Western Australia

in association with Khon Kaen University, Thailand and Bansomdejchaopraya Rajabhat University, Thailand.,

2. Cahn M. Stewan (2011), Moral Problems In Higher Education, Temple University Press
3. Gandhi M.K.(2011), Moral Education, APH Publishing Corp.
4. Martin Trow,(1976), Higher education and moral development, American association of university professors,
5. Sharma Chanderkanta,(2011) Moral Philosophy contemporary perspectives, EBH Publishers (India) Guwahati,
6. Simpson Evan,(1989) Good Lives And Moral Education, Houghton Mifflin Company, Boston
7. http://www.compact.org/advancedtoolkit/pdf/bringle-all.pdf
8. http://www.mayflowerpri.moe.edu.sg/Departments/CharacterDevelopment/CivicsandMoralEducation/LearningOutcomes.aspx
9. http://www.character.org/more-resources/other-helpful-links/research-and-higher-education/

19

Shifting role of Teachers in Higher Education System

*Dr. Kuldeep Kaur**

Abstract

Higher Education is very important for building up a nation. In the world of today, competition in any field is a competition in knowledge. The agricultural, industrial and scientific growth of this country depends upon creating a crops of well trained professionals in these areas and this can happen only with quality higher education. We need not belittle what we have achieved. However there is an inescapable need to strengthen higher education in terms of quality and effectiveness. This new environment also involves a change in the roles of both teachers and students. The role of the teacher will change from knowledge transmitter to that of learning facilitator, knowledge guide, knowledge navigator and co-learner with the student. The new role does not diminish the importance of the teacher but requires new knowledge and skills. Teachers are being challenged to utilize new approaches and methods in an effort to improve learning outcomes. They have to seek improved ways of teaching by developing new programmes and instructional strategies such as enquire approaches, simulation games, computer-assisted instructions and programmed learning materials. The educators at the levels should endeavor to emphasize the need for discipline, character building and inculcate among the young minds the feeling of national integration.

Keywords: *Trained professionals; knowledge transmitter; learning facilitator; knowledge navigator.*

Introduction

Higher Education is very important for building up a nation. In the world of today, competition in any field is a competition in knowledge. The agricultural, industrial and scientific growth of this country

* Assistant Professor, Guru Nanak Khalsa College for Women, Ludhiana

depends upon creating a crops of well trained professionals in these areas and this can happen only with quality higher education. We need not belittle what we have achieved. However there is an inescapable need to strengthen higher education in terms of quality and effectiveness.

Higher education is generally understood to cover teaching, Research and Extension. In the opinion of Ronald Barnett (1992) there are four predominant concepts of higher education.

(i) Higher education as the production of qualified human resources.

(ii) Higher education as training for a research career.

(iii) Higher education as the efficient management of teaching provision.

(iv) Higher education as a matter of extending life chances.

It has thus become a prime necessity for the centres of higher learning to strive and achieve the desired quality of high academic standards comparable to global norms.

This new environment also involves a change in the roles of both teachers and students. The role of the teacher will change from knowledge transmitter to that of learning facilitator, knowledge guide, knowledge navigator and co-learner with the student. The new role does not diminish the importance of the teacher but requires new knowledge and skills Students will have greater responsibility for their own learning in this environment as they seek out, find, synthesize, and share their knowledge with others. ICTs provide powerful tools to support the sift to student centred learning and the new roles of teachers and students.

Main objective of the study is to know the changed Role of Teacher in Higher Education system to shape and mould the personality of students.

This study emphasizes that strict monitoring of teaching, learning and evaluation processes at institutions of higher education will bring the desired quality in higher education in our country to compete internationally and to face the challenges of twenty first century.

Role of Teacher

The teacher is the key person on whom the future of children and the mankind depends. He plays an important role in shaping and moulding the personality of a child. We are convinced that the most important factor in the contemplated educational reconstruction is the teacher his/her personal qualities, his educational qualification, his/her professional training and the place that the occupies in the school as well as in the community, remarks the Secondary Education Commission 1952-53.

In the higher education system, the role of teacher has been changing due to the pressure of social and economic changes. The expected role of teacher has assumed new dimensions and the society expects his/her leadership in the task of making education an effective instrument in the process of nation building. A teacher is required to generate that energy in oneself and handle it in one's work of educating the boys and girls that report to him or her. A teacher has not only to instruct but also inspire the students; she has to influence the life and character of his or her students and equip them with ideas and values.

Today, the teacher required to concern himself with the total development of the child and not only with one or two aspects. S/He must be philosopher, illuminating the way of his intellectual and spiritual progress s/he must be his guide in his moral and aesthetic advancement. In fact, he must be all things to all his pupils-a physician concerned about their physical health, a mental hygienist leading them carefully to sound mental health, a philosopher guiding them painstakingly in their search for truth, a moralist assisting and encouraging them to acquire goodness, an artist helping them to find beauty. The success of student depends essentially upon the competence of the teachers, their sense of dedication and the identification with the interests of the students committed to their care.

Encourage Thinking

The teacher is now expected not only to inculcate knowledge but also to encourage thinking. S/He has to become more of an advisor, a partner to talk to, he has to help seek out conflicting arguments rather than hand out readymade truths. For this, he will have to devote more time and energy to productive and creative activities.

Teachers are being challenged too utilize new approaches and methods in an effort to improve learning outcomes. They have to seek improved ways of teaching by developing new programmes and instructional strategies such as enquiry approaches, simulation games, computer assisted instructions and programmed learning material. The educators at all levels should endeavor to emphasize the need for discipline, character building and inculcate among the young minds the feeling of national integrator. It will also make student's intellectual and imaginative powers to produce an enquiring, analytical and creative mind.

The Information Provider

A traditional responsibility of the teachers is to pass on to students the information, knowledge and understanding on a topic appropriate at the stage of their studies. This leads to the traditional role of the teacher as one of provider of information in the lecture context. Lecturing has always been a central role of higher education teacher. The lecture remains as one of the most widely used instructional methods.

The essence of quality implementation lies in the proper transfer of knowledge from teachers to students, which needs to be done so effectively that there is least loss in the transmission process. The teachers have a very responsible role to play in the regard. They have to generate and disseminate knowledge of high standards with a high quality of teaching methodology. Unless this is done, it is difficult to achieve the desired quality of education needed to equip the students to compete internationally.

The Role Model

The importance of the teachers as role model is well documented. The teacher should model or exemplify what should be learned. Students learn not just from what their teachers say but from what they see in the practice and the knowledge skills and attitudes they exhibit. Students follow the teacher how she stick to the principles. Teacher should exhibit the good moral character which student picks up from him. Teacher should prove to the students an indispensable by having more knowledge and ten steps ahead from the students.

Teachers as a Facilitator

The key role to teacher is as a facilitator and a support to ensuring learning. Teacher is the one who facilitates learners to realize their potentials, articulate their personal and context specific experiences in ways that are acceptable in the wider context of our nation. Students require personal attention of the teachers not only for the studies but also for career guidance and counseling. They want a right mix of skills along with knowledge through a system to gain employment opportunity in the market. This can be done by promoting entrepreneurial education and activities by educational institutions and mgt. Schools with a multi disciplinary approach and cross-curricular teaching methods.

Teacher as a Participant in the Learners Efforts

Teachers have to recognize that in a learner centered situation curriculum evolves and is not pre-designed teacher is merely prepared for providing possible supports in the process of learning. Every subsequent learning situation cumulatively provides better insight to teacher is discerning learner needs and created pool and identifies varied learning supports. In this sense, teacher is a participant in the learner's efforts at evolving learning experience and helping to develop programme for learning. Teacher is to convince the earner that information is power and it is within their reach.

Teacher to Find His Own Teaching Style

There is no one method that is effective in causing all learners to learn in similar ways. Each teacher has to find one's style of teaching through perceptive practice but recognize the fact that all learners learn in their in their own ways. But now a days to made your teaching more individualized interactive, informative and innovative, teachers can integrate ICT in teaching and can made prepare pupils for rapidly changing world.

Recognize Himself as a Professional

Teacher needs to recognize himself/herself as a 'professional'. S/He should be endowed with the necessary knowledge, attitude, competence, commitment, enthusiasm, spirit of seeking new ways and means, capable of reflection and sensitive. S/He should be perceptive not only to the learners and the institution but also to the emergent concerns in the larger social perspective within which one functions. Teacher should create think tank useful to the society.

Teacher's Sensitivity to Student's Needs and Problems

One of the most important characteristics of good teacher is the ability to identify student's problems and needs. When students are comfortable or at ease with the teacher, they can give their full attention to learning. The good teacher does not place emphasis wholly upon academic achievement but recognises and appreciates many other types of abilities and leadership qualities in students. When teachers are sensitive to the needs of students, they are quick to notice the ones who seen unable to excel in anything, who are afraid to talk. Teacher who knows something about the factors that have influenced the lives of students are better prepared to accept them without reacting adversely to their undesirable behaviour. At least the teacher is expected to be more patient, sympathetic and understanding.

The Assessor

As in the twelfth plan period, there is a focus on expansion, equity, excellence, governance, funding and monitoring. Those aspects have to be implemented in the right spirit for the higher education. Teachers have to play an important role in all the spheres.

The assessment of the student's competence is one of the most important tasks facing the teacher. The teacher has a responsibility not only to plan and implement educational programmes and to assess the students' learning, but also to assess the course and curriculum delivered. Monitoring and evaluating the effectiveness of the teaching of courses and curriculum is now recognised an integral part of the educational process. Evaluation can also be interpreted as an integral part of the professional role of teachers, recognizing teachers' own responsibility for monitoring their own performance.

The Planner

Curriculum planning is an important role for the teacher. Most colleges and universities has education committees charged with the responsibility for planning and implementing the curriculum within their institution. Teachers employed by the colleges and universities may be expected to make a contribution to curriculum planning. Curriculum planning presents a significant challenge for the teacher and both time and expertise is required if the job is to be undertaken properly.

The teacher is now expected no only to inculcate knowledge but also to encourage thinking. S/He has to become more of an advisor, a partner to talk to. S/He has to help seek out conflicting arguments rather than hand out readymade truths. For this, s/he will have to devote more time and energy to productive and creative activities. Teachers have to aim for sunrise and ignore sunset policies for betterment of students.

The Researcher

Teaching and Research are found to be inseparable and mutually supportive to each other. Research makes learners achievement oriented. Every Professor is to act like a scientist, in search of new knowledge Education and research both are required to provide quality education. Innovation in Indian education is conspicuously absent, students do not get perspectives. The cure to all these problems is research orientation to education. For this purpose, teacher should use Institutional structure. But the system required that teacher should do research in extra time not substituting the teaching Schedule.

Conclusions

To play this role effectively, the teacher faces a greater challenge today than at any time in history. As an interpreter, the teacher has to place new knowledge and new experience within the context of what is already known and understood by the students. In order to be a good mediator, he has to understand a great deal about the way in which people at various ages and stages of development perceived the world around them. As a guide, s/he has to teach the students 'how to learn' rather than stuff his mind with factual information.

Teachers are being challenged to utilize new approaches and methods in an effort to improve learning outcomes. They have to seek improved ways of teaching by developing new programmes and instructional strategies such as enquire approaches, simulation games, computer-assisted instructions and programmed learning materials. The educators at the levels should endeavor to emphasize the need for discipline, character building and inculcate among the young minds the feeling of national integration.

BIBLIOGRAPHY

1. Dewery, J. (1952). The` Child and Curriculum, University Chicago Press, Chicago.
2. Waller, William (1950). The Sociology of Teaching, John Wiley, New York.
3. Ryans, David G. (1965) Characteristics of Teachers, The American Council of Education, Washington.
4. Bhaskara Rao, Digumati, (Ed.) (2004). Teacher's in a Changing World, Discovery Publishing House, New Delhi.
5. Biggie Moasis, L. (1968), Learning Theory of Teachers; Universal Book Stall, Delhi.
6. Simpson, E.J. (1966). The Classification of Educational Objectives, Prentice Hall, New York.

20

Sustainable Development in Perspective of Environment Education in India

Dr. Madhuri, S. Rishi*

Abstract

This paper discusses the nexus of sustainable development concept in perspective of the environment education scenario in current times. All the conventional energy resources like coal, petroleum, wood on which we depend are non-replenish able and our sustainability quotient drives us to develop alternatives. As humankind is dependent on mother earth for its survival and meeting their livelihood needs a balanced approach is required. This approach is rightly answered through the process of sustainable development which means meeting the needs of everyone and discarding the greed of few. Thus sustainable development is a broad umbrella term which is panacea for all the ills evolved through human brazenness and unmindful development. Eventually incorporation of this concept in environment education sector along with primary and middle will give boost towards research, innovation, technology development for a better tomorrow. Though the policy makers have included this concept while formulating various policies on environment education sector yet its proper implementation is the need of hour.

Keywords: *Sustainable development, Environment education, Research, Innovation, Technology*

Introduction

Sustainable development is development that meets the needs of the present without compromising the ability of the future generations to meet their own needs. In precise terms it clearly means that we have

* Director, Academic Staff College and Professor, University Business School, Panjab University, Chandigarh

to live our lives using the resources like water, coal, oil, fossil fuel in such a way that our children and grandchildren and all the generations coming after them will also have the same chance of living a sustainable life like us. This term has gained popularity in recent times due to surging population and rapid urbanization which is posing a grave threat for the sustenance of all living beings on this blue-planet called earth. The concept of sustainable development was envisaged to bring environmentalist ideas into the central theme of economic development policy. It sought to modify the kind of unsustainable development strategies that were being pursued. Sustainable development combines the two terms of 'sustainability' and 'development' to indicate a pattern of growth, which strengthens both the national capabilities to care for their people in relation to their total relationship with the resources of the earth.

Broad Objectives

- What do we understand by sustainable development?
- Why it should be linked with environment education?
- How this contribution can be made most effectively?

Sustainable development is generally considered to be that which is:

- viable,
- has an equitable impact on society, and
- an acceptable impact on the environment

It is imperative to consider the three components both individually and collectively to achieve an acceptable balance. Sustainability can be considered at a variety of scales – from project to nation or continent. Sustainability is often illustrated as three pillars or three interlocking circles which broadly encompasses social, environmental and economic coexistence in a harmonious manner. It is henceforth recognized that these three pillars are of equal importance and if any one aspect is ignored or given higher priority than others, the repercussions will unbalance and destabilise all three aspects because all three are interconnected and interdependent.

Sustainable development is essentially a value-system and not a scientific formula that can be intellectually or mechanically applied

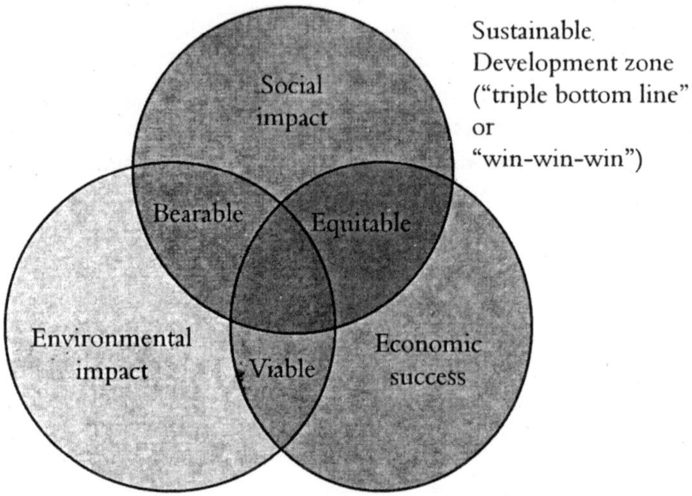

Diagram after Adams, W.M. (2006). "The Future of Sustainability: Re–thinking Environment and Development in the 21st Century". Report of the IUCN Renowned

to a situation. This concept is an evolutionary step forward in human consciousness, awareness and behaviour leading to a more holistic and balanced value system.

Methodology

A detailed literature review was done from secondary sources like research papers, environmental portals, various websites, government and non-government reports. Thus through assessment of a detailed overview of the concept of sustainable development was elucidated accordingly as per this review paper.

Background

The origins of the concept of sustainable development can be tracked back to the 1960s when, the writer and scientist Rachel Carson published her book The Silent Spring (1962). This book drew public attention to the destruction of wildlife by the use of pesticide DDT (dichloro diphenyl trichloroethane). This work was a turning point in the understanding of the interconnections among the environment, the economy and social well being. Gradually, in this period, the fear of global environmental limits began to emerge. Soon after, the animal population biologist Paul Ehrlich published the book Population Bomb (1968) on the connection between human population, resource exploitation, and the environment. In 1969, a non-profit organization, Friends of the Earth was formed which was dedicated to protecting the environment from degradation and empowering citizens to have a voice in decision-making. The governments of the Northern countries began to recognise that the process of industrial development was damaging the environment. In 1971, the OECD council enacted a Polluter Pays principle where it said that those (countries) causing pollution should pay the costs. The report, Limits to Growth (1972), published by a group of young scientists (Club of Rome) from Massachusetts Institute of Technology (MIT), immediately took the world by storm gaining enormous media coverage. It predicted dire consequences if growth was not slowed down.

The United Nations Conference on Human Environment (UNCHE) was organized in Stockholm (1972). For the first time, the idea that the environment was a critical development issue was placed on the international agenda. It led to the establishment of United Nations Environment Programme (UNEP). The first director of UNEP, Maurice Strong coined the term 'eco development' which integrated development with environment protection. Since then, many milestones have marked the journey towards sustainable development. The concept of 'Sustainable Society' emerged at a study conference on Science and Technology for Human Development, convened by the World Council of Churches (1974). Interestingly, the concept did not deal with environmental conditions but started with the principle of equitable distribution, which subsequently became the cornerstone of the Brundtland Report in 1987. 'Sustainable Society' also involved the concept of democratic participation, which became important nearly twenty years later at the Rio Earth Summit (1992). 172 governments participated, with 108 sending their heads of state or government. Some 2,400 representatives of non-governmental organizations (NGOs) attended, with 17,000 people at the parallel NGO Forum, who had so-called Consultative Status.

The Earth Summit resulted in the following documents:

- Rio Declaration on Environment and Development
- Agenda 21
- Convention on Biological Diversity
- Forest Principles
- Framework Convention on Climate Change

It is pertinent to note that both Convention on Biological Diversity and Framework Convention on Climate Change were set as legally binding agreements whereas the other three had no legal binding.

The Rio Declaration on Environment and Development supports Agenda 21 by defining the rights and responsibilities of States regarding these issues. Among its principles:

- That human beings are at the centre of concerns for sustainable development. They are entitled to a healthy and productive life in harmony with nature;
- That scientific uncertainty should not delay measures to prevent environmental degradation where there are threats of serious or irreversible damage;
- That States have a sovereign right to exploit their own resources but not to cause damage to the environment of other States.
- That the full participation of women is essential for achieving sustainable development.
- That the developed countries acknowledge the responsibility that they bear in the international pursuit of sustainable development in view of the pressures their societies place on the global environment and of the technologies and financial resources they command.
- That eradicating poverty and reducing disparities in worldwide standards of living are "indispensable" for sustainable development;

Education for Sustainable Development

United Nations General Assembly proclaimed the UN Decade of Education for Sustainable Development, 2005-2014 (DESD) based on the proposals by Japan and Sweden at its 58th Session in December 2002 emphasizing that education is an indispensable element for achieving sustainable development. The vision of Education for Sustainable Development (ESD) is a world where everyone has the opportunity to benefit from quality education and learn the values, behaviour and lifestyles required for a sustainable future and for positive societal transformation. ESD equally addresses all three pillars of sustainable development – society, environment and economy with culture as an essential additional and underlying dimension. By embracing these elements in a holistic and integrated manner, ESD enables all individuals to fully develop the knowledge, perspectives, values and skills necessary to take part in decisions to improve the quality necessary to take part in decisions to improve the quality of life both locally and globally on terms which are most relevant to their daily lives. ESD focuses on the underlying principles and values conveyed through education and the content and purpose of education. Chapter 36 of Agenda 21 specifically discusses re-orienting education towards sustainable development and encompasses all streams of education both formal and non-formal, basic education and all the key issues related to educating for sustainable human development.

Education for Sustainable Development In Indian Education System

India has integrated sustainable development into its planning process and has several programmes directed towards this goal. In order to achieve the goals of sustainable development, one of the first steps taken was in the direction of environment conservation and protection by promoting environment education. This strategy was adopted post Stockholm conference by setting up Centres of Excellence for Environment Education under Ministry of Environment in the early 1980s. Later Government of India recommended Ministry of Human Resource Development to integrate environmental concerns into all aspects and levels of education.

Thus Indian vision for ESD is deeply rooted in preserving our age-old traditional knowledge which is rich in sustainability aspect and eco-friendly in true sense. However challenges are still present which needs to be overcome through creating awareness and ensuring people's participation on a large scale. Also required is cooperation and continuous engagement with the international world thus underlying the basic principle of shared consequences with differential responsibility.

ATTITUDES TO CURRICULUM AND PEDAGOGY

- Long before the United Nations launched the Decade of Education for Sustainable Development in 2005, the Indian Supreme Court in 1999 directed that environment education must permeate all levels of education.
- Despite initial delays, most universities had introduced an undergraduate environmental studies course from the 2004 academic year.
- According to Kiran B Chhokar, founding editor of the International, peer-reviewed 'Journal of Education for Sustainable Development', " this was a significant step towards making environmental education and education for sustainable development a reality in undergraduate institutions, which account for 85% of students enrolled in higher education in India."
- Not many countries have made it compulsory to have a course on the environment as part of the curriculum. The supreme court ruling has immense potential to reach out to thousands of students "if it is correctly implemented,"
- However, the potential may be lost due to the limited understanding of the concept of sustainable development among teachers and also because education for sustainable development lacks a holistic approach in higher education.
- The court order is about including the environment as a subject, but what do people understand by environment? Most think it is about pollution, greening, dams etc. But the developmental aspects of environment are not considered and it is thought that it is only a compulsory subject that does not carry any weightage towards the final grades.
- Today education for sustainable development includes a focus on green economy, education for peace, conflict as a result of

competing demands for resources and many other areas. But universities have subject experts in pollution, de-forestation, wildlife etc. Some of them are good at making linkages with social issues. But a majority just confines their lectures to the subject area.

Conclusions

Education for sustainable development has been taken up independently by a handful of higher education institutions in India in the absence of any focused advocacy or associations and it is felt that not enough attention is being given to education on sustainable development even on international platforms. There is the official process that is happening. But most people involved in education for sustainable development have been feeling that there is not much focus being given to education. The solutions to India's development needs will not come from Rio but from strong leadership within the country. Education for sustainable development has the potential to bring this change and our universities can play a significant role.

Bibliography

1. Anonymous (2010) Sustainable Development, Chronicle Publishers, India.
2. Brundtland Commission Report (1987) World Commission on Environment and Development, Our Common Future, Oxford University Press, Oxford.
3. Dernback, J.C. (2002) Stumbling toward sustainability. Environmental Law Institute. p. 608
4. Dresner, S. (2002) The Principles of Sustainability, Earthscan, London.
5. Hirsch, F. (1976) The Social Limits to Grow, Routledge, London.
6. Huckle, J. and Sterling, S.R. (2006) Education for sustainability. Earthscan. p. 139.
7. Jones, P., Selby, D., Sterling, S. (2010) Sustainability Education: Perspectives and Practice Across Higher Education. Renouf Publishing.

8. Lang, J. (2007) How to Succeed with Education for Sustainability. Curriculum Corporation.
9. Li, Z., and Williams, M. (2006) Environmental and Geographical Education for Sustainability: cultural contexts. Nova Publishers.
10. Sims, G. D. (2007) Sustainability Education: where does it belong? Minnesota State University.
11. Tilbury, D. and Wortman, D. (2004). Engaging People in Sustainability. IUCN, Gland, Switzerland.

21

Issues, Challenges and Reforms in Higher Education for A Knowledge Society

Dr Maninder Kaur*

Abstract

Knowledge is the sum total of education, experience, research, intelligence and information. It is basically harnessed in academic institutions. They impart in depth knowledge in different walks of life. Presently there are 654 Universities and degree awarding institutions in the country. There are 1522 degree granting engineering colleges in India (2011) with an annual student intake of 5,82,000 and 1244 polytechnics with an annual intake of 265000. The country has been facing a number of challenges and there are various issues that stand before the system of Higher education. The role of higher education institutions in this emerging scenario of knowledge economy is very crucial and multifaceted. The major challenge before the Indian higher education is now to create new strategies, policies and programmes of revolutionary nature that would align the two pulls in the same direction. A knowledge society has two very important components societal transformation and wealth generation. To overcome the present the upcoming challenges some initiative has been taken by central Government and regulating bodies like UGC, AICTE, NCTE. Hence, it is high time for planners, policy makers and practitioners of higher education to ponder over it and make necessary reforms in the course and strategies so that employability skills can be development among the students.

Keywords: *Knowledge Society; New strategies; policies.*

* Assistant Professor, Guru Nanak Khalsa College for Women, Ludhiana

INTRODUCTION

Well defined objective oriented consistent effort to produce knowledge empowered manpower is the need of the society. Knowledge is the sum total of education, experience, research, intelligence and information. It is basically harnessed in academic institutions. They impart in depth knowledge in different walks of life. In the present day knowledge society where the world is highly competitive, it is only the higher education that provides qualified and trained human resources to keep pace with the fast changing world. The higher education system of India has witnesses many fold increase in its institutional capacity since independence. After the independence, Government initiated a plan for the development of higher education in the country as a result of which University Grants Commission came into existence in 1953. During this period, institutions like IITs and IIMs were established and contributed quality higher education to the Indian talents. Drawing on Nehru's vision and articulating most of his key themes, the Kothari Commission (1964-66) was setup to formulate a coherent education policy for India. After around two decades of National Policy on Education (1968), in 1986, Rajiv Gandhi announced a New Education Policy, the National Policy on Education (NPE), which was intended to prepare India for the 21st century. The policy emphasied need for change. The 1986 Policy was reviewed by a Committee Constituted in 1990 under the chairmanship of Acharya Ramamurti. On the basis of the recommendations of this Committee certain provisions of 1986 Policy were modified in 1992.

The objectives of the study are:

1. To study the challenges in Education in knowledge society.
2. To study about the reforms needed in Higher Education.

STATUS OF EDUCATION IN COUNTRY

Presently there are 654 Universities and degree awarding institutions in the country. The number of 30 universities and 695 colleges (23 per University) in 1950 has gone up by 30 folds to 634 universities and whereas college by 50 folds to 33,023 (55 per university) in 2011-12, thus putting huge pressure on the university administration in managing them. There are 1522 degree granting engineering colleges in India (2011) with an annual student intake of 5, 82,000 and 1244 polytechnics with an annual intake of 265000.

Higher Education: Issues and Challenges

In our national development process higher education system has a very important role to play. After independence, we wanted to build a modern, strong dynamic and self-reliant India which could stand abreast with the developed nations. While working towards this end, the country has been facing a number of challenges and there are various issues that stand before the system of Higher education. Some broad issues are like knowledge economy, complexities of India Federalism (central-states relations), political and legal inertia, politicisation of policy communication and implementation funding, privatisation, quality assurance, organisational cultures. internationalisation of higher education.

The role of higher education institutions in this emerging scenario of knowledge economy is very crucial and multifaceted. The agenda of higher education institutions (universities) in this scenario may include opening new vistas of learning, new frontiers of researching, academic restructuring, sharing of expertise, innovation, technology transfer, knowledge management, training, employability, entrepreneurship, media convergence and meeting social, cultural and economic challenges thrown by the forces of globalisation, Issues like access, equity, inclusion, quality and excellence are very complex and intertwined with political, economical, demographic and international dimensions.

Quality in higher education is another burning issue, which can be ensured through regular review of the function of the institutions either through self assessment or throughout side agencies and by accrediting the institutions. The expansion of higher education over the years has also resulted in educational malpractices which exist in the form of capitation fees being charged by private institutions at the time of admissions. Also there has been a spurt in activities of Foreign Educational Institutions operating in India since mid 1990s.

Major Concerns

- Over-centralization: Lack of institutional autonomy and accountability; very slow response to changes.

- Variable quality; market mismatch' inflexibility.
- Little knowledge creation-little interaction with economy, society and other academic/research institutions.
- Difficulties in recruitment and retention of qualified teachers in critical areas.
- Diminishing and skewed public funding; system inefficiencies.
- Limited access and regional disparity.

The major challenge before the Indian higher education is now to create new strategies, policies and programmes of revolutionary nature that would align the two pulls in the same direction.

The 21st century has been widely acclaimed as 'knowledge century era'. Every nation is finding itself to be performing in an increasingly competitive and globalised international environment where the information infrastructure, research and innovation systems, education and lifelong learning, and regulatory frameworks have become critical parameters. The beginning of our Journey in the 21st century has made us realize the development taking place and likely to take place would require a knowledge society that will bring a balance between scientific, economic and knowledge development with equity, liberty, freedom of the individual sustainability while ensuring the values, ethics and the great cultural heritage of the country. The explosion in knowledge has impacted society and economy to such an extent that many have begun to measure themselves in terms of knowledge. Dr. A.P.J. Abdul Kalam rightly stated that "21st Century belongs to the knowledge age, where acquisition, possession and application of knowledge are the most important resources. Knowledge has been the prime mover of prosperity and power; it empowers and enriches people, causes societal transformation, encourages discoveries and innovations, causes goodness in all spheres of the society resulting peace and prosperity."

A knowledge society has two very important components societal transformation and wealth generation. The societal transformation has to be through large scale development in education, healthcare, agriculture and governance. These in turn will lead to employment generation, high productivity and prosperity. Creation of new knowledge primarily depends on the education system, promoting research, innovation in laboratories and trapping of foreign sources of knowledge through open access. It is envisaged that knowledge and wisdom shall shortly become the drivers of tomorrow's economy. The role of universities in this scenario is multifaceted. Declining in the standard of higher education is due to :

- The inability of the system to meet the growing demand
- Considerable evidence of poor teaching
- Ineffective quality control
- 'Reutilization' of Distance Education
- Poor graduate outcome ('unemployability' of most graduated from college)
- Declining Research performance and productivity

Low Status of Indian Universities in International Ranking Systems

Widespread corruption in appointments of faculty and selection of students:

Poor governance (cumbersome bureaucratic impediments to reform);

Further there are certain threats in the system of higher education, which are mentioned below:

- Skill shortage and high graduate unemployment;
- Regulatory system fails to maintain standards despite formidable entry barriers;
- Chaotic and unplanned expansion;
- Poor standards of academic research.

Strategies for Reforms

Here are few strategies for restructuring and reforming the higher education:

Empowerment and Accountability of Institutions

- Academic
- Administrative
- Financial

- Managerial

Optimal Utilization of Resources

- Build on and share existing resources
- Improve system efficiency
- Encourage competitive funding
- Mobilization of Additional Financial Resources
- Enhance cost recovery
- Provide incentives for resource generation
- Encourage private funding

Improving Quality and Effectiveness

- Quality and effectiveness of teaching learning processes
- Faculty development
- Curriculum reforms
- Performance evaluation and accreditation of institutions

Networking to Enhance Capacity, Improve Quality and Produce Excellence

- Networking of institutions with each other with R&D labs, industry and service sector
- Promotion of excellence
- Resource sharing of expertise, facilities
- Networking of libraries

Increasing Access and Reducing Regional Imbalances Developing Employability and Employability Skill

To overcome the present the upcoming challenges some initiative has been taken by central Government and regulating bodies like UGC, AICTE, NCTE. UGC five cardinal principles for XI plan trie to focus J.P. Naik's Trangle of Q3 ie, quality-quantity-equity. The Yashpal Committee and also the National Knowledge Commission (NKC) have dealt with various issues affecting the higher education system in the country and both have suggested definite frame work for improvement by way of institutional and policy reforms.

Once these reforms are formulated and accepted it will be a paradigm shift for most of the traditional universities in terms of its functioning and activities-its teaching and research, its service to the society, its financing mechanisms. Thus a concerted effort is needed on the part of higher learning institution to make a transition from the traditions of the past to the challenges of the present, and ensure the entry into the future success will lie only with such institutions. These institutions will be necessitated to adopt the modern terms of:

- Making teaching programmes more relevant.
- Programmes to meet the societal needs relevant to present day society.
- Constant updating of its programme and courses.
- Encouraging student mobility and programme diversity.
- Accepting horizonal mobility programme.
- Accepting credit transfer system.
- Developing strategic partnership within universitites and with the industry.
- Establishing networks and alliances with private funding institutions.
- Floating foundation to meet the demands of higher education in terms of research needs and infrastructural development.
- Valuing the talent and quality requirements.
- Keeping motivation high on agenda.

The higher education system of the 21st century should accept the challenges of change and motivate their faculty and the society to do the same. The institutions of higher learning preparing to enter the new era will have to accept the fact that the systems of today are demanding, competitive and accountable.

Hence, it is high time for planners, policy makers and practitioners of higher education to ponder over it and make necessary reforms in the course and strategies so that employability skills can be development among the students. In this regard, following guidelines may be suggested:

- The programme of higher education should be restructured giving more importance the task relating to employability skills.
- Continuous and comprehensive evaluation should be introduced so that all the basic, higher-order and affective employability skills get due place in both internal and external examination.

- There should be collaboration between higher education institutions and the employers both public and private so that students get opportunities for active interaction.

CONCLUSIONS

Now it is the time to bring a qualitative change in the scenario of higher education in India. India has a demographic advantage in the form of a huge number of young people. To make the best, these young minds need to be provided opportunities for accessing quality higher education. Only quality human resource will ensure emergence of a true knowledge society which will ultimately enhance the country's competitiveness in the global economy.

BIBLIOGRAPHY

1. Chauhan, C.P.S., (2002). Higher Education in India: Challenges of Global Trends, Aligarh Muslim University, Aligarh. University News, 40 (17), April 29-May 5.
2. Communication, 2008, New Challenges before Indian Higher Education, University News, 46 (15) April 14-20.
3. Dhar, B.B. (2001). Higher Education Scenario in the 21st Century: Accepting Challenges to Change, University News. 39 (35), August 27- September 2.
4. Goel,C, and Goel (2002) R.P. Rationalisation of Higher Education, The M.S. University of Baroda, Vadodara.
5. Kasinath, H.M., and Patted, G.M. 1995, Pre-Induction Training Course to Improve Teaching in Higher Education Karaatak University, Dharwad. University New, Monday, January 9.
6. Patil, L.A., 2002, Higher Education: Challenges, Excellence and Future, Partap College, Amalner. University News, 40(27), July 8-14.
7. Shamshad, H. (2000). Challenges Before Higher Education, University News, 38 (38), September 18.

22

Sustainable Development of Higher Education through Open and Distance Learning

Dr. Manmeet Kaur*

Abstract

UNESCO defines education for sustainable development as the device to allow every human being to acquire the knowledge, skill, attitudes and values necessary to shape a sustainable future. The Education for All (EFA) movement is a global commitment to provide quality basic education for all children, youth and adults. At the World Education Forum 164 governments pledged to achieve EFA. India has registered a mammoth growth in the number of higher education institutions. Therefore, for expansion of higher education in the country, there is an emerging need to bank upon an alternative system in order to reach the target of 20% GER by end of the XII Plan and 30% by 2020. At present India has with 677 universities, near about 35,539 colleges, more than 9.34 lakhs teachers, 218 lakhs student enrollments. Keeping in view the increasing demand of higher education and depleting funding for the same, it is essential that there is an emergent need to strengthen the non formal system of education. Appropriate use of open and Distance learning allows, to increase access, improve quality and cut cost - all at the same time. For these set of emerging realities, open and distance learning is a perfect fit.

***Keywords:** Sustainable development; Education for all.*

Introduction

UNESCO defines education for sustainable development as the device to allow every human being to acquire the knowledge, skill, attitudes

* Assistant Professor, Guru Nanak Khalsa College for Women, Ludhiana

and values necessary to shape a sustainable future.

Therefore, the needs and demands of today's social milieu is varied and ever changing \which warrants an educational system in a non formal way and in a learner centric environment contrast to a conventional pattern of class room teaching learning system. This has happened as the clientele of education today is not confined to a particular age group.

The Education for All (EFA) movement is a global commitment to provide quality basic education for all children, youth and adults. At the World Education Forum (Dakar, 2000), 164 governments pledged to achieve EFA.

Governments, development agencies, civil society and the private sector are working together to reach the EFA goals. Investment in education is yielding results. In India, the higher education system is more broad based today. The landscape of Indian Higher Education is changing in an unprecedented manner over the past few years bringing explosion in knowledge. After the success of the green and the white revolution in the country, India's knowledge prowess has come to be recognized and accepted throughout the world as knowledge revolution.

Objectives of Open Distance Learning (ODL)

(a) To educate the clientele in a non-formal way and in a learner centric environment.

(b) To bridge the gap between unsatisfied demand for education versus actual supply of educational services.

(c) To provide quality basic education for all under the global Commitment of Education for All (EFA) movement.

Growth of the Institutions

India has registered a mammoth growth in the number of higher education institutions.

At present India has with 677 universities, near about 35,539 colleges, more than 9.34 lakhs teachers, 218 lakhs student enrollments. The target of reaching 15% Gross Enrollment Ratio by 2012 set for the XI Plan has almost been achieved.

However, this growth of higher education is still unable to cater to the increasing number of aspirants to higher education. Notwithstanding an impressive growth of higher education institutions, India's Gross Enrolment Ratio (GER) in relative terms compares quite poorly with 60% in USA and Canada, over 40% in several European countries and more than 20% in many developed and developing countries. International experience shows that no country has been able to become an economically advanced country, if its enrolment ratio in higher education has been less than 20%.

Therefore, for expansion of higher education in the country, there is an emerging need to bank upon an alternative system in order to reach the target of 20% GER by end of the XII Plan and 30% by 2020. This necessitates the strengthening the Open and Distance Education (ODE) which currently is contributing 25% to the GER in Higher Education.

Development Through ODL

The non formal system has made its position felt as it is increasingly being preferred by a varied group of clientele that includes housewives, retirees, police personnels, defence personnels, prisoners, disadvantaged groups etc. With the massive growth of the ICT sector, Distance learning has opened up new vistas for learners, providing them a flexible and cost-effective education system.

The distance education system unlike the conventional education system has an edge as it may reach to the needy, disadvantaged and to those sections of the working group desires to acquiring higher qualifications for the pursuit of knowledge.

Institutional Growth in Distance Education:

Year	Open Universities	Distance Education	Total Distance Teaching Instructions
1962	-	1	1
1970-71	-	17	17
1975-76	-	22	22

Year	Open Universities	Distance Education	Total Distance Teaching Instructions
1980-81	-	33	34
1985-86	2	38	40
1990-91	5	46	51
1995-96	7	50	57
2000-01	9	70	79
2005-06	13	104	117
2009-10	14	186	200
2010-11	14	250	264

Growth of Enrolment in Open Universities (OU) and DEIs

S. No.	Year	SOUs	DEIs	Total
1	1962-63	-	1,112	1,112
2	1980-81	-	1,66,428	1,66,428
3	1990-91	1,02,820	4,89,994	5,92,814
4	2000-01	5,22,506	8,55,494	13,78,000
5	2009-10	16,29,732	20,07,012	36,36,744

However student enrolment was not that encouragement between 1962 and 1975 in the ODL system. Between 1975-76 and 1980-81, enrolment in the formal university system indicating an increase of 2.65 percent per annum during the five year period, whereas enrolment in distance education indicating an increase of 31.8 per cent per annum during the same period. The high percentage of growth in ODL system in this period is attributable to low cost plus convenience and flexibility involved in ODL system.

Diversification of Open and Distance Learning (ODL) Programmes

There has been consistent diversification of programmes in the ODL system over the period of five decades starting from 1962, when the first Distance Education Institution (DEI) attached to Delhi University launched the BA programme to start with. During 1970-80, apart from liberal Arts programmes, B. Com, M Com and professional courses like B Ed and M Ed were launched by several DEIs. This was the time when many institutions were accorded approval for PG courses in Law. During the next decade 1980-1990, with the Open Universities coming into existence, professional certificates programmes were offered besides general programmes. It was also the time when M Phil and PhD programmes were also launched by some of the Open Universities. The first MBA programme was launched by Punjabi University, Patiala, in 1985. During this period, IGNOU launched Diploma in Management and Diploma in Distance Education programmes in 1987.

Besides the traditional courses, a number of non-conventional courses were introduced such as certificate and diploma programmes in the teaching of English, Banking, Labour Laws, Cooperation and Rural studies, Distance Education, Financial Management, International Marketing, Journalism, Library Sciences, Management of Public Enterprises, Operational Research, Land Management, Public Accounting Tourism and Hotel Management, Company Law etc. IGNOU being the role model of the ODL system in the country has been breaking new grounds in programmes offering.

Enrollment in Open Universities

SN	Name of the University	Total enrolment for the Year July'II
1.	Dr. B.R. Ambedkar Open University, Hyderabad	1,80,516
2.	Krishanakant Handique State Open University, Guwahati	36,911
3.	Nalanda Open University, Patna	41,000 (approx.)
4.	Pt. Sunderlal Sharma Open University, Bilaspur	12,995
5.	Dr. Babasaheb Ambedkar Open University, Ahmedabad	43,628
6.	Karnatka State Open University, Mysore	1,13,220
7.	M.P. Bhoj Open University, Bhopal	93,178 (for the year 2009-10)

SN	Name of the University	Total enrolment for the Year July'II
8.	Yashwantrao Chavan Maharashtra Open University, Nasik	4,25,908
9.	Varddhaman Mahaveer Open University, Kota	56,622 (for academic year 2010-11)
10.	Tamil Nadu Open University, Chennai	57,150 (for the year 2009-10)
11.	U.P. Rajarshi Tandon Open University, Allahabad	24,780
12.	Uttarakhand Open University, Kolkata	7,393 (for the year 2010-11)
13.	Netaji Subhas Open University, Kolkata	40,214(for the year 2009-10)
14.	Indira Gandhi National Open University, New Delhi	30,16,770 (Student on Rolls)*

Need Based Progrmmes of Open Universities

The Open Universities have been quite responsive to market forces in designing their programmes. These universities have an added advantage contrast to the DEIs of conventional Universities. They being autonomous are free to innovate. The OUs have designed courses which are skill oriented and need based. Courses are offered by the OUs at certificate, Diploma, PG Diploma, UG, PG and Research level in various general as well as professional courses. To mention a few, these programmes are of varied nature including programmes designed for different groups of clientele such as programmes of Literacy and Community Development, Herbal Products and Herbal Home Remedies, Programmes in Motor Insurance. Fire Insurance, Medical Insurance Life Insurance, Tailoring, Mobile Repairing, Motor Rewinding Certificate in Beauty Parlour Management, Interior Designing and Decoration, Electrician & Cyber Security, Agro Journalism, Preparatory for Army personnel, Mother and Child care etc.

Potential of the Distance Education Units of the Conventional Universities (Dual Mode Universities)

Apart from the open universities, the distance education units of the conventional system are also contributing in the big way. The DEIs of premier universities like Panjab University (Chandigarh), Utkal University (Orissa), Delhi University, Delhi, Jamia Millia Islamia (New Delhi), Allahabad University (Allahabad) are some of the potential DEIs offering programmes and having a sound enrolment in these programmes. Some of the DEIs under Central, State and also Deemed Universities are registering large student enrollment in programmes at various level.

Unexplored Opportunities Through ICT

It is generally found that some of the DEIs of premier universities are still continuing in the old correspondence style and are yet to include technology in their teaching learning methodology. It is despite the fact that under the UGC-INFONET connectivity programmes during the XIth Plan, more than 180 universities have been benefitted and also with the launch of National Knowledge Network (NKN) and National Mission on Education through ICT (NME-ICT) that provides I GBPS connectivity to all universities, almost all universities have migrated to NKN/NME-ICT connectivity programme and are availing higher network bandwidth. The universities having the distance education divisions should take full advantage of such schemes for increasing enrolment and improving the teaching learning methodology in the distance education programmes besides providing effective student support services. Development Grants to IOUs and DEIs

All the Open Universities and some of the DEIs which receive development grants from Distance Education Council (DEC) have better opportunities to explore the areas of innovation and thereby contributing to the development in distance education. The DEC provides development grants to the Academic Staff, development of learner support system, staff training and development, adoption of ICT etc.

Conclusions

Keeping in view the increasing demand of higher education and depleting funding for the same, it is essential that there is an emergent need to strengthen the non formal system of education. Appropriate use of open and Distance learning allows, to increase access, improve quality and cut cost - all at the same time.

To improve the quality of distance education in the country and also increase its accessibility in a well-organized and structured way, intensive research in various components of distance education is required.

Student Support Services are to be strengthened. The vocational and skilled based programmes should be provided with adequate facilities for practical training and orientation.

Learning systems will have to adjust to the pace of the learner. Learning is locating itself off campus, to the home, the workplace and the field. For these set of emerging realities, open and distance learning is a perfect fit.

Bibliography

1. Aderinoye, Rashid and Ojokheta, Kestar (2004) Open-Distance Education as a Mechanism for Sustainable Development: Reflections on the Nigerian Experience, University of Ibadan, Nigeria IRR ODL
2. Daniel, John (2005) After-dinner remarks at Vancouver, Open and Distance Learning for Development - The Role of ODL in delivering MDGs
3. Education For All Goals http://www.unesco.org/new/en/education/ themes/leading-the-international-agenda/education-for-all/efa-goals/
4. Panda, Santosh (1999) Development, Networking and Convergence in India, Higher Education Through Open and Distance Learning (ed) by Keith Harry, London and New York, Common Wealth of Learning
5. Report of the Madhav Menon Committee (2010) to suggest Measures to Regulate the Standards of Education being

Imparted through Distance Mode, Ministry of Human Resource Development, Govt of India

6. Srivastava, Manjulika, (2012) Open Universities-India's Answer to Challenges in Higher Education, New Delhi, Vikas Publishing House.

7. Table: complies from various source (DEC rdatabase & Srivastav, 2012 *Report of VC on 26th Convocation of IGNOU, 12th April, 2013

23

Special Education Zones A reform for Higher Education in India

*Dr. Minakshi**

Abstract

"India needs to build excellence in the educational system, especially in the sphere of higher education, to meet the knowledge challenges of the 21st century and increase India's competitive advantage in fields of knowledge"

—National Knowledge Commission Report

Keywords: *Knowledge commission; educational system.*

Introduction

India has come a long way from being a labor-led economy and is on the verge of transforming itself to a major knowledge economy. Availability of skilled manpower is a critical success factor for driving the services sector which in turn fuels the development of a knowledge economy. If India wants to become a Knowledge Superpower in the 21st century, then this can only be achieved if a large portion of its working-age population consists of skilled manpower. In order to create a large pool of skilled manpower, a powerful higher education system is required. An deep insight is required to analyze the current status, problems and solutions pertaining to the state of higher education.

The main purpose is to figure out the major roadblocks India is facing in expansion of higher education .Secondly, to find out the solutions which can help in attaining this much required objective of quality education . Lastly, to have an understanding that how special education zones can be a beneficial measure to boost higher education.

* Assistant Professor, MTSM College for Women, Ludhiana

Current status of Higher Education in India.

India is ranked 3rd globally, after only USA and China, in terms absolute number of students enrolled in higher education institutions. India current gross enrollment ratio (GER) from 18% and aims to increase its to 30% by 2020. During the 12th five year plan (2012-2017), it has been proposed to create an additional enrolment capacity of 10 million students, including one million in open and distance learning. The main emphasis while achieving this target should be on " quality", the need of the hour is inclusive growth and empowerment of a large section of the population.

Startling facts about this point is India's GER in higher education (18 %) if compared to Korea's (100%), US's (83%) and China's (30%) we are far behind. Undoubtedly large numbers of students are needed to be enrolled into the Higher Education System, but is constrained by various rigid academic challenges, some of which are discussed below.

1. Regulations

There are various regulations which govern the course introduction, curriculum to be followed and content to be taught. Introducing a new course within this regulatory system is a very difficult proposition. This also leads to curriculum for traditional sectors not being updated and no specific guidelines available for courses on emerging sectors resulting in significant reduction of the employability levels of students.

2. Dearth of talented faculty:

Teaching is not seen as an attractive option amongst students. Often cited reasons include unattractive remuneration ,lack of good research facilities etc .

3. Lack of adequate freedom in operational issues

Most of the operational aspects of an education institution including admission process, intake numbers, fee charged, the courses that can be taught are regulated by the government. This leaves the institutions with little operational flexibility.

4. Dependence for funds

Most institutions are highly dependent on revenue from tuition fees for managing their operational and developmental activities. This is in sharp contrast with educational institutions in other countries, which have much diversified revenue stream.

5. Unclear FDI norms:

There are 2 separate ways for FDI in education sector in India.

- ❖ Automatic Route: According to Press Note 2 (2000 Series), FDI up to 100 percent is allowed on Automatic Route, without any sectorial cap.
- ❖ FIPB Route: Press Note 2 (2000 Series) also mentions that the investor may choose to make an application directly to Foreign Investment Promotion Board (FIPB) without availing automatic route.

This leads to confusion amongst potential investors on the route to investment in education.

6. Multiple regulatory authorities with overlapping functions:

The Indian higher education sector has a complex regulatory environment with multiple regulatory bodies and their overlapping functions. At the highest level is UGC, which was started as a grants distributing body. There are other statutory bodies such as AICTE, Medical Council of India, Bar Council of India etc, which handle specific higher education streams. Apart from this, there are state level professional councils whose work often overlaps with that of their central counterparts. In order to address this issue, National Knowledge Commission had, in fact, recommended the setting up of an Independent Regulatory Authority for Higher Education (IRAHE) to single-handedly coordinate the system.

7. Students going abroad for studies:

With limited number of seats available in good quality institutions, students take recourse in foreign institutions. Most of the students leave India to pursue higher education, especially in the field of medicine, technology, research and management. Thus, India loses a substantial amount of foreign exchange due to cash outflows for studies abroad.

Need for a Comprehensive Solution:

Indian Higher Education System is confronted with severe challenges for which there is no one-point solution. The improvement in higher education can be brought through restructuring academic programmes to ensure their relevance to modern market demands; domestic and global linkages with employers and external advisory resource support groups.

Experience of countries which had overcome such challenges indicate that they have adopted a multi-pronged approach to revive their higher education sectors.

There are different ways with which the problem can be tackled viz

(i) unshackle the system and allow private partnership on a massive scale to energise the sector and bring the fruits of education to a mass of India's underserved learners at both ends of the market.

(ii) while the market for higher education is growing, the supply is constricted due to paucity of quality teachers. Academicians must be highly paid but in an environment of accountability. Complete revamping of teaching/learning methods by shifting from traditional repetitive experiments to open-ended design-oriented work for encouraging invention and research; compulsory interactive seminar-tutorials, broadening the content of Science and engineering programmes to strengthen fundamental concepts,

(iii) Allowing universities and institutions the freedom to scale up or down their remunerative models in accordance with their market strengths would streamline the current mismatch in the teaching profession and give a fillip to deserved, merit-based employment to teachers.

(iv) setting up of Special Education Zones as a cluster concept seeking to build a sustainable educational ecosystem.

The last initiative can be very fruitful provided proper implementation is there.

What are Special Education Zones (SEdZ)

Special Education Zones can be defined as "Specific geographic regions in the country where the rules and regulations relating to set up and operation of educational institutions are liberal than in other parts of the country." Special education zones will have collaboration with international universities to help create facilities for imparting world-class vocational education. It would have a cluster of reputed colleges affiliated to international universities imparting education in sunrise sectors like information technology, biotechnology and pharmacy.

With a steep fall in employment levels due to shortage of soft skills, the National Association of Software and Services Companies (Nasscom) has mooted the idea of special education zones to overcome the problem way back in 2006. The special zones will liberate education from bureaucratic forces and make it market-driven. They will go a long way in improving the employability of college-leaving youth, according to Nasscom president.

Even in 2009,National Knowledge Commission (NKC) chairman Sam G Pitroda has favored setting up of special education zones (SEZ) in the country to promote access to higher education and improving the quality of education. Interacting with stakeholders in higher education at the CII Education Summit via videoconferencing from Chicago, Pitroda said he had already spoken to union commerce minister Kamal Nath on the need to establish special education zones. "I think the special education zones can be set up on the lines of technology parks and special incentives can be granted to promote them. I would encourage you to set up one or two SEZs to explore how it works, it is worth doing it," he said.

There are a number of stakeholders who need to work in cohesion in order to improve the standards of Indian Higher Education System. SEdZ can bring together the stakeholders in order to form an educational ecosystem will create the required synergy.

Objectives of SEdZ

- To improve the quality of education being imparted through
- Increased autonomy in course design, development and delivery
- Increased autonomy in operational aspects of managing an institution
- Increased interaction between industry and academia
- To infuse private capital into the sector, both domestic and foreign,
- To enable education institutions to be sustainable
- To attract reputed global institutions to set base in India and reposition India as a Education Hub

There are several critical success factors that are required for a SEdZ to succeed. To implement these critical success factors, it is proposed that the Special Education Zone should have the following features:

❖ Single window SEdZ approval Mechanism:

It is proposed that SEdZ should have a single window clearance to expedite the approval procedure. This could help to alleviate the bureaucracy and time delay in getting the approval.

❖ Freedom in academic aspects:

It is proposed that institutions operating out of the SEdZ should be given greater autonomy in the courses offered, pedagogy followed and the content that is delivered and the duration of the courses. This involved relaxing the regulatory control on academic aspects of education so as to encourage innovation on the intellectual front, offering education that is market oriented.

❖ Greater operational autonomy:

Institutions located in the SEdZ should have greater autonomy in deciding the admission process in such a manner that meritocracy and equity prevails over economic power. Institutions would also have autonomy in fee aspects as long as the fee charged is justifiable. Reservation can be given to students from economically challenged classes.

❖ High quality research infrastructure:

Reputed industry players will be attracted to set their R&D and operations base in SEdZ provided they house high quality research and support infrastructure.

Features of the Proposed SEdZ:

❖ Fiscal Incentives:

In order to facilitate the financial viability of educational institutions, the government could look to providing tax/ fiscal incentives similar to what is available for units operating out of Special Economic Zones.

❖ Invitation to reputed Foreign Institutions:

Reputed international universities like the Harvard, MIT, Yale etc., could be given an open invitation to invest in Indian education sector by setting up branch campuses in these SEdZ.

- Special tax allowance for foreign faculty/researchers:

Government could consider offering special tax allowance for faculty/ researchers from leading global universities. This move would encourage active participation of global faculty in the Indian academic system.

- Clear guidelines on FDI in Education:

Clear guidelines should be made available for investments in education in terms of modes of entry, operation and repatriation of funds.

- Infrastructural benefits :

The state governments and the local bodies should focus on providing basic infrastructural facilities (water, power etc) required for the entities located in the SEdZ. Similar to Special Economic Zones, SEdZ can also have sector specific focus. This could lead to the emergence of two variants.

- Inter-disciplinary SEdZ:

These SEdZ would not have any specific industry focus and would offer courses across most streams like general engineering, general arts and science etc.

- Industry-specific SEdZ:

These SEdZ would have strong industry focus and hence would co-exist with an industry-specific Special Economic Zone. Ideally, these SEdZ would operate as part of a SEZ in their non-processing zone.

E.g.: A Biotechnology SEdZ located in a Pharmaceutical SEZ or an IT SEdZ in an IT/ITES SEZ

- benefits to stakeholders:

Establishment of SEdZ is expected to lead to overall improvement in the system. Some of the specific benefits that could accrue to the stakeholders include the following:

- Benefits to Economy
    a) Improved overall higher education standards through increased interaction between industry and academia
    b) Increased enrolment levels in higher education institutions in India

c) Improved the R&D capability in India through greater collaboration opportunities between Indian institutions, foreign institutions and the industry

d) Increased capital inflow into education sector and reduction in the outflow of foreign exchange through brain-drain

e) Indian education system made more equitable by providing reservation and scholarships to students from weaker economic backgrounds

f) Reposition India as the "Global Education Hub"

❖ Benefits to Students:

a) Opportunity for Indian students to access global standards of education in India

b) Increased choice of institutions, both Indian and foreign, and increased choice of courses

c) Develops diverse student base leading to better understanding and appreciation of intercultural aspects

❖ Benefits to Indian Educational Institutions:

a) Easy clearance procedures for setting up educational institutions

b) Increased academic and operational autonomy

c) Increased options to source faculty – from industry and foreign institutions

d) Better sustainability through diversified revenue sources and increased access to funds.

❖ Benefits for the Industry:

a) Sustained availability of manpower

b) Access to talented faculty and quality infrastructure for joint R&D

c) Tax incentives for collaborative research with academic institutions.

❖ Benefits for the Society:

a) Cluster dynamics driving institutions to improve their standards

b) Global education at Indian doorsteps

c) Employment generation.

Challenges in Implementing SEdZ:

While there are significant challenges for establishing a SEdZ, benefits far outweigh the negatives. In fact, SEdZ as a concept has already taken root in India. Though Special Education Zones as a concept is relatively new in India, there have been many instances in the recent past where many state governments have taken steps to set up specific areas demarcated for education institutions. The following are some of the attempts by various state governments to set up education zones.

- Jawaharlal Nehru Education City, Chandigarh
- Rajiv Gandhi Education City, Haryana
- Andhra Pradesh Special Education Zones
- Madhya Pradesh Special Education Zones
- Himachal Pradesh Special Education Zones
- The Pondicherry Special Education Zones

Here the one such zone is studied "Rajiv Gandhi Education City, Haryana":

The Rajiv Gandhi Education City (RGEC) is an ambitious project of Haryana Government to develop a hub of higher education institutes in the state. It is being set up in the Sonepat district of the state and more than 2000 acres of land has been allotted for it.

Educational Societies and Trusts having track record of over ten years and Institutes of higher education run by business houses having annual turnover of Rs 5000 crore provided they are run on no-profit-no loss basis. Site for institutes of international repute, and private reputed institutions & universities would be allotted on lease hold basis. The site for other educational institutions would be allotted on free hold basis.

On 10th June 2012 Haryana Chief Minister Shri Bhupinder Singh Hooda laid the foundation for this much-awaited, ambitious projet. The campus will house some of the country's best educational institutions and Universities.

These institutes include Pune's Bharti Vidyapeeth University, Ashoka University, Asian Education Society Skyline Business School, Foundation for Organisation Research and Education (FORE), Manav Rachna International University, NC College of Engineering and Research, Hindu School of Architecture, RIMT Technical Campus, Shri Balwant Rai Institute of Technology and Research and SRM University.

Indian Institute of Technology Delhi has taken possession of 50 acres of land offered free of cost from Haryana government. Manav Rachna University and SRM University are also among the Universities who have started the projects of establishing their campus in the city.

Courses offered by institutions in the Education City would include Avionics, Environmental Sciences, Bio Medical Engineering and Medical Robotics, Information Technology and Artificial Intelligence, Cutting-Edge engineering and Technologies, Management and Finance, Textile Technology, Biotechnology, Nano Technology and Defence Research, Art and Cultural Studies, Habitat Studies, Film and Media Studies, Pure Sciences and Fashion Technologies.

Conclusions

Special Education Zones could adopt a multi-pronged approach to confront the challenges posed for the Indian Higher Education System. SEdZ models a sustainable educational ecosystem designed to benefit the stakeholders involved in the system. However, reaping the potential benefits of SEdZ is largely dependent on effective implementation of the system, which will require proactive action on the part of the stakeholders, especially from the government.

Bibliography

1. "NASSCOM for special education zones" The Hindu Tuesday, Dec 19, 2006
2. "Sam Pitroda favours special education zones" Times of India Feb 14, 2009.
3. "Govt mulls special education zones" Tribune News Service, October 1, 2009

4. "M.P. to set up Special Education Zones", The Hindu, July 8, 2010.

5. Annual Report MHRD 12-13

6. "IIT campus to come up in Rajiv Gandhi education city in Haryana" Jun 10, 2012.

7. "Haryana govt to develop Kundli- Sonepat as new hub" Express News Service, Apr 27, 2013

8. "30% gross enrolment ratio our target by 2020: MM Pallam Raju" Times of India July 2013.

9. "Higher education ignored" The Hindu, September 3, 2013

24

Higher Education in India at Crossroads-Needed Reforms

Dr. Namita Kohli*

Abstract

Higher education in India is emerging as the strongest instrument for the development and humanisation of mankind. An ever improving higher education system along with the demographic dividend make a perfect recipe for India to be a knowledge super power in the 21st century. But sadly enough, our government has not paid adequate attention to it. There is no coherent long term policy on higher education. Our whole system needs to change with the changes in society and the stakeholders need to accept the flaws and work towards wading them off. The number of universities in India as on December 2011 increased to 634, the number of colleges increased to 33,023(UGC Report, Feb., 2012). But this is not sufficient for a population of 1200 million. The total spending by the government on education accounts for a dismal 3.7% of GDP (2009-10). India is far behind in development of higher education because expenditure on higher education is small as compared to other developed countries. With the expansion of private sector, quantitatively much expansion has taken place in higher education in India. But we have not been able to achieve goals of access, equity and excellence. While India has the second largest system of higher education in the world next to US, the student enrolment ratio in higher education is just 17.9%. India has the largest target market in the world with a population of 234 million in the age group of 15-24 years. Our young demography is an asset and we should prepare this population for their future by making a transition into a knowledge economy that creates, disseminates and uses knowledge to enhance its growth and development. The Ministry of Human Resource Development has set a target of achieving 30% GER in higher education by 2020. There is a

* Assistant Professor,Guru Nanak Khalsa College for Women, Ludhiana

need to provide at least 1.5% of the total GDP for higher education in order to compete successfully in the knowledge based economy of 21st century. The present number of universities, colleges, resources and facilities are insufficient to cope up with the growing demands of higher education. More funding and public support are essential to ensure balanced achievement of educational and social missions.

Keywords: *Higher education-Gross Enrolment Ratio-Public expenditure-Access- Equity-Excellence-Quality-Knowledge economy.*

INTRODUCTION

Higher education plays a vital role in imparting in-depth knowledge and understanding to students about the new frontiers of growth in different walks of life. Education in general and higher education in particular is the strongest instrument for the development and humanisation of mankind. In the present day knowledge society where the world is highly competitive, it is only higher education that provides qualified and trained human resources to keep pace with the fast changing world. Therefore, investing into higher education is highly rewarding in order to strengthen the society and nation as a whole.

Hon'ble President of India, Shri Pranab Mukherjee said, "education is the true alchemy that can bring India its next golden age." So he described Education as the key to golden age. An ever improving higher education system along with the demographic dividend make a perfect recipe for India to be a knowledge super power in the 21st century. But sadly enough, our government has not paid adequate attention to it. There is no coherent long term policy on higher education. Most of the policy issues in education were confined to literacy and elementary education ignoring higher education. As the demand of funds for primary and secondary education increased, the government felt that there was no way it could continue to support higher education on the same scale as it used to do earlier. Moreover, there are other concerns of quality access, finance, reorientation of curriculum, accreditation of institutes etc. to be taken care of. Our whole system needs to change with the changes in society and the stakeholders need to accept the flaws and work towards wading them off.

The Objectives of the study are:

- ❖ To study the impediments in smooth growth of higher education in the phase of neo-liberal policies

- To study the recent changes in the higher education scenario in India.
- To look into the much needed reforms to uplift higher education in India.
- To suggest ways and means to improve the quality vis-a-vis excellence in higher education.

Slow Growth of Higher Education

Before independence, access to higher education was very limited and elitist, with enrolment of less than a million students in 500 colleges and 20 universities. Since independence, the growth has not been very impressive. The number of universities as on December 2011 increased to 634, the number of colleges increased to 33,023(UGC Report, Feb., 2012). This is not sufficient for a population of 1200 million.

Neo Liberal Policies and Higher Education

Introduction of neo-liberal economic policies in early 1990's facilitated the growth of private sector at the cost of public higher education. These policies that required stabilization and structural adjustment required a drastic cut in public expenditure on higher education. Higher education was defined as non-merit good that did not deserve to be financed by the state. Allocation for higher education in eighth and ninth five year plans touched all time low. Hardly 7% to 8% of the total planned expenditure was devoted to higher education in these plans. A drastic decline in public expenditure per student in real prices was recorded both in general higher education as well as in technical and professional education.

More than 40 years ago a panel set up by the government- The Kothari Commission, had recommended stepping up public spending on education to six percent of the Gross Domestic Product (GDP). However, the total spending by the government on education (Centre and State combined) accounts for a dismal 3.7% of GDP (2009-10). India is far behind in development of higher education because expenditure on higher education is small as compared to other developed countries. Private sector got a fillip starting the mid 1980's coinciding with the reducing investment by government of India with the neo-liberal economic policies in 1990's. By 2006 the share of private institute went up to 63.2% and student share went up to 51.5%. With the expansion of private sector, quantitatively much expansion has taken place in higher education in India. But we have not been able to achieve goals of access, equity and excellence.

Major Concerns

- Access to higher education is restricted to a limited population.
- India's GER of 17.9% was much below the world average of 27% as well as that of other emerging countries such as China 24% and Brazil 36%.
- There is a wide disparity in the GER of higher education across states, urban and rural areas and gender and community wise.
- NASSCOM report found that a mere 25% of technical and 10% of non-technical graduates are actually employable.
- Almost two-thirds of universities and 90% of colleges were rated average on the basis of NAAC Accreditation Report.
- The quality of higher education in India does not match the global quality standards. Not even a single Indian university found mention in the top 200 universities of the world.

Low Rate of Enrolment in Higher Education

Currently 17 million students are admitted in the 33023 colleges and 634 universities across the country. While India has the second largest system of higher education in the world next to US, the student enrolment ratio in higher education is just 17.9%. However, this rate is very low as compared to other developed nations. The GER is 86% in USA, 55% in France, 35% in UK, 24% in China.

The faculty wise enrolment is 80% in traditional courses such as Arts, Commerce and Science and only 20% in professional courses out of which 10% is for Engineering and technology, 3% in Medicine, 3% in Education (B.Ed), 2% in law and 2% others. There is a serious problem of quality and access in higher education. Moreover, the private engineering and medical colleges are merely profit making institutions and there is dearth of funds in engineering and medical colleges opened by government.

Recent Developments

Recently it has been realised by the government that series of qualitative deficiencies exist in Indian higher education system. Perhaps the clearest and boldest statement of this issue can be found in the "Report to Nation,2006" of National Knowledge Commission (NKC) which concludes that there is quiet crisis in higher education in India that runs 'deep' and it has to do away with both quantity and quality of higher education in India.

India has the largest target market in the world with a population of 234 million in the age group of 15-24 years. India's youth population aged 18-24 years is going to increase by over 2005-2020 as against the world average of 4%. Over 70% of Indians will be of working age in 2025. Our young demography is an asset and we should prepare this population for their future by making a transition into a knowledge economy that creates, disseminates and uses knowledge to enhance its growth and development. Realizing this, the Ministry of Human Resource Development has set a target of achieving 30% GER in higher education by 2020.

Eleventh plan was declared as educational plan. Allocation to higher education was scaled up and major expansion was planned. As many as 30 new Central Universities were to be set up. Plans for expansion also included setting up six new Indian Institutes of Management, Seven Indian Institutes of Technology, 20 National Institutes of technology, nearly 2000 colleges of engineering and technology, 1300 polytechnic, and many other institutions.

The student loan scheme has been further reformed with liberalized conditions and a subsidy of interest to students belonging to lower social strata. The government is also considering setting up 14 world class or "innovation" universities.

The twelfth plan places an unprecedented focus on the expansion of education, on significantly improving the quality of education imparted and on ensuring that educational opportunities are available to all segments of society. The objective of 12th plan is to raise GER from 17.9% in 2011-12 to 25.2% by 2017-18.

Other Highlights

- The share of private sector in GER increased from 54.2% in 2006-07 to 58.9% in 2011-12.
- During the eleventh plan, 98 private universities, 17 private deemed universities, 7818 private colleges and 3581 private diploma institutions were set up.
- 12th plan states, "Private initiative in higher education, including viable and innovative Public Private Partnerships (PPP) models will be actively promoted."
- It further stresses on the need for removal of entry barrier to private participation and self- funding of courses by the institutions.

Needed Reforms

The drawbacks of higher education system underscore the need for reforms in order to create an employable workforce to harness its demographic dividend to maximum extent. Here are a few suggestions:

❖ The government should spend 6% of GDP on education out of which 1.5% must be spent on higher education.

❖ Some minimum proportion of budget should be kept for- (a) Merit scholarship (to promote excellence); (b)Merit cum mean scholarship (to promote equity).

❖ An appropriate regulatory structure to discipline the unbridled profiteering in private sector is a must. Strong regulations to check the quality and governance in education are the need of the hour.

❖ In order to ensure quality, faculty recruitment should be based purely upon excellence.

❖ Apart from salary, working conditions, academic freedom, research and study also should be modified and incentivized. More and more faculty development programmes should be initiated.

❖ For promotion and enhancement of research in higher education it is necessary to upgrade laboratories & infrastructure. Moreover, exposure to global standards and research with international collaboration should be encouraged.

- There should be regular revision of curriculum to ensure updation and relevance of knowledge imparted to students. Experimental learning, moral education, community service, creative thinking should be included in the curriculum.
- There should be greater transparency and accountability in higher education. The issues like corruption, political inkling, nepotism etc. should not be allowed to interfere in academic organisations by imposing a proper set of rules and code of conduct.

Conclusion

Higher education in India is faced with numerous issues which are multi faceted and complex. The present number of universities, colleges, resources and facilities are insufficient to cope up with the growing demands of higher education. The greatest weakness today is lack of commitment. More funding and public support are essential to ensure balanced achievement of educational and social missions. Hence, the need for a legal and regulatory framework which can guarantee a transparent and credible relationship between public and private sector is critically needed. There is a need to provide at least 1.5% of the total GDP for higher education in order to compete successfully in the knowledge based economy of 21st century.

Bibliography

1. B.S. Nagendra Prashar, "Deemed/Private Universities: Shattered Dreams," University news, Vol. 51 No. 06, February 11-17, 2013.
2. Bhushan Sudhanshu, "Higher Education in 12th Plan- Paradigm Shift in favour of 'FOR PROFIT'," Economic and Political weekly, January 26, 2013.
3. Jandhyala BG Tilak, "Higher Education Policy in India in Transition," Economic and Political Weekly, March 31, 2012.
4. Ernst Young, "Higher Education in India: Twelfth Five Year Plan (2012-17) and Beyond," FICCI Higher Education Summit, 2012.

5. Jeelani, "Challenges and Opportunities in Higher Education in 12th Five Year Plan," University News, Vol. 50, No.21, May 21-27,2012.

6. Shaikh Saleem, "Higher Education in India at the Crossroads," University News, Vol. 50, No. 50. December 10-16, 2012.

7. The Economic Times, Pune, July 20, 2012.

8. The Hindu Business Line, June 8, 2012.

25

KHAP PANCHAYAT AND HIGHER EDUCATION

Dr. Ajay Ranga★

ABSTRACT

In this era of democratic modernization internet and technology, middle-aged orders of khaps are not acceptable in society and revolt against these orders has been started long back. In this paper, an attempt is made to trace the history of Khap Panchayat, examining its working and its role in the promotion of Higher Education.

Introduction

Khap Panchayat means community panchayat. It is as old as caste and family system in India. It is a traditional institution engaged primarily in dispute resolution and in regulating the behavior of individual or groups in rural North India. Khap Panchayats are self-styled guardians of social morality violating the human rights and Indian Constitution.

Institution of Khap Panchayat is very old but they attracted the attention of scholars only when the print and electronic media highlighted their certain illegal decisions which were violating the human rights of individuals. This paper is written to see the historical development, structure, working, of Khap Panchayats and their role in the promotion of higher education in society.

This research paper is based on the personal experience, observations and discussion with the persons familiar with the working of Khap Panchayats. Researcher is resident of that part of Haryana where these khap are very powerful and having first -hand information about the structure, working of khap panchayta in this modern society. In

★ Assistant Professor, University Institute of Legal Studies, Panjab University, Chandigarh addition to above said resources various books, articles available of the topic and information available on internet have also been taken into consideration.

The Khap Panchayat was a system of social administration and organization in the republics of Northwestern Indian States such as Haryana, Punjab, Rajasthan, and Western Uttar Pradesh. The

concept of Khap is ancient; written reference are found as far as Rig Vedic times 2500BC. The ancient Kshatriyas have always organized themselves into clans or under panchayat system; both typically Aryan. A clan was based on one large gotra or a number of closely related gotras under one elected leader whose word was law. Mutual quarrels of any intensity could be settled under his order.

Some well known occasions, when arms and funds were marshaled under the aegis of khaps, are:

(i) The battle against attack of Timur in 1398 AD was led by Veer Jograj Singh Gujjar, the Gujjar landlord of Saharanpur (UP) and the commander of Sarv Khap Army.

(ii) Battle of Miltan against Huns in Vikram Samvat 564(507 AD).

(iii) Battle of taraori against Muhammad Gohari in 12th Century AD.The battle at the confluence of Hindan and Kali river against Alauddin Khilji in the 13th century AD in protest against imposition of heavey taxes and interference in private affairs.

Presently, Khap Panchayat is mainly based on the following three things:

(i) **Gotra (clan):** Khap based on a single gotra of a particular caste is called Gotra Khap Panchayat. For example- Dahiya Khap, Malik khap, Sangwan Khap, Sheoran Khap, and Balyan Khap in the Muzaffarnager district of uttar Pradesh etc. These khaps had between 40-80 villages.

(ii) **Caste:** Khap based on single caste and multi-gotra is called Caste Khap Panchayat. Almost all castes from upper caste to lower caste in society are having their own caste panchyats. For example – Jat khap Panchayat, Gujjar khap panchayat, Chamar Khap Panchyat, Balmiki Khap Panchayat etc.

(iii) **Area:** Khap based on multi-caste and multi-gotras living in a particular geographical area or group of villages based on different castes and clan were organized into one unit which is known as Area based Khap Panchayat. For example - Meham Choubisi (group of 24 villages),Baawal Chaurasi(group of 84 villages), Kandela Khap (group of 28 villages). Panchgrami (group of 5 villages), Danoda Khap (group of 52 villages), Hooda Khap (group of 24 villages) etc.

Broadly speaking, on the basis of above said detail Khap Panchayats can be categories into two categories:

(i) Khap Panchayat (Based on single gotra, caste and particular geographical area)

(ii) Sarv Khap Panchayat (Based on the combination of multi-gotra, multi-caste and different geographica area based Khap panchayats)

Working of Khaps:

Main role khap panchayat in society is to maintain the traditional moral code of conduct which means bhaichara (brotherhood). These khap panchayats are making their own laws based on social morality, traditions and custom, executing them in society and if any person violates these laws, then punish that person as judicial authorities. Before independence their authority was not challenged by any ruler but after independence Indian Constitution has set up the three tier system which establish three organs of state i.e. Judiciary, Executive and Legislature. Through three tier system Indian Constitution has establish the Rule of Law in society.

Each khap had a pradhan, which was a post sometime hereditary and sometime nominated on the basis of the pradhan's reputation for fair play, his power of argument and his socioeconomic position in the area. Meeting of khap is depending on the magnitude of matter in dispute. Generally meetings are called in open where any person belonging to that gotra, caste and area is allowed to participate in the meeting according to the nature of Khap Panchayat. If the dispute was inter-caste, it was decided by the khap panchayat of the upper caste or clan, in which the lower caste people also participated. The lower castes were expected to follow the norms and traditions of the upper castes who fell under the jurisdiction of the khap. Women were not allowed to participate in panchayats at any level. Women were not even allowed to put their views in the panchyats in the cases related to women.

Role of Khap Panchayats in the Promotion of Higher Education:

After independence, education, the recognition of individual rights, adult franchise, the introduction of panchayati raj institutions at village, block and district levels, state and Parliamenty election, urbanization, economic independence and other such factors provided opportunities to the individuals to come out of traditional system and the moral ideology of bhaichara.

Khap Panchayats do not permit same gotra marriage and inter-caste marriage, where as Indian Laws permitting such kind of marriages. Khap leaders believe that modernization and education is responsible for the violation of their moral traditional code of marriage. They belies that highly educated people don't bother about the morality of society and they do not respect the decisions of Khap Panchayats. So they are not in favor of spreading higher education in the society. Today, Khap Panchayats are powerful in rural area. Khap leaders are politically and economically powerful in rural society, but none of them is running any higher educational institutions.

Conclusion

During Mugal and British rule Punjab was covering the area from Peshawar to Delhi. Both the rulers keep themselves away from the working of Khap Panchayats, infect they recognized the working and remarkable work done by khap in social sphere of Punjab specially. Same was the situation in Rajasthan and Western Uttar Pradesh. Due to long dominance over the social disputes resolution system they become very powerful in this part of country. After 1950 when democratic election system for making government was established, the color of caste, religion and areas was shown on the election system. Politicians recognized the powers of Khap Panchayats in democratic system and found that whatever order is passed by the Khap leader that was followed by the entire caste, gotra (clen) or area. Then politicians started protecting and promoting khap leader and their decisions to get benefit in the elections. From here Khap Panchayats forget their role of social responsibility and started playing political role in society. when Khap Panchayats started passing fatwa's of cutting hands, head, expulsion from village or caste, end to sharing huqqa, water or meals, and excommunication or ostracism from the caste or group or even from the villages or khap, that time politicians remains silent in matters of Khap Panchayats. This conduct of politician instigates and promotes the middle-aged fatwa's of khaps. Khaps were exploited by politicians for vote politics.

In this era of democratic modernization internet and technology, middle-aged orders of khaps are not acceptable in society and revolt against these orders has been started long back. Indian Constitution and Government do not permit these extra Judicial unconstitutional bodies in the form of Khap Panchayats.

The major considerations which the khap panchayats are facing are that they still hold tradition and a particular morality very dear. The cases relating to marriages where the individuals or families have violated the old traditions of village and gotra bhaichara on the other hand legal system favours the action taken by these individuals or families. The intervention of the courts in these cases has challenged the authority of the Khap Panchayat for having taken decision which violates the rights of individuals.

Khap Panchayats are losing faith of the society because they are not changing themselves according to the changing need of the society. If Khap Panchayats wants to retain their respect and honor in the society then they have to change their morality according to the changing needs of the society. They have to irradiate social evil of castism, dowry, female feticide, unnecessary expenditure on marriages, child marriage etc. They need to promote education in society. They have to look forward for the welfare of the public in the changing modern scenario of society.

Bibliography

1 Pardhan, M.C., 1966, The Political System of Jats of Northern India, Oxford University Press, Delhi, p. 97.

2 Thapar, Romila, 1984, From Lineage to State Bombay, Oxfor University Press, Delhi, p 64.

3 Walker, Gordon, 1884, Ludhiana Settlement Report, pp45,79.

4 Dorairaj, S., 2009, Spreading Meance: The Syatem of Dispensing Justice through Kangaroo Courts Continues in Rural and Urban Tamil Nadu Despite Court Directives to End Practice, Frontline, p.46

5 Mandelbaum, David G., 2005, Society in Inida: Continuty and Change; Change and Continuity, Popular Prakeshan, Bombay, p.73.

6 Kumar, Varinder, March14,2010, Vicissitudes of Gotra Row: Sustain the Crusade against Khap Panchayats, The Tribune, p.13.

7 Chawala, Salja, April 16,2010, What Honour in Killing: Lesser Crimes do not Bother Us, The Tribune, p.9.

8 Singh, Preet, May 1,2010, Hounded by Khap, Couple Wants to Embrace Death, The Tribune, p.2.

9 Singh, Ranbir, March15,2010, Khap Panchayats are Violating Human Rights, The Tribune, p.9.

10 Kumar, Ajay, January 28,2012, Khap Panchayats : A Socio-Historical Overview, Economic & Political Weekly, pp.59-64.

11 Available on www.wikipedia.org, visited on 14/12/2013 at 8pm.

26

Women in science: Cause of Under-representation and Remedies

Dr. Akhlash P Singh*

Abstract

The women is the inevitable part of the healthy human society and she should not be ignored in any walk of life and her talent must use for the national development process. Due some social ill-will women participation in the science has been meagre but with the passage of time they made their presence felt in different areas of science. Although, traditional biases have been already abolished and new types of discriminations will also remove in future. In this endeavor different government effort play a significant role and it provide large number incentives to women students in terms of fellowships and flexibilities at work place. But most challenging tasks before the women scientist is to established a balance between science and family. This paper briefs the types of discriminations and their remedies for women workers in science.

Key words: Women in science, social discrimination, fellowships and incentive for women.

Introduction

According to mythology the Nature has created two most important creatures i.e. male and female on the earth. Although, initially they were created for the perpetuations of human race on the earth and they had played equally significant role in this endeavor. But as the civilizations developed in different part of the world, men had adopted different professions like agriculture; domestications and industries for their sustenance, hence labor of divisions were created. During

* Assistant Professor,Department of biochemistry, GGD SD College 32 C, Chandigarh

this course of time, role of women had been specialized, moreover, particular in the fanatic, religion-based and feudal society in 17, 18 and 19 centuries consequently, this restricted women to parental care and domestic work. Naturally, this make women lag behind in different walk of life which lead to the generation of male dominated professions or society. Simultaneously, the popular perceptions had been developed that, women is suitable only for parental care and house hold works. It created extreme dearth of women workers in the area of science (Phalkey, 2013).

Historically, despite the strong adverse and unfavorable working conditions prevailed for long time, women have had made their way in science, technology, engineering and medicine (STEM). Several name of repute in field of science can be noticed. For example, Lilavati (Bhaskaracharya's daughter, 1114-1185 AD) was great women scientist in the area of algebra and mathematics. Rusa, another women scientist who wrote a great text on women related diseases. There were also some famous women scientists in British era in India such as Kadambini Ganguly, the first Indian lady doctor. More recently, we have large number women scientist and entrepreneurs like Kalplana Chawla (great astronomer, March 17, 1962 – February 1, 2003) Kiran Mazumdar-Shaw (Biotechnology) and Tessy Thomas (Agni Putri).

Internationally, Marie Curie, Rosalind Franklin and many more women Nobel laureates who did excellent work in the area of science. Total 16 women have been awarded the Nobel Prize in physics, chemistry, physiology or medicine (http:/ / nobelprize. org/ nobel_ prizes/ lists/ women. html). But these are some specific example and do not reflect sorry state of affairs which is low representation women in science in India and world. It does not also fulfill the requirement of healthy impartial human society from the human right point of view. Currently in India, only 18 % women are employed in science including the scientist, professors, postdocs and technical assistant. http://www.nistads.res.in/index.php?option=com_content&task=view&id=197&Itemid=110).

Refer to fig no 1and 2 for women representation in science in major world's economies. But the question arises why the sufficient representation of women in science or gender equality is essential? There are few reasons can be put forward (1) from the human right perspective that society must of free from discrimination; (2) women talent must be used; (3) increase in scientific force; (4) economic augmentation of different countries ; (5) diversity in research without consideration of religion, caste, creed and gender.

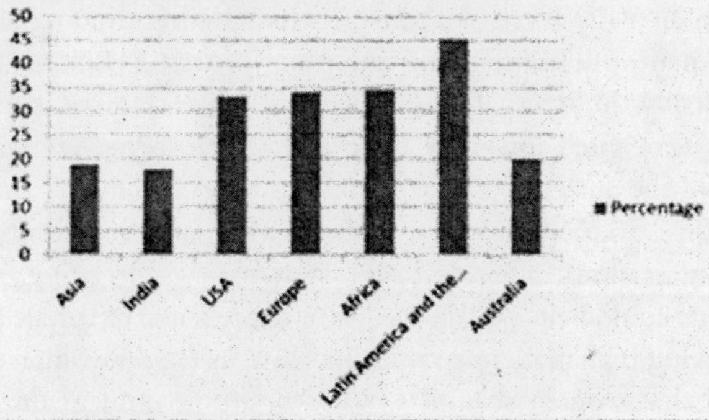

Fig No 1. Percentage of Women in the World of Science

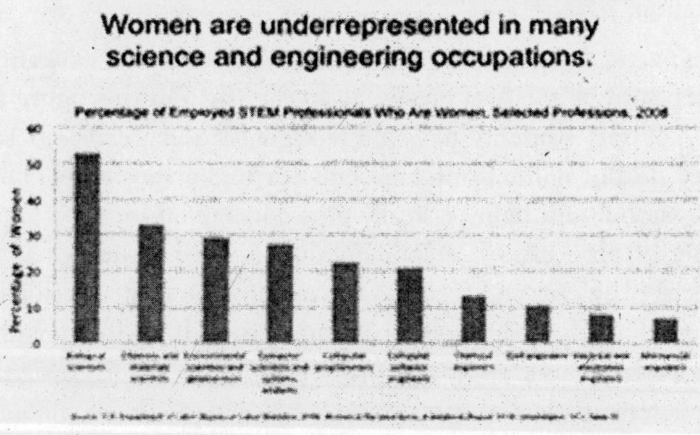

Fig NO 2. Women under-reperesentataion in STEM

In view of above facts, this paper reviewed the reasons of under-representation in science educations and research and remedies which can be used to meet these challenges. Identification of areas of under-representation

These areas are particularly math intensive areas such as chemical, mechanical, computer, electrical, civil engineering and physics and physical chemistry. However, female make felt their substantial presence in biological science and medicine (fig.2). The root of these problems can be trace out in math-intensive fields that is not due to discrimination in these subjects, but rather to sex differences in resources attributes, abilities, and choices. There are also some areas where women also discriminated such as in grant and manuscript reviewing, interviewing, postdoc, and hiring. Generally people do not hire women scientist than a men with equal qualification. It is now recognized that biases function at many levels within science including funding allocation, employment, publication, and patenting process (Hunt et al, 2013). Traditionally, Substantial research shows that resumes and journal articles were rated lower by male and female reviewers when they were told the author was a woman. Similarly, a study of postdoctoral fellowships awarded showed that female awardees needed substantially more publications. Therefore, the systematic underrating of female applicants could help explain the lower success rate of female scientists in achieving high academic ranks. In some instances women scientists claimed that women scientists suffer discrimination in these arenas rest on a set of studies undergirding policies and programs aimed at remediation.

To understand the dearth of women scientist in higher education can be understand by the data presented in the (fig.3 in this figure a large number of girl students passed their graduation degree in science but they do not entered into the labs for higher positions. This can be understood with help of "leaky pipe concept". Under this concept high rate of drop ratio is responsible or in other words you can say that, social problems and scenario force them enter into small jobs and family, particularly in developing countries in India. Other possibilities may be husband and family and prevailing situations play a significant role in determination of carrier and employment for women. These types of results had emerged after the analysis of personal life events of women scientists (Genome Biology, doi: 10.1186/gb-2012-13-3-148). This study was conducted when the women identified balancing a career in science with a personal life as a struggle. For many women, the point at which they are making these career choices coincides with the time at which they will be getting married and starting a family. There is urgent need to identify the causes during and after graduate school and beyond that may add difficulty to obtaining and maintaining a career in science by girl students. Because the women who face such types of discriminatory situations can leads to confidence loose toward the carrier building in the area of science.

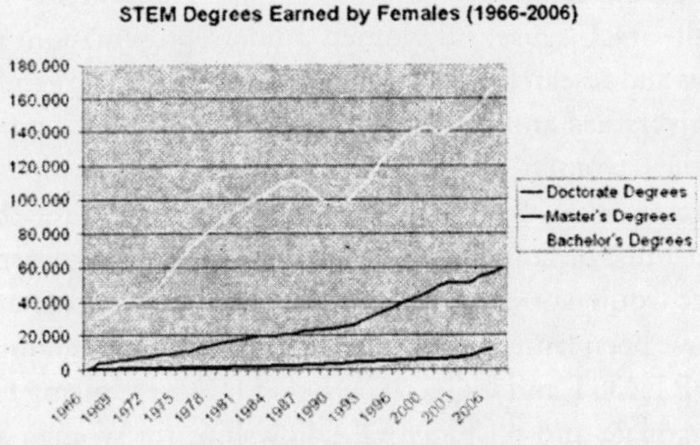

Fig No 3. Leaky pipe concept

REMEDIES

The overall problems faced by the women workers in the science can be distributed into traditional and current problems. It can be proved with the help of several studies that, traditionally problems have been solved and presently no such type of discrimination as mentioned above has been noticed. In other words current efforts going on which are part of course correction for the past disparities were prevailed in the society (Ceci et al, 2011). Additionally, women choose generally teaching oriented jobs which do not offered more research resources hence so less scientific publications. The problems related to paper acceptance, reviewing and findings are solved completely in the era of blind folded review process by funding agencies and editorial committee.

The women scientists need the exceptional role models who can motivate them for determinations and stay in the science. The leaky pipe concept shows that, a large number of women cannot pursue their carrier in science attributed to lack of balance between carrier and family life. It can resolve with help of support provided by family and government to provide the fund for the child care as in case of western countries. The mentor can help a lot the women by providing the right kind of carrier advice and research proposal. According some scientist, women candidate generally got demoralize and have less level of confidence in adverse conditions therefore, need to be more confident.

The governments of different countries need to frame the policy which promote the women in science such as legislation for the women recruitments, constitute national committees which can suggest the real cause of women underrepresentation in science educations and research. Governments must ensure the gender balance in the universities and research institutes. Even in exceptional cases new national women specific science centers can be open to make their representation. Special training and fellowships for the women candidates must be launched. In this direction Indian government and world over women oriented fellowships and training programmes have already have been launched. In India various national funding agencies such as DBT, DST and UGC, ICMR and ICAR are giving fellowships for postgraduate and postdoctoral fellowships for women student so they can pursue higher studies in sciences. Additionally, government also providing the leaves from the works places for two years for child care after that, women scientist or professor can restart her carrier. With these measures the representation of women in the science will increase and according the estimation the women will represent the STEM in large number in 2018.

Conclusion

However the women has left behind in the field of science and technologies due to some social reasons and but they have made felt their presence in biological sciences and medicine. Simultaneously all traditional biased related to women in science almost has been abolished. Due to substantial efforts on the part of different governments has make situation conducive for women. But the greatest challenge is to establish a great balance between science career and family life. It is certain hope that in coming years there will be heavy presence of women in the science.

Bibliography

1. Phalkey, J (2013) Focus: science, history, and modern India Isis. 2013 Jun;104(2):330-6
2. http://www.nistads.res.in/index.php?option=com_content&task =view&id=197&Itemid=110)
3. Nobel Prize Awarded Women (http:/ / nobelprize. org/ nobel_ prizes/ lists/ women. html)

4. Genome Biology 2012, 13:148 doi:10.1186/gb-2012-13-3-148
5. Hunt et al, (2013) why are women underrepresented amongst patentees. Research Policy 42 (2013) 831– 843
6. Ceci SJ, Williams WM(2011) Understanding current causes of women's underrepresentation in science Proc Natl Acad Sci U S A. 22;108(8):3157-62

27

Social Inequality – A Challenge to Higher Education in India

Dr. Pallavi Manik*

Abstract

Higher education in India is passing through a phase of unprecedented expansion, marked by an explosion in the volume of students, a substantial expansion in the number of institutions and a quantum jump in the level of public funding. The past century has been characterized by a massive worldwide educational expansion. Increasingly complex economies demand a better-educated workforce. The distribution of education both in terms of quality and quantity is highly uneven in most societies. Indian society suffers from substantial inequalities in education, employment, and income based on caste and ethnicity. Inequality in opportunities for education is found not only with reference to individuals and social classes but also in terms of regions and territorial regions such as urban and rural areas. With widespread inequality in opportunities for education resulting from the operation of socio-economic factors education seems to have failed as an effective equalizing factor. However it is not that education has not contributed at all to the process of upward social mobility but the momentum has been slow considering the social fabric of the country. By educational inequality we mean a system under which all the sections of society are not given equal opportunity to get education. In India changes in political, economic and social life are as a result of educational inequality. Taking all these points in to consideration an attempt has been made to find out the causes of social inequalities in higher education in India and suggest some measures to improve them.

Introduction

Education, especially higher education is one of the sector that has undergone tremendous changes in the last two decades. Private

* Assistant Professor, LRDAV College, Jagraon

universities, market based and new generation courses, decreasing public spending, public private partnership, setting up of foreign universities especially in higher education sector, how far these has impacted a section of society that does not have access to higher education historically would unfold educational and economic inequality with in the Indian society. How far this jumps where distributed among all the communities and groups in India have to be examined to understand how unequal the development that took place in the arena of higher education was. The national policy adopted in 1986 has emphasized on three basic elements "Access, Equality and Expansion". But the process of development is exclusionary for the sections like SCs, STs and other backward Classes.

Social Stratification in India along the lines of caste, ethnicity and religion is also reflected in educational attainment with a vast quantity of literature documenting inequalities therein. These inequalities have been a cause of concern to both the government and civil society. The government has put in place strong and affirmative action to redress many of the historical injustices. Some of these have led to resentment and protests from more privileged sections of society.

Reservations get some attention. Recently, a news report about entrance to the IITs mention that 1,403 students got admission under the scheduled caste category, only two dalit students could secure admission under general category. The figures also showed that if there was no reservation for the OBCs, the IITs would have had only 17% students from this social group that comprises around 45% population of the country. Official statistics did not reveal how many upper caste Hindu students make it to the IITs, but a simple back-of-the-envelope calculation shows that despite reservations, their share is anywhere between two or three times their share in population.

The inequality is being perpetuated by notoriously unequal access to education between the poor (whose ability to pay for better quality private services is very limited) and the rich. In fact, inequality in access to education is so glaring, that in HDR 2013, India's education index loses more than 40 per cent of its value once adjusted for inequality. These have to do with misplaced policy priorities of the Government that are only aimed at short-term benefits with an eye towards political gain. Thus, while the Indian Government spends less than five per cent of the GDP on education, it spends close to six per cent of GDP on (leaky and poorly targeted) subsidies (which, according to the IMF, benefits the rich more than the poor) and interest payments. Higher expenditure on subsidies (which doesn't help in capacity-building) and interest payments comes at the cost of health and education for the teeming millions, thereby blunting future growth potential.There are many issues relating to higher education such as Expansion, Equity and Excellence. In the following discussion effort is to look at the issue realted to Equity.

The Objectives of the study are:

1. To have an overview of social inequality in terms of gender, rural-urban and communities.
2. To identify the challenges in Indian higher education system due to social inequality.
3. To suggest measures to overcome these challenges.

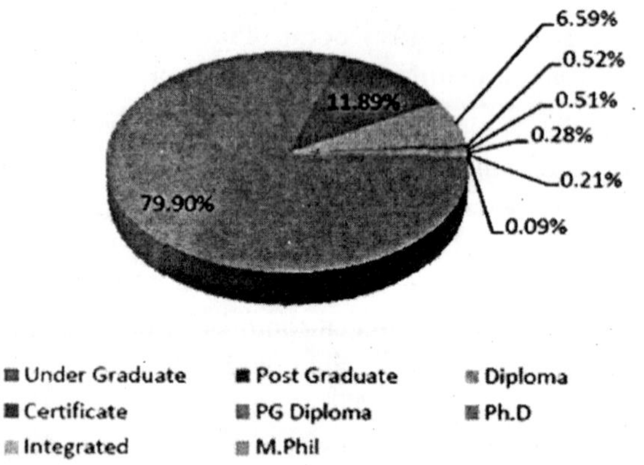

Figure 1: Student Enrolment by levels for the year 2011-12

Source: All India Survey on higher Education 2010-11

Total student enrollment has been classified in 8 levels across all the states of India i.e PhD,M.Phil, PG, UG, PG Diploma, Diploma, Certificate and Integrated. The highest number of students are seen enrolled at UG level across India. Out of total 2,74,99749 students a vast majority of 2,19,72,260 students ar enrolled in UG sweeping 79.9 pc. 11.9 pc are enrolled at diploma level.

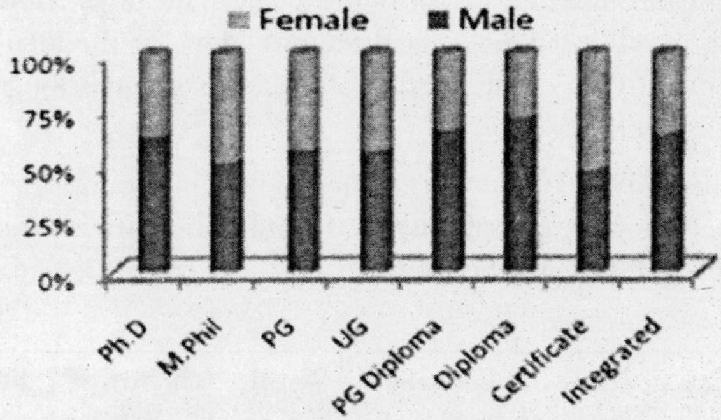

Figure 2: Gender Distribution at Different Level

Source: All India Survey on higher Education 2010-11

Taking a look at the male-female ratio at each level. The trend is of higher males than females in almost at every level except M.Phil, which is almost equal. While in certificate course, the female enrolment is slightly higher at 53.4 pc versus male enrolment 46.6 pc. Students at UG and PG has a similar trend with around 55 pc males and 45 pc females. PG diploma has an unbalanced distribution. Similarly Ph.D and integrated levels, both have an unequal around 62 pc male and 38 pc female. Diploma students project the most lopsided picture with 71 pc male and 29 pc female.

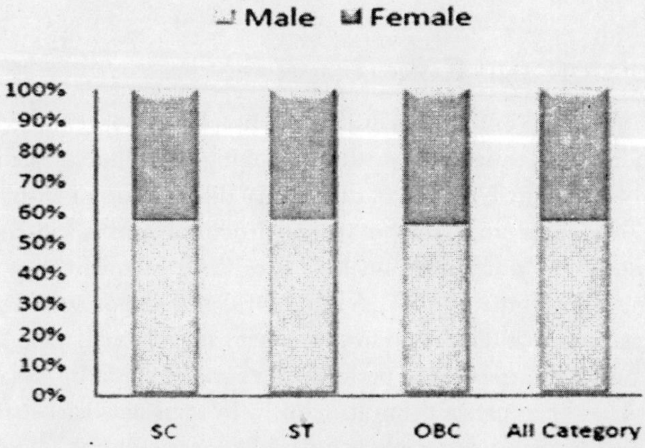

Figure 3: Social Categories and Gender Distribution in Student Enrolment

Source: All India Survey on higher Education 2010-11

SC student enrollment is 11.1 pc of the total.On the other hand student belonging to ST categories constitute only 44pc of the total student enrollment with 57 pc male. 27.6 pc of the total student belong to OBC 55 pc male students.

Among minority, 3.8 pc sudents belong to muslim minority and 1.8 pc from other minority communities. Muslim minorities has more male students than females. Whereas other minority has more females than males.

Category	Male	Female	Total	% out of Total	Female per hundred male
Total	26507	27468	53975		104
SC	1835	2919	4754	8.8	159
ST	965	413	1378	2.6	43
OBC	5796	7346	13142	24.3	127

Figure 4: Category Wise Distribution of PWD Students

Source: All India Survey on higher Education 2010-11

53975 PWD students are enrolled in higher education. Out of which 26507 are male and 27486 are female students, this having more female students.

Discussion and Conclusion

Even though the enrollment pattern is not indicating equity. Caste and gender differentials are worth mentioning. Enrollment rate is not equitably distributed. Causes of differential distribution of enrollment can be explained in terms of socio-structural and socio-cultural background. In India, traditionally, caste based inequality has been depriving large segments of SC, ST and OBC. Education was legacy of upper castes only and it ceased for those who are at lower strata. Lower caste people were assigned to perform all degrading task. In India caste and class has been present simultaneously. In agrarian social structure in India all lower caste people were landless agricultural labour and belonged to lower stratas of class hierarchy. In post independence era the tradition continues. Existing socio-economic condition pulls them into backwardness and do not let them move toward upward mobility.

Marginal group in the country are submerged in poverty. Earning is prior to higher education. Further the expenditure incurred for higher education cannot be borne by them. Although there is provision of post matric scholarship but it is allowed to only those who belong to BPL level. The amount of scholarship is not substantial enough to meet all the requirement of higher education.

It is observed that, cultural capital is not favorable to marginal groups. Most of the SC students are either first generation educated or second generation educated. As a result they are neither motivated nor helped by family in comparison to upper caste peer. The term cultural capital was used by Pierre Bourdieu. In this theory cultural reproduction makes effective use of word cultural capital which refers to the form of knowledge, skill, education and any advantages a person has which gives him a higher status in society. Cultural reproduction passed from one generation to the next. Thus, unfavorable cultural capital of lower caste may further contribute to their less participation.

To ameliorate the embedded problem of social inequality, successive governments have introduced caste based reservations in the institutions of higher education. At present the caste based reservation applicable only in Government funded institutions, and amount to approximately 49 pc of the total seats. Union Government has launched a number of schemes and programmes for the purpose of enhancing participation of deprived classes in higher education. India has about 21,902 institutions of higher learning including universities, institutions of national importance and colleges. It is compulsory for all these institutions to provide 15 pc reservations to SC, 7.5 reservations to ST. Additionally provision of the Central Government has now provided for 27 pc reservation to OBC. Apart from reservation, there is also a relaxation given in the minimum qualifying marks for admission for these students. Many other facilities like scholarship to SC/ST students, free remedial coaching and hostel facilities are also given.

Although the enrollment rate of girl student does not signify gender disparity at UG level. But a dismal situation prevails at PG and research level. It also indicates an increase in the enrollment of women in the higher education institutions in 2010-11 by nearly 30pc in all India level. This is of immense importance for development. But quiet a substantial number of girls especially in rural areas are motivated to enroll in the higher education for engagement and to earn qualification for marriage. Their proportion is however meager in PG and research level. Motivations of competition and career orientation to girl students are real challenges of society. Girls are yet to come out from the status of inferiority in relation to men. Men are bread earners and women are objects of domestic work this traditional value persuades many girls to drop out of study.

A national study by AC Nielsen and NGO Plan in 2012 India revealed as many as 23 percent of girls in India drop out of school when they attain puberty. Where girls remain in school a lack of facilities causes' widespread absenteeism each month, with the report showing that girls miss an average of 50 days of school each year because of menstruation

Recommendations

In order to improve the situation the following recommendations should be adopted:

1. Provide education for the learners who are deprived as well as for those who wants to pursue further education, to further and intensify the process of democratization of education, etc via Distance and open learning. In fact, distance and open learning is an important strategy that can promote accessibility and equity particularly in higher education in our country.
2. Instead of just talking about inequalities, we need to pay careful attention to the various dimensions of inequalities and how they interact with one another. This would mean targeting subgroups such as scavenging and nomadic communities on the one hand and identifying groups that lie at the intersection of many inequalities.
3. Talk about equity must be backed by resources. In particular there is a need for a quantum jump in the volume, range and amount of student support measures like scholarship, stipend, assistantship and loans for disadvantaged students.
4. Reservation needs to be supplemented by a range of smart equity designs such as multidimensional index of disadvantage for students and a diversity index for institutions.

5. Higher education system should take interest in their feeder area or supply chain to improve quality and drop out as a priority need of the community and duty of higher education system and for their own growth i.e., higher education system.
6. Enhance the amount of scholarship of SC
7. Provide adequate infrastructural facilities in SC villages.
8. Make provision for further motivation of individual dignity, self respect and values of education especially to women.

Conclusions

In this globalized world, for promoting social security through development in education, economic as well as social life, we need to enhance the skills and capacities of the vibrant human resources of our country. So ensuring the access of higher education by all (in order to create knowledge economy) should be the priority agenda for the Government as well as for the various private bodies in India.

We cannot expect that expansion of higher education will automatically reduce inequalities. Over the years, the access to higher education has improved for all social groups, but their relative disparities have not reduced substantially. While rapid expansion of private educational institutions has helped to meet the acute need for increasing the capacity, it has also accentuated inequalities by reducing the scope of state action in favour of the disadvantaged. The entry of dis-privileged social groups has shifted the site of deepest imprint of social inequa-lity from the lower end of higher education to its upper end.

Bibliography

1. All India Survey on Higher Education, 2010-11, Govt. Of India, MHRD, New Delhi.
2. Bora, Abhijit; "Higher Education Consolidation of existing facilities", academe, Vol.XV.No.1. January, 2012, ASC, HPU.
3. Deka, K.K; "Higher Education: some concerns", Assam Tribune, edit page, August 13, 2012.
4. Siddique, M.A. (2010), "Rural-urban Disparity in Higher Education", University News, Vol. 48, No.28.

5. Bose, B & Chakravarty; "New vigilantism in higher education", The Hindu, April 1, 2011.

6. Saxena V, Kulsrestha S, and Khan B; "Higher Education and Research in India", International Journal of Educational Research and Technology, Vol. 1 [1] June 2010:pp.91-98.

7. Bordoloi, R.; "Accessibility and Equity: A Challenge for Higher Education in India"; Journal of Economics and Sustainable Development, Vol.3, No.4, 2012.

8. Padamwar U.D & Patil S.S.; "Quality Enhancement in Higher Education: Achievements & Failure; with Special Reference to the Rural Colleges", International Indexed & Referred Research Journal, ISSN- 2250-2556; Vol.-I, ISSUE-1, April, 2012.

9. Adi. S. Mukta. 2007. "Higher Education in Rural Areas", University News, 12 (March 19-25):16-17.

28

USE OF SOCIAL MEDIA, BLOGS AND FILE SHARING SITES IN HIGHER EDUCATION

Dr. Pooja Mohan*

ABSTRACT:

Social media generally refer to media used to enable social interaction. It is seen merely as a way to pass the time or stay connected to friends and family. However, its use is rapidly expanding into the educational sector as instructors look to technology to mediate and enhance their instruction as well as promote active learning for students. The term social media technology refers to web-based and mobile applications that allow individuals and organizations to create, engage, and share new user-generated or existing content, in digital environments through multi-way communication. This paper provides an overview of how technologies are being used to support teaching, learning and research, highlights some of the risks and the benefits faced by staff with a role in higher education. Various issues and challenges faced in managing new means of communications will be addressed by this study.

Keywords: *Facebook, Twitter, LinkedIn, Learning, Education*

INTRODUCTION

In recent past, higher education has witnessed adoption of emerging technologies like internet in spreading knowledge among students through a variety of platforms. After online distance education showed how physical boundaries could be blurred, social networking sites (SNS), blogs (Weblogs) and micro blogs (Twitter) and file sharing sites are offering new ways to share information in a cost-effective, convenient and faster way. On big shift in social-media-enabled education is the shift in focus from teacher-to-student to student-

* Assistant Professor, GGDSD College, Chandigarh

to-student interactions. Once information has been put out in cyber space, it can be discussed, shared and reacted to using the social media.

Experts have expressed concerns over social media education coming at the cost of traditional face to face communication that comes with the advantages of physical presence in classrooms. There are also doubts about whether older faculty member would be open to use of social media. Issues such as concerns over credibility of information put out on social media, need for moderation of offensive content and in-built handicaps of SNS like 140-character limit on Twitter, anonymity of those who comment on blogs and possible misuse of information shared on Facebook walls need to be tackled.

However, use of social media in higher education is becoming imminent in view of the changing profile of students, who spend a lot of time online, sharing content on social platforms. Given the large number of adult students who are now online, educations institutions are expected to share online space with them and put out updates that could be checked on the go with the convenience of smart phones and laptops by students.

Where use of social media for programmes aimed at reaching out to masses in general are criticized on count of 'digital divide', it doesn't hold much ground in case of higher education. Most students who reach college or university are expected to be connected to the Internet in some form and at some place. Even if they hail from rural areas, connectivity at campus library or hostels is a big possibility.

Almost all top universities worldwide have official pages or fan pages or communities of students on Facebook, researchers and faculty members write blogs and students give real-time updates of academic events with live tweeting. Social media is used to fulfill cognitive needs with universities giving information about lecture schedules, uploading course curriculum and other updates and at the same time students experience community bonding by sharing notes, links, audio and video among themselves. Similarly, scientists and researchers too strive to be connected with like-minded people.

The Objectives of the study are:

- Which social media and file sharing platforms are most used to supplement classroom teaching, learning and research and how?

- ❖ Benefits for both stake holders (students and teachers) for social media to promote higher education.
- ❖ Concerns/Challenges related to these community networks
- ❖ To find out if social media use is only hype. Is it actually effective
- ❖ To look at the future use of this interactive medium

Literature Review

Social Media Network: Definition and Usage

Social media has been described as "Internet and mobile-based tools and devices that integrate technology, telecommunications and social interaction enabling the construction, co-construction and dissemination of words, images (static and moving) and audio." The Educause Center for Applied Research (ECAR) Study of Undergraduate Students and Information Technology, 2008 defines social networking sites as "Web-based services that allow [individuals] to 1) construct a public or semi-public profile within a bounded system, 2) articulate a list of other users with whom they share a connection, and 3) view and traverse their list of connections and those made by others within the system.

In social networking systems the individual user (or groups of users) can decide what they wish to discuss and who they wish to work together with. This means that social networking systems truly have the capability to deliver a platform for learning where the student is potentially at the centre of activities.

A multi-platform approach

- ❖ **Blogs** to share Classroom material
- ❖ **YouTube** videos for 'how-to' guides for students
- ❖ **Slide share** for sharing PPTs on academic projects
- ❖ **Facebook** for online communities of students/teachers
- ❖ **Twitter** for sharing links of educational websites/blogs, live updates of events like conferences
- ❖ **LinkedIn** for finding jobs/business opportunities
- ❖ **Wikis** and **Google Drive** for project collaboration

Usage of Social Network in Higher Education

The usage of SN media in higher education can vary from marketing media, information media, communication media, feedback, complain, announcement, sharing, task assignment and examination.

Many universities jumped at the opportunity to create an official Facebook, and also some of sub organization in the university, for example library, student's association, student's forum, etc. Fan pages can creates viral marketing effect, because it can catch the interest from the friends of people who already become fan.

Utility of social media and internet in general for promotion of higher education is still a matter of debate. The divergent views were brought out in a survey conduct by Pew Research Centre on 'the topic 'The future of higher education.' It pointed out that where "experts expected more efficient and collaborative environments; they worry about massive online courses the shift away from on campus life." Moran, M., Seaman, J., & Tinti-Kane, H. (2011) in their study found that there was not much difference in levels of awareness about popular SNS between senior and younger faculty. But there are some variations – younger faculty is likely to know about Slideshare and platforms like LinkedIn are more popular with male members.

Highlighting the participatory nature of Facebook, which promotes sharing of user generated content, Pempek, T. A., Yermolayeva, Y. A., & Calvert, S. L. (2009) claim that "like traditional media such as television and film viewing, Facebook consists of a one-to-many communication style, where information presented reaches many "viewers" at a time. Users are now the creators of content, and they view one another's profiles and information rather than viewing mass-produced content made by large corporations." The study also highlights 'online lurking' by college students, where they passively go through information put up on the SNS without actually commenting on or sharing it.

Among the many studies reporting statistics related to Facebook adoption and usage, 90% of undergraduate college students were reported to have Facebook accounts. Study found that 94% of their college students were users of Facebook spending an average of 10–30 min on the site and having 150–200 friends.

Social media acts as a communication tools for stand-alone departments, administrative offices, and even individual faculty. For instance, some admissions offices have begun to use student blogs to showcase current student experiences as a recruitment tool for prospective students

Underlining the need for an "innovative approach of using blogs and social media for technical educational purposes", Strnad, G. (2012) launched a personal blog and social media specifically for the study in 2008 by the name 'Tehnological Land'. In 2012 the blog was followed by 89.6 % of students enrolled in the course who found the blog useful for their technical knowledge improvement.

College and university faculty have also used blogs as a pedagogical strategy. Recent studies have investigated the use of blogs in academic disciplines including the sciences, teacher education, and business.

Using Twitter, Institutions can create live, up-to-the-minute notices of commencement programs, homecoming events, class reunions, and live chat sessions as well as campus emergency alerts

Tess, P. A. (2013) too points out that the wide presence of social media comes with immense possibility and "potential role for social media as a facilitator and enhancer of learning is worth investigating."

As part of a research on the effects of introducing Facebook as the course communication tool versus a learning management system (i.e., WebCT) by Schroeder, J., & Greenbowe, T. (2009), posts of 128 undergraduate students enrolled in an introductory inorganic chemistry lab at Iowa State University were examined at the end of the semester. It showed that only 41% of the students enrolled in the Facebook group for the course, the number of discussion posts was nearly four times (67 versus 17) those in the WebCT forum.

But it will not be a cakewalk to spread the use of social media in higher education. A case in point is finding of research by Jones, N., Blackey, H., Fitzgibbon, K., & Chew, E. (2010) about "a large distinction in student perceptions regarding technology use in the personal space versus the learning space. While more than 70% of the students reported having a social networking account, they also indicated that they rarely used social media for educational purposes."

Social media in research

Apart from user-to-user interactions by students, the social media platform can also be used effectively for promoting research in colleges and varsities. Getting insights into the lifestyle of a top researcher on his blog or twitter account can be beneficial for the budding researchers who look upto him. When it comes to organizing conferences with shoe string budgets, online (virtual) participation can bring together minds for intensive brainstorming.

This has been successfully illustrated in many conferences that used video streaming of plenary sessions and Twitter back channels broadcast conference presentations allowing virtual delegates to participate and engage in the conference discussion and pose questions to keynote speakers. Like other events, videos of keynotes and plenary talks are uploaded to YouTube or Vimeo whilst PowerPoint presentations may be uploaded to Slideshare or Google Drive or Google Sites and viewable to a wider audience there.

SNS sites like LinkedIn are an ideal platform to meet fellow researchers for possible collaborations and the in—built system of references can go a long way in forging a credible alliance.

Sites such as CiteULike, Mendeley, Zotero and Colwiz all support groups and different levels of collaboration. Group collections can be followed via RSS feeds pushing information to individuals rather than them having to constantly check for what's new. Most journals now support sharing buttons allowing individual readers to share an article to a reference tool, social bookmarking tool, Twitter, Google+, LinkedIn, and Facebook.

Benefits of Social media in Higher Education

A teacher can share detailed visual (pics and videos, graphics) content with students through YouTube for which there may not be time in classroom. Subject specific links to websites/blogs can be shared on twitter and Facebook. Online discussions among students of FB communities can be triggered. Even an introvert student get a chance to speak, they can use pseudonym (fake name) or post comments anonymously. Various other benefits are one-to-many connection, Problem- and inquiry-based informal learning. Students can get Personal and professional support and mentoring by sharing advice by a teacher on these medias. 'Hypertextuality' feature of Web 2.0 (They can go from one link to another) can help students for online research on a topic.

Concerns/ Challenges/ Solutions

Social media education should not come at the cost of traditional face-to-face communication. There are some of the challenges in effective implementation of these in classroom teaching environments. There is a debate over whether classroom attendance will be replaced by online presence. Students can post offensive comments. They are more addicted towards facebook for sharing entertainment stuff than studying. Students may not be comfortable in sharing their personnel space on facebook and twitter with their teachers. Professional training of student/faculty around social media would be required. Social media tools and networking sites encourage students to engage with each other and to express and share their creativity.

Teachers can create separate account for each class to identify with whom they are interacting. By doing this they can keep a check who is posting offensive comments. They can manage their privacy settings properly. They can create blog for their class and published notes, posted them on facebook by tagging all the students. They can also use Open Source Social Media that allow collaboration between individuals. It allows customization, enabling educators to host the platform on their own institutes' servers.

CONCLUSIONS:

Social media in higher education is still a new phenomenon and there is need for more research to come up with insights into pros and cons of the virtual interface that brings together teachers and students in an informal set-up where there is less rigidity and reactions and clarifications are encouraged due to the interactive format of social media. Future research on how to increase the active participation of students in content creation for blog and dedicated social media pages and also in another innovative educational approach is required. Reluctance of senior faculty members to take up social media to interact with students in cyber space, especially when they are not using SNS for personal accounts, patchy penetration of internet and ignorance about the possibilities that the network offers are issues that need to be tackled. If getting students to classrooms is a problem in real world, platforms such as Facebook are virtual spaces where youth spend most of their time. The key lies in coming up with engaging content and elements of hypertextuality, interactivity and mixing of text, pictures, audio and video messages can give a new dimension to higher education. The rapid growth of SN usage in higher education, we have no other choice than adopting it in higher education in the most effective way.

Bibliography

1. Anderson, J. Q., Boyles, J. L., & Rainie, L. (2012), "The Future Impact of the Internet on Higher Education: Experts Expect More Efficient Collaborative Environments and New Grading Schemes; They Worry about Massive Online Courses, the Shift Away from On-Campus Life", Pew Internet & American Life Project.
2. Dabner, N. (2012). 'Breaking Ground' in the use of social media: A case study of a university earthquake response to inform educational design with Facebook. The Internet and Higher Education, 15(1), 69-78.
3. Jones, N., Blackey, H., Fitzgibbon, K., & Chew, E. (2010), Get out of MySpace! Computers & Education, 54(3), 776-782.
4. Moran, M., Seaman, J., & Tinti-Kane, H. (2011), "Teaching, Learning, and Sharing: How Today's Higher Education Faculty Use Social Media" Babson Survey Research Group.
5. Oradini, F., Saunders, G., (2008), "The use of social networking by students and staff in higher education", iLearning Forum.
6. Pempek, T. A., Yermolayeva, Y. A., & Calvert, S. L. (2009), "College students' social networking experiences on Facebook", Journal of Applied Developmental Psychology, 30(3), 227-238.
7. Rosmala, Dewi (2012). "Study of Social Networking usage in Higher Education Environment", Procedia-Social and Behavioral Sciences 67, 156-166.
8. Schroeder, J., & Greenbowe, T. (2009), "The chemistry of Facebook: Using social networking to create an online community for the organic chemistry laboratory". Innovate: Journal of Online Education, 5(4), 1-7.

9. Strnad, G. (2012), "The Use of Blogs and Social Media for Technical Education in Specific Field of Materials Processing", Procedia Economics and Finance, 3, 337-342.

10. Tess, P. A. (2013), "The role of social media in higher education classes (real and virtual)–A literature review", Computers in Human Behavior, 29, A60–A68

29

Implications of Commercialization of Higher Education

Dr. Priyanka Malhotra

Abstract

From the time when education started with the first phase of commercialisation the responsibilities of the teachers have been compromised. People view it just as a well paid profession. With the opening up of many private institutes by many corporates and foreign collaborations with the private institutes has raised the challenge for the government to have control on higher education and make it more affordable and inclusive to all sections of the society. Is higher education being devalued or enhanced by commercial interest and success is the question which will be perused in the following paper. It is a secondary data based research highlighting the implications of commercialization of higher education and the remedies that can be offered.

Keywords: Commercialization; corporates.

Introduction

"Higher Education must lead the march to the fundamentals of human relationships, to the old discovery that is ever new, that man does not live by bread alone."

—John A. Hannah

The Indian Higher Education system has expanded at a fast pace adding nearly 20000 colleges and more than 8 million students in a decade from 2000-2001 to 2010-2011. as of 2011, India has 42 central universities, 275 state universities, 130 deemed universities, 90 private universities, 5 institutions established and functioning under the State Act and 33 institutes of National Importance. Other institutions

* Assistant Professor, Deptt. of Commerce, GGDSD College, Chandigarh

include 33000 government degree and private degree colleges. Apart from these there are distance learning education and open universities. While the students who graduate from secondary school(10 million annually), there are only places for 20% of them at tertiary level, and only a few are admitted to elite institutions (Short, 2008a,2.10) Only 10% enrolled in HE (Cheeney et al.2005, p1) 9 in 10 students pursue bachelor's degree, 1 in 10 pursue PG degree (Cheeney et al .2005,p17) Estimates suggest that there are about 160000 students from India studying abroad. Average spending on fees and maintenance is $25000 per student per year (National Knowledge Commission,2006, p13) The All India Council for Technical Education (AICTE), Ministry of Human Resource Development (MHRD) launched the National Vocational Education Qualification Framework (NVEQF) implemented in polytechnics, engineering colleges and other colleges in the university system from 2012-13. This is expected to cater to at least 5 million students applying for vocational degrees and diplomas every year. The higher and technical education in India is increasingly privatized in multiple ways. The joining of corporates and opening up of many private institutions in the so called 'business of education' have led to the commercialization of higher education.

The Objectives of the study are:

1. To understand the concept of commercialization of Higher Education
2. To study the implications of commercialization of Higher Education
3. To give suggestive measures to reduce the negative impact of commercialization on Higher Education

Commercialization of Higher Education

"Commercialization is the term used to designate the tendencies and practices that create increasing connections between colleges and universities and the economic sector. It also refers to the process of driving public educational institutions to operate as if they were private". It is estimated that about 63% of all tertiary education (including TVET) in India is now provided in the private sector (Short, 2008a, p. 12).The relevant indicator of commercialization of Higher

Education is the rapid expansion of 'international trade' in education services. The World Trade Organisation and General Agreement on Trade in Services (GATS) is proposing to regulate educate jus like any other trade in commodities. Education has become market oriented. The corporate language views students as customers and products, teachers are service providers, learning guides and education managers, evaluation becomes quality control and education is coined as the production process. As the public funding decreases, 'user-pay' increasingly replaces it. In response to calls for "cost effectiveness" and "value for money", new managerial doctrines have been adopted in the university sector. The success of Higher Education reforms is merely measured by lesser degree of state intervention, while increased management autonomy and market oriented instruments are playing a far significant role (World Bank, 1994) Under the strong tide of managerialism, universities have become more· managerialist and bureaucratic in nature (Currie, 1998).

Commercialization of Higher Education has been characterized in the following manner:

1. The spread of market discourse and the use of economic market as a model
2. Massification of higher education
3. Increasing number of private providers of HE and research
4. Rise of global market for education and research
5. Rising costs of expanded tertiary education systems
6. Changing balance of private and public funding
7. Pressure for management efficiency
8. Increased regulatory and policy pressures

Beginning of Commercialization in Education

The National Policy on Education, 1986, aimed at development, consolidation and expansion of educational facilities, considering education as a base for economic development. The resources were proposed to be raised by "mobilizing donations"' "raising fees", "effecting some savings by efficient use of facilities", "levying a cess on user agencies". Further, it added that 6% of the National Income will be contributed towards education from the Eighth Five Year Plan onwards whereas nothing of this sought has been done till date. Rather the government took a step back and started privatizing and deregulating the education sector. The World Bank (1994), with reference to developing countries stated that Higher Education should not have the highest priority claim on incremental public resources available for education. In 1995 it stated that the benefits of higher Education were received only by young students from high income families. The Annual Report of The National Knowledge Commission (1996) caters to the demands of the big business, has given recommendations regarding reforms in existing public universities, undergraduate colleges, regulatory structures, financing, quality, creation of National Universities as centres of academic excellence and access to marginalised and excluded groups. However all the "prescriptions" are contrary to its purpose. The entire structure of Higher Education in India presented in the NKC Repot is highly elitist and will not benefit a vast majority of young people below the age of 25.. it will decrease the enrollment instead of raising it to 15% by 2015 raising the student fees to 20% of the recurring expenditure, financing pattern, private investment, salary differential, regulation by IRAHE with enormous powers, bias against the disadvantaged sections, autonomous colleges, elitist National Universities based on commercialization etc are retrograde recommendations which will lead to privatization and commercialization of the Higher Education in India.

Instead of meeting the demand of Higher Education and ensuring the growth of the country, the socio economic policies of the successive union governments, the ideological commitments of ruling classes, proactive role of judiciary and vested interests of the business houses have created a dismal situation in the Higher Education scenario.

Policy Regime supporting privatization of Higher Education

1. 100% FDI in education allowed through automatic route.
2. A high-powered advisory body - National Knowledge Commission (NKC) set up
3. NKC recommendations tremendously successful in increasing Government's focus and plan outlay on education

4. NKC has recommended that the number of universities increase from the present 370 to 1500 by 2015, considered a highly ambitious target, but inadequate to meet demand for quality education
5. Government has identified expansion, inclusion and rapid improvement in quality throughout higher and technical education system as the core focus of its 11th Five-Year Plan (2007-12)
6. For higher education, an expenditure of USD 37.13 billion has been projected to achieve the proposed objectives during the 12th Five Year Plan (2012-17)
7. In December 2010, AICTE notified regulations for grant of approval of technical institutions. The AICTE permitted Section 25 Company to act as a sponsoring body of a technical institute with the rider that no foreign investment (directly or indirectly) will be permitted in such a company.

Government resource allocation is inadequate to meet its own targets (30% GER by 2020) leaving enough scope for private participation. The Eleventh Five Year Plan (2007-12) allocation for technical and higher education has been raised by almost nine fold to USD 18.8 billion from USD 2.1 billion in the Tenth Plan. However, this is still a fraction of the estimated requirement for achieving the targets.

Issues and implications in commercialization of Higher Education

The privatization of Higher Education front is posing many issues and challenges which have negative implications. These negative implications being grave need perusal.

1. **Fees:**

The fees charged by these commercial institutions are very high which is beyond the reach of students making the Higher Education highly exclusive and within reach of those who can afford it. This has also led to a rise in the reliance on educational loans. Loans are being preferred over scholarships.

2. **Self financing courses and seats:**

Self financed courses, self financed seats in normal courses and distance learning courses have come in vogue with the sole aim of generating revenues. The distance learning courses have started mushrooming all over India, thereby, deteriorating the quality of education. If this trend continues then a time may come when the higher education system will be restructured to offer only self financed courses to be self reliant. This will not only truncate the growth of higher education but also weaken the society.

3. Deteriorating quality of education:

These institutions do not hesitate to admit students with poor academic credentials. They attempt to be financially efficient by reducing the costs on vital components which adversely affects quality. 'Higher education is far too expensive to be made privately profitable unless it is reserved for the rich or is of very poor quality' (Patel 2003:151)

4. Internationalization of Higher Education:

Foreign institutions are entering in the country taking advantage of differential and excess demand for Higher Education. Majority of them are mediocre and try to cash in the craze for foreign degrees. They charge very high fees on which even the government have no control.

5. Unethical businesses:

Driven by market opportunities and entrepreneurial zeal, many institutions are taking advantage of the lax regulatory environment to offer degrees not approved by Indian authorities. With competitiveness in the global market getting increased significance, institutes of higher learning are viewing education as a commodity; the growing commercialization is thus posing a challenge to moral and ethical values. According to George Haddad, Director of UNESCO's Higher Education Division," marketisation can be seen as damaging to the intrinsic values and ideals that education represents".

6. Exploitation of teachers:

In lieu to earn more profits, commercialized colleges will exploit teachers and professors by building a culture of adhocism and contractual posts so as to pay less and get more.

7. Poor regulatory framework:

The lack of govt. contribution and intervention and faulty reforms has made HE more exclusive and the GER which was supposed to rise shows a dismal position.

Recommendations

1. A public and private ownership should be there so that the government has a certain amount of control on the working and policy matters of the higher education institutions.
2. Recourse to quality private Higher Education, both university and non university is essential.
3. There is a need for financing of Higher Education for students, especially from low income households to make HE more inclusive.
4. There should be a regulatory setup to have control on cheating w.r.t fees and also imparting good quality education and enhancing research and innovation.
5. More access to national scholarships should be provided so as to decrease dependence on educational loans and encouraging meritorious students also.
6. Building an Industry academia relationship so as to fulfill the needs of both the parties.
7. The Swaminathan Panel has suggested building a reservoir of funds by collecting education cess from industries and other user organisations.
8. Setting up of an Educational Development Bank of India initially with shares of Rs. 1000 crores each by State Governments, Central Government and international financial agencies has been suggested.

Conclusions

It is known that providing increased access to education, meeting the challenge of equity and improving the quality of education entails huge investment which has been difficult for the government, therefore, the need for private investment has arisen. But privatization and deregulation through negative commercialization is leading to serious consequences of exclusions and deterioration in the quality of education. A coherent policy framework, an enabling regulatory framework and appropriate financial incentives can encourage student mobility by developing open systems that offer recognition of relevant prior experience, degree equivalences, credit transfer, tuition exchange schemes, access to national scholarships and student loans, comprehensive qualifications and a lifelong learning framework. Conscious considerations need to be made on the Higher Education front so as to meet the major objectives of making education inclusive, delivering quality and solving the purpose of public interest. The government needs to play a major role for the same.

Bibliography

1. Anand.C.L., Privatization of Higher Education: Rationale and Perspectives, Astha Bharti,July to September,1999, Volume 1 No.1
2. Sanat Kaul, Higher Education in India: Seizing the opportunity, Working Paper No. 179, Indian Council For Research on International Economic Relations, May 2006
3. Sharma Vijender, A Decade of Aggressive Commodification of Higher Education in India, Wordpress
4. Ved Prakash, Trends in Growth and Financing of Higher Education in India, Economic and Political Weekly, August 4, 2007
5. Sharma Vijender, Indian Higher Education Commodification and Foreign Direct Investment, The Marxcist, April to June, 2007, Vol. XXIII, No. 2
6. Chandwani Vinod. S., Bhome Shraddha M., A Study of Impact of Commercialisation of Education in India, Episteme, March 2013
7. www.legalservices.com/articles/he.html
8. indiaeducrises.wordpress.com
9. www.jstor.org/stable/3518092
10. www.igidr.ac.in/conf/ysp/JB1.pdf

30

Hindrance in Achieving Quality in Higher Education in India

*Dr. Rajendra Swain**

Abstract

Indian higher Education system is the symbolic relationship between education and national development. For the growth and development of human resource which can take the responsibility for social, economic and scientific development of the country attained by higher education. The vision of Indian Higher Education System is to attain the countries human resource potential with equity and inclusion, Indian Higher Education System need to provide greater opportunities to all eligible and in particular to the vulnerable section of the society. The aim is to remove the regional and other imbalances that exist at present. In recent years so many developments for higher education like, National Knowledge Commission (NKC), RUSA and many proposal made by 12th FYP like greater focus on performance, curricular reforms, better human resource management and to promote high quality research. The Hindrances lies in improving quality of teaching learning in a majority of non-elite universities and colleges which are fail to Justice to more number of talented students. This would require high quality research and continues appointment of faculty. The strategy for promoting quality at all levels need initiate innovative measures to provide much needed vibrancy to the system to enhance access, promote international quality and excellence to fulfill the objective of higher education.

Keywords: *Knowledge commission;Inclusion*

Introduction

Indian Higher Education System one of the largest in the world. When

* Assistant Professor, Deartment of Chemistry, PGGCG, Sector 42, Chandigarh

India attained Independence there were only 20 universities and 500 Colleges with 0.1 million students at present we have around 600 universities (Central, State, Private,Deemed Universities, Agricultural Universities and Institute of National Importance) around 32000 colleges, 14.6 million students and more than 9.33 lakh teachers covering all the disciples like humanities, basic sciences, engineering, medical and management. In addition to this the 12th year plan document proposes 184740 crores from 84743 crores in the 11th plan. In the new plan there is more for everything like construction of new universities, IITS, IIMS, NITS, model college, college cluster universities. There is a good dose of amount for agriculture management and medical institute.

In spite of this number can we say we are lack in higher education? Definite the answer is yes because we are far behind as compared to the developed countries in terms of quality as well quantity. The main purpose of 12th year plan to increase GER to 27% by 2020 from 17% right now.

For national economy excellence of work force is pre requisite for sustain growth and development which is only come from quality higher education, very few Indian institutions have global recognition in terms of being centre of excellence in their field. The toughest challenge of excellence lies in improving the quality of teaching, learning in universities and colleges but at the present time India suffers from quality deficit in the following respects.

Shortage as Faculty

Faculty being the most critical factor responsible for the overall quality and excellence in higher education, The unacknowledged crisis of Indian higher education is 40 % teachers are temporary and due to this quality of education is badly hit. It is a matter of grave concern that a large number of faculty positions remains vacant due to either non-availability of suitable qualified persons or due to procedural/ restriction fund constrains and freeze on new full time appointment in many colleges and universities. The recent research shows

- 40% of them are contractual teachers.
- Salaries range from 4000 to 30,000.

- No benefits like, PF, medical, accommodation, leave, etc.
- Teach 6-8 months/ 89 days contract.
- At managements mercy for contract renewal, extension, etc.
- Large no. of contractual teachers have no M.Phil, Phd Degrees and not clear NET.

Under such circumstances the teachers of this category are more concerned about their future job rather than teaching.

More Colleges with Single University

There is a lack of proper co-ordination between colleges and universities because there are so many affiliated colleges under a single university. The document says large university with more colleges are unsustainable. Osmania university has more than 800 colleges, while Mumbai, Pune and Banglore varsity have around 500 colleges. Some of these universities conduct more than 1000 examination annually. These are becoming agencies for conducting examination and award degree but more or less concerned about the quality of the education. It has been observed some smaller universities are well managed and maintain their quality.

Teaching Standard

The teaching standard in colleges and universities in India way behind the west. As a student advances to the higher level the responsibility and involvement should increases with teachers but which is hard to find in most of the cases. Sometimes due to lack of quality of our teaching students prefer to spend time away from classroom rather than inside it. The overcrowded classes' particularly in undergraduate level creates problem for the more interaction with the teachers. During independent the teacher student ratio was 1:40 and now it reached to 1:80. The proportion of teachers who prepare serious for their classes is very very small. Even in some cases the quality of teacher is high but the active interaction with the individual student is less. In some colleges particularly situated in small towns and rural area, in which teachers are bunking more classes than students.

Infrastructure

The quality of education also related to the infrastructure of the institution. Except some few universities and colleges in most cases the standard is very very poor as far as infrastructure is concerned. The modern technology based classrooms equipped with AC, sound system, power point etc. dream for some institutes. The gap between the colleges of urban area and rural bases so high that the students are more affected about study.

Financial Assistance

In spite of various scholarships and other financial benefits more students from poor and lower middle class families not getting opportunity in professional courses and even sometimes in normal undergraduate courses due to financial constrain. As a result some quality remains hidden in poor families and rural areas which is overlooked by the policy makers. If the system does not extract the talent from each corner of the country then which type of higher education it is?

No Uniform of Syllabus and Examination

Student these days have tendency to move from one university to other but the syllabus of the university are differ from each other. There is no uniformity in the syllabus and mode of examination in the different university by which students are affected more. .

More Interest in Abroad

There are many graduates well trained in technology have chosen not to contribute their skills to the technology sector in India. Perhaps most of them leave the country to pursue advanced study abroad and do not return. At the same time 86% of students in science and technology field from india who obtain degree in outside do not return home immediately following their study. Our best doctors and engineers go to America. This is not complaint against America. I am only saying that we have an enormous loss of brain power.

Central Funded Institute

In the name of few central funded universities most of the state universities facing problem about finance matter, infrastructure, appointment of faculty and grants under different heads. The finance conditions of some states are so poor that they difficult to maintain the quality of the universities.

Lack of Accreditation

To control the quality of institution UGC has set up NAAC (National Assessment and Accreditation Council) but till today (for the past 17 years) only 1415 Colleges out of 32000 and 75 out of 611 universities have been covered for their accreditation. Out of this number very few universities and colleges have got A grade and five star status. This figure indicates how our higher educational institutes maintain their quality.

Political Interference

Many colleges and universities are created by the local communities and politicians. So in every issue starting from student intake to faculty appointment there is interference of politicians. So the head of the institute is out of the decision maker. A very few colleges are getting autonomy power.

Lack of research

Due to the declining admission in basic science the quality of research activity in higher education declines day by day. Unfortunately the promotion and financial benefits in colleges as well as in universities based on the no of years rather than the quality of teaching and research work carried out by the teachers. This is the main reason why teachers are not actively taking part in research work and as a result the contribution of our research work in world science is not more than one percent.

It is very much clear without basic science there can be no technology and the growth of technology based in science. But students are crazy about engineering course leaving behind the study of science. A course of science does not appeal to many. The same thing will soon be seen in the field of engineering, ME, M.Tech, and Ph.D. where students will be on decline. Our main competitor china which produce MBA and PhDs almost ten times more than India. This one reason why there are so many products coming out from this country.

Conclusions

Finally to improve the quality of Higher education starting from Dr. RadhaKrishna report other proposal like Kothari commission, NKC, Yashpal Committee report and very recently RUSA report placed before Govt. of India. But quality of education can be improved by appointment of good faculty qualitative research, good infrastructure and active participation of every teacher in the system of higher education.

Bibliography

1. 12th Five year plan report.
2. Times of India, November10,2013
3. Yashpal Committee Report
4. A heart full of Burden, T.N. Seshan(2005) ,Page-83
5. The Hindu April 12, 2005

Chemistry Education: Challenges in Higher Studies

Dr. Ramesh Kataria*

Abstract

Chemistry is an incredibly fascinating field of study. Because it is so fundamental to our world, chemistry plays a role in everyone's lives and touches almost every aspect of our existence in some way. Chemistry is essential for meeting our basic needs of food, clothing, shelter, health, energy, and clean air, water, and soil. Chemical technologies enrich our quality of life in numerous ways by providing new solutions to problems in health, materials, and energy usage. Thus, studying chemistry is useful in preparing us for the real world. Teaching and learning chemistry can be challenging, and may often be complicated by students developing misconception of the chemistry they are taught. Although there have been challenges to higher education in the past, these most recent calls for reform may provoke a fundamental change in higher education. This change may not occur as a direct response to calls for greater transparency and accountability, but rather because of the opportunity to reflect on the purpose of higher education, the role of colleges and universities in the new millennium, and emerging scientific research on how people learn. This article reports structure, challenges and some suggestion for chemistry education at higher level.

Keywords: *Challenge, misconception, Laboratories and Instruments etc.*

Introduction

Chemistry education is a comprehensive term that refers to the study of the teaching and learning of chemistry in all schools, colleges and universities. Topics in chemistry education might include

* Assistant Professor,Department of Chemistry & Centre for Advanced studies in Chemistry, Panjab University, Chandigarh

understanding, how students learn chemistry, how to teach chemistry, how to improve learning outcomes by changing teaching methods and appropriate training of chemistry instructors, with many modes, including classroom lecture, demonstrators, and laboratory activities. There is a constant need to update the skills of teachers engaged in teaching chemistry, so chemistry education speaks to this need. There are at least four different philosophical perspectives that describe how the work in chemistry education is carried out. The first is what one might call a practitioner's perspective, wherein the individuals who are responsible for teaching chemistry (Teachers, Instructors and Professors) are the ones who ultimately define chemistry education by their actions. A second perspective is defined by a self-identified group of chemical educators, faculty members and instructors who, as opposed to declaring their primary interest in a typical area of laboratory research (Organic, inorganic and biochemistry etc.), take on interest in contributing suggestions, essays, observations and other descriptive reports of practice into the public domain, through publications, books, and presentations. A third perspective is chemical education research (CER) like science education researchers, CER practitioners tend to study the teaching practices of others as opposed to focusing on their classrooms practices. CER research is typically carried out in situ using human subjects from secondary and post-secondary schools. CER utilizes both quantitative and qualitative data collection methods. Quantitative methods typically involve collecting data that can then be analysed using various statistical methods. Qualitative methods include interviews, observations, journaling, and other methods common to social science research. The last perspective called the scholarship of teaching and learning (SOTL), although there is a debate on how to best define SOTL, one of the primary practices is for mainstream faculty members to develop a more informed view of their practices, how to carry out research and reflection on their own teaching, and about what constitutes deep understanding in student learning.

The Objectives of the study are:

i) To study the structure of chemistry education at Higher level

ii) To study the challenges in chemistry education at Higher Level

iii) To suggest ways and means to address these challenges in Indian contest

System of Chemistry Teaching at Higher Level

India is vast country with about approximately 1.25 billion people and different languages are spoken by the peoples of the various states as a result of the education could not be brought to uniformity throughout the country. The government of India had set up an autonomous commission, the university grant commission (U.G.C.) to look after the higher education and research. Although education is largely decided by the states, they follow the norms set by the UGC in matters related to the higher education.

Course and Name of the Examinations	Duration of the Course
1. Bachelor of Science (Pass)	Three years course. Equal weights for three combination subjects are given, e.g., (Physics, Chemistry, Mathematics), (Chemistry, Botany, Zoology) etc. Chemistry is taught and practical training is provided for three years
2. Bachelor of Science (Honours)	Three years course. Students majoring in chemistry, study the subject in detail for three years. They are to take two more subsidiary subjects (pass subjects) as in 1 above. Rigorous practical training is also given.
3. Master of Science	Two years course. First year gives emphasis to all main branches of chemistry. The second year is devoted for specialisation in any one of the major branches e.g., organic, inorganic, physical, polymer and analytical. Rigorous practical training is given. Master degree in subjects based on chemistry eg. Bio-chemistry, and agricultural chemistry, etc. is also offered in many universities.

Course and Name of the Examinations	Duration of the Course
4. Bachelor of Technology, Master of Technology and Integrated MSc	In some universities, there are 4 year B. Tech. course and after successful completion of the course 2 years M.Tech. Course in chemical technology, chemical engineering or allied topics are provided. Chemistry is taught in these courses giving emphasis on Industrial aspect of the subject. In IIT's and IISER's there are 5 year Integrated MSc course in Chemistry is also taught.
5. Doctoral Programme	Many Institutes and Universities provide doctoral programme to students after MSc or M.Tech degree. Students have to carry out their research work under the guidance of a supervisor and submit thesis for the award of the Ph.D. Degree. Institutes like IIT, IISc etc have also integrated Ph.D. programme where students, after passing B.Sc. examination, are admitted. Now a day's most of the institutes emphasize on course work and the dissertation work is considered as partial requirement for the Ph.D. Degree.

CHALLENGES IN CHEMISTRY EDUCATION

i) **Basic Laboratories:** The large enrolment has complicated the task of laboratory management by making heavy demands on space and on basic facilities like power, gas, distilled water etc. A serious problem is escalating cost of chemicals and glass ware. The allocation of teaching laboratories have not kept peace with the galloping prices of even routine reagents, solvents, and other chemicals required for run an average course.

ii) **Teaching Style:** The greater concern is the fact the teaching style has retained the traditional outlook. For example only qualitative and quantitative analysis of organic and inorganic compounds and physical experiments which are the main mode of practical experiments so far emphasize the traditional technique.

iii) **Outdated Instruments:** Chemical industry and research today is dominated by the instrumentation culture, the roots of which lie in electronics and computers but this technological revolution is yet to touch the chemical education scene in India. The high cost of commercial models is again the reason why student laboratories are starved of even simple equipment.

iv) **Teacher/student Awareness:** The lack of familiarities of a teacher/student with basic of instrumentation and electronics generates a 'black box' mentality and results in poor output.

v) **Syllabi:** Heavy and sometimes useless syllabus, focus of examination on rote learning with little emphasis on in depth understanding leads to the down grading of standard of chemistry education.

vi) **Library:** Our School, College and University libraries have not sufficient collection of books. Our Libraries are also not efficient due to lack of online facilities.

vii) **Collaboration of institutes with industries:** lack of collaborative approach of the chemistry institutes with industries affects the development of the research ability of interested students.

viii) **Financial Assistance:** Unavailability of regular funding by the government to the institutions for involvement in research activities.

Suggestions for Improving Quality of Chemistry Education

i) **Industry and Academia Connection:** Industry and Academia connect necessary to ensure curriculum and skill development, which is very crucial to ensure employability. Vocational and Diploma courses need to be made more attractive to facilitate specialized programs being offered to students. Industries should allow visit of student on regular basis.

ii) **Internship:** Offering internship to the students will prevent the needy ones from taking up other jobs and subsequently losing interest in subject.

iii) **Exhibition and Advertisement:** Counselling parents of the students during open day in institutes and holding career exhibition for chemistry with advertisement of vacancies for chemistry graduates and postgraduates will increase awareness for the scope of the subject.

iv) **Examination Reforms:** Shifting from the terminal, annual and semester examinations to regular and continuous assessment of student's performance in learning should be implemented.

v) **High-tech Libraries:** The libraries should have a good collection of latest books, research articles and must be online for effective study. There are more than 8000 chemistry journals in the world and manually going through even some of them is very tedious job. Implementation of ICT in the form of electronic data base will extensively beneficial for the researchers to be aware of most recent finding in their respective fields.

vi) **Student-Centred Education and Dynamic Methods:** Methods of higher education also have to be appropriate to the needs of learning to learn, learning to do, learning to be and learning to become. Methods of teaching through lectures will have to subordinate to the methods that will lay stress on self-study, personal consultation between teachers and pupils, and dynamic sessions of seminars and workshops.

vii) **Public Private Partnership:** There must be some effort by the University Grants Commission, Ministry of HRD and the private education institutions to develop the teaching staff at various levels. To achieve excellence, we thus need to create a real partnership between government, educators and industry that can provide our high-tech industries with skilled workers who meet the standards of their industry.

viii) **Funding:** Financial Assistance to Colleges, Universities and National Research Laboratories by the government should ensure the involvement of institutes in research activities to facilitate availability of latest sophisticated equipment and other basic requirement.

ix) **Job-Oriented Courses:** Interdisciplinary courses should be introduced so that such courses could be useful for the students to get jobs in some companies which would reduce unnecessary rush to higher education.

x) **World Class Education:** Many national universities like in the USA, UK, Australia, etc. allow studies in higher education for foreign students in their countries and through correspondence courses as well. In the same way Indian Universities can also offer courses to foreign students taking advantage of the globalization process. To achieve that goal it should adopt uniform international syllabus in its educational institutions.

xi) **Stipends to Research Fellows:** The number of Ph.Ds from Indian Universities should increase with proper standards. This should be seen in the context of extremely low fraction of Ph.Ds in India in relation to M.Sc./B.Tech., as compared to what it is in USA, UK, Germany, Japan etc. Meritorious doctoral students should be recognized through teaching assistantships with stipends over and above the research fellowships.

xii) **Fair Quality Assurance System:** Colleges and Private institutes should set up Internal Quality Assurance Cell and must follow a minimum standard to give degrees. It is also important that all institutes of higher learning must make public the acceptability of their courses and degrees.

xiii) **To increase Quantity of Universities:** We need more universities because we are more in number and present number of universities is too less.

Conclusions

Indian universities should concentrate more on providing quality education which is comparable to that of international standards. No doubt we have had some eminent chemists but whether they are because of the system or in spite of the system is a big question mark. Chemistry education pedagogy in this country will have to shift its present focus from the examination to the understanding of the chemistry, creating interest and nurturing innovation and creativity amongst students. We need chemists who are creative minds rather than rote learners. All this is possible only if the teaching profession at all levels attracts the best talent, retains them and works for their professional development. For this, teaching profession will have to be made more attractive. Teachers like researchers should be duty recognised for their contributions in the form of awards, fellowship, and for their innovation and excellence in teaching. During the last few decades, chemistry has made advancements both in basic front as well as in application front. We are moving towards an era which would be defined by the parameters of knowledge and wisdom in order to become a developed nation by 2020 and knowledge power by 2015. When India can provide skilled people to the outside world then we can transfer our country from a developing nation to a developed nation very easily and quickly.

Bibliography

1 Bakhshi A.K. and Rarh Vimal, Chemistry education in the 21st century: Challenges and opportunities, Science Reporter, 2012, 38-42

2 Sane K.V., Chemical education in coming decades-Challenges and opportunities, Proceeding of the Indian Academy of Sciences-Chemical Sciences, 1994, 106, 1389-1398

3 Jandhyala B.G. Tilak, Absence of policy and perspective in higher education, Economics and political weekly, 2004, 39, 2159-2164

4 Agarwal Pawan, Higher Education in India: The need for change, Indian council for research on international Economics relations, 2006, 180

5 Report of the National Knowledge Commission, 2006-2009

6 Approach Paper on Higher Education for the 12th FYP, UGC, 2011

32

Higher Education in Science: Challenges

Dr. Samriti Dhawan★

Abstract

Higher education is drawing tremendous attention in both developing and developed countries. To maintain their competitive superiority, the developed countries are investing heavily in R&D both in the private as well as the public sector. India cannot remain behind. Our unprecedented recent economic growth, the values of knowledge and education shared by a billion diverse people, and the investments made over the last half century, all point to India's potential future as a knowledge economy with high level man power in the science and technology driven global village. At our present stage of growth, when there is increasing international pressure for knowledge based, value-added development of major areas like pharmaceuticals, drugs, biotechnology, nanoscience/technology, healthcare, genetics, information/computer technology etc, it is clear that both in terms of numbers and quality, a vast expansion and intensification of higher level education embedded in research is essential. Challenges faced in the past need to be anticipated for concrete reforms in taking India to a leading position. The main thrust for the recommendations is to facilitate development of human resource that is capable of utilizing available knowledge to create wealth and of generating new knowledge and innovation.

Keywords: *Gross Enrolment Ratio, R&D/ Academia Partnership, Quality Education.*

Introduction

India faces enormous social challenges as well as opportunities for

★ Assistant Professor, Department Of Biotechnology, GGDSD College, Chandigarh.

rapid development in the new millennium. India's huge pool of young people might be considered its biggest strength. Unfortunately, India is far from having its act together when it comes to figuring out how to educate these young people. Government data suggests that only one out of every seven children born in India goes to college. What's more, the nation suffers from both a crippling quantity, as well as a quality challenge when it comes to higher education. Other countries visualizing a similar future, are investing massively to improve both the quality and quantity of higher education and research, some to give their societies a competitive advantage, and others to preserve their advantage.

India is one of the leaders of the developing world. In the times of global slowdown, Indian economy is likely to grow by 6% in the year 2013-2014. India has suffered in the past because of severely suboptimal investments in these areas. The present juncture is critical for Indian science: major positive steps would enable it to flower and play a key role in taking India to a leading position in the future, but inaction or sub-optimal action would accelerate the national decline. If India wants to enter into the league of developed nations, it has to strengthen the pillars of scientific research.

The Objectives of the study are to make India more competitive globally, skilled workforce is indispensable for rapid socio-economic progress of our country. It is essential to assess challenges faced in the past and which are still lying ahead.

- Poor Gross Enrolment Ratio (GER)
- Lack of Quality Education
- Lack of R&D/ Academia Partnership
- Faculty Crunch

Poor Gross Enrolment Ratio (GER)

India has one of the poorest Gross Enrolment Ratios (GER) for higher education in the world. According to recent data, India's GER was a meager 17.9 percent, compared with the global average of around 26 percent. Countries like Australia, Russia and the U.S., to name a few examples, have GERs upwards of 75 percent. Although the Ministry of Human Resources & Development had set a target of a 30 percent GER for India by 2020, that target is unlikely to be met.

Statistics show that there is a huge gap between the demand and the supply. Increasing and improving the 'supply side' of the scientific & technological community will be able to fill this gap. However, a major change is needed to attract a large number of young Indians to science based careers. The various opportunities in this large and central area need to be explored for present as well as in future. These opportunities could be in existing institutions, in research and development, in new institutions, in the industry as well as in new areas where we have advantages and potential for competitive growth, e.g bioengineering and biotechnology, pharmaceuticals, nanotechnology, etc. Besides, the HRD ministry says that the foreign institutions could fill this gap to a large extent. Close to 50 Foreign universities may enter India in near future. But realistically speaking, the foreign institutions could not fill this gap. This is the third attempt being made by government to liberalize education system. Two attempts were made in 1995 and 2006 to bring foreign universities to India. Anybody is lining up to take a part in India's $15 billion higher education market just isn't correct. As, universities in the West are facing their own financial crisis. As a potential market, India could have supplemented these universities' incomes at home. But our Foreign Education Provider's Bill prohibits foreign universities from taking surpluses out of India. In short, there are no shortcuts to fix our higher education problems.

Lack of Quality Education

Increasing the quantity alone is not going to address the problem. Both quantity and quality of highly specialized human resources determine their competence in the global market. The development in the field of science and research is rooted in university-level pure science courses. Unfortunately, the conventional educational practices followed in an average Indian university can be described as: A prescribed syllabus, with no changes introduced from last so many years with number of theoretical concepts to be memorized. Easily accessible reading material, obtained from the seniors or dictated class notes from some faculty members. Students refer the test papers of last five years to get an idea of possible questions. Once you are able to reproduce theories as in the "reading material", your first-class is confirmed, possibly with a gold medal. Probably more than 50% of the syllabus is unread even by the toppers of the college/universities because of the liberal choice in the question paper. Students often strategize what not to study and leave out subject-content in "option". This method may efficiently produce trainers who can pass on their memorization techniques to the younger generation, but how can it produce scientists and researchers? This leads to lack of innovation. The reason of a few exceptions that can be seen in the society can be either student's strong intrinsic motivation for learning or a presence of a dedicated faculty member. Given this absence of research culture, it is not-at-all surprising that the Indian universities hardly ever appear in the list of top universities of the world. Moreover, Lack of practical knowledge, interdisciplinary approach, inadequate examination and teaching resources and mushrooming of shoddy Institutions, further deteriorate the problem of quality education. As a consequence of such educational practices, India has not yet participated in the global competition in the field of science and research.

The first non-professional degree (viz., B.Sc.) in which millions of students are enrolled, unlike professional degrees, of not much value or societal attractiveness unless it is of educationally good quality, obtained in a lively research environment, and is supplemented by a professional edge (e.g., additional skill building that adds to employability) or research experience. According to the National Council of Applied Economic Research (NCAER, 2005), out of total unemployed graduates, 22.3% are pure science graduates. The proportion of pure science pass outs is 62.8% among total unemployed post graduates. This may be a major reason why students avoid pure science programmes after completion of their high school studies (as suggested by NCAER, 2005). So this is another area of challenge to the higher education in India. Urgent steps need to be undertaken to enhance the perceived status of conventional B.Sc. degrees in colleges/Universities as a career option. Currently, the low morale of B.Sc. students in the country is a very worrying feature of the higher education scenario in the country. A large number of college students pursuing B.Sc. degrees, several of them talented and motivated, feel 'left out' and 'discarded' by the system. Most of them pursue their degrees without any enthusiasm or motivation and are constantly looking for opportunities to change to the 'professional' streams. An important measure to address the problem of low morale in B.Sc. degrees to initiate post-B.Sc. 2-year B.Tech. programs, followed by 2-year M.Tech. programs. This will provide greater choices in career development to the meritorious students with undergraduate degrees in Science. These schools would offer B. Tech. degrees in frontier areas of industrial R&D like robotics, design, microelectronics, materials and nanomaterials.

Lack of R&D/ Academia Partnership

Research and higher education are complementary to each other. According to the available official statistics from Battelle, R&D Magazine, the expenditure on R&D in the field of Science & Technology as a percentage of gross domestic product (GDP) was mere 2.1 percent during the year 2009 in India as compared to 12.5 % and 12.6 % of China and Japan. Moreover, India's higher education institutions are poorly connected to research centers/Industries. Only 10 % of manufacturers in India offer in-service training to their employees, compared with an over 90 % in China. According to the Science Report 2010 of UNESCO, India's contribution to the world research publication is only 3.7 %, whereas China's contribution is 10.6% and United States' contribution is whooping 27.7%. R&D/ Academia/Industry needs to be substantially strengthened through increased financial outlay and major administrative reforms.

Faculty Crunch

According to a recent report of HRD Ministry, even premier educational institutes like the Indian Institute of Technology (IITs) and the Indian Institute of Management (IIMs) are facing a faculty crunch with nearly one-third of the posts vacant. According to a report published in IANS, around 35 percent posts are vacant in the central universities, 25 percent in the IIMs, 33.33 percent in the National Institute of Technology (NITs) and more than 35 percent in other central education institutions coming up under the Human Resource Development (HRD) Ministry. However in order to overcome this, government is planning to have short-term measures like raising the retirement age in teaching posts from 62 to 65 years and enhancement in salaries and other benefits for teachers. Also some long-term measures have also been initiated for attracting young people to opt for this (teaching) career. These include enhancement in fellowships and attractive start-up grants in various disciplines.

Modern education in India is often criticized for being based on rote learning rather than problem solving. The development and present scenario of higher education in India in context with science and Technology is presented by analyzing the various data and reports.

Key initiatives from the government side include the establishment or increase in number of universities including IITs, IIMs and NITs during 11th five year plan and increase in the number of seats in existing institutions. Concrete steps need to be taken to:

Improve the overall quality of existing institutions by ensuring that all institutions conform to prescribed norms and standards and adopt a mandatory quality assurance framework.

Conduct transformative reforms in the state higher education system by creating a facilitating institutional structure, promoting autonomy in state universities and improving governance in higher educational institutions.

Ensure academic and examination reforms in the higher educational institutions.

Enable conversion of some of the universities into institutions of excellence at par with the best in the world.

Create opportunities for the states to undertake reforms in affiliating system in order to ensure that the reforms and resource requirements of affiliated colleges are adequately met.

Ensure adequate availability of quality faculty in all higher educational institutions and ensure capacity building at all levels of employment.

Improve quality in higher education by providing adequate opportunities of higher education to socially deprived communities, minorities and to combat gender inequalities.

The Government has recently launched Rashtriya Uchattar Shiksha Abhiyan (RUSA) to provide strategic funding to State higher and technical institutions, with a vision for enhancement in quality and skill based education, and to further meet these challenges.

BIBLIOGRAPHY

1. Gupta D and Gupta N. (2012) Higher Education in India: Structure, Statistics and Challenges Journal of Education and Practice. 3(2).
2. Kaul, S. (2006). Higher Education in India: seizing the opportunity. Working paper no. 179.
3. National Council of Applied Economic Research. (2005). India Science Report. Retrieved 18. 12. 2013.
4. http://www.going-global-edu.in/educationsystem.html. Retrieved 18. 12. 2013
5. http://www.dst.ac.in. Retrieved 18. 12. 2013.
6. http://sciencecongress.nic.in/html/everymans/science.php. Retrieved 18. 12. 2013.
7. http://www.ias.ac.in/academy/misc/docs/sci/edu-insa/ias.pdf. Retrieved 18. 12. 2013.
8. http://www.fairobserver.com/article/indias-21st-century-challenge-scientific-education. Retrieved 18. 12. 2013
9. http://www.mu.ac.in/rusa.pdf RUSA Presentation of Ministry of MHRD. Retrieved 28. 12. 2013

33

Institutional Planning: A milestone in a journey towards Improvement of Education

Dr. Sapna Nanda★

IP is a milestone in the journey towards the improvement of education

—E.W. Franklin

Abstract:

Quest for excellence is the most innate need of human being. The sensitization and concern of ministry of human resource development put this need of human being in the central policy framing with respect to the education. Twenty first century has posed to be a big Challenge for education due to its new implications of the present scenario. The higher education institutions at present are sufficient for GER of 19%, which is quite below the international average of 30%. Thus, the higher education of India has three pronged problem with quality, expansion and cost as the three prongs. With the launching of Rashtriya Uchchtar Shiksha Abhiyan (RUSA) in October, 2013, a new centrally sponsored scheme to bring reforms in the state higher education sector, using central funds in a strategic manner to ensure holistic planning at the state level and the enhancement of allocations to the state institutions to address the issues of equity, access and excellence in higher education. In this direction, Institutional Planning is a milestone in the journey towards the improvement of education.

Keywords: Institutional Planning, Qualitative improvement, Higher education.

Introduction

Planning is vital in every walk of life i.e. teaching, organizing, administration, business etc. It may be educational planning, industrial,

★ Assistant Professor, Govt. College of Education, Sec-20-D, Chandigarh

town and community or family. It is a major instrument in any social system. In educational administration, it is restricted to institutional planning.

Planning is a Key factor for the success of any management process followed by organization, implementation and evaluation. Planning means to get ready to decide or act upon some problem or a piece of work.

It is a goal oriented and an intelligent activity to arrive at decisions, which lead to actual course of action. If an activity is to be executed successfully, planning is must. Planning ensures:

1. Recognition of goals
2. Proper use of resources
3. Prevention of wastage, overlapping and duplication of efforts
4. Efficiency and economy
5. Definiteness and orderly execution of any enterprise.

According to **American Association of School Administrators**, Planning involves

1. Definition and classification of purposes and its scope of operation.
2. Investigation of several conditions affecting achievement of purposes.
3. Analysis and forecast of effect of possible courses of action on achievement of purpose.
4. Decision making as indicated by processes of purposes, defining, investigation and analysis.

Planning must be:

1. Flexible and adaptable
2. Consistent and stable
3. Uniform as well as reserving appropriate scope for experimentation.

The Objective of the study is to study the role of institutional planning in the improvement of education.

In educational system, it is restricted to institutional planning. However, global concern of IP is to improve the quality of education. The

Indian Education Commission (1964-66) has observed,' In view of the great need to improve the standards of education, a nation-wide programme of improvement should be developed in which conditions will be created for each institution to strive continually to achieve the best results of which it is capable. No comprehensive programme od educational development can ever put across unless it involves every educational institution and all the human efforts connected with it- its teachers, students and the local community- and unless it provides the necessary inducements to make them put in their best efforts.

The **Indian Education Commission (1964-66)** has further said," Even within its existing resources, however limited they may be, every educational institution can do a great deal more through better planning and harder work, to improve the quality of education it provides. Here, the emphasis should not be so much on physical resources, as on motivating the human agencies concerned to make their best efforts in a coordinated manner for the improvement of education, and thereby offset the shortcomings in the physical resources.

Dr. V.K.R.V. Rao, our former education minister, emphasized the importance IP for qualitative improvement in schools. He remarked, "Each institution will have to learn to plan its development on its own individual lines within the broad framework of national policy of education."

This approach of IP has been supported and promoted on priority basis by union minister of education, planning commission, NCERT and state governments.

With the increasing recognition of need of IP, there is a rising concern for its implementation. Education commission has suggested that every institution should prepare its own plan of improvement and development.

At a national seminar on IP held at Bhopal in November,1986, **Prof. M.B.Buch** remarked," A programme of improvement and development prepared by an educational institution on the basis of its felt needs and the resources available or likely to be available with a view to improve the school programme and school practices constitute a plan for an institution. It is based on the principles of optimum utilization of resources available in the school and community. The plan may be of longer or shorter duration.

Major Objectives/Purposes Of Ip:

1. Improvement of Curriculum transaction
2. Improvement of library equipment and facilities
3. Improvement of Co-curricular activities
4. Optimum utilization of existing resources
5. Harnessing community resources and goodwill to improve and develop the institution
6. Providing opportunity of student, staff and local community to join hands to improve
7. Developing creative ability of teachers
8. Recognizing the initiative of teachers
9. Exploring, locating and mobilizing all possible available resources
10. Imparting realism and concreteness to educational planning

Characteristics/ Requistics Of Good Ip

1. **Need based:** the plan is prepared on the needs of the institution as identified by students, faculty and the community.
2. **Practical:** the plan should be feasible to be carried out under local conditions with the available resources.
3. **Optimum utilization of resources:** It is based on the principle of optimum utilization of resources available with in the institution and the community.
4. **Co-operative affair:** it is a cooperative venture of the community, management, staff and the students.
5. **Goal oriented:** It is a goal oriented activity with well defined objectives.
6. **Prospective plan:** It is for future plan of action aiming at improvement.
7. **Specific plan:** it is specific for an institution. There can not be a plan for all the institutions.
8. **Improvement and development:** it aims at qualitative improvement and development.
9. **Continuously developing:** it is continuously developing and is an ongoing process.

10. **Democratic procedures:** It results into establishment of democratic procedures within the institution.
11. **Rapport with the community:** It results into a better rapport with the community.
12. **Eliminates wastage:** It prevents wastage of material and human resources.
13. **Flexible:** An institutional plan cannot be rigid.
14. **Forward looking:** It results in increased motivation on the part of teachers, students, community and the management.
15. **Conforming to national policy:** Though the plan is specific but it should be in conformity to the national policy of education.

Scope Of Ip

Everything that relates to an institution is an area of IP—**J.P.Naik.**

1. Improving the physical infrastructure
   - Provision of more amenities to pupil- drinking water, sanitary facilities, medical aid, transportation, book bank etc.
   - More and better equipment- library, reading rooms, laboratories, teaching aids, research facilities etc.
   - Maintenance of building- voluntary labour, contributions etc.
   - Providing adequate space in the institution.
2. Improvement of instruction
   - Supervised study and special coaching facilities
   - Visiting faculty from teaching fraternity as well as from outside.
   - Support to faculty development programmes like in-service training, refresher courses, summer and winter schools etc.
3. Improvement of CCA
   - Social service projects like NSS and community development projects.

- Work experience through participation in community projects
- Literary activities
- Games, sports, athletics etc.

4. Improvement of community programme
   - Literary and awareness generation programmes
   - Adult education programmes
   - Youth service activities
5. Other areas
   - Improvement of academic programme
   - Administrative area
   - Discipline
   - Teaching learning materials
   - Community relations
   - Professional growth of teachers
   - Investigation and research

Advantages Of Ip:

1. **Betterment and qualitative improvement:** teachers and head to act as planners and executors of educational improvement.
2. **Proper direction to educational planning:** IP should be in upward direction from bottom to top and involve everyone.
3. **Maximum utilization of resources:** optimum utilization of scarce resources with increasing needs and demands.
4. **National development:** educational planning must fit into overall national planning for development purposes.
5. **To encourage initiative of individual teacher:** IP encourages initiative, freedom, and creativity of teachers and motivates them for excellence.
6. **Democratization of IP:** Centralized and decentralized system
7. **Making plan task oriented, not finance oriented.**

How To Prepare An Ip:

The technical and procedural aspects of educational planning at institutional level cannot be rigidly defined or specifically laid down.

Being essentially institution- centered, it accommodates a wide range of differences in conditions and methods of operation. However, the cardinal principles of planning and techniques of implantation should identify the following stages in the institutional planning procedure:

Following are the steps of preparation of an IP

1. **Identification of the needs of school and demarcation of its lines of operation:**
   - IP should be need based.
   - Identification of problem through surveys.
   - Discuss pros and cons of each problem in staff meeting.
   - Analyze the present situation with respect to needs.
2. **Estimating resources available and resources harness-able for the improvement and development of the institution:** A survey of existing resources, scrutiny of their use and an assessment as to how much can be mobilized. Three types of resources need to be surveyed and examined
   - Resources available in the institution
   - Resources available through govt./ management/board
   - Resources available in the community.
3. **Determination of priorities and Preparation of improvement plan:** Two types: short term and long term plan. Each plan is defined in terms of :
   - Its utility for the institution
   - Its financial implications
   - Difficulties, limitations and delimitations.
   - Involvement of school population{partial/total}
   - Evaluation and follow-up
4. **Implementing the Plan:** Execute the plan
   - With the existing facilities and resources utilized to the maximum extent
   - With maximum effort through cooperation of all
   - Division of labour, where required

- Committees and sub- committees to be formed
- Time schedule to be prepared.
- Expert guidance and facilities to be sought

5. **Evaluating the project:** After completion of project, the end product/ output/ results are evaluated quantitatively and qualitatively to see whether the objectives are achieved or not. Periodical review of work and an assessment of performance will not only help in identification of problems but also help in solution of conflicts.

Defects In The Present Educational Planning:

According to **Kothari commission**," One of the major weaknesses of our planning system is that it begins at the top and hardly decends down to the institution level. Consequently, most of the institutions remain unconcerned with educational development plans at state or national level.

Its defects are as follows:

1. **It is centralized.** Top level makes plans and sends down to lower level for implementation.
2. **Teachers should be taken into confidence** otherwise they fail to catch the spirit behind the plan.
3. **Real improvement or development** of school is pushed into the background.
4. It is **rigidly uniform**. Same educational plan is followed by all institutions, irrespective of conditions or circumstances of the institutions.
5. It is **finance oriented** and not task oriented.
6. It does not take into account the **available resources** of each individual institution.
7. It does not encourage **planning at the level of institution**.

Conclusions

To conclude, it is suggested that SWOT Analysis for the tasks which need to be undertaken at Institutional level so as to enable the Institution to prepare its improvement and development plan, initiation of academic reforms, initiation of Governance reforms and the initiation of research, innovation and quality improvement. Secondly, to improve the quality of institutions and enhance existing capacities of the institutions to become dynamic, demand-driven, quality conscious, efficient and forward looking, responsive to rapid economic and technological developments occurring at local, state, national and international levels.

BIBLIOGRAPHY

1. Kandula, Srinivas R. (2009) Human Resource Management in Practice. PHI Learning Private Limited, New Delhi.
2. Sharma, O.P. and Khan, N. Modern Approach to Development of Education System in India . Modern Publishers.
3. Sodhi, T.S. and Suri, A. (2002) Management of School Education. Bawa Publications, Patiala.
4. Sodhi, T.S. and Suri, A. (1999) Issue in Education and National Development. Bawa Publications, Patiala.

How Godly is the God Particle? (A peep into the Realm of High Energy Physics)

*Dr. Sheojee Singh**

Abstract:

This paper is an attempt to understand the mystery of 'Higgs boson', the so called God particle, discovered through a series of LHC experiments at CERN, Geneva on July 4, 2012 in the simplest possible terms. The author compiles various related facts and theories in a coherent manner to make a sensible picture of the importance of this discovery for the common person. Introducing the concept of elementary particles and the Standard Model, it has been illustrated how the discovery of this god particle provides a clue to the initial stages of the origin of the universe after the Big Bang thereby attempting to solve a longstanding mystery postulated by the Standard Model. Also, it has been attempted to establish how this particle has nothing to do with religion or spirituality as such, and the popular name 'God-particle' is just the result of a co-incidence in the publication of the book by a famous physicist showing the elusive nature of this the-then postulated particle. The paper concludes with the assertion that this discovery is a milestone in the field of science and technology and a victory of human imagination, sincere collective effort and patience; and thus has a significant lesson for higher education in all disciplines.

Keywords: *Godly; God particle; Elementary particles.*

Introduction:

God-particle or the famous Higgs' boson for which the world was so excited in July, 2012 that the Swedish Academy of Sciences announced

* Assistant Professor,Govt. College of Education, Sector 20, Chandigarh

2013 Nobel Prize of Physics to Francois Englert & Peter Higgs for their 50 years old vision (for the theoretical discovery of a mechanism that contributes to our understanding of the origin of mass of subatomic particles recently confirmed through the discovery of the predicted fundamental particle) in order to complete the Standard Model of particle physics.

Now, a basic question arises as what is this Higgs Boson, which has been widely acclaimed as the clue for understanding the building of the universe? Also nicknamed as God-particle, let us find out some of its features! Let us try to answer the question: How Godly is this particle? What is the significance of this discovery for the future of science and the future of mankind's search for knowledge and for higher education as such?

Let us go a bit slow as most of us are non-physicists either by choice or by chance. But, surely we have some interest in knowing the mystery behind the so called God particle for which the sane world seemed to have lost all sanity in spending billions of dollars in global collaborative research which may not yield much fruitful advantages for the suffering humanity.

This paper has the following objectives:

i) To acquaint the reader with basic (rudimentary) idea of Elementary Particles, High Energy Physics and the Standard Model of Physics,

ii) To explain, in the simplest possible terminology, the significance of the discovery of Higgs' boson for our understanding of the origin of the universe,

iii) To explain the mystery behind the so called God particle, and explain how this God-particle has nothing directly to do with religion or spirituality as such,

iv) To discuss how the euphoria behind this so called great discovery is not the end of road for our scientific research at the frontier of high energy physics; and to establish the importance of this discovery for science, mankind and higher education in particular.

"We go about our daily lives understanding almost nothing of the world. We give little thought to the machinery that generates the sunlight that makes life possible,

to the gravity that glues us to an earth that would otherwise send us spinning off into space, or to the atoms of which we are made and on whose stability, we fundamentally depend."

Prof. Carl Sagan(Cornell University)

Elementary Particles:

A series of basic questions raised by Stephan Hawking in his book 'A Brief History of Time' begins with: Where did the universe come from, and where is it going? Did the universe have a beginning and if so what happened before then? Recent breakthroughs in physics, made possible in part by fantastic new technologies, suggest answers to some of these longstanding questions. Some day these answers may seem as obvious to us as the earth orbiting the sun. The experimental confirmation of discovery of Higgs boson is one such milestone in our journey towards a better understanding of the universe, which proves the correctness of a very important scientific theory known as Standard Model. Before we proceed further, a few words about a scientific theory will be pertinent here.

A scientific theory is just a model of the universe or a restricted part of it, and a set of rules that relate quantities in the model to the observations that we make. It exists only in our minds and does not have any other reality. A theory is a good theory if it satisfies two requirements:

1. It must accurately describe a large class of observations on the basis of a model that contains only a few arbitrary elements, and
2. It must make definite predictions about the results of future predictions.

Any physical theory is always provisional, in the sense that it is only a hypothesis, one can never prove it. Now, let us turn our attention to the prevailing theory of the constituents of matter!

Like all matter is made from atoms, all atoms are made from even smaller particles. Physicist discovered that similar to the `Periodic System of Atoms', there is a list of subatomic particles called elementary particles.

It is believed that matter – everything created in the universe by the Big Bang some 14-15 billion years ago- is made up of 12 fundamental particles (except Higgs boson, the other particles had been detected/

found earlier) and six (6) force carriers. Higgs boson gives matter its mass and holds the universe together. This picture of the constituents of matter at sub-microscopic level and its governing interactions make up the Standard Model. The standard model is the best mathematical framework that physicists have been able to construct in order to describe the building blocks of matter and the fundamental forces of nature. It is one of the biggest achievements of the 20th century physics, one of the major goals of which has been to unify the forces that are widely disparate in their strength of interaction and range of influence in a single mathematical framework.

Particles and Fields

Besides the basic particles (called fermions' after E. Fermi) of the matter, there are also the basic forces between them. We now know through various studies, four different forces (sorted by their relative strengths):

The Gravitational Force (e.g. between Sun and Earth)

The Electromagnetic Force (e.g. between electric charges and magnets)

The Weak Force (e.g.in nuclear decays like radioactivity etc.)

The Strong Force (e.g. binding the nucleons of the atom)

The constituents of the universe, according to the Standard Model, come in two categories- the field sector and the particle sector. In the field sector, we have the 12 gauge fields: the four electroweak fields that include the photon (γ, W+,W-,Z) and the eight gluon fields (G1,G2,... G8). Their quanta are all particles with one unit of the quantum attribute called 'spin' (spin 1 particles), exactly like the first and most familiar among them, the photon. All such particles having integral spin belong to the family of particles called "bosons" and obey what is called Bose Einstein statistics).

The particle sector consists of spin ½ particles belonging to the other great family of "fermions" (particles that obey Fermi Dirac statistics).

The quarks make up the nucleon and the nucleons make nuclei. Nuclei and electrons make atoms, molecules and all known matter.

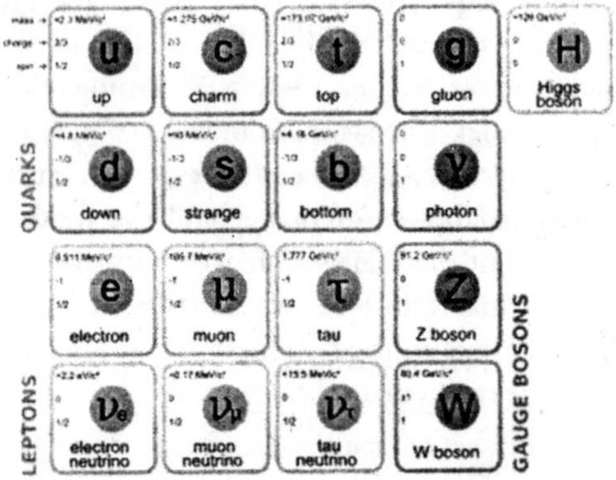

Fig.1: The Standard Model of elementary particles, with the three generations of matter, gauge bosons in the fourth column and the Higgs boson in the fifth.

The weak radioactive decays involve the neutrino. Thus, the quartet of particles consisting of a quark doublet and a lepton doublet seems to be sufficient to make up the whole universe. However, nature has chosen to repeat this quartet two more times so that there actually exists three generations of particle quartets, each consisting of a quark doublet and a lepton doublet.

One surprising result of the last 50 years of research was, that one can describe those forces with the exchange of particles. For example the **photon** is created in electromagnetic processes. We also know it as normal **light**. Those particles (called 'bosons', honouring S.N. Bose) can also be **produced** in current experiments. Up to now, gravitation can not be completely described in this way, but the theorists are working hard to achieve this goal.

What is High Energy Physics?

'High Energy Physics' (HEP) or 'Particle Physics' searches for the fundamental particles and forces which build the world around us.

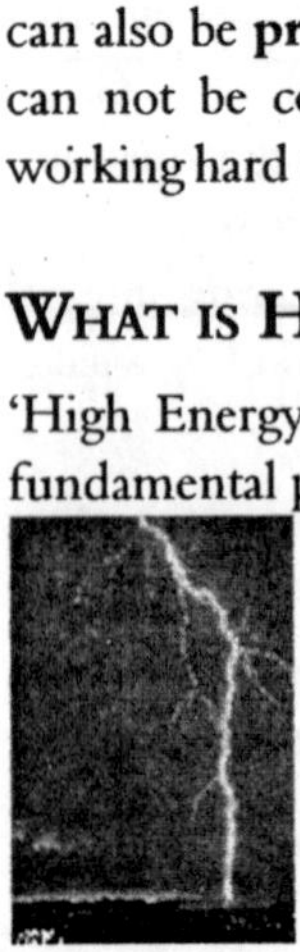

We create those particles (which are not a normal part of matter we encounter everyday) by using the famous 'Einstein Law' that relates energy and matter: $E = mc^2$. Compared to natural processes on earth, like the creation of a lightning or the energy released in a nuclear decay, the energy per particle is many magnitudes higher in such experiments. That is why this field is called 'High Energy Physics'.

Higgs Boson: The Elusive Particle:

The search for the Higgs boson, the missing key link in the standard model, has been going on for the last several decades or so. And, now finally one has got experimental results confirming the existence of this particle. On July 4, 2012, scientists of ATLAS and CMS experiments working at CERN' s Large Hadron Collider (LHC) announced the discovery of a sub-atomic particle called the Higgs boson with a mass of 125-126 GeV, which is nearly one hundred thirty times the mass of a hydrogen atom. This particle is expected to help in understanding why matter has mass which results in giving an object its weight due to gravity.

The existence of three generations of particles seems to be related to matter-antimatter asymmetry, which can solve the cosmological puzzle-how did the universe, which started as a fireball (with Big Bang) with equal proportion of matter and anti-matter, evolve into a state which has only matter?

There is a vast disparity between electromagnetism and the weak forces: one is infinite in range and the other is short-ranged. Then, how does electroweak unification cope with this breakdown of the electroweak symmetry that is intrinsic to unification? This is explained by a spontaneous breakdown of symmetry (SBS) engineered by the celebrated Higgs Mechanism, which keeps photon massless while raising the masses of W and Z to finite values. Thus, weak interaction gets a finite range. The experimental discovery of W and Z with the masses predicted by the electroweak theory in the 1980's was a great triumph of the theory.

The idea of SBS in High Energy Physics originates from the Yoichiro Nambu although he applied it in a different context. But, the stumbling block was the Goldstone theorem, which predicted the existence of a massless spin zero boson as the consequence of the SBS and prevented the application of SBS to construct any physically relevant theory, since such a massless particle is not seen. Thus, apparently, one has to choose between the devil (massless W boson) and the deep sea (massless spin zero boson).

It was Peter W. Higgs, who in 1964, showed that this is not correct. He showed that there is no Goldstone theorem if the symmetry that is broken is gauge symmetry. The devil drinks up the deep sea and comes out as a regular massive spin one gauge boson. No massless spin zero boson is left. This is called the Higgs mechanism.

The Higgs mechanism postulates the existence of an all-pervading field called the Higgs field and this field, which gives mass to W and Z, also gives mass to all the fermions of the particle sector, except to the neutrinos. Thus, in particular, the masses of the quarks and the electron come from the Higgs field.

But there is ***an important byproduct of the Higgs mechanism:*** a massive spin zero boson, called the Higgs boson, must exist as a relic of the original Higgs field. High energy physicists searching for it in all the earlier particle accelerators had failed to find it. In order for the Standard Model of leptons and quarks to be mathematically consistent, the Scottish physicist Peter Higgs showed that a field, now called the Higgs field, must exist everywhere in space. The Higgs field turned out to have an additional significance: by interacting with it, particles acquire their characteristic masses. The stronger the interaction, the greater the mass. As with other fields, a particle- here the Higgs boson- mediates the action of the Higgs field.

The Higgs particle is a massive scalar elementary particle theorized by Robert Brout, François Englert, Peter Higgs, Gerald Guralnik, C. R. Hagen, and Tom Kibble in 1964 and is a key building block in the Standard Model. It has no intrinsic spin, and for that reason it is classified as a boson (like the gauge bosons, which have integral spin).

The Higgs boson plays a unique role in the Standard Model, by explaining why the other elementary particles, except the photon and gluon, are massive. In particular, the Higgs boson would explain why the photon has no mass, while the W and Z bosons are very heavy. Elementary particle masses, and the differences between electromagnetism (mediated by the photon) and the weak force (mediated by the W and Z bosons), are critical to many aspects of the structure of microscopic (and hence macroscopic) matter. In electroweak theory, the Higgs boson generates the masses of the leptons (electron, muon, and tau) and quarks. As the Higgs boson is massive, it must interact with itself.

Because the Higgs boson is a very massive (relatively speaking) particle and also decays almost immediately when created, only a very high-energy particle accelerator can observe and record it. Experiments to confirm and determine the nature of the Higgs boson using the Large Hadron Collider (LHC) at CERN began in early 2010, and were performed at Fermilab's Tevatron until its closure in late 2011. Mathematical consistency of the Standard Model requires that any mechanism capable of generating the masses of elementary particles become visible at energies above 1.4 TeV therefore, the LHC (designed to collide two 7 to 8 TeV proton beams) was built to answer the question of whether the Higgs boson actually exists.

On 4 July 2012, the two main experiments at the LHC (ATLAS and CMS) both reported independently that they found a new particle with a mass of about 125 GeV/c^2 (about 133 proton masses, on the order of 10−25 kg), which is "consistent with the Higgs boson." Although it has several properties similar to the predicted "simplest" Higgs, they acknowledged that further work would be needed to conclude that it is indeed the Higgs boson, and exactly which version of the Standard Model Higgs is best supported if confirmed. On 14 March 2013 the Higgs Boson was tentatively confirmed to exist. The discovery comes at a cost of around $13.25 billion to the world community.

Although, it seems a very important milestone in the advancement of our knowledge and it has aided the development of serviceable stuff like the world-wide-web, medical imaging and Cloud Computing, as quantum mechanics has a huge quantum of solaces, the transistors, lasers, PC's etc, only the future will prove its further value. The collaborative efforts of scientists all over the globe resulted in this fantastic discovery and it has had huge advantages for the progress of higher education and research, it promises to be a boon for furthering human imagination in pursuit of knowledge.

Why is it called God particle?

The 1988 Nobel laureate physicist, Leon Lederman unwittingly gave the Higgs boson what may be its most-disliked descriptor with the title of his book, 'The God Particle' (***The God Particle:*** If the Universe is the Answer, what is the Question?). Lederman likes to joke that he actually wanted to call the Higgs boson the "goddamn particle" because it had been so darned difficult to find. His manuscript of the book was revised by the publisher and the title insisted by the publisher became the nickname of the elusive particle. The nickname makes for the attention-grabbing headlines, but it also makes most particle physicists cringe (have a feeling of dislike).

So, physicists have welcomed the announcement on July 4, 2012 that the Higgs boson has been sighted finally at a mass of 125 GeV at the LHC at CERN, Geneva.

In the past four decades, experiments have succeeded in confirming every component of the full Standard Model with three generations of fermions. The Higgs boson was the only missing piece. With its discovery, the Standard Model has emerged as the standard theory to describe nature. This is a great scientific achievement.

Conclusions

Thus, it can be safely concluded from the discussion that the Higgs boson or the so called God particle is one of the important stages in our understanding of how this universe was created; and is not the magic particle to understand the whole of the universe as comes the signal from the popular impression of the coverage given to this discovery in the news. This particle is neither Godly nor mystic; rather it is an important milestone in the long journey of scientific research for our better understanding of the universe at basic level.

Bibliography

1. Ganguly, S.N.(2013): Higgs boson-the success story of the Standard Model; Bulletin IAPT, 5(1), Jan-Feb.2013, p 24-25;
2. Ramdas (2012): God Particle; Bhawan's Journal, 59(10), Dec.31, 2012, p. 87.
3. www.cern.ch; CERN stands for Conseil Europeen pour la Recherche Nucleaire, the European Organization for Nuclear Research, the world's largest particle physics centre based in Geneva. India has an observer status at CERN; (retrieved on 15th Dec.2013.)

4. Venkataraman, G.(2001): the Big and the Small-Journey into the Microcosm (The Story of Elementary Particles); Universities Press, Hyderabad, p.208-9.
5. Khanna, M.P.(1999): Introduction to Particle Physics; Prentice Hall of India Pvt. Ltd., New Delhi, p 215, 219.
6. Ramchandran R.(2012):The Higgs hunt, Frontline, July 14-27, 2012., p 7-8.
7. Rajasekaran, G. (2012): The Long Journey, Frontline, July 14-27, 2012, p 124-125.
8. Hawking, S.(11989): A Brief History of Time; Bantam Books,, London, p.67, 74-75;
9. Beiser, A. (1995): Concepts of Modern Physics, Tata Mc Graw Hill, New Delhi; p 499-500.

Mother Tongue Interference & Related Issues in Teaching English in Higher Education

*Dr. Shweta Ahuja**

Abstract

The changing times have witnessed the growing importance of English language in all walks of life. The use of the English words in everyday conversation is an ample proof of that. A very important reason for regarding English as a world language is that the world's knowledge is enshrined in English. Language learning is a natural process for the natives but for the students of other languages, conscious efforts are required to learn a foreign language. Language acquisition is both a process of analogy and application, nature and nurture. The present paper enlists some of the problems faced by Indian students in learning English as a second language. The paper also tries to deliberate some of the strategies which can help the students and would be effective in dealing with the problem. If these problems are tackled, the standard of students will certainly improve and the knowledge of English would be used for higher legal, technical and scientific education and research in all branches of learning. The students who are undergoing training at various institutions will be admitted to certain vocations when they have access to the treasures of knowledge, have the ability to read with facility and understanding the works of English writers.

Keywords: *English language;Natural process; treasures of knowledge.*

Introduction

It is a known fact that English plays an important role in India today. It is important for a person who wants to excel in any stream of human

* Assistant Professor,D.A.V. College(Lahore), Ambala City

activity to know, to be able to read and write in English. As such English is taught as a compulsory subject in higher education. This has created problems for Indian students where the subject is taught at a very late stage in some of the schools. Besides this, the students are well versed in their mother tongue. Its very obvious that these students experience problems in learning English as a second language and they lag behind their counterparts who are learning English from primary levels. When these students reach the level of higher education the gravity of the problem increases manifold.

The Objectives of this study are:

1. To discuss the issue of mother tongue interference and difficulties of the learners while learning English as a second language.
2. To deal with other problems in teaching English in higher education.

English is considered as the most important language having communicative and educative value. English symbolizes in Indian minds, better education, better culture and higher intellect. It takes up the role of an international language, as a window to the outside world, as a library and as a link language both in India and abroad, the role of English cannot be undermined. The virtuosity and towering status of English has been fathomed by a scholar in these words in *Effective Methods of Teaching English*, "English is our major window on the world. It provides us distilled essence of modern knowledge in all fields of human activity." English has co-existed in the Indian subcontinent alongside thousands of local languages but for the vast majority, it remains the second language. English spoken by such speakers is heavily influenced by speech patterns of their ethnic language. Consequently, different set of pronunciations and speech patterns are visible.

Language is used for expressing our thoughts and ideas by modulating the sounds. It is used for communicative purpose to interact at various levels such as personal, social and intellectual. Language is a system related with sounds, words and structures where articulation is required to pronounce the words. It has its own system of rules which should be followed to understand it.

First language or the mother tongue is the language by which the child makes an acquaintance with everything with which he wants to communicate. This is a natural process. The language skills listening and speaking are learnt at home and then child is sent to school for learning other skills such as reading and writing of the language. When a child learns his mother tongue, there is no hindrance from any other language in the process but when he tries to learn a new language, the habits of his mother tongue conflict with those of foreign language. Mother tongue is learnt after birth but the process of second language acquisition which is known as foreign tongue is quite different. It is an artificial process which needs training and practice. When a child learns the mother tongue his mind is raw and clean so he learns the mother tongue easily by imitating others. When he learns the second language i.e. English he faces difficulties of accepting the rules which is distinct from the rules imbibed by him within his mother tongue. The differences in the sounds, stress, rhythm and intonation makes it difficult for a child to acquire correct English pronunciation and understanding. This becomes a problem area for child. If the problem is checked at a proper time it can be minimized. Otherwise the difficulty in comprehending and speaking English can affect the students in higher classes and consequently in later life activities. The students from the rural areas especially encounter this problem as they have different backgrounds and different set of conditions to face. Their speech is highly infused by their regional dialects which is exhibited in their pronunciation and speech which needs to be checked.

The scenario at the college level is entirely different. Students find themselves unable to express themselves in English. They don't know proper pronunciation, spellings and grammatical structure. They don't have the idea of the proper sentence structure. Their sole objective is to clear the exams. They don't realize the importance of learning English as a language. They opt for the cramming method. Such an approach is not useful as it only helps them to pass the exams but their understanding of the subject is poor.

The problem of declining standards of English is clearly visible. The aims of English education and teaching are certainly high but there is a dearth of the means to realise those aims. The Indian policy makers have forgotten that English is not the mother tongue of Indians. They do not realise the hindrances and problems which Indians have to face in acquiring a new language. The worth of English as an international language is already known. We Indians are trying to imbibe the rich legacy which has been bestowed to us. University syllabi doesn't specify the present objectives of teaching English. Those who prescribe the syllabi try to raise the standard of teaching and understanding English and prescribe difficult works but they forget the handicaps of Indian students. Books often describe and reflect English life and culture but are less appreciated and understood by students. Books are beyond the comprehension of the students and create a distaste for reading English. As a result faulty spellings and incorrect sentences are markedly visible. Grammatical errors can be found in simple sentences. The inapt use of sms language among students is very high. The shortened forms of the words are largely used like plz, bcoz and in addition contracted words are widely used like mst, 2morrow, 2day etc which has aggravated the problem. At times, the words used in mother tongue are written in English like home-ghar, ration-saman etc. V.K. Gokak, a scholar in his book *English in India: Its Present and Future* has summed up the attitude of people towards English as follows:

The English language has lined India with the outside world, outside to India from India to the world. We are blessed with the two way traffic that English has afforded us. We have paid a heavy price in the past for this privilege. But in our indignation over the price that has been paid, let us not throw away the privilege that is already ours.

There are some people who oppose the compulsory study of English. They are of the opinion that English is a difficult language and a majority of students fail in different exams because of their failure in English. The problem can be tackled not by discarding English but by creating the interest and motivation among the students. Students have a problem learning English as the students have very little knowledge about the rules. The students don't comprehend the importance of English as a medium of instruction. They lack the confidence to speak in English. Their expression in the language is weak. They have been taught English through Translation method. This method makes them dependent on mother tongue. During the time of exams, they memorise the expected questions but they can't even write a single sentence on their own. While writing the answers, they rely on the readily available material from the help books. The output is obvious and the standard deteriorates.

At this stage, the aims of teaching of teaching English have to be understood. The main aim of teaching English should be to concentrate on the fundamental skills of the language ability of the students that is, listening, speaking, reading and writing. It is the responsibility of the teacher to decide, how and when to teach a particular topic. The objectives of teaching should be practical and in keeping with the standard of the students. The orderly presentation of language to students is influenced by several factors. The teacher is to keep in mind the age of the student, his native language, his cultural background and his previous experience with English.

At times, it has been observed there is slackness on the part of the teachers. The teacher of English is incompetent to realise the need for significance of English in the new perspective. They fail to revise their aims in the new setting and also to teach English most effectively within a short time. The teachers in the colleges do not keep themselves abreast of the latest happenings in the fields of linguistics and theories of learning and teaching, without which they cannot teach effectively. Even, in the professional courses, the teaching of English is an important part of the curriculum but it is a common practice that whatever teacher gains towards the completion of their course or as an educational ability for seeking a job, it becomes stagnated. The process of teaching is not updated even after the passing of many years.

The Indian examination system is faulty. In this pattern of question settings, it is easy to predict what type of questions can be asked and which books to read. The students only memorise the important questions. Students are not able to develop the power of written and oral expression in a classroom situation. The hackneyed, stereotyped and traditional pattern of exams aims at learning of English not as a language but as a subject. The number of students in the classes everywhere is considerably large and the students participation in the class is difficult to manage. The ratio of the students versus teacher is not proportional. As there is shortage of time and the teachers have to rush in to complete the syllabus on time, there is little scope of interaction with the students. This way the students who are weak and have to be supervised for their disabilities are neglected.

The methods and techniques employed by the teachers are not up to mark. The activities like role play, play way, dramatisation in the class are ignored. The teacher delivers through lecture method. There is insufficient provision of audio-visual aids in the classrooms. As such the infrastructure of the institutions is weak. The students learn better by the techniques which use questions, illustrations and simple practice drills.

Motivation is the force which determines how the learner embarks on a task, how much energy he devotes to it and how long he preserves it. It demands individual drive, need for achievement and success, desire and curiosity on the part of the students. Lack of creativity is also been observed in the students. Power of self expression should be given due consideration. The expression in essay writing, letter writing and précis should be given importance. Students should be given guidance to improve their expression.

Another important problem in English language teaching is that English is pronounced in a different way from almost all other languages of the world. Every region of the world wherever English is spoken has a different accent. People who are not used to these accents find it difficult to understand English. Even a south Indian has a different accent from a North Indian. Besides that, there is British English, American English and other models to follow. Indians are confused out by varieties which English has to offer.

Then, there is the problem of correlation of English with other subjects and life. English has to be related with other subject like history, geography, sociology etc, so that students realise the importance and utility of English in real life situations. The teachers are not relating the subject with other streams not providing enough examples or relating it with present situations. Had they done it, the poetical interpretation of different geographical locations, how the writers have discussed the social lives of their times and how they all are relevant today, would have made the difference and made the study more interesting.

CONCLUSIONS

Various sorts of solutions can be provided to deal with the problems of English language teaching A systematic approach has to be followed. The teachers should aim at teaching knowledge skills for good listening, speaking, reading and writing. Some ways to keep students enjoy their language activities and building their confidence should be followed.

a. Practice and drill should be given from the grass root level i.e. the primary classes. Grammatical rules and concepts should be made clear.

b. To tackle the problem of vocabulary in the students, productive and receptive use of words should be kept in mind. The students should be made to learn simple words. This will help them in inculcating a habit of learning new words in them.

c. English language should be taught in the language lab for proper pronunciation and mother tongue interference where students can practice through techniques.

d. Self study and self assessment programmes to be suggested. Group discussions, debates, speech competitions, seminars should be organised frequently.

e. Different methods and techniques of teaching English should be employed. Oral method, audio lingual approach should be practised to improve the speech and pronunciation of students.

f. Improvements in the teaching facilities should be made where teachers have the liberty to exercise their will to choose the appropriate method. They should not be restricted by the time limit and pressure of syllabus.

g. Regular tests and checks have to monitored.

Improvements in education system have to be carried out. All sorts of barriers in language communication should be discarded to enhance the progress. It is said that the interference of mother tongue in acquiring a second language continues throughout the life but it can be certainly minimised by constant practice and effort. The inter-disciplinary relation of teaching and learning can solve the problem if we concentrate on the causes of the problems which affect the performance of students.

Bibliography

1. Bhandari, Supriya. Problems of Teaching English at College Level in India. 24th May 2009. <http://www.boloji.com/index.cfm.

2. Goodman, W.R. "Place of English in India." English Literature for Competitive Examinations. Delhi:Doaba Pbs.2001.

3. Gokak. V.K. English in India: Its Present and Future. Bombay: Asia Publishing House,1984.

4. Hanumantharao, Chirivella. "Teaching English language : Problems and Remedies." Indian

5. Streams Research Journal.Vol.1,May2011.eng.<http:// www. isrjinet/May/ 2011/English_Teaching_Language.aspx.

6. Sethi, J., and P.V. Dhamija. A Course in Phonetics and Spoken English. New Delhi: Prentice

7. Hall of India, 2001

8. Tyagi, R. A. Effective Methods of Teaching English. New Delhi: Alpha Pbs.2006.

36

Higher Education in Life Sciences in India: Challenges, Scope and Direction

Dr Sonali Guleria*

Abstract

Scientific research in our country continues to lag behind and we need to considerably improve our research capabilities and then only we would be able to improve our nation's competitiveness. The research and innovation capabilities can be improved by improving the standard of higher education in our country. However, the current higher education system of our country especially in the field of life sciences has many issues of concern, like financing and management including access, equity and relevance, quality of higher education together with the assessment of institutions and their accreditation. The decline in enrolment in life science courses over last few years is also a matter of concern. These maladies should be rectified and a number of steps should be taken to improve higher education system of our country. Higher education should have an excellent teaching and learning experience for the students whereby they are informed by up-to-date research and facilitated by a high-quality learning environment, with state-of-the-art learning resources, such as libraries, laboratories, and e-learning facilities. A number of steps have been initiated by our government to improve upon higher education and the future looks promising.

Key words: *Life sciences; higher education; information and communication technology; innovation; research*

* Assistant Professor,Department of Botany, DAV College, Sec-10, Chandigarh

Introduction

Despite the impressive economic growth, scientific research in our country continues to lag behind and we need to considerably improve our research capabilities. Our first prime minister had aptly stated that the "science alone can solve the problems of hunger and poverty and the future belongs to science and those who make friends with science". In the current global scenario, the only way to improve the nation's competitiveness is through better science and technical education and flourishing scientific research, technological development and innovation.

The research and innovation capabilities can be improved by improving the standard of higher education in our country. The Indian higher education system is one of the largest systems of higher education in the World and also boasts of a large number of degree awarding institutions and colleges. However, the current higher education system as a whole has many issues of concern at present, like financing and management including access, equity and relevance, quality of higher education together with the assessment of institutions and their accreditation. The current higher education system produces graduates that are unemployable, though there are mounting skill shortages in a number of sectors. The standards of academic research are also low and declining.

This malady in higher education is even more pronounced in the field of life sciences. The contribution in the field of life sciences by India is very small considering the population of our country and the research in this field is being done only by few selected universities. Moreover, more stress has been laid in the fields of physics, math, and engineering and therefore India has produced more internationally recognized scientists in these fields compared to life sciences. In contrast to research in the field of physics and chemistry that was initiated in our country in middle of 19th century, the modern biological research started much later. The decline in enrolment in life science courses over last few years is also a matter of concern. Also, world-class institutions in India are mainly limited with most of the Indian colleges and universities lacking high-end research facilities.

India has two distinct advantages as compared to the rest of the world: an enormous domestic market and a large talent pool. To be a world leader India needs to promote home-grown innovation and to achieve this goal, develop a higher education system of highest quality. If this is not done, this advantage will be lost and India will lag behind the other countries.

The Objectives of this study is to enumerate the challenges and issues facing the higher education in field of life sciences in our country and look at possible measures needed to improve the standards of higher education and research.

CHALLENGES IN HIGHER EDUCATION IN LIFE SCIENCES

The field of life sciences has enormous challenges and the potential of this field are enormous like food supply and natural resources, microbial lifestyles and the microbial metagenome, stem cells, infectious diseases, regulations, systems biology, synthetic biology and education. Research in the Life Sciences can contribute practical solutions to crucial societal problems and this can be achieved by improving higher education standards and quality.

The first non-professional degree (viz., B.Sc.) by itself is, unlike professional degrees, of not much value or societal attractiveness unless it is of educationally good quality, obtained in a lively research environment, and is supplemented by a professional edge (e.g., additional skill building that adds to employability) or research experience.

Another important problem is the inadequate funding and as the demand far exceeds the supply, and therefore the money is used only for the most basic education and scanty budget is available for innovative programs and ideas. Shrinking state budgets with increasing private funding leading on to commercialization of higher education has further compounded the problem. Other important concerns are:

- ❖ Over-centralization, lack of autonomy and accountability
- ❖ Access to education, removal of gender and regional disparities as currently there is large rural-urban and gender divide. The institutions of higher education located in rural and socio-economic backward areas are lacking in the implementation of best practices in higher education and quality.

- • High rate of dropouts and failures
- Poor quality of production and lack of relevance
- Poor exposure to research and innovation in current undergraduate courses: The college biology teachers have little, if any, experience in scientific research. As a result, college undergraduates learn facts from textbooks and do not understand the excitement of research and are not taught the latest scientific developments. Being physically separated from research Institutes and Universities, college students also are not exposed to the leading scientists in India. The separation of teaching and research contrasts the situation at top US universities, where undergraduates are taught by and can do research internships with the best scientists in the world. A growing and increasingly popular track in colleges is a BSc Biotechnology degree, but sadly, most graduating students are ill prepared for jobs in the biotechnology industry or for graduate-level education.
- Lack of information and communication technology (ICT) infrastructure as well as low technology/people readiness
- Poor quality of digital content, especially in regional languages
- Lack of qualified faculty, limited funding for research as well as poor linkages between academic institutions and industry/ Government R&D labs
- Multiplicity of regulators with overlapping roles

Improvement of higher education in life sciences

1. Use of information technology in higher education: The use of IT tools in teaching will make the learning process simple and affordable.
2. Increase funding in higher education: Encourage private sector investment in education through the development of innovative public private partnership models. Provide tax incentives and simplify norms to attract private investments. The introduction of performance based funding by Government and rationalization of tuition fees structures can also improve research. Enhancing student financial support should be done for maintaining equity in the system

3. Incentivize research in universities, while creating an enabling environment in terms of lesser teaching hours for researchers, greater budgets and access to better infrastructure. Also increase the number and quality of doctoral students through the launch of innovative programs, provision of attractive fellowships and enhanced industry collaboration
4. Create a single independent agency for regulating higher education and simplify the regulatory framework. This will help in providing a conducive environment for the entry & growth of a large number of high quality higher education institutes.
5. Igniting bright young minds at school level to pursue life sciences as a career
6. All students must have access to teaching that has been kept up to date and relevant through scholarship, research and professional development
7. Produce and Retain More Graduate Students with Interdisciplinary Training: Need to produce and retain more young life scientists who have training in business, management, information technology and regulatory affairs.
8. Include research as a key criteria for faculty promotion and compensation, setting easily measurable targets such as publications in high quality journals. Provide fast track growth to the most promising researchers in government universities
9. Create 'research awards', which selects leading researchers amongst the faculty of both public and private sector education institutions through a fair and transparent process. These researchers should be provided with significant financial assistance to take their research forward
10. Examine possibility of relocating R&D institutes to university campuses, while ensuring all further infrastructure expansion in Government R&D institutes is done at university campuses
11. Invest in creating a strong ICT backbone linking all Indian universities and providing a large digital repository of journals and publications to researchers across a range of institutes.
12. All research and scholarship in higher education institutions should enhance the quality of undergraduate and postgraduate

teaching. The structure and design of PhD programmes should incorporate generic skills and be formulated with direct engagement with employers.

13. Develop closer collaborations between biology and its extensive physical science enterprise

Changes Initiated by the Government

- The setting up of Central Universities, with high quality of infrastructure for teaching and research
- Setting up Indian Institutes of Technology and Indian Institutes of Management, which are leaders in Technical and Management Education in the country
- Opening up the Professional Education Sector to large scale private investment and permitting the investors cost recovery from student fees
- Permitting some deemed Universities to open campuses both in other states and abroad
- A number of innovative schemes have also been in operation in the Higher Education sector, some promoted by the University Grants Commission, others by the Technical education division of the Ministry of Human Resource development and All India Council Of Technical Education, and yet others by Indian Council of Agricultural research and several other Departments of the Central Government dealing with Science and Technology
- Setting up of the Indian Institutes of Science Education and Research (IISERs) and their five-year combined bachelor's/ master's programs for training in science education and research, admitting a relatively small, select class

Conclusions

Higher education should have an excellent teaching and learning experience for the students whereby they are informed by up-to-date research and facilitated by a high-quality learning environment, with state-of-the-art learning resources, such as libraries, laboratories, and e-learning facilities. The roles of teaching and research should be balanced and this should be reflected in resource allocation, in promotion criteria, and in the metrics used to assess performance at individual, institution and system level. In the decades ahead, higher education will play a central role in making our country recognised for innovation, competitive enterprise and continuing academic excellence and this is more so true for the field of life sciences.

Bibliography

1. Altbach, Philip G. (2006) The Private Higher Education Revolution: An Introduction. University News. January 2-8, 2006. Vol. 44 No.01.
2. Agarwal, Pawan (2006) Higher Education in India: The Need for Change (ICIER Working Paper No. 180). New Delhi: Indian Council for Research on International Economic Relations, (http://www.icrier.org/publication/ working_papers_180.html)
3. Carl Dahlman and Anuja Utz, (2005) India and the Knowledge Economy: Leveraging Strengths and Opportunities (World Bank Report No.31267-IN),Washington DC: W. Bank)
4. Sanat Kaul, Higher Education in India: Seizing the Opportunity (ICIER Working Paper No. 179). New Delhi: Indian Council for Research on International Economic Relations, May 2006 (http:// www.icrier.org /pdf/WP_179.pdf) available on 25.1.2011
5. Higher Education in India: Issues, Concerns and New Directions http://www.ugc.ac.in/pub/heindia.pdf.
6. Higher education in India and Yashpal Committee recommendations http://www.jnu.ac.in/Yash_Pal_Committee. pdf.April 18, 2009, available on 25.1.2011
7. All India survey on higher education. Main Report 2010-11. Available on http://aishe.nic.in/aishe/reports
8. National Knowledge Commission, Report to the Nation 2006. New Delhi: National Knowledge Commission, 2007 (cited as NKC 2007) (http://knowledgecommission. gov.in/report2006/ default.asp)
9. Jandhyala B.G. Tilak, Absence of Policy and Perspective in Higher Education. Economic and Political Weekly Vol. 39, No.

21 (May 22, 2004), 2159-2164 (http://www. epw.org.in/epw/uploads/articles/7650.pdf)

10. Chatterjee, Jayanta, How to improve India's higher education and research quality? http://www.nature.com/ 04 November 2008

11. Singh JD. Higher Education in India: Issues, Challenges and Suggestions. http://www.gvctesangaria. org/websiteimg/publications/jdarticle.pdf

12. Joshi S. Sustainable Development of the Higher Education Sector in India for Catalyzing Services-Driven Growth. Working papers 2012/01, Maastricht School of Management. http://ideas. repec.org/p/msm/wpaper/ 20 12-01.html

37

Innovative Teaching Methods to Enhance English language learning: Practical Steps

Dr. Sunita*

Abstract

English has become a global language. A deficiency in this language may result in hurdles in one's personal and professional growth. In India it is mostly taught as a second language. But it has been found that in schools and colleges' students consider it as a subject and not as a language. Our present educational system also focuses more and more on the students' writing skills and not on the interactive and communicative aspect which is the chief feature of any language. To enhance their English language learning, four skills i. e. reading, writing, listening and speaking need to be equally emphasized. The present paper deals with the problems or reasons which impede this enhancement and how by taking a few practical steps to make language teaching learner centered, the desired results can be obtained.

Keywords: *Four skills (i.e. reading, writing, listening and speaking), enhancement of learning, communicative competence, innovations.*

Introduction

English has unmistakably been proclaimed as Lingua Franca of the world. In India it occupies a prestigious position as it is used by Indians as a link language to communicate with people from India and all over the world. Acquisition of English language as a skill has become almost a necessary evil with the phenomenon of globalization. It has become a 'Must' to get access to the world of science and technology,

* Assistant Professor, PGGCG, Sector 42, Chandigarh

to get jobs and to promote business interests. It is a pre-requisite for success and advancement in career. As such there is a shift in our aims and objectives of learning English; the primary aim being to interact and communicate effectively. In India it is primarily being taught in schools and colleges as a foreign or second language. But unfortunately years of English language and literature teaching has not been able to bring expected results. And teaching of English language in Indian classrooms is still a challenge.

The objective of this paper is to understand the reasons behind this failure of teaching of English particularly to the students who come from rural or semi urban areas of Panjab in India in spite of the great efforts put in. The study also aims at suggesting some innovations in teaching methods to enhance the learning of English language at undergraduate level.

Present Scenario: Today though the teaching of English language begins relatively at an early stage but even after studying it for 14-15 years ,students' language proficiency is not up to the mark. This is especially in the case of students coming from rural or semi urban areas. Sometimes they don't have any idea of proper sentence structure. This specimen makes the picture clear.

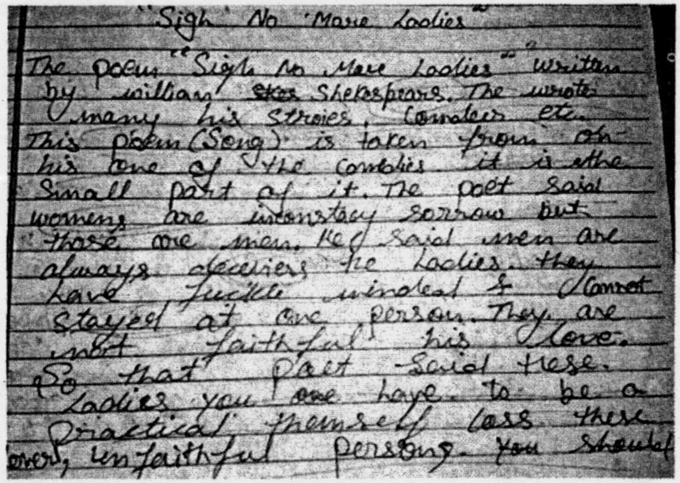

"Sigh" No "More Ladies"

The poem "Sigh No More Ladies" written by william Skes Shekespears. The wrote many his Stroies, Comdeis etc. This poem (Song) is taken from on his one of the comdies it is othe small part of it. The poet said womens are inconstacy sorrow but those are men. he said men are always deceivers he ladies. they have fickle windeal & connot stayed at one person. They are not faithful his love. So that poet said these ladies you one have to be a practical themself loss these lovers, unfaithful persons. You should

Teaching such students is very challenging for teachers also. There are some evident reasons for this scenario.

REASONS FOR THE PRESENT SCENARIO:

- **Grammar Translation method:** This method makes the students dependent on their mother tongue. As a result they don't have sufficient vocabulary of English words and there is a lack of spontaneity of expression.
- **Overcrowded Classes:** Most of the teachers have this grievance that they cannot pay individual attention to the students. If a language teacher has to teach a class of 100 or in some cases more than 100 students, how can the teacher justify? In a language classroom each student has his /her special needs and in overcrowded classes it becomes difficult for the teachers to cater to their individual needs.
- **Faulty Evaluation:** Where students are evaluated only on the basis of writing skill. They hardly take any pains to go through the texts even. They just mug up from the cheap help books and vomit out in the exam. They merely pass the subject and never learn the language. Teachers are more concerned about the results only. As a result they evaluate the answer sheets so leniently that a student who hardly knows anything about the language, easily gets through.
- **Supremacy of Literature:** Language is taught through poems, plays and novels. The area of learning remains limited to text books only. The students often find the contents of the text books uninteresting. Moreover students having no command over language are not able to appreciate literature also.
- **Teaching Confined To Syllabus only:** Teachers are in a hurry to complete the syllabus. They are hardly left with any time for the language activities. Due to this constraint the enthusiasm of the teacher is dampened.
- **Apathy on the Part of Students:** Students don't have a choice and study English language under compulsion. Majority of the students show lack of interest. Mother tongue interference and phobia of using rules of grammar de-motivate them so far as English language learning is concerned.
- **Lack of Teacher Training Programmes:** Most of the training programmes focus on literature only and nothing is done to equip the teachers in language.

But teaching of English in classrooms can be made more meaningful provided the teacher has the willingness, enthusiasm, patience and interest to make his or her class interesting. With some innovations in his teaching methods he can kindle the spark of learning in his students. Teachers can provide ample opportunities to practice language in the classroom as well as outside the classroom. No doubt the teacher plays pivotal role but certain modifications in the system also are required.

Innovations in Methods To Teach English Language:

(i) **Communicative Competence Involving 4 Skills to Be Emphasized:**

How To Develop Reading Skills: Students should be encouraged to read good books and then talk about them in the class. They should be encouraged to go to the library. They can be asked to read the text in the class. Reading competitions should be there. To encourage the students the teacher can give small prizes from his own pocket. This will inspire the students a lot. All this will lead to their reading fluency and an increase in their vocabulary.

Writing Skills: Creative writing needs to be promoted. They can be given some situations to make appropriate sentences e.g. they can be taken to college lawns and asked to write a paragraph on it. Later on they will speak out and share these sentences in the class.

Listening Skills: Students should be asked to listen to news bulletins on T.V. Teacher can record certain bulletins and debates from T.V and can make them listen in the class. Audio tapes by native speakers of language are very effective in improving the listening skill.

Speaking Skills: English language environment is to be created. Teachers should speak simple English as much as possible and should encourage students to respond in simple short sentences. Group discussions on current topics and various language games can also enhance this skill.

(ii) **Comprehensive Assessment:** Assessment should be made continuous and comprehensive. Only one annual exam is not sufficient. Initially the students should be motivated. When they know that they will be assessed continuously, gradually they will start taking interest in language learning.

(iii) **Use Of Dictionary:** It can go a long way to enhance their language learning. It inculcates in them a habit of learning new words and enhancement of vocabulary automatically leads to better and spontaneous expression. Students should be asked to find 5 new words in the newspaper daily and then they have to look up those words in the dictionary. Next day in the class they have to speak out these words so that others may also note down. Then they should be encouraged to make these words a part of their own vocabulary by using them again and again.

(iv) **Presentations and practical Assignments:** Though in Functional English Students are given presentations and practical assignments but in compulsory English there is no such practice. These assignments can be situational or based on self study.

(v) **Use of multimedia:** Use of mass media can make the teaching and learning of language interesting. A lot of language practices can be given to the students through mass media.

(vi) **Newspapers:** They are very easy to use. They can be used for developing reading comprehension, critical and writing skills.

(vii) **Radio:** A lot of radio programmes can contribute to language learning. It can help the students to improve their pronunciation, stress, intonation and pitch of voice.

(viii) **Movies:** As we know that task based teaching always aims to create a need and a desire to learn and use language. Movies are a step towards that. Today they are an indispensable part of the young people's lives. They can increase their visual and critical awareness. Students can be shown various English movies (Initially with sub-titles) depending on their age and interest. After watching students can be asked to comment on various things. Their experiences and reactions are very important. Group discussions in small groups can also be held. They can be asked to write down newly heard words and expressions.

(ix) **Power Point Presentations:** These can help the students to speak freely and have an eye contact which makes them confident. They can be used by teachers as well as by students.

It is agreed that sometimes it is difficult to bring multimedia in the classroom. Moreover no doubt this teaching will break the monotony of the class and stimulate the enthusiasm of the students but it cannot take the place of a teacher.

(x) **Grammar to Be Taught Inductively:** Students should be given examples first. Then they should be asked to apply the rules. This will ensure the correct use of language by students. If a teacher wants to tell 'what is a noun', students can be asked to take a look around the room and name the different things. Then classification can be there accordingly. The teacher's discretion can teach the students other parts of speech also in a very different and novel way.

(xi) **Lesser Syllabus:** Most of the times teachers have to make the basics clear to the students even at college level. At the same time they are in a hurry to complete the syllabus also. They cannot find time for task based teaching. This problem can be solved if syllabus is not that much.

(xii) **Revision of Syllabus:** Syllabus should be revised after a period of time. Feed back and suggestions from the concerned teachers should definitely be taken. This should be ensured whether the present curriculum is suitable for the students to achieve their goals.

(xi) **More Stress on Language Than Literature:** Once they learn language ,they can appreciate literature also. Literature should be used as a tool to learn language and should not be taught in isolation.

(xii) **Phonetics To Be Introduced:** In compulsory English phonetics should be introduced in the curriculum. Language laboratories are also required.

(xiii) **Teacher Training Programmes:** Frequent teacher training programmes should be there so that teachers become aware and can update their knowledge in technology and various teaching methods. Teachers should be trained in the Refresher Courses.

Conclusion

The job of a language teacher is a challenging and an important one. Teacher should always try to be student centred. Working conditions should also be improved so that the teachers find sufficient time to improve the students' skills. With the aforesaid innovations in teaching methods better results in the teaching and learning of English language can be achieved. Students will be able to use English as a language of communication. But one or two teachers can't do anything. Everyone concerned has to take the responsibility.

Bibliography

1. Bhandari, Supriya. Problems of Teaching English at College Level in India,(http://www.boloji.com)
2. Murali, M. Teaching English As A Second Language In India: A Review. Modern Journal of Applied Linguistics,(www.mjal.org)
3. Rathore, Bharti. Innovations in Teaching English. The Journal of English Language Teaching, Volume 51/1, Jan.-Feb. 2013
4. Saravanam, V. Dealing With Difficult Classroom Situations. The Journal of English Language Teaching, Volume 49/1, Jan.-Feb. 2011
5. Shingore, Akshay & Padmavat, Nirmala Shivram. Indian Education System and English Language Teaching. ELTWEEKLY Online Newsletter, Volume 5, Issue 11, (http://www.eltweekly.com)
6. Thirunavukkarasu, S. & Vidhya Lakshmi, C.N. Moving to Movies: Teaching ESL Through Movies. The Journal of English Language Teaching, Volume 50/2, March-April 2012.
7. www.lkcjal.org/files/elt.pdf

38

Teacher's Training: An integral part of Higher Education

Ms. Navleen Kaur*

Abstract

The study highlights the importance of training for the teachers of colleges and universities at the level of higher education. It gives an overview of the content and module of the training required for the teachers to enhance their analytical skills, communication skills, reasoning skills, teaching skills and also making them well apprised of the use of latest technology in higher education. The soft skills are given much importance for the teaching to be effective. The training plays a pivotal role in having the positive impact on the outcome of the students shaping them into budding professionals with the aid of teacher's practical knowledge about the subject and the latest teaching pedagogy. It also enhances the scope of promotions for the teachers adding to their academic performance index. The objectives of the study are to study the impact of training of the teachers on their students and also to discuss the effective content and module of the training.

Keywords: *Teaching skills, Technology, training module, teaching pedagogy*

Introduction

Higher education plays the role of leadership in a society. Higher Education incorporates new ideas in a society and plays the role of a change agent. It brings change in the life style of the people constituting that social group. It influences the economic condition of the people which results in the economic prosperity of that country. Higher education serves as foundation of the entire system of education. Higher education is mostly imparted by a number of public and private

* Assistant Professor, Department of Business Management, Sri Guru Granth Sahib World University, Fatehgarh Sahib.

universities. Quality of higher education cannot be achieved without quality teachers. Faculty is the heart and soul of the university, and without an active and well qualified faculty it will not be possible to have meaningful development in this sector. Faculty development cannot be viewed in isolation and must be considered together with the development of an environment conducive to academics, as well as research and development in the universities. Faculty development programmes must also address factors pertaining to retention of qualified faculty in the public sector higher education institutions. Since teacher is the nucleus of the whole educational system and the most important figure for initiating radical and effective changes in the learning process, all attempts have to be made to generate creative teachers who are qualitatively skilled and empowered through a continuous professional development process. (Ordonez and MacLean, 1997).

Teaching is a skill and like any other skill it requires training and practice. A person may acquire vast amounts of knowledge and information, but yet may be in dark about the techniques of transmitting it properly. Knowing something and letting it be known to others are not the same thing. Helping others to learn effectively is a performing art as well as a skill. Throughout the world a lot of research has been done in this area. New methods, techniques and innovations on teaching and learning are being discovered regularly. It is popularly believed that there is a positive correlation between the qualities and qualifications of the teacher and the achievements of the students. In order to enhance the qualities and qualifications of the teachers and also to make him/her more skillful in teaching, teacher education programs are offered. He or she is initiates revolutionary steps for the betterment of education of the country. To him or her new experiences are learning experiences contributing to his or her treasure of knowledge. All the above attributes could be inculcated through rigorous continuous Training.

The purpose of this study was to investigate the in-service training needs of the university teachers and to explore the essential competencies for the professional development of university teachers. More specifically, the following objectives guided this study:

(1) To discuss the impact of training on enhancement of various skills.

(2) To study the use of effective modules of training.

Importance of Training

The importance and effectiveness of faculty training programs lies with enhancing and elevating faculty members' professional abilities in teaching. The training programme aims at improving the teaching qualifications of the assistant professors. One of the objectives is for the assistant professors, after the completion of their assistant professorship, to be able to plan, carry out and evaluate teaching in a manner that optimally supports student learning in relation to the learning objectives that have been formulated for the subjects. The assistant professors are also to be capable of contributing to the development of the study programmes for the specific subject and the institution in general. The assistant professor must be able to reflect on their own teaching practice in relation to student learning; and on that background be able to adapt their teaching. The assistant professor teacher training programme requires the application of a broad teaching concept such that the assistant professor gains insight in a variety of teaching forms. The assistant professor teacher training programme is to include practical and theoretical aspects of subject-specific and general competencies as well as possible participation in measures aimed at further developing teaching. Some institutions mandate in-service training for all faculty members; others require certificates in teaching. Furthermore, faculty professional development should be looked at as a lifelong learning process. Based on a number of in-depth interviews, Gibbs and Coffey (2000) developed a framework that lays out the rationale for conducting a faculty training program. Their rationale is based on the improvement of teachers' skills, the development of teachers' conceptions of teaching and learning, and the consequent changes in students' learning.

Development of Teaching Skills: Training deals with aspects of teaching and learning, focuses on five broad areas known as learning outcomes domains for inculcating required skills in the teachers . These are:

Knowledge: The ability to recall, understand, and present information, including: knowledge of specific facts, knowledge of concepts, principles and theories, and knowledge of procedure.

Cognitive skills: the ability to apply conceptual understanding of concepts, principles, and theories and apply procedures involved in critical thinking and creative problem solving, both when asked to do so, and when faced with unanticipated new situations.

Interpersonal skills and responsibility: including the ability to take responsibility for their own learning and continuing personal and professional development, work effectively in groups and exercise leadership when appropriate, act responsibly in personal and professional relationships, act ethically and consistently with high moral standards in personal and public forums.

Communication, information technology and numerical skills: including the ability to communicate effectively in oral and written form, use information and communications technology, and use basic mathematical and statistical techniques.

Psychomotor skills: which are required in some fields of study such as medicine, music and fine art.

Training Methods:

1. **Workshops :** It is an educational seminar on series of meeting emphasizing interaction or exchange of ideas.It is a small group that meets to explore some subject, develop a skill or technique, carry out a creative project.

2. **Orientation Courses:** The University Grants Commission, in pursuance of the National Policy on Education 1986 and its programme of action, had set up 66 Academic Staff Colleges (ASCs) in different Universities/

   Institutions in the country. The Academic Staff Colleges so established are conducting specially designed orientation programmes for newly appointed lecturers and refresher courses for in service teachers. The Orientation programme is intended to inculcate in the young lecturers the quality of self-reliance through awareness of the social, intellectual and moral environment as well as to discover self-potential and confidence. The orientation programmes contributes to the teacher awareness of the problems of the Indian society and the role of education, higher education leaders and educators in the resolution of these problems to achieve desired goals in national development.

3. **Refresher Courses:** The Commission has identified 5 Universities/Institutions on the recommendation of Expert Committee as UGC refresher course centers' to run Specialized Refresher courses during the year 2009-2010 around the country on the basis of requests received from number of Universities/ Institution of Higher Education and Research. The Refresher course provides opportunities for serving teachers to exchange experiences with their peers and mutually learns from each other. It will be a forum to abreast of the latest advances in the subjects, technological spin off etc. The eligibility for attending Refresher course for teachers who have not attended earlier Orientation programme has been reduced to "two years" from "five years".

4. **FDP's: Faculty Development programme:** The FDP is designed for management teachers and researchers working in management schools, universities, colleges and professional institutes which teach management and allied subjects like economics, statistics, computer applications, commerce, banking, sociology and labor relations. Participants should have post-graduate level teaching experience in management or research experience of at least two years. Preference will be given to participants less than 45 years of age. Past experience indicates that participants in the early stages of their teaching or research careers benefit most. Since the FDP is offered in the English language, participants are expected to be fluent in English.

❖ **Objectives:**

The major focus of the FDP is on upgrading the teaching, training, and research skills of management teachers— especially those teachers who have not had an opportunity to acquaint themselves with recent developments in teaching and research methods. The programme enables participants to develop competence in general management education as well as in management research and pedagogy.

4. Academic skill-related courses (e.g., Research Methods, Statistical Analysis, Communication for Management Teachers and Introduction to Case Writing)

5. Elective courses in specialized areas.

- **Educational approach**

  The FDP relies on a variety of learning settings like classrooms, workshops and seminars, and a participatory approach to learning. There is an emphasis on the case method of teaching and learning. Other educational methods such as lectures, small group exercises, management games, and presentations are also used. Computers, statistical kits, and audio-visual aids complement these methods. Participants are also encouraged to develop insights into curriculum planning and academic administration.

5. **Seminars:** It is a meeting for an exchange of ideas. The word seminar comes from a latin root that reflects this: Seminarium, a seed plot. The seminar is where you plant a seed or an idea and than work with that seed to develop it over a period of time through a dynamic and interactive process.

6. **Conferences:** It can be at the national level and the international level, which can have any number of the participants from the different field or from the same field depending upon the theme/ subthemes of the conference. It is a platform where academicians, research scholars gather at the same platform to share their knowledge and views about the specified theme

7. **Exchange programs:** It is a FDP where teachers of one institute can visit another institute/ institute of another city/ state or country to exchange their ideas and knowledge of their systems, structure, plans and policies and best practices at a common platform in the areas of academics, research & development, innovative practices and the like.

Impact of Teachers training on the students:

1. **Behavioral understanding:** It helps them to understand the psychological needs of the students which vary from one student to another and can become better guides and mentors for their both personal and academic issues.

2. **Soft skills/ communication skills:** The soft skill is the expression and the tone used by the communicator and can have the better and long lasting impression on one's mind. With improvement in the communication skills of the teacher, there would be better understanding of the concept.

3. **Analytical Skills:** The trained teacher would justify the improvement in the ability to analyze the situations and thereby taking better decisions at time of emergencies or contingencies.

4. **ICT skills:** The knowledge about the use of latest integrated technologies can make teacher well versed with the content which helps to disseminate the information to the students more effectively and efficiently.

The above all mentioned improvement in the skills can lead to the holistic development of the students. It will groom and polish the personality of the students with the help of mentors. Hence will make them more productive and well performed.The students will be able to get better placed by getting counseled from the trained teachers in their concerned fields. The students may get enlightened on the importance of the body language while facing the interview board. Today's current problem lies with the relationship building which can be taught and made to learn by the guide who is well versed with the ways to improve the interpersonal skills.

Conclusions

Faculty members' competency encompasses knowledge of subject matter, teaching skills and professional attitudes. Obviously, knowledge based on a subject matter is not enough to claim competency in teaching. Besides subject matter, teaching professional competency requires additional "nonacademic" knowledge (i.e. social, administrative and technical). Teachers need to re-learn with new modern inclusions, for what they have learned from the traditional era. The policy of liberalization though has lead to the mushrooming of many private institutes, focusing just on the quantity and not on the quality. The word "Excellence" has become the word of extinct. The rapid reform in the quality of education on the part of the government is the need of the hour. The policies in terms of TQM – total quality management needs to be framed. Even, in the latest RUSA document, there is hardly any provision for the faculty development programmes which has been really thought out in terms of quality instead of just numbers. The massive work needs to be done in improving the skills of the teachers which in turn would lead to the better performing results of the students. The sad story begins with API and ends with API, which is also responsible for the deterioration of the quality education as it has lead to the rat race for fetching more points for API. The only solution can be the self realization of the teachers as well as the government to reframe the policies, with more inclination towards the development of the faculty.

Bibliography

1 Abdulghani A. Al-Hattami a *, Omar M. Muammar a and Ismail A. Elmahdi a, (2013),"The need for professional training programs to improve faculty members teaching skills", ISSN: 2147-6284, European Journal of Research on Education, 1(2), 39-45.

2 Bartunek, J. M. and M. K. Moch (1994), "Third-Order Change and the Western Mystical Tradition," Journal of Organisational Change Management, 7 (1), 24-41.

3 Elahi, Nizam (1997) Teacher's Education in India New Delhi, APH Publishing Corporation

4 Kundu, C.L. (1998) Indian Year Book on Teacher Education New Delhi, Sterling Publishers Privatization Ltd.

5. McNergney, Robert F. and Herbert, Joanne M. (2001) Foundations of Education : The Challenge of Professional Practice Boston Allyn and Bacon.

6. Misra, K.S. (1993) Teachers and Their Education Ambala Cantt., The Associated Publishers.

7. National Council for Teacher Education (NCTE) (1998) NCTE Document New Delhi, Published by Member Secretary, NCTE.

8. www.hec.gov.pk

Role of Biotechnology in Higher Education and Social Development

Dr. Neetu Thakur*

Abstract

For centuries, biotechnology has been at the forefront of developments for food, feed, fiber and medicine. In fact, biotechnology refers to "any technique which uses living organisms or parts thereof to make or modify products, improve plant and animal productivity or to develop micro-organisms for specific use". But recent developments in molecular biology have given biotechnology new meaning, new prominence, and new potential. Biotechnology is on the front lines generating new and brighter futures for humankind. The application of biotechnology in agriculture and food production promises global agriculture that is both more productive and environmentally sustainable.

Keywords: *Biotechnology, Higher education, career, social development*

Introduction

For centuries, biotechnology has been at the forefront of developments for food, feed, fiber and medicine. Traditional biotechnology used for many years in the food industry, for the production of beer, rum, vinegar and cheese, to ago-industry, for the micro- propagation of disease-free plants, and to the field of medicine for the development of pregnancy test kits and the production of insulin. In fact, biotechnology refers to "any technique which uses living organisms or parts thereof to make or modify products, improve plant and animal productivity or to develop micro-organisms for specific use". But recent developments in molecular biology have given biotechnology new meaning, new

* Assistant Professor, Department of Biotechnology, GGDSD College, Sector 32, Chandigarh.

prominence, and new potential. The modern biotechnology has captured the attention of the public and can have a dramatic effect on the world economy and society. "High end" biotechnology, involves recombinant DNA, cell fusion and novel bio-processing and engineering techniques, such as gene transfer, embryo-manipulation and monoclonal antibodies.

The Objectives of this paper are :

1. To highlight the higher education in Biotechnology
2. To highlight the role of plant biotechnology in social development

Biotechnology is the use of biological processes, organisms, or systems to manufacture products intended to improve the quality of human life. The earliest biotechnologists were farmers who developed improved species of plants and animals by cross pollenization or cross breeding. In recent years, biotechnology has expanded in sophistication, scope, and applicability. Biotechnology is an enormously wide field of science and technology. It embraces many branches, from techniques to improve crops productivity to the manipulation of human genes. Thus, in an attempt to comprehend all biotechnological activities, the following definition is provided: A set of biological techniques developed through basic research and now applied to research and produce development.

Different types of biotechnology

Biotechnology is roughly divided into three main parts:

- Green biotechnology
- Red biotechnology
- White biotechnology

Green Biotechnology: Agricultural Processes

It is a very important field of modern biotechnology. The foundation of green biotech is crop improvement and production of novel products in plants, which is achieved by implanting foreign genes to plant species that is economically important. It contains three main areas Plant tissue culture, Plant genetic engineering and Plant molecular marker assisted breeding.

Red Biotechnology: Health Care Processes

It uses the human body's own tools and weapons to fight diseases. Red biotechnology is of great importance in traditional drug discovery and also in creating new possibilities for

treatment, prevention and diagnosis (by using new methods). Biotech medicines account for 20% of all market medicines. The continuous growth of knowledge, new discoveries and investments in this field, result in the fact that the opportunities for curing broaden too. It includes cell therapy, Stem cells, Gene therapy and genetic testing etc.

White Biotechnology: Industrial and Environmental Processes

This field of biotechnology is connected with industry. White biotech uses moulds, yeasts, bacteria and enzymes to produce goods and services or parts of products. It offers a wide range of bio-products like detergents, vitamins, antibiotics etc. Most of the white biotech processes results in the saving of water, energy, chemicals and in the reduction of waste compared to traditional methods. However, this area is not new, since such processes have been used for thousands of years in the production of wine, cheese, bread and many others. Using eco-efficient enzymes speeds up some processes in certain chemical processes (for example, transforming one substance into another) with consuming less water, raw materials and energy than the traditional one. It is a cleaner solution for industry, with the environmental impact minimized, a better product and lower costs.

Biotechnology and Higher Education

Biotechnology is a recent development in the field of science and technology. Biotechnology as the name suggests is the combination of Biology and Technology and is an applied science. It is concerned with variety of subjects including Biochemistry, Genetics, Microbiology, Chemistry and Engineering. There is a great scope for career in biotechnology in India as well as abroad. Career in Biotechnology offers various employment opportunities in research, marketing and production in the fields like medicine and healthcare, animal husbandry, agriculture and environment industry. Some of the best universities in the world to pursue a degree in biotechnology include Harvard University, University of Tokyo, University of London, University of California, Penn State University, John Hopkins University, Stanford University, Yale University, University of Washington, Duke University, National University of Singapore and University of Western Australia.

Top 10 Indian colleges offering Biotechnology

S.No	Name of the Institute	Address
1.	Rajiv Gandhi Center for Biotechnology, Trivandrum	Trivandrum, Kerala
2.	School of Life Sciences, University of Hyderabad	Hyderabad, Andhra Pradesh
3.	National Dairy Research Institute, Karnal	Karnal, Haryana
4.	Institute of Chemical Technology, University of Mumbai	Mumbai, Maharashtra
5.	Department of Biochemical Engineering & Biotechnology, Indian Institute of Technology	New Delhi
6.	University School of Biotechnology, Guru Govind Singh Indraprasths University	New Delhi
7.	Department of Microbiology & Biotechnology Centre, Faculty of Science, The Maharaja Sayaji Rao University of Baroda	Vadodra, Gujarat
8.	Department of Animal Biotechnology, Madras Veterinary College, Tamilnadu Veterinary and Animal Sciences University	Chennai, Tamil Nadu
9.	University Institute of Engineering & Technology, Punjab University	Chandigarh
10.	Department of Plant Molecular Biology & Biotechnology, Tamil Nadu Agricultural University	Coimbatore, Tamil Nadu

CARRIER OPTIONS

Biotechnology has wide areas of application in Agriculture, Animal Husbandry, development of Medicines and Vaccine, treatment of prolonged disease, pollution control and waste management and ecological conservation, energy production and conservation and many more. Because of such utilities Biotechnology is a preferred career option among youngster. Multiple career options are waiting for biotechnology professionals. They can be employed in pharmaceutical companies, chemical, agriculture and allied industries. Research laboratories whether run by government or corporate sector are the preferred place for many bio-technologists. There they work as research scientists or assistants. There are also many employment opportunities for bio-technologists in government and private sector collages and universities. In private sector they many find employment in company such as pharmaceutical farms, food processing industries, aquaculture and agro based industries. They can also be hired as environmental specialist by various government agencies and private institutions. Biotechnologists also have the option to join media houses as Science writer.

Some companies that hire biotechnologists are Hindustan Lever, Thapar Group, Indo American Hybrid Seeds, Bincon India Limited, Bivcol, IDPL, Indian Vaccines Corporation, Hindustan Antibiotics, Sun Pharma, Cadila etc.

FUNDING AGENCIES

At present in India, there are six major agencies responsible for financing and supporting research in the realm of biotechnology apart from other sciences. They are Department of Science and Technology (DST), Department of Biotechnology (DBT), Council of Scientific and Industrial Research (CSIR), Indian Council of Medical Research (ICMR), Indian Council of Agriculture Research (ICAR) and University Grants Commission (UGC), Department of Scientific and Industrial Research (DSIR). DST, DBT and DSIR are part of Ministry of Science and Technology while ICMR is with Ministry of Health, ICAR with Ministry of Agriculture and UGC with Ministry of Human Resource and Development. DSIR is the funding agency for CSIR and both of them independently fund biotechnology related research programme.

Biotechnology and Social Development

Biotechnology has a critical role in developing and processing value added products of enhanced nutritive quality and providing tools for ensuring and monitoring food quality and safety. With a global population of nearly 7 billion expanding every day, feeding the world with nutritious foods via sustainable agriculture is an intense challenge. Agricultural biotechnology is leading the charge in meeting this challenge providing solutions that increase crop yields, preserve and improve soils, enhance the control of pests, weeds and harmful diseases, and produce more healthful food with enhanced vitamin and nutrient levels. Biotechnology inventions such as herbicide tolerant crops, insect resistant crops and disease resistant plants have revolutionized modern agriculture while greatly reducing the need for a diverse range of agricultural chemical pesticides. Furthermore, agricultural biotechnologists are bringing to market the next wave of biotech plants with a host of new and exciting production characteristics such as drought tolerance, cold tolerance, saline tolerance, and plants with enhanced nitrogen-use efficiency—reducing the amount of fertilizers needed for high levels of productivity. Key categories of benefits from biotechnology in agriculture include, for example:

- Increased agricultural yields and agricultural productivity;
- Reduced environmental impacts of agricultural production;
- Increased farmer incomes;
- Enhanced food safety, nutrition, and health; and
- pportunities for new and expanding industries in the sustainable production of biobased fuels, chemicals, plastics and materials from agricultural and forest biotech crops.

Biotechnology is on the front lines generating new and brighter futures for humankind. The application of biotechnology in agriculture and food production promises global agriculture that is both more productive and environmentally sustainable. According to the eleventh annual Indian Biotech Industry survey by Biospectrum-ABLE

(Association of Biotechnology Led Enterprises), the Indian biotech industry grew by 15.1 % in 2012-13, increasing its revenues from 204.4 Billion INR (Indian Rupees) to 235.24 Billion INR (3.94 B US$ - exchange rate June 2013: 1 US$ approx. 60 INR)(figure 1).

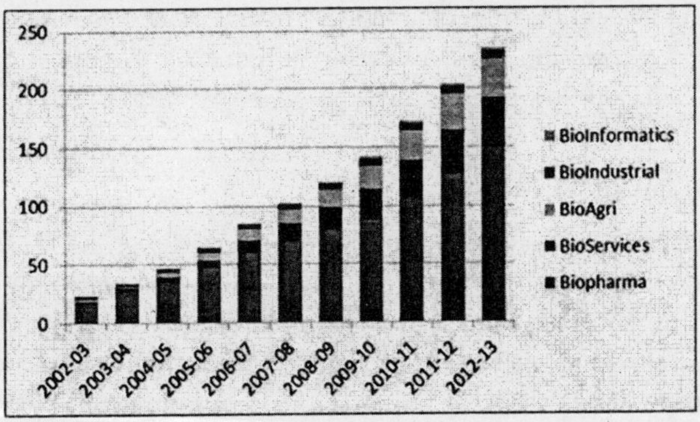

Figure 1 showing Indian biotech industry 2012-2013(www.biospectrum.com)

Applications of Plant biotechnology

Whether in the developed world or the developing world human nutrition is a matter of great public health concern. One-sixth of the world's population suffers from hunger; and Over half of the global population suffers from "hidden hunger" due to the poor nutritional quality of available staple foods. Billions of people in the developing world simply do not have access to a well-rounded and diverse diet. What is needed, in lieu of such a diet, is an approach to fortifying their staple crops with the nutrients that are typically missing from their diets. Biotechnology is helping achieve this goal.

Golden Rice

Vitamin A Enrichment. Vitamin A deficiency is a leading cause of blindness in the developing world and is particularly prevalent among children. To combat this deficiency, biotech processes are being used to enrich staple crops with β-carotene (provitamin A). β-carotene is produced naturally in rice plants, but Safer, Healthier, More Nutritious Foods for Consumers only in their green tissues, not in the rice grain that people eat. The development of the biotech crop "Golden Rice," however, used genetic engineering to get β-carotene expressed in rice grains. At its current stage of development, Golden Rice could provide half the required daily intake of Vitamin A for a 1 to 3 year old child in a 2.5 ounce serving. Biotechnologists are also working to incorporate increased expression of β-carotene in potatoes, canola, tomatoes, carrots and cauliflower.

Flavr Savr tomato

The Flavr Savr tomato was the first commercially grown genetically engineered food to be granted a license for human consumption. By adding an antisense gene, the California-based company Calgene hoped to slow the ripening process of the tomato to prevent softening and rotting, while allowing the tomato to retain its natural flavor and color.

Bt cotton

(Bt) cotton was created through the addition of genes encoding toxin crystals in the Cry group of endotoxin. These crystalline proteins are ingested by the insects while feeding on the cotton plant. High pH level of the insect's stomach activates the cry toxin. The now dissolved and activated Cry toxin molecules attach themselves to specific locations on the receptor present on the epithelial cells of the midgut and creates ion channels formation of cells . Due to the formation of Cry ion channels sufficient regulation of potassium ions is lost and results in the death of epithelial cells and ultimately the death of organism.

The use of Bt-Cotton in India has grown exponentially since its introduction. Recently India has become the number one global exporter of cotton and the second largest cotton producer in the world. India has also bred Bt-cotton varieties such as Bikaneri Nermaand hybrids such as (NHH-44), setting up India to benefit now and well into the future. Socio-economic surveys confirm that Bt-Cotton continues to deliver significant and multiple agronomic, economic, environmental and welfare benefits to Indian farmers and society including halved insecticide requirements and a doubling of yields.

EDIBLE VACCINE

Plant and animal protein structures are almost similar. Biotechnology is finding novel uses beyond food. Potatoes, tomatoes, rice, tobacco, lettuce, safflowers, and other plants have been genetically engineered to produce insulin and certain vaccines. The plant-based vaccine production method works by isolating a specific antigen protein, one that triggers a human immune response from the targeted virus. A gene from the protein is transferred to bacteria, which are then used to "infect" plant cells. The plants then start producing the exact protein that will be used for vaccinations. Edible vaccine can be one of the alternatives of the traditional vaccines as they can overcome all the problems associated with traditional vaccines. Edible vaccines are targeted to provide mucosal as well as systemic immunity today, micro-organisms are used to produce vaccines. However, plants can easily be made to produce some pharmacologically important antigens, and can economically be used as an alternative method. There are some reports on vaccine production against cholera and malaria by transgenic plants. The demonstration that vaccine antigens can provide new opportunities for bio-farming of vaccines, If the antigens were orally active, food-based 'edible vaccines' could allow economical production and delivery in developing countries. Astonishingly, the vaccines containing edible plants may be developed and will be commercially available, and in the very near future, children in developing countries will be eating tailor-made polysaccharide containing potato as a nutrient, as well as a vaccine to protect them from cholera. The 'edible vaccine' plant foods will be one of the most amazing new products of the next century.

CONCLUSIONS

The applications of biotechnology are so broad, and the advantages so compelling, that virtually every industry is using this technology. Developments are underway in areas as diverse as pharmaceuticals, diagnostics, textiles, aquaculture, forestry, chemicals, household products, environmental cleanup, food processing and forensics to name a few. Biotechnology is enabling these industries to make new or better products, often with greater speed, efficiency and flexibility. Biotechnology holds significant promise to the future but certain amount of risk is associated with any area. Biotechnology must continue to be carefully regulated so that the maximum benefits are received with the least risk .

Bibliography

1. Biotechnology for Socio-Economic Development: A Policy for Jamaica (2006). Draft developed by the National Commission on Science and Technology, 17 pp
2. Biotechnology Research Subcommittee (1995). Biotechnology for the 21stCentury: New Horizons, Chapter 6. National Agricultural Library, Washington, D.C.
3. Madhavan Guruprasad, Oakley Barbara, Kun Luis (2009) Career Development in Bioengineering and Biotechnology: Series in Biomedical Engineering an official publication of the International Federation for Medical andBiologicalEngineering. Springer,584pp
4. What is biotechnology, http://www.europabio.org/what-biotechnology
5. Careers in Biotech after Graduation, http://www.biotecnika.org/biotech-career-guide/career... in-biotech/graduation
6. Grants in India, http://www.indiabioscience.org/ grants_in_india
7. Tang G, Hu Y, Yin S, Wang Y, Dallal GE, Grusak MA & Russell RM (2012) β-carotene in Golden Rice is as good as β-carotene in oil at providing vitamin A to children. American Journal of Clinical Nutrition, 96: 658-664pp.
8. Choudhary, B. & Gaur, K. 2010. Bt Cotton in India: A Country Profile. ISAAA Series of Biotech Crop Profiles. ISAAA: Ithaca, NewYork
9. James, Clive. 2009. Global Status of Commercialized Biotech/ GM Crops: 2009. ISAAA Brief No.41. ISAAA: Ithaca, NewYork
10. Weasel, Lisa H. 2009. Food Fray .American Management Association, New York Publishing, 256 pp.
11. Landridge ,W.2000. Edible vaccines. Scientific American, 283:66-71pp
12. Mason H S, Arntzen C J.(1995). Transgenic plant as vaccine production system. Trends in Biotechnology ,13:388□92pp.
13. NorthCarolinaBiotechnologyCenter."AboutBiotech". http://www.ncbiotech.org/aboutbt/ main.cfm

Higher Education in Manipur: Issues, Challenges and Expectations

*Dr. M. Rameshwor Singh**

Abstract

Education is an essential and inevitable part of human life. Whether in the days of Vedas or in the contemporary world, whatever may be its forms and objectives, everyone has felt its importance. Realizing the importance of education in general and higher education in particular, the Government of India has launched certain ambitious schemes one after another like SSA, RMSA and RUSA etc. These schemes and their implementation certainly have far-reaching implications in the arena called 'Education' extending in every nook and corner of the country. There are not only issues and challenges, but also certain hopes and expectations from these schemes if properly implemented. The present paper attempts to highlight some of the issues and challenges associated with higher education in Manipur. The objective of writing this paper is to figure out some of the pertinent facts and harsh realities associated with education sector in the state of Manipur, which is replica of the states located at the receiving end. It aims to address those issues and suggest the ways and means to rectify them so that the real objectives of any educational schemes may be fulfilled in the real sense of the term.

***Key words:** Education, Schemes, Objectives, Implications, Issues, Challenges.*

Introduction

"Education is not the filling of a bucket, but the lighting of a fire" –W. B. Yeats

In the life of a man, from cradle to grave, Education is an essential entity. Considering its importance, the Government of India, under Article 21(A) of the Constitution, has declared for the universalization

* Assistant Professor,DM College of Arts, Imphal

of primary education for the children between the ages 6 to 14 years (RTE, 2009). The Government has already launched the much-hyped and ambitious schemes like the Serva Shiksha Abhiyan (SSA) for the lower primary and upper primary education and Rashtriya Madhyamik Shiksha Abhiyan (RMSA) for middle school and secondary education. However, these are not the end of the road, particularly keeping in view the needs of the individual as well as the societal demands. There is also the need for universalization of higher education to establish a knowledge-based society. Keeping this hope alive, the Government has now announced the Rashtriya Uchchatar Shiksha Abhiyan (RUSA). In order to make the mission successful, in addition to upgrading the status of the existing higher educational institutions, 278 new universities and 388 colleges have been proposed to establish throughout the country. However, ironically, without the internal quality assurance, the mere establishment of institutes of higher study could not fulfill the dream of having a knowledge-based society.

The main objectives of imparting education in India change from time to time through the ages. During the days of Vedas, the main objectives were to teach the pupils the lore of the weapons i.e. Asthasashtra and the teaching of Vedas i.e. Vedasashtra. During the British period the main objectives as envisaged by the colonial masters were to give the natives the knowledge of 3 R's i.e. Reading, Writing and Arithmetic, so that the natives could be employed conveniently and trainthem the master's language i.e. English, to perform their menial and clerical jobs. After independence, the objectives of education in India have changed. Education commissions after commissions have recommended more or less the same directives. All of them converge to the goal, which is invariably the production of good citizens of the country, having the basic qualities of the 6 Hs -Head (logical and critical thinking), Heart (empathy), Hand (skill), Health (sound health for sound body), Humanity (looking beyond self), Harmony (balance), etc. In the 21st century, the war of ideas dominated the scene and the wherewithal for it, no doubt, is higher education.

Background of Higher Education in Manipur

The history of higher education in Manipur is of recent origin. The first institution of higher education in Manipur was established in 1946 due to the hue and cry of the students who have completed the secondary stage of education. It was an undergraduate college established with the initiative of some local educationists. Later on, it was taken over by the Government and was named after Maharani Dhanamanjuri Devi for her generous donation towards the development of the college. With the establishment of the college, 60 students could receive collegiate education in Manipur. Dhanamanjuri College (D.M. College) played a vital role in the history of higher education in the state. The college was first affiliated to the Calcutta University; later it followed the curriculum and educational programmes of the Guwahati University. The first batch of graduates of D. M. College received their degrees in 1950. D. M. College also served as the nucleus of many other institutions, such as B. T. College, G. P. Women's College, P.G class of J. N. University centre. Later on the college has been bifurcated into Arts College, Science College and then a college of Commerce stream is added. Up to 1948, there was no college for imparting professional education such as Law, Agriculture, Medicine, Engineering, Fine Arts, Dance and Drama, etc.. However, in 2005-06 there are 16 professional institutes under Manipur University.

Higher education has expanded over the years in Manipur. The number of institutions and the students enrolled there also increased manifold. As per record, in the academic session 2012-13, there are 22,968 students enrolled in the government colleges, 12,115 in government-aided colleges and 6525 in the private colleges.From only one college in 1946, today the state has two full- fledged Central universities and another regional centre of a central university (Indira Gandhi National Tribal University with its headquarter at Amarkantak, Madhya Pradesh). The two central universities are Central Agricultural University, Iroisemba, Imphal with various constituent colleges located in all the north east states including Sikkim, and Manipur University, Imphal, having one constituent college and 76 affiliated institutions of higher studies including two medical colleges, one central and another state owned. The Manipur University is located at Canchipur, Imphal, the capital city of Manipur. The University is spread over an area of 333.33 acres of land which has the complexes of Administrative building, Humanities, Social Sciences and Science blocks, Teachers' Quarters, Students' Hostels, Post Office, a Bank, Canteen and Co-operative store, a Recreation Hall, a Health Centre, an Auditorium, a Library building etc.. It was established on 5th June, 1980 under the Manipur University Act 1980 as a teaching-cum-affiliating University at Imphal with territorial jurisdiction of the whole of the state of Manipur. Later on, Jawaharlal Nehru University, New Delhi centre of P.G studies at Canchipur, Imphal was merged with the Manipur University in 1981. On 13th October 2005, Manipur University was converted into a central university. The following are the category of colleges/institutes affiliated to Manipur University:

Sl. No.	Types of colleges/institutes; Nature of affiliation	No. of colleges/ institutes
1.	Permanent affiliated Govt. colleges/institutes (including one constituent college)	35
2.	Government aided colleges/institutes	08
3.	Permanently affiliated private colleges/institutes	18
4.	Private affiliated colleges/institutes	07
5.	Permitted private colleges/institutes	09

The Government of India has already initiated several reforms in the higher education sector, which encompass not only reforms in governance but also in the regulatory structures of the higher education system. According to Radhakrishnan Commission(1948-49), "The most important and urgent reform needed in education is to transform higher education, to endeavor to relate it to the life, needs and aspirations of the people and thereby make it the powerful instrument of social, economic and cultural transformation necessary for the realization of the national goals." The University Grants Commission was established in 1956. In order to assess and accredit institutions of higher education, to facilitate the volunteering institutions to assess their performance viz-à-viz set parameters through introspection, the Government of India established NAAC, an autonomous body, in 1994 with its headquarter at Bangalore.It is the outcome of the recommendations of the National Policy on Education (1986), having aimed to address the issues of quality of higher education by an independent national accreditation body.

In Manipur, the total number of NAAC accredited colleges is 14 out of 77 colleges/institutes. The percentage is very low if we compare it with some other advanced states in the country. The detail is given below:

Sl. No.	Type of college/institute	Total no. of colleges/ institutes	NAAC accredited colleges/ institutes
1.	Government colleges	28	11
2.	Private colleges	31	03
3.	Aided colleges	08	00
4.	Technical institutes and others	10	00
	Total	77	14

Quality education is one of the most hackneyed notions, which is yet eluding a clear-cut definition not only in the parlance but also even in the academic circle. Still more elusive is the idea of quality higher education. To give a quantitative measure of the quality of education achieved by a student is a really hazy concept. Many academic authorities are still groping to find the appropriate devices to quantify the achievements of their graduates. Although there has been a qualitative expansion, the progress of higher education in the state in terms of quality is not encouraging. The quality of education provided in the colleges has deteriorated due to the mushroom growth of private colleges in the state. These colleges are without proper infrastructures and proper facilities.

At the individual level, majority of the students in the colleges of Manipur appear to have anticipated at the time they entered the college that their higher education at the secondary school stage would help them better their employment prospects. They seem to continue their study without definite objective. Many of them do not have keen interest in higher learning. They come to the colleges in the hope of getting mere degrees and jobs for which only such education would qualify them. The number of competent teachers in the college is short of requirement. There are a large number of part-time and guest teachers. The norms set out by the UGC are often, ignored in recruiting the teachers. The gap between the students and teachers, and students to students has also widened in Manipur. The academic interactions between teachers and students and among students themselves have been very limited. Even the serious-minded students do not have much chance of developing their potentialities.

Higher Education in Manipur: Issues and Challenges

Since higher Education in Manipur has been introduced very lately, it has many shortcomings and hence faces many problems. Some of the serious issues can be cited here:

Lack of clear-cut educational policy: There is no clear-cut policy on Higher Education in Manipur. The increase in number of institutions is not in tune with the socio-economic system of the state. The Education Survey Report mentions that the state of higher education in Manipur is not an encouraging one. The expansion at this level has been mostly in Arts and Humanities rather than Science and Professional courses.

Mis-governance and malfunctioning of the Education department: In Manipur, at present, the Directorate of University and Higher Education is headed by a Director (now Commissioner, Higher Education as ex-officio Director) who is assisted by 1 Additional Director, 1 Joint Director and 5 Officers on Special Duty. It is a very small team of Officers, who are always over-burdened with administrative works and supervision of higher education in the state. Moreover, unfortunately such an important department has been running without a regular Director for the last 10 years or more. Running an academic department without academic head and leaving it at the mercy of the cumbersome bureaucracy is just like doing a great disfavor to the development of quality higher education in the state.

Politicization of Education: Frequent bandhs, strikes and boycotts in the state make itvery difficult to maintain proper academic calendar in the schools, colleges and other institutes of higher studies. The law and order maintenance is a state subject; however, wherever and whenever the state fails to do the needful task, the educational institutions always remain the soft target. The miscreants or aggrieved parties always take the advantage to target the educational establishments. Here, mention may be made of the complete closure of the entire educational activity in the state for roughly four months in connection with the infamous fake encounter in the heart of the city in broad daylight in July 23, 2009 (reported in The Tehelka Magazine) and its resultant effect. The most disturbing situation is the lack of proper academic atmosphere in the institutions and the attitude of both the teachers and the students. Another disheartening feature is extreme and active participation of students in politics. Besides the Students' Unions in the respective institutions, there are more than 10 students' organizations operating actively in the state. Their noble agendas and contributions in academic surveillance are noteworthy; however, having so many organizations sometimes create more problems and confusion than solving the problems. Their ideological clash and struggle for existence and dominance often hamper the academic atmosphere in the institutions. Here also, mention may be made of the killing of a Manipur University professor in 2009 and the brutal assault of the two college professors by the miscreants belonging to some students' organizations in connection with Students' Union Election, 2013 on the very unfounded ground of whether votes already casted should be counted or not. It is the extreme case of students' disrespect to their gurus under the influence of dirty politics. Ideologically, students' participation in politics in democracy seems very good, but when the ideal is derailed, it rather pollutes the young minds and makes them indiscipline and irresponsible, as power is poison.

Issue of Rationalization: Many institutions spread in the state are starved of resources – funds, infrastructure, teachers and students. The prevailing situation is pathetic and harmful. External factors like globalization and comparative advantage, coupled with internal deficiencies in higher education sector in the state, factored in student migration. In order to enhance the standard of higher institutions in the state and stop this large-scale student migration proper rationalization is necessary. It is high time to measure the strengths and weaknesses of each of the institutions, decide the parameters of performance appraisal with 100 percent objectivity and act without any prejudice and political bias. On this line of rationalization, if necessary, certain nearby colleges with poor percentage of enrollment should be merged to avoid double wastage and allocation of funds. So far, no concrete action has been taken in this matter.

Problem of infrastructure development: With the introduction of semester system in Manipur University and its affiliated colleges, there is a big crisis of acute shortage of infrastructure and manpower needs, especially in the colleges. More teachers, books, reading rooms of libraries, classrooms, hostels, uninterrupted power supply, internet facility, adequate teaching aids, etc., are required. State, having its own financial crisis, could not provide the required infrastructure. Mention may be made here that before the introduction of semester system in 1997-98 there were 2898 teachers working in the colleges of Manipur, it was reduced to 1267 in 2000-01. After the introduction of semester system in the colleges, at present there is 1019 teachers working in the Government colleges. The actual sanctioned post is 1303, and as per Manipur University Syndicate approval in 1997, the number should be 1551.Hence, there is a shortfall of 532 posts of teachers in the government colleges. Where there is an increase in demand, the supply is reduced. What an irony it is? UGC is also moving at the wrong direction because instead of providing funds in basic things of education like construction of well-equipped classrooms and classroom equipments, libraries, seminar halls and staff rooms, funds are being provided more for the construction secondary needs like Auditorium and Swimming Pools. Is it ideal to neglect the basics and promote the secondary things?

Administration by In-Charge Principals: As per the requirements of NAAC, the head of the institution should be regular and fulltime. Unfortunately, all the head of the institutions in the state, either Government or Government Aided colleges, happen to be the In-Charges. This malpractice has been continuing since the last 10 years or so. The In-charge Principals actually cannot exercise full authority and they cannot properly help in the smooth functioning of the institutions. If the Government of India and UGC have the least concern for the development of higher education in the state, they should have fixed and reprimanded the state Government for this years-long malpractice.

Lack of proper transfer and posting policy: There is no fix and proper transfer policy in the higher education department. Without any valid reason at any time and any place, teachers are being transferred. As there is no state transfer policy, in such a mishap, the teachers are forced to spend a huge chunk of money to be transferred or to get their transfer order stayed. The teachers are always at the receiving end of the process of victimization. The undue and untimely transfer of teachers seriously affected the academic atmosphere of the colleges and it also demoralizes the teachers.

Non-implementation of UGC schemes: While teachers are expected to render their noble task to mould the society and the nation, the country pays least respect and acknowledgement for their divine service. They are the least corrupt but the most neglected group of employees in the state. While salary and other entitlements are not givenon time to the teachers as per UGC norms, at the time of placement to the next level the UGC API score has been imposed. Is not it injustice? The onus lies on UGC for not making its regulation mandatory to all the state governments and giving the states room for violating its norms.

Engagement of part-time/guest teachers in lieu of regular teachers: In almost all the Government colleges, there is acute shortage of regular teachers and non-teaching staff. In order to fill up the vacuum, the state government already committed a big blunder of appointing part-time/guest teachers. The principals in the colleges have the difficulty to assign and fix duties and responsibilities to those part-time/guest teachers like the limited regular teachers. There is also low level of job satisfaction among them since their service condition is not so good. At present, there are 478 part-time/guest teachers under the Department of Higher and Technical Education, Government of Manipur.

Quality maintenance: Quality of higher education in Manipur suffers due to faulty admission procedures, mushrooming growth of colleges, scarcity of teaching faculties, excessive utilization of part-time teachers, recruitment of incompetent teachers (in private and aided colleges), lack of facilities such as libraries, laboratories, etc. The admission process of undergraduate and graduate of colleges under Manipur University is not uniform as different colleges are having separate system of admission process based on either mark basis and written examination. The intake capacity of students of each college is also not the same. Most of the colleges located at the rural outskirts and hilly regions are facing the problem of shortage of students whereas some of the colleges at the heart of the city are over-burdened. The norm set out by UGC is often violated while recruiting the teachers, especially in the private colleges. The newly established colleges face acute financial hardships. The UGC grant does not reach many institutions, and as such, standard cannot be maintained.

Lack of Guidance, Counseling, and problem of educated unemployment: There is lack of students' knowledge and skills necessary to cope with the demands of their courses. The parents and teachers play an important role in sensitizing the students about their educational and career options. Students are to be informed of the modern avenues and changes from time to time. There is a need of regular and consistent contact with the students to motivate them. No substantial efforts could be seen in this regard in the academic institutions of Manipur. There are very few formal counseling centres in the colleges and less information is being disseminated to the students properly about their educational and career choices. The present higher education system has contributed to the problem of educated unemployment in the state. There has been increase in the number of graduates in the faculties of Sciences, Arts and commerce. There were 32,479 graduates and above who were unemployed in 1994 and it increased to 55,349 in 2005. There is lack of professional and technical institutions. State government cannot provide employment to all the graduates coming out from the colleges. The state has no large-scale industries to absorb these educated youths. These create an educated unemployment problem in the state.

Lack of Research and Extension activities: Higher education, in the real sense of the term, refers to three important areas of knowledge – Teaching, Research and Extension. At the current juncture, a thrust is needed to improve higher education in Manipur to prepare the youths to face the challenges of the 21st century. For it, research activities in the colleges and university are necessary. However, ironically, research facilities in the colleges remained virtually non-existent. It would be worthwhile to remember President Pranab Mukherjee's lament echoed in the annual convocation of Sikkim University in 2013 and in rewarding 25 Indian Global Living Legends, which was sponsored by NDTV, that since C.V. Raman no Indian researcher working in the Indian Universities is getting the prestigious Novel Prize.

EXPECTATIONS:

Birds migrate for a favourable climate. Likewise, students who have just passed their secondary examinations are looking for better education in other states or abroad. Youthful energy thirst for a happening place and a college campus is one such place. Our colleges are not built up to the mark. The energy in the youth is made dull and dormant with very limited vision in the state. These can be solved by making our state an educational hub. The dream of an educational hub could be fulfilled if we can stop the larger percentage of migrating students. If the Government, the department concerned and various stakeholders are ready to accept this challenging task with the right step and rectify the previous wrongdoings, the climate will change. In this knowledge age and knowledge economy, our students should dance to the best tune. Therefore, what every students and their parents are expecting is that let our college goers enjoy well-equipped colleges; let them play in the big campus; let them have the best teachers; let there be world-class interactions through invitation lectures; let them surf the globe. If the environment is not conducive and disturbing let there be residential colleges for them. Let there be very less political and bureaucratic interference in the functioning of these colleges. Let there be more autonomy. Let us observe and witness the ability of these resourceful youths. Let there be a congenial atmosphere for growth.

Education in a knowledge driven world, which is already flattened by a strong brainwave, needs to be reoriented keeping in view the imperatives of SCALE (thinking big), SKILL (professionalism) and SCIENTIFIC TEMPER (experimenting with truth, research, discovery and invention). We need to encourage our young minds "out-of-well-thinking", imagination and innovation. The investments made in education should be considered as long term investment for humanity.

We have good teachers and resourceful students but we lack investors in higher education. Planning and investment should be solely demand driven. Contractor oriented ventures create wastage of public expenditure. The various institutions in the state are at different levels of development, and their needs and demands are different. It would be an excellent idea to create a "Knowledge pool" with resource persons drawn from surplus institutions to cater to the needs of deficit institutions. Besides, academic exchange programmes should promote knowledge sharing and sense of fraternity among the teachers as well as the institutions.

SUGGESTIONS:

A number of suggestions or solutions to the problems of higher education and graduate unemployment can be put forward. These include the qualitative improvement of the college curricula, restricting the intake capacity into the degree colleges, introduction of more professional and vocational subjects/courses, setting up of more career-counseling units in the colleges with latest information bulletins about the development of the prospective careers etc. Parents and teachers, besides guiding them, can serve as the effective and motivating forces of the students. Improvement in higher education system in the state can be brought when students and teachers do their own academic works, there is strict adherence of proper academic calendar and proper regulations to increase expenditure in education and adequate attention of the Government on education.

At the organizational and administrative level, there should be a proper and clear-cut higher education policy in the state, misgovernance and malfunctioning by the department officials should stop, rationalization process initiated earlier should be materialized and there should be no politicization of education. If the government has the least concern for education, it should initiate to appoint the Head of the Department from among the academicians, appoint the regular principals for better administration, address the issues of part-time/guest teachers. There should have proper transfer and posting policy in the state. The state should follow and abide by UGC regulations and implement its schemes in toto and that is also on time.

CONCLUSIONS

The time has come for a total reassessment of our weaknesses, strengths and achievements. What is required is critical but impartial reassessment made not by the politicians or the bureaucrats, not by the technocrats or trade union leaders, but by the people themselves and by those who are associated with the academia To make the entire system of higher education in the state, productive and meaningful one, all options that can make the desired kind of education possible must be explored, and for it, no stones should be left unturned. By witnessing the kind of resources (human) available in this part of the region and the kind of opportunities provided, one may observed that the state has tremendous prospects. The only thing, that is required at the moment is to explore all options available to provide a congenial atmosphere for growth and channelization of the dormant potentials. At the current juncture, RUSA is a silver lining, a hope for inclusive growth, and for enhancing both quality and quantity of higher education and restoring the dignity of the academicians.

Bibliography

1. Annual Administration Report for the year 2009-2010, Department of University and Higher Education, Government of Manipur.
2. Annual Quality Assurance Report of Manipur College for the Academic Year 2008-09.
3. Devi, Jamini.(2006)Education in Manipur, Imphal:RaiPravina Brothers.
4. Report of the Manipur State Higher Education Commission, 2003(Part I and II).
5. Report of the Academic Reforms Committee, 2008, Directorate of University and Higher Education, Government of Manipur.
6. Website of Ministry of HRD, Govt. of India: www.education.nic.in
7. Website of NAAC: www.naac.gov.in,
8. Website of UGC: www.ugc.ac.in

41

Inclusion in Higher Education: Challenges in Disability Sector

Dr. Sukhwinder Kaur*

Abstract

Inclusion is a dynamic process, not a static condition; it is a journey, not a destination. Students with disabilities who experience difficulties in learning are often marginalized and moreover excluded from the higher education system. Moving out of high school into university or college is an exciting and tense experience for all students and their families. The move from a secure environment, where teachers and friends are close at hand, into an environment which is free, the responsibility of attending the classes is on themselves, the teachers become lecturers, may be scary to some students. The same experience for students with disabilities is even more difficult. If the colleges and universities take the initiative and provide effective inclusive education, enrolments of students with disabilities into higher education will increase. In order to combat the alienation of students with disabilities, the university must identify student peers and faculty mentors in a position to reach out to students with disubilities who feel alienated. The goal of inclusive education is to act as a catalyst to ensure access, achievement, presence, participation of all students including those from diverse backgrounds. Inclusive education, accepts all challenges ahead and with the cooperation of all stakeholders it will surely be successful on the realization of its objectives. The paper attempts to present various challenges towards inclusive education in higher education in disability sector and also suggests strategies to address the challenges that Indian administrators and educators face in the move towards facilitating inclusive education for easy transition into higher education.

Keywords: *Inclusive education, disability, challenges, strategies*

* Guest Faculty, Department of Community Education and Disability Studies, Panjab University, Chandigarh

Introduction

Students with disabilities who experience difficulties in learning are often marginalized and moreover excluded from the higher education system. Moving out of high school into university or college is an exciting and apprehensive experience for all students and their families. The move from a secure environment, where teachers and friends are close at hand, into an environment which is free, the responsibility of attending the classes is on themselves, the teachers become lecturers, may be scary to some students. The same experience for students with disabilities is even more difficult. Students with disabilities are routinely edged out of an education system that's hesitant to acknowledge diversity. This happens in spite of the fact that there have been number of attempts to create awareness about inclusion through many of the major governmental programs. The high number of policies in support of inclusion, unfortunately, is in no way indicative of the current situation in the country, there is a world of difference between the law and its implementation. Undoubtedly, legislation can eventually bring about a substantial change in a uniform manner in the lives of students with disabilities. But only legislation cannot radically change the fabric of a society. This is a sacred duty of every citizen to support and to help to bring down barriers for fuller participation of students with disabilities in all activities of the society. Government as well as private organization's support to increase accessibility of the disabled to education and employment may enable them to lead an independent life. Although there is a widespread support for education of students with disabilities at a philosophical level, there are some concerns that the policy of inclusion is difficult to implement because teachers are not sufficiently well prepared and supported to work in inclusive ways. If the colleges and universities take the initiative and provide effective inclusive education, enrolments of students with disabilities into higher education will increase. Inclusive education is the responsibility of everyone involved in a child's education – parents, teachers, administrators, community and government.

One mark of a great educator is the ability to lead students out to new places where even the educator has never been. Inclusion requires some changes in how teachers teach, as well as changes in how students with and without disabilities interact with and relate to one another.

National Council for Promotion of Disabled Persons reveal that only 0.1% disabled are in mainstream educational institutions at the university level. The broad aim is to encourage institutions to develop high quality provisions for students with disabilities to increase the participation for students with all types of disability. Inclusive education practices frequently rely on active learning, authentic assessment practices, applied curriculum, multi-level instructional approaches, and increased attention to diverse student needs and individualization. Universities pride themselves on providing access to all students with ambition and the potential for achievement. Yet despite the urgency of ensuring access to inclusive education, the higher education is falling behind. Research suggests that recent graduates wanted more time to practice teaching within diverse settings during pre-service education programmes (West & Hudson, 2010). The objectives of this paper are:

- To discuss the challenges towards inclusive education of students with disabilities at higher education level.
- To recommend strategies to overcome the challenges towards inclusive education of students with disabilities at higher education level.

Inclusive Education

Inclusion is a dynamic process, not a static condition; it is a journey, not a destination. It is a never ending process dependent on continuous pedagogical and organizational development. Inclusive education brings all students together in one classroom and community, regardless of their strengths or weaknesses in any area and seeks to maximize the potential of all students. Inclusion is an educational approach and philosophy that provides all students with community membership and greater opportunities for academic and social achievement. Inclusion is about making sure that each and every student feels welcome and that their unique needs and learning styles are attended to and valued. Inclusive education is defined as a strategy to ensure "education for all" (Ainscow et al, 2006).

Inclusion in Education of Children and Youth with Disabilities (IECYD, 2005), focuses upon inclusion of children and young persons with disabilities in all regular schools from Early Childhood to Higher Education. Its goal is to ensure the inclusion of children and youth with disabilities in all available general educational settings, by providing them with a learning environment that is available, accessible, affordable and appropriate.

Inclusive education is primarily an attitude, a value and a belief system... Not merely a set up of actions...The word 'include' implies being a part of something, being embraced into the whole (Puri and Abraham, 2004). The goal of inclusive education is to act as a catalyst to ensure access, achievement, presence, participation of all students including those from diverse backgrounds (UNESCO, 1994). The feeling of belongingness among all community members – teachers, students and other functionaries is developed through inclusive education. Inclusive education is for all, irrespective of any social community, caste, class gender and (dis-) ability of the child. Inclusion is an effort to make sure that diverse learners – those with disabilities, different languages and cultures, different homes and family lives, different interests and ways of learning – are exposed to teaching strategies that reach them as individual learners. Inclusion solicits teachers to provide appropriate individualized supports and services to all students without the stigmatization that comes with separation.

Education of children with disabilities has always posed a challenge to educators. Rule 6 of the UN Standard Rules for Persons with Disabilities states: States should recognize the principles of equal primary, secondary and tertiary educational opportunities for children, youth and adults with disabilities in integrated settings. They should ensure that the education of persons with disabilities is an integral part of the educational system. General education authorities are responsible for the education of persons with disabilities in integrated settings. Education for persons with disabilities should form an integral part of national educational planning, curriculum development and school organization.

Challenges in Inclusive Education

Barriers always block the way to achievement of goal. Inclusive education is also a difficult process full of various obstacles which need to be studied thoroughly. Following are some of the challenges which are being faced while providing inclusive education at higher education level:

- **Resistance to accept change:** Some people are very rigid and resist to change. They think that inclusive education will bring about a Herculean change. The social changes are not readily accepted, because novelty always demands a different and difficult adjustment for which people generally are not prepared and for that an adequate span of time is needed.
- **Negative attitude:** Society in general thinks about the disabled and handicapped students in distorted way. Most of the people of any society take impairment as a curse of God and show their helplessness in this regard. A substantial number of respectable individuals are the severe critics of inclusive education.
- **Teachers' responsibilities:** An additional burden: In our country, many of the teachers generally do teaching work half-heartedly, that is why they perceive inclusive education as a very difficult process. They have already so much work and no time is left to this type of activity. Moreover, there is lack of practical exposure to teaching in inclusive classroom. Regular teachers have been provided with professional development focussing on inclusive education; however, there is still a lot of work to be done to change the attitudes of teachers towards students with special educational needs. (Ahuja & Ibrahim, 2006).
- **Scarcity of trained teachers:** In universities and colleges, there is acute shortage of trained teachers. There is lack of awareness to deal students with diverse needs in the classroom. This is one of the most hazardous conditions.
- **Rigid and inflexible curriculum:** Teachers and persons associated with education develop a rigid attitude towards what actually exists in the present and are quite resistant to bring about a change in that. Inclusive education needs a lot of change in the curricula, teaching strategies, dealing with students and in planning and making policies. The fundamentalists react to it and criticise this approach. Findings of an action research (Malak, 2012) indicated that pre-service special education teachers were not satisfied with their experiential learning facilities

and demanded more hands-on experience prior to practicum placement.

- **Less sensitivity towards disabilities:** Teachers, administrators and organizers etc. are less sensitive towards disabilities. The society shows ignorance towards various aspects of disability. Research revealed that the principals of several teacher training colleges acknowledged challenges in providing effective practicum facilities in inclusive settings for pre-service teachers as inclusive schools were unavailable (Ahsan et al, 2011).
- **Emotional problems:** Sometimes the sarcastic comments of parents, peers and teachers lead to the development of inferiority complex among students making the problem more acute and difficult. The behaviour of students with disabilities becomes so deviated that they fail to benefit from the educational opportunities despite all the best efforts of teachers and universities.
- **Educational barriers:** Educational barriers are generally related to acceptability, availability, accessibility, adaptability, attention etc. Keeping in view the educational needs of students with and without disabilities, teachers are lacking these characteristics in their attitude and behaviour towards the students.
- **Economic barriers:** Funding provision for education has always been problematic. Even if the system is well resourced overall, there is almost always a feeling that resources are inadequate to meet the learners' needs. Moreover, the teachers are not adequately aware about issues related to the provisions and policies for the students with disabilities.
- **Physical barriers and lack of equipment:** The lack of disability friendly transportation services and accessible buildings are considered by some to be far greater problems than social prejudice and negative attitudes. (Chatterjee, 2003).
- **Spending grant-in-aid in a wasteful manner:** Many scholarships and stipends are being released for students with disabilities which are not spent in a meaningful way. The money can be spent for developing a barrier free environment e.g. ramp or alternations in toilet or purchasing something good for the supporting aid or resource room etc. But many of the teachers

do not find it worthwhile to use that money purposefully. They have certain malafide intentions to spend that money. Moreover, very often this fund is disbursed in the month of March, which makes another rationalized excuse to spend for some thought of melange purpose.

- **Apprehension about lowering down the quality of education:** A substantial number of teachers view inclusive education a process of lowering down the quality of education and thus hampering the status of education in society.
- **Inclusive education hampers competitiveness:** Inclusive education supports co-operative learning and interactive social activities. The critics opine that inclusive education does not prepare students for the modern competitive world to progress. Consequently such students may face many adjustment problems in occupation and society.
- **Disabled and handicapped are not educable:** Not only the parents of normal students but also of students with disabilities feel that many of the students with disabilities are not educable. It is true only in case of profoundly mentally retarded children. But other students with disabilities can be helped to get their potential developed to the optimum level.
- **Attitudes of the parents of non-disabled:** Bringing disabled students to normal classes is considered to be withholding the progress of normal students. Many parents emphatically view that their children will certainly be losing their academic worth if the inclusive education system is implemented. They think that their children would be ignored in inclusive education.
- **Non-availability of the parents:** Inclusive education is a joint venture, a practicality based big group initiated activity for which all the stakeholders share their responsibility. Parents are not readily available to put committed efforts for the well being and progress of their children. Hence inclusive education is not so enthusiastic to get cooperation and participation of parents in making this educational system a success.

So, it is clear that inclusive education has a very difficult path to cover. Therefore, it should be prepared to accept all challenges and with the cooperation of all stakeholders it will surely be successful on the realization of its objectives.

Recommendations to Overcome the Challenges Towards Inclusive Education

The following strategies are recommended to address the challenges that Indian administrators and educators face while facilitating inclusive education for easy transition into higher education:

- **Start with the three R's**—Respect, respect and respect. Make it clear that treating everyone with respect is both imperative and non-negotiable.
- **Eliminate Stigmas:** Sensitize that inclusive education is not a bad thing and that some students need inclusive education services because of their unique learning needs. Alur (2001) found that disability in India is not seen as something 'normal' or 'natural'; rather it is seen as an 'evil eye'. Guilt, stigma and different kinds of fears tend to be paramount in families.
- **School-University partnership:** The multi-lingual, multi-cultural and multi-religious nature of India is often cited as a challenge in implementing any educational reforms. Local universities in each of the states may play a significant role in overcoming this challenge. Pilot projects involving local schools could be initiated by universities to explore strategies that may be appropriate for each region. Moreover, practical strategies may be produced in the common language spoken by educators in each of the states.
- **Establishment of National Resource Centre:** There is also a greater need to have a National Resource Centre for Disabilities. Such a centre would work to collect and disseminate information on various aspects of disability (Sharma, 2001). The centre would provide information through various TV and radio programs as well as through internet.
- **Create awareness:** Universities should provide support and counselling for students with disabilities at universities and all lecturers should receive awareness training on how to adapt their teaching appropriately.

- **Provide scholarship:** Universities should provide scholarship for students with disabilities to attend the classes. More seats should be reserved for students with disabilities.
- **Acknowledge Learning Differences Positively:** Create awareness that everyone learns differently and that some students need specialized educational services to help them learn best.
- **Embrace Diversity:** Help to develop a profound appreciation of diversity. Highlight the contributions each student brings to the classroom community. Encourage students to share their talents with the class. Impress upon students how fortunate they are to be able to share with and learn from each other. Correlate the style of teaching to the learning styles of all students.
- **Teach Tolerance:** Teach tolerance, patience, kindness, compassion and empathy explicitly so that students may develop these habits by heart implicitly. Bortoli et al (2009) reported that teachers' confidence and efficacy improved because of the increased exposure to teaching students with special educational needs in practicum placement.
- **Promote Acceptance:** Talk to students individually and as a group about what acceptance means. Tell them that in order for a classroom community to thrive, all of its members need to be fully accepted and appreciated.
- **Involve parents:** The parents' involvement should be encouraged.
- **Restructure education:** For effective delivery of education in the inclusion mode, all teacher education (in-service and pre-service) must be restructured. In order to encourage changes in the attitudes of teachers, it is necessary to design practice teaching programmes explicitly (Malak, 2012).
- **Practical exposure both at pre-service and in-service levels (to handle diversity in classrooms):** Pearce (2009) considers practicum as a significant factor in preparing teachers for better inclusive practices. Research shows that practicum assists pre-service teachers to enhance their understanding and professional skills regarding teaching and learning strategies for inclusive practice (Golder et al, 2009).

- **Team work:** Emphasize concept of team work between general and special teachers. Roni and Leyser (2006) reported the correlation between early experience of working with students with SEN and more positive attitudes about the benefits of inclusion.
- **Curricular modifications:** Teachers must learn methods and curricular modifications that respond to the diverse learning needs of all students in classroom.
- **Access to teaching-learning material:** When providing sensitizing courses to general teachers, special attention should be paid to development of teaching-learning material required for different categories of students. Ensure that all aspects of the university are accessible to students with disabilities including physical access and access to all teaching modes and materials, and should include sign language interpreters.
- **Assistive Technology:** Assistive Technology has opened up exciting avenues for the students with disabilities. Universities should provide assistive technologies and all necessary resources for students with disabilities who attend classes.

Hence, if there is provision of relevant information, knowledge and skills, the pedagogical skills required in inclusive classrooms may be geared up at higher education level.

Conclusions

Inclusion is a challenge to the long-standing, traditional approach that regards students with disability as marginal or an afterthought, instead inclusion promotes that disability is a common experience of humanity and should be a central issue in the planning and delivery of human services such as education. Inclusive education must respond to all students as individuals, recognizing individuality as something to be appreciated and respected. Inclusive education responding to special needs will thus have positive returns for all students. In order to combat the alienation of students with disabilities, the university must identify student peers and faculty mentors in a position to reach out to students with disabilities who feel alienated. Thus, universities and colleges are the most crucial builders in providing support for students with disabilities from a wide variety of backgrounds as they proceed towards higher education.

Bibliography

1. Ahsan, M.T., Sharma, U. and Deppeler, J. (2011). Beliefs of pre-service teacher education institutional heads about inclusive education in Bangladesh. Bangladesh Education Journal. 10 (1), 9-29.
2. Ahuja. A. and Ibrahim, M. (2006). An assessment of inclusive education in Bangladesh. Dhaka: UNESCO.
3. Ainscow, M., Booth, T. and Dyson, A. (2006). Improving schools, developing inclusion. Abingdon: Routledge. 15.
4. Alur, M. (2001). Inclusion in the Indian Context. Humanscape, 8(6), 1-8.
5. Bortoli, A., Brown, P.M. and Hsien, M. (2009). Teacher qualification and attitudes towards inclusion. Australasian Journal of Special Education. 33(1), 26-41.
6. Chatterjee, G. (2003). The Global Movement for Inclusive Education. Retrieved 7th January, 2014 from http://www.indiatogether.org/2014/apr/edu-inclusive.html
7. Golder, G., Jones, N. and Quinn, E.E. (2009). Strengthening the special educational needs element of initial teacher training and education. British Journal of Special Education. 36(4), 183-190.
8. Maitra, K. and Saxena, V. (2008). Inclusion: Issues and perspectives. New Delhi: Kanishka Publishers.
9. Malak, M.S. (2012). Pre-service special education teachers' preparation for inclusive education in Bangladesh: An action research. Journal of Education and Practice. 3(14), 91-100.
10. Pearce, M. (2009). The inclusive secondary school teacher in Australia. International Journal of Whole Schooling. 5(2), 1-15.
11. Puri, M. and Abraham, G. (2004). Handbook of inclusive education. New Delhi: Sage.
12. Roni, S. and Leyser, Y. (2006). Exploring inclusion, pre-service training needs: A study of variables associated with attitudes

and self-efficacy beliefs. European Journal of Special Needs Education. 21(1), 85-105.

13. Sharma, B.L. (2001). United Nations expert group meeting on disability-sensitive policy and program monitoring and evaluation. Country paper-India, New York: UN Headquarters.
14. United Nations Educational, Scientific and Cultural Organisation (1994). The Salamanca statement and framework for action on special needs education. Available at http://www.unesco.org.
15. Virk, J., Arora, A. and Sood, R.S. (2010). Fundamentals of inclusive education. Patiala: Twenty first century publications.
16. West, E.A. and Hudson, R.F. (2010). Using early career special educators voice to influence initial teacher education. International Journal of Whole Schooling. 6(1), 63-74.

Problems of Management Education in Punjab

Dr. Kapil Dev* & Prof. Rakesh Gupta**

Abstract

Management education carries a lot of importance in the minds of students particularly in the country like India. Economic and industrial growth has paved the way for management education to flourish. However, management education can produce quality managers only if it is facilitated by good faculty, infrastructure, a carefully designed curriculum and evaluation system and finally a mutually rewarding relationship between industry and management institutes. Keeping this theme in mind, this paper focuses on various problems and challenges faced by management institutes and management students in Punjab region of India. A sample was selected and respondents were asked about problems and satisfaction from facilities. Results indicate severe problems in management education in Punjab. Institutes must focus on such problems to develop managers who can accept global challenges.

Keywords: *Management education; Curriculum and evaluation system*

Introduction

Management education is a broad term and may be subject to multiple interpretations. Management education is that branch of education, which offers all necessary tools equip one with the necessary techniques of successfully handling various business management related issue. Management education enhances the managerial skills by sharing of ideas, the acceptance of others ideas and many of healthy discussions.

* Dr. Kapil Dev, Assistant Professor, GGDSD College, Chandigarh

** Prof. Rakesh Gupta,Professor (Commerce & Management) & Director, USOL, Panjab University, Chandigarh

Learning from other approaches is not always a natural and single study process. It has to come with active participation in a group of people and it happens in the management courses. Faculty and other students challenge statements, attack and defend ideas. The assimilation of other approaches forms an important part of the learning process. Students coming from different spheres of life, bring with them all the advantages disadvantages, fairness and prejudice of centuries of cultural heritage. These characteristics manifest themselves sometimes, in very different approaches towards solving business problems and learning fundamentals of management. From all of these approaches there is something to learn. A multi-cultured institute enhances the benefits gained from the participatory learning approach.

Unfortunately, in the country like India, there are few management institutes like IIMs, which can produce skilled and analytical managers with the help of good faculty, good infrastructure, quality curriculum and evaluation system and finally good interaction with industry. There are many business schools, which are unable to bring the similar output. MBA and PGDM courses have become extremely popular in India. It has caused mushrooming of management institutes in India. However, the point of concern at this time is to examine if such business schools are equipped with infrastructure and good faculty to develop managerial skills among students. That is why the effort in this study has been made to examine various problems faced by students in terms of infrastructure, faculty, curriculum and evaluation system, fee and other related issues and finally their interaction with industry.

The study has been restricted to management institutes in Punjab only. Primary objective of the study has been to find various problems faced by management students in Punjab. Specifically, problems in relation to basic infrastructure of the college, faculty, curriculum, examination and evaluation, fee and interaction with industry have been covered in this study.

Concerns for ensuring quality in management education have been paramount ever since management education started in India and the same has been reflected in print media, academic and professional journals and other publications. Payle (1967) presented certain facts regarding the evolution and growth of management education in India. He concluded that there was a lack of collaborative efforts between educational institutions and industry especially in the field of management research. Business World (1983) conducted a comprehensive survey of the Indian Corporate sector's perceived strengths and weaknesses of MBA's. Findings revealed strengths such as theoretical knowledge, broad perspective of business and industry, analytical and conceptual abilities and weaknesses; superiority complex, poor ability to adjust with non-MBAs, very high expectations and over confident.

Some researchers like Sudharshan Kumar (1983), Bhardwaj, (1983) and Bharati, Sharma (1988) found that the status of Northeastern region had not made any conscious efforts and plans to promote the growth and development of management education in right perspective. Recently there has been increasing concern on the quality of management education. Authors like Bhardwaj, (1983), Chand, Bidhi, (1993), Karamjeet (2006), Gill Suveera (2006) and Arya, P.P. (2006) stressed on the major challenges in the field of management education in India. He found that there is mushrooming of institutes imparting management education. He emphasized that the affiliation of a new institute should be done strictly on merit. Lakshmi (2007), Mukherjee (2008), Dr. Priya (2008), Jain (2008), Laha (2009) and Venugopal (2010) concluded that the vast imbalance between the supply and demand for high quality education had opened up an enormous, untapped global market. All agreed and stressed on the question of educational values created through the online learning environment and knowledge sharing.

Thus, almost all the researchers have agreed that there has been a vast majority of institutes providing management education in India. However, concerns about the quality of management education have remained there throughout all the years of research.

To achieve the objectives of study, 20 institutes each from Punjab were selected based on systematic sampling. Further 10 students were selected systematically (5 each from 1st and 2nd year) from each of 20 institutes. Two faculty members were selected from every institute. One management representative was also selected from each institute. Primary information was collected through questionnaires and interviews. Three different questionnaires were designed for students, faculty members and management representatives. Basic statistical tools like mean and standard deviation were used to get descriptive results. Besides, chi-square test was used to examine the association between various respondents and their perception over the quality of infrastructure, faculty and other factors.

FINDINGS

Concerning infrastructure, students perceived that there were problems of non-availability of good books and good journals. Computer labs were also not up to the mark. There were problems with the capabilities, and qualities of teachers in management education. In addition, the teachers lack adequate corporate exposure. Curriculum of management education lacks orientation towards industry. Examinations standards are also average and do not encourage students to work hard. Table-1 below shows the brief results of three categories of respondents.

Table-1: Relative Scores of Satisfaction

Problem Areas	Mean (Students)	Mean (Faculty)	Mean (Mgt.)	F-value
Library	4.04	1.92	3.84	25.382*
Computer Laboratory	1.37	2.58	3.58	18.953*
Class Rooms	2.47	3.56	4.33	22.869*
Other Infrastructural Facilities	3.57	3.78	3.95	0.985
Curriculum	4.67	3.46	3.83	13.476*
Student Evaluation	2.86	3.25	3.12	7.398*
Examination Standards	4.56	1.46	3.13	28.573*
Summer Training	1.35	2.15	4.26	16.347*
Final Placement of Students	1.47	2.12	3.73	13.826*
Faculty	2.25	3.68	3.63	9.254*
Fee Structure	3.67	3.65	3.54	0.632

*** F-value significant at 5% level of significance.**

There were severe problems with industry-institute interface in management education in Punjab. It is a known fact that industry institute interface plays a big role to make students fit for the corporate world. However, it was been found that companies rarely took summer training seriously. Trainees seldom felt that they had learnt anything from training. Even attendance was not made compulsory in companies for trainees during summer training. This resulted in students having no or least practical knowledge of industry. Thus, most of the fresh management graduates tend to be big misfit for industry.

However, F-value suggested that there were disagreements on the satisfaction from infrastructure, faculty and other parameters. In case of library books and facilities, students and management representatives were satisfied. However, faculty members did not seem to be satisfied with facilities of libraries, examination standards and training & placements of students. Similarly, students were found to be highly dissatisfied from the available facilities in computer labs, classrooms, training & placement. Thus, it can be said that there are definitely problems about infrastructure, teaching skills of faculty, curriculum and examination standards and finally training and placements of management students. However, in certain cases where f-values are significant, it develops an idea that there might be problems of expectations not met.

In today's scenario, there are many management institutes, which have been closed or are on the verge of being closed due to vacant seats. In such cases, the concern might move towards the cost savings and financial viability, which may eventually hamper the objective of good quality management education. Hence, focusing on long run targets, the institutes must make efforts to understand problems of management education and try to develop good managers who can meet global challenges.

Conclusions

Therefore, it can be concluded that the existence of an institution shall depend upon the quality of education and training offered in coming years in Punjab. Now principle of Darwin holds well even today that fittest that would survive. On one hand, there have been vacant seats of management education in institutes, which raises issues of financial viability. On the other hand, there are problems and challenges before institutes in management education. In this scenario, institutes in Punjab should try to handle problems of management education to survive in the long term. To ensure quality in management education, inclusion of BPR, IDR & ISO9000 and ISO1000 etc. can be utilized. As per the words of Cyrus Guzdev, CEO, Airflight Express, the state of management education in India, "The B-schools are not sufficiently in touch with the real world, and the pace of change, which is challenging management through today, is threatening their credibility". So, it is an immediate requirement to shape the management education in accordance with the global changes to improve competitiveness with the total quality management.

Notes

1. Rao, S.L., (2007), ""From Servants to Masters? The evolution of Professional Management in India", Global Business Press, February 2007.
2. Chakravartty, Aloke. (2008), "Concept of Business School" accessed at http://sites.google.com /site/swapna mukherjee273/ conceptofbusinessschool
3. Bhatnagar, Deepti. & Bhatnagar, Subhash.,(2006), "Management Education in India: Trends and Challenges." Accessed at www. iimahd.ernet.in/~subhash/pdfs/management%20education.pdf on 04-11-2011.

Bibliography

1. Arya, P.P.(2006), "The Quality of Management education – The Challenge of Changing Scenario", Higher Education and Global challenge Dee's Deep Publications Pvt Ltd., pp. 87-91.
2. Bhardwaj, (1983), "Some thoughts on management education in India" Management and Business Education, Rawat Publication, pp. 201-214.
3. Bharti, Sharma, (1983), "Management education in north-eastern region", Management. and Business Education, Rawat

Publication, pp. 307-315.Management and Business education, Rawal Publication PP 307-317.

4. Business World (1983), 14-27, March.
5. Chand, Bidhi, (1993), "Business Education in India Adequacy and Effectiveness", Management and Business Education, Rawat Publication, pp. 172-174.
6. Dr. Priya,A.,(2008)"Global World & Quality of Management Education in India", available at: http://www.indianmba.com/faculty_column/fc631/fc631.html(accessed 25 October 2010).
7. Gill Suveera (2006), "Governance It Management School", Higher Education and Global challenge Dee's Deep Publications Pvt Ltd., pp 192-206.
8. Jain, Dipak.,(2008), "All the world is a market" Business Standard, 10 November 2008. p. 6.
9. Laha, A.K. (2002), "Quality in management education- A Meta analysis of recent B-school surveys", Paper presented at the national conference on quality of life organized by IAPQR and Viswa Bharati at Santiniketan, W.B.
10. Lakshmi, K. (2007), "Essential Attributes of Faculty of Management Education: Students' Perspective", Available at SSRN: http://ssrn.com/abstract=1350186
11. Mukherjee J. (2008) "An Integrated Approach to Management Communication at the T.A. Pai Management Institute" Business Communication Quarterly, Vol. 68 (2), (237-246) The Association for Business Communication, NY: Sage
12. Payle, M.V. (1967), "Management Education in India" Management Science, Vol.13, No. 10, June, 1967, pp 209-217.
13. Singh, Karamjeet (2006), "Quality of Management education – Challenges Ahead" Higher Education and Global challenge Deep & Deep Publications Pvt Ltd. pp 81-86.
14. Sudharshan Kumar (1983), "Universities and Management Education: Problems and prospects", Management and Business Education, Rawat Publication, pp. 193-200.
15. Venugopal, Pingali, (2006), "Management Education: A Framework for Grading" Management and Labour Studies, Forthcoming. Available at SSRN: http://ssrn.com/abstract=905166

43

Higher Education in India -Challenges and Solutions

*Prof. Harpreet Singh Dua**

Abstract

India is the land of great thinkers and planners who from time to time have worked towards community upliftment and generated ideas to kindle our lives with meaning and purpose. This has been true in the realm of higher education. Universities are important means for exploring, generating, conserving and transmitting knowledge. Today universities and other institutions responsible for higher education have a specially critical role to play.

The task of creating new social order which has assumed paramount importance today cannot be overlooked by the university community. Thus the goal of university education has a dual character, firstly the pursuit of knowledge and the attainment of excellence in different disciplines, and secondly the development of a sense of ethos which makes the university community conscious of its obligations to the community at large.

The university system has important responsibilities to the society as a whole as well as to the educational system itself, the significance of the traditional functions of acquisition, preservation, dissemination and extension of the frontiers of knowledge, the balanced education of individuals and the training of high level personnel for all walks of life is obvious.

The keystone of effective motivation is the mounting awareness and use of the technique of participation, i.e. permission granted to the members of staff – either supervisors or non- supervisors – to take effective part in the planning, discussion, communicating or decision-making by providing free and frank environment in which they become accustomed to apply their intelligence rather than to receive instructions on every detailed step or task. A teaching atmosphere thereby replaces the command atmosphere.

* Assistant Professor Gujranwala GuruNanak Khalsa, College,Civil Lines, Ludhiana.

Higher education in India is facing an acute resource crisis. Ever since India became independent, attempts have been made to improve the quality of higher education and extend it to all socio economic level of her population. The importance of higher education has increased several folds with the realization that in a world order based on science and technology, it is the quality of higher education that decides the country's pace of economic and social development. In order to provide better education financial problems should be tackled efficiently. The requirements of funds for higher education have increased substantially mainly due to its rapid expansion whereas the allocation of funds to this sector has declined considerably in recent years.

Key words: *Knowledge attainment; community conscious.*

Introduction

India is the land of great thinkers and planners who from time to time have worked towards community upliftment and generated ideas to kindle our lives with meaning and purpose. This has been true in the realm of higher education. Education is the most crucial input for socio-economic development.[1] Universities are important means for exploring, generating, conserving and transmitting knowledge. Today universities and other institutions responsible for higher education have a specially critical role to play. The University Education Commission headed by Dr. S. Radhakrishnan in its report entrusted universities with wide responsibilities. "They have to provide leadership in politics and administration, the professions, industry and commerce. They have to meet the increasing demand for every type of higher education-literacy and scientific, technical and professional. They must enable the country to attain, in as short a time as possible, freedom from want,disease and ignorance, by the application and development of scientific and technical knowledge. India is rich in natural resources and her people have intelligence and energy and are throbbing with renewed life and vigor. It is for the universities to create knowledge and train minds who bring together the two material resources and human energies.[2]

1 Gopalan, K. (1995) Higher Education in India- Prospects and Perspectives, University News, New Delhi, Vol XXXII,9th Jan 2001.

2 Chaturvedi, O.N, 'University Objectives in Changing World', Indian Journal of Public Administration, Vol XXXII,No 3, July- Sept.,1986, p. 647.

The task of creating new social order which has assumed paramount importance today cannot be overlooked by the university community. Thus the goal of university education has a dual character, firstly the pursuit of knowledge and the attainment of excellence in different disciplines, and secondly the development of a sense of ethos which makes the university community conscious of its obligations to the community at large. As the Report of the Education Commission (1964 – 1966) so aptly points out, the university education should have a three fold emphasis;[3]

- Internal transformation so as to relate it to the life, needs and aspirations of the nation ;
- qualitative improvement so that the standards achieved are adequate, keep continually rising and at least in a few sectors, became internationally comparable; and
- expansion of educational facilities broadly on the basis of manpower needs and with an accent on equalisation of educational opportunities.

The university system has important responsibilities to the society as a whole as well as to the educational system itself, the significance of the traditional functions of acquisition, preservation, dissemination and extension of the frontiers of knowledge, the balanced education of individuals and the training of high level personnel for all walks of life is obvious. But a modern university, specially in a developing country has to undertake several other functions as well. It must, for instance:

i. serve as the conscience of the nation and from this point of view they should encourage individuality, variety and dissent within a climate of tolerance;

ii. inculcate and promote basic human values and the capacity to choose between alternate value systems;

iii. preserve and foster our great cultural traditions and blend them with essential elements from other cultures and peoples;

iv. promote a rational outlook and scientific temper;

---

3 Report of the Committee on the Governance of Universities and Colleges, Part- I, (New Delhi : University Grants Commission Publications) pp.50-51

v. enrich the national language(s) and promote their use as important means of communication and for national development and unity;

vi. promote the development of the total personality of students and inculcate a commitment of society through involvement in national service programmes;

vii. act as an objective critic of society and assist in the formulation or national objectives and programmes for their realization;

viii. promote commitment to the pursuit of excellence;

ix. promote the development of science and technology and of indigenous capability to apply it effectively with special emphasis on national problems;

x. contribute to the improvement of the entire educational system so as to sub serve the community;

xi. shake off the heavy load of their early tradition which gives a prominent place to examinations and strive to improve standards all round by symbiotic development of teaching and research;

xii. create at least a few centers which would be comparable to those of their type in any other part of the world and thus help to bring back the 'center of gravity' of the academic life within country itself;

To achieve these objectives, a well conceived plan for the development of higher education should be drawn up which should include, among others the following programmes on a high priority basis[4]:

1. A radical improvement in the quality and standards of higher education and research
2. Expansion of higher education to meet the man power needs of national development and to some extent, the rising social ambitions and expectations of the people.
3. Improvement of university organization and administration.

Types of Universities

At present, the following four types of institutions of higher learning are existing in India,

---

4 Development of Higher Education and Research in the Universities-1980-85,(New Delhi: UGC Publication),pp. 50-51

1. Affiliating Universities
2. Unitary Universities
3. Federative Universities
4. Deemed Universities

Affiliating Universities: This type of universities are ones which exercise control in varying measures over the large number of affiliated colleges which are scattered over a particular specified area to secure certain minimum conditions but this main service they renders is still that of providing syllabi and holding examination.

Unitary Universities: In a unitary university almost the entire teaching is done by the university in its own departments. This type of universities generally are restricted to a single town or its immediate neighbourhood, for e.g. JawaharLal Nehru University and Banaras Hindu University .

Federative Universities: The federative university is a variation from the above. While this is also restricted to a town, there are number of colleges which generally work under the direction of, and in co-operation with, the university. The University of Delhi and agricultural universities are its example.

Deemed Universities: Some of the prestigious institutions were established in India as separate institutions with private as well as government management. They include Tata Institute of Social Science Research, Bombay; Indian Institute of Science, Bangalore etc. These institutes are full fledged ones and they provide teaching as well as research facilities. They satisfied some of the conditions laid down for the recognition of a university, the University Grants Commission recognized them as institutions as deemed to be universities.

Problems/Challenges of Higher Education

Several problems in the field of education are:

1. **Explosion in the number of students**

   The number of students is rising at the rate of 13 percent per year.[5] The national policy on education adopted in 1968 laid down that

5 Kapur, J.N.,' Current issues in Higher Education in India', (New Delhi; Sultan Chand and Company,1975), p.44

the number of full-time students enrolled in university education should be limited in accordance with the physical facilities and staff. But inspite of all there appears to be no check in this regard.

2. **Student unrest and indiscipline**

In some of campuses of the universities the atmosphere is explosive that any cause or protext is good enough to lead to a disturbance. The other problem from the students is indiscipline. This has several manifestations, for e.g. students disrupting classes, interfering with management functions, indulging in voilance during elections and engaging in 'Unfair' practices at the time of examination.

3. **Inferior Faculty**

Persons having poor background with no spirit of dedication and inferior qualifications are appointed to the faculty positions. Such persons often resort to favoritism in student evaluation, encourage factionalism, etc., and this create hurdles for sincere and dedicated teachers.[6]

4. **Irrelevance of Education**

Another problem of higher education is irrelevance of education as it turns out 'Unemployable 'graduates. This raise a host of questions bearing on curriculum, the competence of graduates and the capacity of the economy to absorb the output of the system.

5. **Qualitative Decrease in the Standards of Students**

The foundation of students seeking admission to university education coming from higher secondary schools, having extremely poor facilities, is very weak. It is felt that only those students like to continue post-graduate or research education, who are unable to get openings elsewhere.

Besides, on account of social pressures universities are forced to admit sub-standard students. Moreover, such students resort to unfair means to compete with the intelligent ones which results in several ills.[7]

---

6 Chaturvedi, O.N.,'University objectives in Changing World', Indian Journal of Public Administration, Op.cit.,p.646-657

7 Ibid p. 646-657

6. Teacher – Politician

It is the teacher-politicians who have brought disgrace to the faculty and eroded the cherished values in academic field. The agitations launched by teachers have particularly pernicious effect on university life and morale, since they tend to destroy the image of teachers in the eyes of students and thus encourage all round lawlessness.

7. Prolifieration of Higher Education

The post independence period witnessed an enormous expansion of colleges by private agencies as well as government and these colleges were established for reasons or considerations other than quality of education.[8]

8. Inadequate Funding

The other challenge of higher education is that of inadequate funding due to which universities are facing several financial crisis. The problem is more severe in case of state universities. Some times it is even become difficult to pay salaries to the staff and meet other day to day expenses. This position is causing deep concern to academicians as well as administrators of the universities in India.[9]

9. Autonomy and Accountability

Academic freedom is the very life-breath of the university. Autonomy includes the right of the university to determine who shall teach what and to whom. But, now-a-days, the autonomy of the universities is mostly affected by the interference of the government in the day- to – day affairs of the university. University autonomy has to be distinguished from academic freedom which signifies freedom of expression for professionals. Autonomy in universities has three aspects, viz., financial, administrative and academic. "The real threat to autonomy does not come from the state as much as it does from within the members of the faculty

---

8 Reddi, O.S.,' The Unrest in Universities', The Hindu, 20th May,1986, p. 19

9 Rao, K.V., Prasad, G., & Kiranmayi,Y.S.,' Can universities Continue to Relegate Financial Admisnistration to the Background'?, Vikalpa, Vol. 12, No. 2, April- June, 1987, p 29

who use their position of power and influence to promote the interests of their relations or kinsmen and those who instigate students against their own colleagues or authorities and some fail to observe high standards of integrity required of the academic profession --- in teaching, conducting examinations and in making appointments --- are the real enemies of university autonomy".[10]

10. Lack of Motivation for Teachers to keep up – to – date

After one year of probation, every employee gets a tenure and thereafter he gets his increments regularly. Very often the promotions are by seniority and not by merit. According to some teachers there is stagnation in the universities due to lack of promotional avenues. According to them the merit promotion scheme introduced by the University Grant Commission after considerable delay is not enough, and it should be automatic and more liberal rather than be based on merit.[11]

University Grants Commission has deliberated on 12th (Five Year Plan) and has submitted a report titled ' Inclusive and Qualitative Expansions of Higher Education', to the Human Resource Development Ministry and Planning Commission. The report suggests reforms in achieving the target of 25 percent General Enrolment Ratio (GER). The existing enrolment pattern of public universities is concentrated in the conventional disciplines whereas, the enrolment pattern of private universities is restricted to market – driven disciplines which needs immediate introduction of strict check and balances mechanisms.

University Grants Commission in its report on 12th (Five Year Plan) felt concerns over:

- ❖ Poor performance of the majority of our higher educational institutions in the area of quality on a relative global scale,
- ❖ Quality and the provision of relevant education is another major challenge for the higher education sector.

---

10 Kolhatkar,M.R., 'Administration of Institutions' of Higher Learning: Purposes, Problems and Remedies', Indian Journal of Public Administration p.367.

11 Report of the Committee to Enquire into the Working of Central Universities, Op. cit,p.75.

- Emphasized for regular revision and upgrading of curriculum, introduction of semester system.
- Choice based credit system and examination reforms which are yet to be implemented.

In consonance with the targets of 12th (Five Year Plan), UGC in its above said report has proposed to launch a **national level mission 'Rashtriya Uchch Shiksha Abhiyan (RUSA)'** aimed to achieve national level gross enrolment ratio in different steps.

Firstly, upgradation of autonomous colleges, colleges with potential for excellence and colleges which have 'A' grade accreditation from NAAC (National Assessment and Accreditation Council) into university level institutions;

Secondly, RUSA will promote the concept of evening classes or universities;

Thirdly, introduction of under- graduate programmes in the universities as integrated under- graduate/ postgraduate programmes;

Fourthly, enhancing the intake capacity of the existing institutions of higher education;

Fifthly, RUSA would be developing 'College Cluster Universities' regionally;

Sixthly, 'Meta University Complexes', in association with public and private sector undertakings would be a part of their corporate social responsibilities, on an industry- academia mode.

Participative Management

The keystone of effective motivation is the mounting awareness and use of the technique of participation, i.e. permission granted to the members of staff – either supervisors or non-supervisors – to take effective part in the planning, discussion, communicating or decision-making by providing free and frank environment in which they become accustomed to apply their intelligence rather than to receive instructions on every detailed step or task. A teaching atmosphere thereby replaces the command atmosphere. It symbolizes management by winning consent, as distinguished from management by command. Participation in decision-making gives employees a sense of belonging, and being a party to decisions and therefore, and to be more motivated to live upto them. A number of studies, such as the one by Vroom confirm the view that participation facilities ego involvement, self-control, encourages initiative and a spirit of cooperation among those participating and hence increases higher intrinsic motivation.

Campus Students

More than 50 percent of the time of the administration is being spent on solving the problems of campus students. If the students problems are solved in the universities, a number of other related problems will be solved automatically. The following suggestions are offered in this connection:-

1. The student problems should be solved without any delay. It is good if they are solved at the level of the department or hostel warden or the principal itself without approaching higher authorities for simple reasons.
2. No student should be allowed to join and study more than one course in the university campus. This step is very important and urgent since most of the problems of the universities from the students are mainly because of a few students who continue to stay in the campus for long.
3. In the hostels, no outsider should be allowed to stay for more than one day. The hostel supervisors may be asked to note down and inform about the presence of the outsiders to the concerned wardens. If they fail to do so, they may be warned of the consequences.
4. The conduct of examinations should be decentralized. To start with, all the post- graduate examinations should be conducted in the respective departments under the control and supervision of the concerned head of the department
5. The university authorities may consider the possibility of shifting some of the faculties, which have a very large enrolment of students, from the campus to other areas so as to reduce the pressure of numbers in the numbers, which has been a major cause for student indiscipline.

6. There is every need for improving the student services in many respects. It is no exaggeration to say that student 'services in many universities are far from adequacy giving them a feeling that ' nobody care for them'.

Process Evaluation

Evaluation is a process of discovering the extent to which a given institution or programme has achieved or is in the process of achieving objectives or outcomes it purports to achieve. This is done by measuring the processes, technology ,structures, intermittent or final outcomes attained, etc., and attaching values to them. Evaluation can play a very critical role in guiding the administrators in taking a series of mid-course corrections and ensure the achievement of the programme institutional. Briefly the process evaluation helps:

1. clarity in the statement of objectives
2. design of the programme / institution including its structure
3. understanding of the roles and responsibilities by various constituents of the programme and their commitment to the programme /institution and its success.
4. quality of human resources employed and human processes generated to motivate develop and utilize their competencies
5. leadership styles used at different levels.
6. Technological variables (instructional technology and other technology used and their suitability to goals)
7. availability, generation and utilization of other resources (financial and other forms)
8. the kind of culture (norms and values)developed in the organisation and the extent to which they are conductive to the achievement of goals.

Management Audit

It is a constructive method of assisting management to improve operations of its business by alerting to any breakdown of operational controls, by pin pointing areas of cost reduction, by suggesting potential operating improvements and by pointing out where breakdowns in the implementation of functional responsibilities in various areas have significantly affected these areas. The benefits derived from Management Audit include:

1. An appraisal of strategies, policies, plans and programmes for their potential and realized effectiveness;
2. Identification of areas where improvement is needed;
3. Better utilization of resources;
4. Guidelines for improving inter-group, inter-personal and staff-line relations;
5. Improving the communication system;
6. Strengthening the control system;
7. Improving the utilization of Management, Information system;
8. Streamlining the operations;

Use of Computers

Today computers are being used in many areas of work in the advanced countries and in the developing countries also, they are finding an involving application in industrial and educational fields. Computers have not only accelerated scientific and technological progress, but also have made tremendous contribution to improvement managerial decision-making and solution of complex problems through simulation and quick data processing.

So a new orientation in thinking and practice is necessary to promote the culture whereby creative people can function with freedom for the advancements of knowledge. The administration plays an important catalytic role for creating and developing learning culture which is very essential for the success of an educational institution.

Bibliography

1 Chaturvedi, O.N, 'University Objectives in Changing World', Indian Journal of Public Administration, Vol XXXII,No 3, July-Sept.,1986, p. 647.

2 Report of the Committee to Enquire into the Working of Central Universities, Op. cit,p.75.

3 Gopalan, K. (1995) Higher Education in India- Prospects and Perspectives, University News, New Delhi, Vol XXXII,9th Jan 2001.

4 Kapur, J.N.,' Current issues in Higher Education in India', (New Delhi; Sultan Chand and Company,1975), p.44.

5 Kolhatkar,M.R., 'Administration of Institutions' of Higher Learning: Purposes, Problems and Remedies', Indian Journal of Public Administration p.367.

6 Reddi, O.S.,' The Unrest in Universities', The Hindu, 20th May,1986, p. 19

7 Rao, K.V. ,Prasad, G., & Kiranmayi,Y.S.,' Can universities Continue to Relegate Financial Admisnistration to the Background'?, Vikalpa, Vol. 12, No. 2, April- June, 1987, p 29.

List of Contributors

Sr. No.	Name and Designation	Titles of the Papers
1	**Prof. Karamjeet Singh,** Honorary Director, Academic Staff College & Professor, University Business School, Panjab University, Chandigarh	Higher Education In India: A Perspective Of Twelfth Five Year Plan
2	**Dr. Navleen Kaur,** Chairperson & Associate Professor, Department of Community Education and Disability Studies, Panjab University, Chandigarh,	Exclusive Aspects In Inclusive Society: From Theory To Practice In Higher Education.
3	**Dr. Ashwani Kumar Sharma** Associate Professor, Department of Community Education and Disability Studies, Panjab University, Chandigarh	Issues And Challenges Before Higher Education In India: Policy And Perspectives
4	**Dr. Jayanti Dutta** Deputy Director, Academic Staff College, Panjab University, Chandigarh	Accessing Of Academic Performance Of Higher Education Teachers: Dealing With Non-Linear Situations
5	**Dr. Komila Parthi,** Assistant Professor, D.A.V. College, Sec-10, Chandigarh	Alienation And Depression Among Students In Higher Education: An Overview
6	**Dr. Yajvender Pal Verma,** Assistant Professor , University Institute of Engineering and Technology, Panjab University, Chandigarh	Retention Of Faculty In Institutions Of Higher Education
7	**Dr. Anil Kumar Thakur,** Assistant Professor, Department of Laws, Panjab University , Chandigarh	Challenges Of Legal Education In The Era Of Globalization: A Critique.

Sr. No.	Name and Designation	Titles of the Papers
8	**Dr. Anupam Bahri,** Assistant Professor, University Institute of Legal Studies, Panjab University , Chandigarh	Sexual Harassment Among Girls In India: Within The Framework Of Higher Educational Institutions
9	**Dr. Rohini Thapar,** Assistant Professor D.A.V. College, Sec-10, Chandigarh	Role Of Parental Influence On The Values Of Females In Higher Education:An Overview
10	**Dr. Kanwalpreet Kaur,** Assistant Professor, Institute of Educational Technology & Vocational Education, Panjab University, Chandigarh And **Dr Jitender Grover,** Reader, Dept. of Education, USOL, Panjab University, Chandigarh	Teacher Education At Crossroads In Punjab.
11	**Dr. Harpreet Kaur Vohra,** Assistant Professor, Panjab University Regional Centre, Ludhiana	The Role Of Missionaries In Higher Education In Shillong: Can The 'Local' Compete With The 'Foreign'?
12	**Dr. Ramnik Aurora,** Assistant Professor, Department of French, Panjab University , Chandigarh	Foreign Languages In Professional Courses With Special Reference To French
13	**Dr. Arunachal Khosla,** Assistant Professor, University Institute of Applied Management Sciences, Panjab University , Chandigarh	Relevance Of Soft Skills In Higher Education
14	**Dr. Cute Kharbanda,** Assistant Professor, D.A.V. College Ambala City	Vocationally Viable English In Higher Education

Sr. No.	Name and Designation	Titles of the Papers
15	**Dr. Dipankar Baidya,** Assistant Professor, Nowgong College, Nagaon, Assam	Increasing Cost Of Higher Education In India: Some Reflections On Problems And Prospects
16	**Dr. Gagandeep Kaur,** Assistant Professor, GGDSD College, Sector- 32, Chandigarh	E-Learning: Role In Higher Education
17	**Dr. Rita Kant,** Assistant Professor, University Institute of Fashion Technology, Panjab University, Chandigarh	Widening The Gates Of The Institutions Of Higher Learning
18	**Dr.Amandeep Kaur Sandhu,** Assistant Professor, Master Tara Singh Memorial College for Women, Ludhiana.	Relevance Of Moral Education In Higher Education
19	**Dr. Kuldeep Kaur,** Assistant Professor, Guru Nanak Khalsa College for Women, Gujarkhan Campus, Ludhiana	Shifting Role Of Teachers In Higher Education System
20	**Dr. Madhuri Rishi,** Assistant Professor, Dept. of Environment Studies, Panjab University, Chandigarh	Sustainable Development In Perspective Of Environment Education In India
21	**Dr. Maninder Kaur,** Assistant Professor, Guru Nanak Khalsa College for Women, Ludhiana	Issues, Challenges And Reforms In Higher Education For A Knowledge Society
22	**Dr. Manmeet Kaur,** Assistant Professor, Guru Nanak Khalsa College for Women, Ludhiana	Sustainable Development Of Higher Education Through Open And Distance Learning
23	**Dr. Minakshi,** Assistant Professor, Master Tara Singh Memorial College for Women, Ludhiana.	Special Education Zones: A Reform For Higher Education In India

Sr. No.	Name and Designation	Titles of the Papers
24	**Dr. Namita Kohli,** Assistant Professor, Guru Nanak Khalsa College for Women, Ludhiana	Higher Education In India At Crossroads: Needed Reforms
25	**Dr. Ajay Ranga,** Assistant Professor, University Institute of Legal Studies, Panjab University , Chandigarh	Khap Panchayat And Higher Education
26	**Dr. Akhlash P. Singh,** Assistant Professor, GGDSD College, Sector -32 C, Chandigarh	Women In Science: Causes Of Under-Representation And Remedies
27	**Dr. Pallavi Manik,** Assistant Professor, LR DAV College, Jagraon	Social Inequality: A Challenge To Higher Education In India
28	**Dr. Pooja Mohan,** Assistant Professor , GGDSD College, Sector-32 Chandigarh	Use Of Social Media, Blogs And File Sharing Sites In Higher Education
29	**Dr. Priyanka Malhotra,** Assistant Professor, GGDSD College, Sector 32 Chandigarh	Implications Of Commercialisation Of Higher Education
30	**Dr. Rajendra Swain,** Assistant Professor, Post Graduate Govt College for Girls Sector- 42, Chandigarh	Hindrances In Achieving Quality In Higher Education In India
31	**Dr. Ramesh Kataria,** Assistant Professor, Department of Chemistry, Panjab University , Chandigarh	Chemistry Education: Challenges In Higher Studies
32	**Dr. Samriti Dhawan,** Assistant Professor GGDSD College, Sec-32, Chandigarh	Higher Education In Science : Challenges

Sr. No.	Name and Designation	Titles of the Papers
33	**Dr. Sapna Nanda,** Assistant Professor Govt. College of Education, Sec-20-D, Chandigarh	Institutional Planning: A Milestone In A Journey Towards Improvement Of Education
34	**Dr. Sheojee Singh,** Assistant Professor Govt. College of Education,Sec-20-D, Chandigarh	How Godly Is The God Particle? (A Peep Into The Realm Of High Energy Physics)
35	**Dr. Shweta Ahuja,** Assistant Professor, D.A.V. College Ambala City	Mother Tongue Interference And Related Issues In Teaching English In Higher Education
36	**Dr. Sonali Guleria,** Assistant Professor D.A.V. College, Sec-10, Chandigarh.	Higher Education In Life Sciences In India: Challenges, Scope And Direction
37	**Dr. Sunita,** Assistant Professor Post Graduate Government College for Girls Sector 42 Chandigarh	Innovative Teaching Methods To Enhance English Language Learning: Practical Steps
38	**Ms. Navleen Kaur,** Assistant Professor,Department of Business Management, Sri Guru Granth Sahib World University, Fatehgarh Sahib.	Teacher's Training: An Integral Part Of Higher Education
39	**Dr. Neetu Thakur,** Assistant Professor, GGDSD college, Sector 32 Chandigarh	Role Of Biotechnology In Higher Education And Social Development
40	**Dr. M. Rameshwor Singh,** Assistant Professor, DM College of Arts, Imphal	Higher Education In Manipur: Issues, Challenges And Expectations
41	**Dr. Sukhwinder Kaur,** Guest Faculty,Dept. Of Community Education and Disability Studies, Panjab University, Chandigarh	Inclusion In Higher Education: Challenges In Disability Sector

Sr. No.	Name and Designation	Titles of the Papers
42	**Dr. Kapil Dev** Assistant Professor (Commerce), GGDSD College, Chandigarh and Prof. Rakesh Gupta Professor (Commerce & Management) & Director, USOL, Panjab University, Chandigarh	Problems Of Management Education In Punjab
43	**Prof. Harpreet Singh Dua** Assistant Professor Gujranwala GuruNanak Khalsa College,Civil Lines,Ludhiana.	Higher Education In India:Challenges And Solutions